Black Bodies, White Gazes

Black Bodies, White Gazes

The Continuing Significance of Race in America

Second Edition

George Yancy

ROWMAN & LITTLEFIELD
Lanham • Boulder • New York • London

Published by Rowman & Littlefield
A wholly owned subsidary of The Rowman & Littlefield Publishing Group, Inc.
4501 Forbes Boulevard, Suite 200, Lanham, Maryland 20706
www.rowman.com

Unit A, Whitacre Mews, 26-34 Stannary Street, London SE11 4AB

British Library Cataloguing in Publication Information Available

Library of Congress Cataloging-in-Publication Data

Names: Yancy, George, author.
Title: Black bodies, white gazes: the continuing significance of race
    in America / George Yancy.
Description: Second Edition. | Lanham: Rowman & Littlefield, 2016. |
    Includes index.
Identifiers: LCCN 2016038669 (print) | LCCN 2016041887 (ebook) |
    ISBN 9781442258341 (cloth : alk. paper) | ISBN 9781442258365 (pbk. : alk. paper) |
    ISBN 9781442258358 (Electronic)
Subjects: LCSH: African Americans. | Racism—United States. |
    United States—Race relations.
Classification: LCC E185 .Y32 2016 (print) | LCC E185 (ebook) |
    DDC 305.800973—dc23
LC record available at https://lccn.loc.gov/2016038669

Printed in the United States of America

For all bodies that suffer

Contents

Foreword

How does one live in a post-enslavement culture? Say, a culture such as the United States with a four-hundred-year-old legacy of slavery and barely a generation of (quasi) protected civil rights? Can anyone possibly imagine that their lives, their identities, their economic position, or their subjective selves are free and clear of this long history? Can even those of us who came here well past slavery's demise imagine that we are not affected by the patterns of interaction and systems of beliefs that persist from that era?

This is an important book. And it is important for all of us to read, and to read carefully. What George Yancy provides here is a thick description of subjective interiority inside a racist culture, bringing to life the subjectivity of black bodies under a white racist hegemonic gaze. He deftly and acutely—even painfully—unpacks the multiple layers of meaning that exist within the micro-practices of interracial living, through the use of numerous literary, biographical, as well as first-person real-life examples, from the well-meaning white colleague who admonishes his use of the black vernacular to the painful story of the great actor Ossie Davis who was taken by white cops at the age of six to their station house for a disturbing version of fun and games. There is even a whole chapter on the elevator experience, analyzed with great insight. If you think you know everything there is to know about racism, think again.

Yancy turns a keen, and cold, critical ethnographic eye on anti-black racism, past and present, unearthing new aspects and effecting a useful defamiliarization, in which automatic responses are picked apart and learned habits of the body can become visible and subject to reflection. In the tradition of Jean-Paul Sartre, Frantz Fanon, Maurice Merleau-Ponty, Simone de Beauvoir, and Lewis Gordon, he mines the phenomenological method for its ability to make our everyday world of normalcy become strange and even horrific. He outlines the basic, daily obstacles of living under a white gaze where every action has to be second-guessed for its possible misinterpretation by a hostile or simply uncomprehending onlooker. The very writing of this book, with its focus on the bodily experiences of black people, places theorists like Yancy and myself in a position where it has to be defended against in case it works to support the idea that blacks have experiences, whereas whites have thoughts. And while it should not have to be addressed at all, it is because of the climate of discourse and the effects of racism that make it necessary.

In post-slavery culture, whiteness remains the measure of man, that is, of humanity.

Whites and non-blacks in general may well find themselves resisting Yancy's analysis here. They may see some of his unpacking of white offhand comments as projections on his part more than they are accurate depictions of true intentions. They may be tempted to insist that we need to disaggregate both whites and blacks rather than using such broad brush strokes to characterize psychic life. There are certainly whites, other non-blacks, and blacks themselves who will not recognize themselves here, but it will take some careful reflection to distinguish a defensive response from a true critical engagement. Yancy's book is precisely what will help all of us to augment our reflective capacity and ability to make such distinctions. Whites, as Yancy points out, are much more familiar with the role of the person who sees than of the person who is seen, and their difficulty with his objectification of whiteness may well be grounded in a simple unfamiliarity with the direction of his gaze. Yancy's last chapter addresses in great detail the difficulties and complexities of white antiracist efforts, as well as white defensiveness, using numerous examples from his own teaching and public speaking, including having a student shout "Bullshit!" loudly after one lecture. Yancy offers clear-eyed advice here for whites who aspire to antiracism in what is, I believe, the best discussion of this topic in print.

In some respects, one should read this as a book about Whiteness more than simply about whites in their individual everyday lives. Whiteness here operates analogously to the phallus, as opposed to the penis, that is, a symbolic structure around which values and meanings are organized, rather than a representation of how individual whites feel about their level of social empowerment. One cannot adequately test the validity of Yancy's analysis by introspection or by ethnographic data that focus on self-understandings and conscious attributions. Rather, this is an analysis at the level of cultural semiotics, a sign system that works on objects of all sorts, bodies as well as other kinds, to interject meanings and values and to map relationships, beyond any conscious intent or even conscious awareness. Yet I, like many feminists, want to insist that there is a connection between the phallus and the penis, that these are not completely independent either symbolically or in their effects on material existence. Similarly, we must acknowledge the connection between Whiteness and whites. One of Yancy's central arguments here is that Whiteness is not merely an objective social location entirely independent of the self, but rather, a central feature of subjectivity, or one's lived, interior self. Whiteness is learned, in process, developed over the modern era and still developing, but lived on the inside as well as attributed to one's external appearance.

Yancy's account of identity here is anything but simplistic. Identities are existential projects for him, not found objects. They are historical and social, not essential or fixed, but their historical roots have been laid over generations of practices. Identities are deep rather than on the surface and so take work to unearth and assess. Black people, as he puts it, are not what they seem, sometimes even to themselves. Against eliminativist takes on race and deconstructivist approaches to identity, Yancy argues for a version of realism, a post-positivist, phenomenologically informed realism about black identity. What this means concretely is that for him, blackness is not entirely reducible to, or explainable by reference to, white constructions or representations, it is not a difference that is illusory. Rather, blackness has a substantive identity with its own agential, resistant history, neither reducible to white racism nor unconnected to the historical experience of enslavement. Thus, here Yancy helps black identity emerge or come out from under the white gaze, using the theoretical resources of both feminist and antiracist philosophers to uncover the existential project of blackness itself. He helps to answer the question: what does it mean to be black?

So what am I, a mixed-race Latina who has criticized the hegemony of the black/white binary in critical race discourses, doing writing a foreword to this book, a book clearly focused on white/black relations? The answer is because this is an important book, and its importance comes in no small part because the significations of blackness impact us all, black and nonblack alike. It is a gravitational pull we feel when we come to the United States, not pulling us toward blackness but toward anti-black racism that realigns our sense of identity, of empathic identifications, and of imagined community. The very writing of this book is testament to the fact that George Yancy has not forsaken his hope that a more inclusive community might someday be achieved, even in a post-enslavement culture.

Linda Martín Alcoff
Department of Philosophy
Syracuse University

Preface to the Second Edition

As you hold this book in your hands, I encourage you to take yet another look at the very powerful image on the cover. Even before you read the words between the front and back covers, the text begins with the image. The image itself communicates Black suffering and pain and how this pain and suffering is fundamentally linked to the violence and sadism of white gazes. Ask yourself about what the image communicates, how it is related to the history of white America's way of looking at and gazing upon Black bodies, and how the Black body is and has been dehumanized throughout North American history through the lens of whiteness. Notice how the white hands touch the young Black woman's face, one appearing to be a gentle embrace and another that looks more like a touch out of curiosity. Whether the white hand touches in the form of a gentle embrace or touches out of curiosity, what is important is that the Black woman expresses deep discomfort; she is not pleased, and she clearly does not want or desire to be touched. After all, the history of whiteness demonstrates that curious white hands can lead to violent acts of objectifying and experimenting on Black bodies; and, desirous white hands can lead to violent and unspeakable acts of molestation, where the Black body undergoes tremendous pain and trauma. And notice the white hands in her hair, some literally pulling at her hair, some perhaps trying to pull out her hair. What is certain is that those white hands are touching her hair in ways that are clearly uninvited. The faces of the whites are not shown, but one can imagine the panoply of facial configurations—some looks of white desire, others contorted with white anger and hatred, and others perhaps with mouths open, surprised by the "peculiar" texture of her hair. The hands function as extensions of the white gaze, white affect, white distortion, white malevolence.

The cover of this book powerfully and brilliantly ushers the reader into a racist and racially charged space, a space that exemplifies the violence and mutilation done to Black bodies. The white hands touching and pulling at the Black woman's body are violating the integrity of her Black body, doing violence to her embodied psyche, subjecting her Black body to the toxic dimensions of the white imaginary. Under the pressure of so many white hands touching, grasping, pulling, tearing, ripping, desiring, threatening, testing, and examining, the Black body functions as an exotic object placed on display; it is a spectacle. The image communicates a specific historical arc, one that moves from the brutalities of American slavery, across the larger European racist imaginary, to the contemporary ethical and ontological declaration that *Black Lives Matter*.

The white hands violating this Black woman's face and hair, her body, communicate a form of blatant degradation; the image says that Black Lives Matter, but only in terms of how white gazes value those Black lives. In other words, Black bodies are devoid of intrinsic value; their value is decided upon in terms of white forms of policing and stereotyping. The image of the Black woman on the cover speaks across space and time, capturing how white gazes have attempted to define Black bodies as problem bodies, dangerous and unwanted bodies, desired and hyper-sexualized bodies, strange bodies, curious bodies, always already touchable bodies, violable bodies, freakish bodies, nigger bodies, and dark and mysterious bodies.

The image on the cover of the book exemplifies an ethically corrupt relational ontology. It is a relational ontology that is predicated upon the structure of whiteness. The structure of whiteness is binary. Whiteness requires the so-called degraded and dangerous Black body. It is this structural requirement that reveals both the socially constructed nature of whiteness and its deep fragility. In fact, the white hands on the cover engage in acts of performative gesturing that help constitute the Black body as the focus of confusion; that is, the object, *the thing* to be dealt with, the problem to be confronted. The white hands signify white bodies as "epistemic subjects of control," "masters of meaning," "definers of reality," "the autonomous ones." Yet, at the heart of whiteness, there is a profound instability. The white hands that touch the Black body and that pull at the Black body operate within a performative space that creates the illusion of white stability and white innocence. To believe it itself, to pay tribute to its "innocence" and "normality," the Black body is the sacrificial object, the fantasized projection that whiteness relies upon to remain sutured, whole, intact.

Therefore, the cover on the book actually exemplifies white subject formation as that formation is fundamentally linked to Black deformation. And the arguments, examples, metaphors, and narratives deployed within this text demonstrate the white formational and Black deformational relational dynamics as they are structured through the white gaze. In fact, within this second edition of *Black Bodies, White Gazes*, I demonstrate that the deeply violent and tragic encounters faced by Trayvon Martin, Eric Garner, Eric Harris, Renisha McBride, Michael Brown, Tamir Rice, Sandra Bland, Jordan Davis, and so many others, are inextricably linked to the hegemony and power of the white gaze, which I theorize as an iterative historical phenomenon that is embedded within a larger social and political context of white privilege. Philosophically, I engage these tragic situations through the conceptual framework of what I call the *density project*. It is an approach that engages race and the process of racialization within quotidian spaces of the everyday; it is an approach that remains attentive, many times painfully so, to an embodied relational ontology that presupposes a country, indeed, a world, where the Black body is deemed the damned of the earth, where it is treated like excrement and refuse, and where whiteness continues to function as "normative," "intrinsically valuable," "pure," and "god-like."

The density project is an approach that refuses to allow philosophy and philosophical discourse to remain abstract and distant. So, there is the need to push discourse *to do* more. It also demands more from flesh and blood philosophers who engage problems of race. Those philosophers who attempt to understand the complex processes of racialization must also painfully confront (and live with) what it means to be embodied as raced. Through this framework, there is no way to remain removed from and not implicated in the messiness of race. The density project begins with the fact that Black lives *don't* matter vis-à-vis the white gaze and white "sacred" embodiment, that Black ontology is always already inconsequential, a site of nullification. As such, the density project demands that philosophy engages with the existential tragic lives of Black people within a real world that is structurally dominated by white terror, white injustice, white microaggressions, white power. It demands that Black philosophers and philosophers of color understand that there is no safe world within which questions of race are raised and critically discussed. The topic of race can't be locked away, bracketed out, and only raised as a scholarly topic within the "safe" confines of a classroom or within a journal article, book, or in a conference presentation. Moreover, the density project specifically demands of white philosophers to understand how they carry the historical and contemporary embodied implications of *their whiteness* and admit to how it functions to keep them alive, to keep them flourishing, to keep them safe and complicit with racialized injustice. And even as it is true that poor whites don't unconditionally reap all of the benefits from whiteness when mediated by class, such bodies continue to matter differentially when juxtaposed to *poor* Black bodies. In fact, I would argue that there is a kind of metaphysics of white value that continues to operate through class, disability, and sexual orientation markers that only compound existential and sociopolitical problems for Black bodies.

As we continue to face the tragic deaths of Black bodies and bodies of color at the hands of the state and those who see themselves as proxies of the state (say, George Zimmerman), my hope is that this second edition of *Black Bodies, White Gazes* will help to abolish the illusions of those who would dare to pretend (or convince themselves into believing) that we currently live in a post-racial moment in North America. There is one thing that I can, with tremendous grief and sorrow, count on. Tomorrow, another unarmed Black person will be killed by the state or by its proxies; another unarmed Black body will cease to exist through the actions of those mainly white police officers who took an oath to protect us regardless of race. Some Black mother and father will mourn with a terrifying heaviness as their child's life is deemed worthless by the state. In fact, perhaps, as in the case of Philando Castile (on July 6, 2016), that Black person will be armed and have a permit to carry and yet will still be killed by police. Or, perhaps, as in the case of Charles Kinsey (on July 18, 2016), that Black person will be shot while unarmed and also on the ground with his hands held up and his feet spread apart, saying in earshot of police officers that he is a behavioral Tech and that his client who has Autism has a toy truck in his hand. Kinsey's situation painfully reveals that a Black body, though defenseless, is still perceived as a "violent" body. Even as Kinsey provided an explanation of the entire situation, thus functioning within that situation as an epistemic authority, his Black body remains excessive, a surplus to be disciplined, to be held in check, to be shot.

This second edition of *Black Bodies, White Gazes* continues to be dedicated to *all* bodies that suffer, which must include the police officers killed in Dallas, Texas (in 2016) and their families who suffered as a result of their deaths. Those killings were tragic. I was deeply saddened by them. What we need in this country is a new and radical relational ontology that gets at the roots of what it means to *be-with*, what it means to *dwell near* each other. After all, we are entangled together in a racially saturated social integument that is in desperate need of un-suturing, of undoing, and then re-suturing in ways that are based upon a prior radical troubling of a form of relational ontology that has rendered so many human beings as permanent "strangers," "others," "refuse," and as falling under the category of those whose pain and suffering should not be grieved. This second edition of *Black Bodies, White Gazes* dares yet again to confront the white gaze, to offer the gift of the Black gaze, and to engage in courageous speech, a form of speech that refuses to be beautiful or calm. My hope is that it will continue to encourage a generative space for fearless listening.

The first edition of *Black Bodies, White Gazes* came out in 2008, the same year that we experienced the historic election of the United States' first African American President. The second edition is coming out as President Obama's eight years are coming to a close. Under Obama's tenure, white hegemony, power and privilege continued unabated. Arguably, Black bodies have been under white assault *because* of Obama's presidency, a form of violent pushback, perhaps even retaliation, from those who consciously or unconsciously believed (and continue to believe) that Obama has taken (white) America from them. In 2008, my objectives were multiple. I wrote about race in a style that captured the *lived* reality of race, the dynamic process of racialization, and the deep *embodied* social spaces and social transactions in which racism permeates. I opted for a style of writing that pushed philosophy and philosophical discourse *to do* more on the page. I demonstrated how contemporary philosophy could be honest and courageous, how it could speak to issues that are existentially urgent and that involve existentially high-stakes. I spoke from a space of exposure, a place of passion or suffering. I made it clear that I theorized from an embodied perspective, taking that embodiment seriously as a condition for *doing* philosophy. I dwelled within a place of risk. My objective was to provide a sustained philosophical treatment of Black embodiment and to theorize the contemporary and historical structural violence of the white gaze. The first edition was very successful as a philosophy text. Yet, as a philosopher, a writer, there are times when I've asked if I'm really making a difference. When the first edition began to be significantly referenced and critically engaged in books, articles, PhD dissertations, MA theses, and on multiple websites, I was thrilled. The many book reviews that I read were engaging and expressed an explicit appreciation for the philosophical importance of the book, its introduction of new conceptual frames of reference and vocabulary, and its nuance in terms of writing style. This was very affirming, yet I'm still often haunted by a lingering doubt that I have not done enough.

In 2008, like many, I thought that the historic election of the first African American President would make a huge positive impact on race relations in terms of bringing us closer, as we are such a racially divided nation. However, I was mistaken, terribly wrong. Obama's election to the highest office in the nation, as intimated above, triggered expressions of deep white racist resentment, racist vitriol, and vile caricatures of his person. He was/is the presidential Rorschach test for some of the most despicable manifestations of white racism. President Obama has been depicted as a monkey a la Curious George, as obsessed with eating fried chicken and watermelon, as a terrorist, as emaciated and preferring to drink cheap beer, as a thug and gangbanger, as a witch doctor, as a rat, as someone who likes Kool-Aid, as dressed in drag, as the character Buckwheat in *The Little Rascals*, as the object of perverse homophobic references, and again as a monkey, only this time one being killed by white police. On social media, where whites can hide behind false identities, Obama has also been called a "nigger," one of our nation's most preferred and stable racist epithets. He has also been publically called a liar.

I recall thinking: Only in America! Then again, Obama has also functioned globally as a "simian," as something "dark," "evil," and "malevolent," which are deeply racist and racially coded terms. More recently, in 2016, Donald Trump has referenced Obama, "Barack *Hussein* Obama," as being the founder of ISIS. Within a racially charged context as that in which we live (or have always lived), one where white nationalist discourse runs rampant, and white xenophobia is so pervasive, his claim is profoundly dangerous and irresponsible, despite the later statement that he was being sarcastic. As a birther who believes that Obama was not born in the US, and as one who, as of this writing, has shamelessly exercised his white privilege not only to define Black reality monolithically and in derogatory terms, but to dare to play the role of Black peoples' white savior, Trump continues to add kindling to the fire next time.

As argued above, it is/was during Obama's presidency that unarmed Black people have been killed at shocking rates by those who have sworn to protect and serve. Perhaps I had been naïve. Analogously, I guess that it would have been equally naïve to think that just because a female had become president that somehow the structural and ideological dimensions of sexism would magically disappear. On this score, assuming that Hilary Clinton becomes the next president, there is no reason to also assume that patriarchy will no longer exist. Moreover, there is no reason to assume that the plight of Black women and women of color will radically change for the good. But surely, under Obama's presidency, there was an implied promise to Black people in North America, one that was not naïve, but one that might be said to be reasonably expected and ethically and politically obligatory given the racist history of this country. After all, we are talking about the first African American President after literally centuries of Black enslavement, dehumanization, racist caricature and distortion, mutilation, rape, torture, suffering, bodily and psychic trauma, discrimination, oppression, and death. Imagine the expectations of those hundreds of thousands of Black bodies whose cries and screams have been heard throughout the centuries given white America's brutality toward them. Think of the ethical responsibility that our first African American President had to feel or should have felt. The important question to be asked, one that I will not address here, is: what has Black America gained, politically, economically, socially, psychologically, and existentially, since the election of Obama? While Obama's presidency has had tremendous racial symbolic power, and will continue to do so, I argue that the office of the presidency constitutes a site of white normativity that occludes a Black President from addressing race, racism, and whiteness in a sustained, serious, powerful, and robust way. It might be argued that Obama's need to distance himself from being depicted as "the president of Black people," which I think that most Black people knew could not and should not be the case, actually functioned to flatten out the important differential problems suffered by Black people that he had an ethical obligation to address and significantly remedy. To be Black and President of this nation appears to be mutually exclusive or certainly rife with tension. The white normativity of the Office itself forces a form of bad faith, forcing a compromise with one's own Black self. To be white and presidential, and address race matters, is to be a liberal or a progressive. Well, others might even say, a "nigger lover." To be Black and presidential, and to address race matters, is to be nonpresidential, partial, particularistic, nonobjective, un-American, perhaps even "racist." Therefore, one is backed into a corner to generate just enough discourse about race to give the impression that the needs of Black people are being addressed as the needs of *all* Americans are being addressed. Of course, for many whites, despite the relative paucity of such discourse that came from Obama, any mention of race is enough to have made Obama into a "race baiter." My position here should remind us of the complexity and endurance of the power of race and racism in our nation; it speaks to us of the illusion that we are living in a post-racial America. If anything, Black people are still living in the belly of the beast. White racism is alive and well. The future of race and racism within this country will continue. Personally, I don't see an end, which means that I don't see an end to Black suffering as linked to whiteness, disproportionate Black incarceration rates, structural Black poverty and unemployment, and the disposability of Black life. Whiteness will continue to expand, even as the United States continues to increase in its number of people of color. Indeed, such an increase does not *ipso facto* mean that whiteness, its power, hegemony, and privilege, will dwindle. In fact, it is my sense that whiteness will grow stronger. Sheer numbers of Black and Brown bodies can increase as whites remain in power. Just think of South Africa. I am by no means optimistic. I have felt sickened and emotionally drained by the sheer magnitude of racism in this country. America's collective anti-Blackness has left me in a Sisyphean mode of existence. Perhaps only a god can save us now. And yet, I continue to write, to encourage, and to hope, a hope that these days I often wonder whether or not is a joke.

After eight years since the original publication of *Black Bodies, White Gazes*, I have come to think of this book as prescient, painfully so. As I mourned the death of yet another Black person, a death that was inextricably linked to the white gaze and the ontological truncation of the Black body, I was reminded of how I (in 2008) conceptually framed the problem of race and racism in terms of the "sub-humanity" of Black bodies vis-à-vis the specific structure of the white gaze. I thought about how the white gaze distorts, caricatures, oppresses, and dehumanizes Black bodies. I thought about how Black bodies suffer within everyday social spaces of being stopped, frisked, and criminalized through the racist historic machinations of white gazes and the racist policies of the white state and its policing of Black bodies. While we only need to ask Black people about what it is like to live under constant white surveillance, a gesture that would acknowledge and respect Black people as epistemic subjects who know what it is like to live under the constant threat of being harassed, violated, and traumatized, the Justice Department's reports on both Ferguson's racist deployment of "law and order" and the scathing report into the despicable violations committed by the Baltimore City Police Department testify to the ways in which Black people continue to suffer from daily acts of criminalization and racial injustice.

When Trayvon Martin had been pursued and *a priori* criminalized, and then killed, I felt the weight of the white gaze and how it is mobile. George Zimmerman embodied the white gaze despite his "mixed race" identity. I wept upon hearing what was said to be Martin's cries of help. As Eric Garner cried out—"I can't breathe"—I knew that those white police officers had not "seen" him as they should have. When Michael Brown was seen as a "demon" by a white police officer, the history of the white gaze was historically concretized once again in its violence. When Levar Jones (2014) was shot at and actually hit after reaching into his vehicle to retrieve his license, after being asked for his license by a white police officer, the ontological truncation of the Black body was all too evident. The white police officer did not see an innocent act of following rules, but a Black body on the brink of retrieving a weapon. For Jones, to follow white "law and order" was to risk being killed. Not to follow white "law and order" was also to risk being killed. Either way, he could have been killed. It's not about what the Black body does, but about what the white gaze sees, what it constructs. Recall that LaQuan McDonald (2014) was shot sixteen times by a white police officer as he turned to walk away from police officers with his three-inch blade. His body can be seen moving as a result of the impact of the bullets entering into his body as he was on the ground. My deep fear is that my life (and the life of my Black sons) is in white hands that think about and behave toward our Black bodies in ways that spell out in unequivocal terms that our lives *don't matter*. These white hands have been historically at the ends of ropes, have flayed Black flesh, and beaten Black bodies beyond recognition. When Sandra Bland was stopped and physically forced to the ground by a white police officer, the treatment she received was appalling; the white police officer acted with impunity as he used his white authority, which is linked to the state as a site of whiteness, to threaten her. What he saw was someone who behaved "disorderly," was "recalcitrant," and "refused" his orders. His white gaze set the stage for Bland's righteous anger and her eventual death.

In this new edition of *Black Bodies, White Gazes*, I have tried to be consistent in style and tone. I've refused to allow philosophy to remain trapped in abstract spaces, and, thereby, rendering its human face obsolete. I don't deny theory as such, but the kind of theory that makes itself into an idol, where "to look" becomes a fetish. Philosophy is an embodied *practice*. To do philosophy, at least for me, is to feel the weight of the world, its problems, its silences, its failures, its tragedy, its pain and suffering. Personally, for me, to do philosophy, to love wisdom, is a species of *suffering*. How can it not? I have always known that I approach the world with a certain affect, a certain mood. And that affect discloses the world in certain ways to me. At times, what is disclosed is absolute, inexplicable mystery. At other times, what is disclosed is the suffering of the world. In either case, what is disclosed is heavy to bear. And specifically within the context of North America where Black Americans are continuously despised, hated, and killed by the state and those who are its proxies, a voice that strives to be pleasant, calm, and pure is one that will fail to confront the gravitas of anti-Black racism. My voice must confront the horror of the white gaze head-on. Therefore, it is necessary that I/we critically tarry within the discursive and non-discursive domains of white power and its grotesqueness if we are to be honest about Black pain and suffering under the weight of the white gaze.

In this second edition, I have remained close to the proverbial ground. I've critically engaged contemporary contexts within which Black bodies have continued to suffer under the white gaze and white gazing. I've brought the same style of writing, hopefully with greater effectiveness and descriptive power, to bear upon the horror of unarmed Black bodies that have been tragically gunned down by those whose jobs it has been to serve and protect us. I have continued to engage contemporary white spaces and how such spaces occlude Black bodies from being. Such spaces are normatively white and function to underwrite white gazes and the "truths" that such gazes produce vis-à-vis Black bodies. In two new chapters, chapters 1 and 8, I've introduced new concepts within the critical vocabulary of critical philosophy of race and critical whiteness studies (such as sutured and un-sutured) as a way of rethinking and reimagining whiteness and what is socio-ontologically at stake at the level of white embodied existence and possible white transgression. My hope is that such concepts will engage the broader racist social integument that is always already operative within the structure of racial encounters. Rethinking such encounters has helped me to complicate and further engage sociality as raced. In chapter 3, I've added two new vignettes, one on Jacqueline Woodson, a Black literary figure, and another one on poet, activist, and cultural theorist Audre Lorde. This chapter actually creates an important conceptual space that engages a total of 9 vignettes that powerfully speak to shared forms of anti-Black suffering across gender, space and time, fictional texts, and personally *lived* experiences. In chapter 4, while I continue to argue for the importance of Black resistance, toward the end of that chapter I now rethink the structure of hope that undergirds that resistance. I have also enlarged the scope of my critical engagement of differentially gendered forms of Black embodiment under the white gaze. This has been an important insight for me. As a Black male, I have had to learn how my own treatment of race can slip into forms of privileging my own Black embodiment *as male*. I have heard the critique of Black women's voices (some philosophers and others not) and I have been touched by those critical voices. There are many events that I have not engaged since 2008 in this text, especially those that are racially significant events that the reader may think that I should have engaged. If the reader decides that these are failures, it is my fault and only mine.

My hope is that those readers who appreciatively and critically engaged the 2008 edition of this book will engage this new edition with equal appreciation and criticality. My hope is that I have provided a newer contemporary version of *Black Bodies, White Gazes* that will help readers to understand how Black bodies continue to be marked, ontologically, as problem bodies and how the white gaze continues to mark those bodies through processes of interpellation (or hailing), power, denial, hegemony, and privilege even as so many white people believe that they are innocent of racism. If you are Black, don't be seduced by such a lie; it grows out of a certain problematic and false perspective on how our society is actually organized. Such a lie is constructed from a white perspective, one that dangerously fails to see that the world has been shaped to validate white assumptions and white modes of being—even as those assumptions are blatantly erroneous and those modes of being are complicit with forms of oppression. In fact, I would argue that not only is the structure of whiteness binary, but its structure is constituted by lies that white people desperately feel that they can't live without; indeed, lies that they can't even see or name as lies. To be embodied as Black and to fall for such a lie is to flirt with death.

If you are Black, you can't afford to believe that you are seen as a "neo-liberal subject" free from the force of white racism and its ugly legacy. You must not assume that your life matters in the same way that white lives matter. You must not assume that you are granted unconditional spatial mobility. You must not assume that your body is defined only by you and that such a definition can save you. And you must not assume that you can exercise your right to defend your dignity through "free speech" without dire consequences. Within white racist North America, you must not even assume that you are taken to be human. The history of white supremacy in this country more than justifies my cautionary advice to you.

If you are white, though, know that you are part of a system that would rather you live a lie than risk you seeing the truth. If you are white, you *must* face a certain kind of death—the death of your narrowness of vision, the death of your white narcissism, the death of your "innocence," the death of your neoliberal assumptions, the death of the metanarrative of meritocracy, the death of all of those things that underwrite your white gaze as the only way of seeing the world. This book asks that you die to such lies in order that you might truly live.

Acknowledgments

I would like to thank Rowman & Littlefield for its confidence and enthusiasm for publishing a second edition of this important text. It is an absolute pleasure to work with you. I would like to thank Jon Sisk for his deep appreciation for issues of social justice and for his patience, Natalie Mandziuk for her initial encouragement for a second edition, and Christopher Utter for his logistical assistance. I would also like to thank the two anonymous external reviewers who were incredibly excited about publishing a second edition. Their comments were extremely insightful and helpful. I was especially honored to learn that the two of them used the first edition in their courses. I would also like to thank all of the readers who have found the book helpful as you have struggled to understand the complexities of race and embodiment. I hope that this second edition meets or even exceeds your expectations.

Being the "author" of a book carries traces of "creator." And while language is something akin to *bringing forth*, the truth is that this book owes a debt to insights and influences from a multiplicity of voices. This, I hope, speaks to a level of humility, something reminiscent of Socrates who wanted to make sure that his sons were reproached when they thought that they amounted to something when they did not.

I would like to thank Dr. Ross H. Miller, senior editor at Rowman & Littlefield, for his continued support of my work and his genuine investment in high-quality books in philosophy. Ruth Gilbert, editorial assistant, is thanked for the dedication that she gives to detail. Paula Smith-Vanderslice, assistant production editor, is thanked for her professionalism. Heather Lee Miller for her excellent copyediting. Dawn Vogel is to be thanked for her excellent indexing and keen eye. I would like to thank the anonymous reviewers for Rowman & Littlefield who strongly supported the publication of this project and argued for its significant contribution to multiple areas of critical inquiry.

I would also like to thank the Wimmer Foundation, through Duquesne University, for awarding me a writing grant for the summer of 2006 to complete research for this project. Related to this, I thank former Dean Francesco C. Cesareo and my colleague and chairperson Jim Swindal for their enthusiastic reception of my scholarship and for providing financial support. There are many colleagues I would like to thank who have read parts of this text over the course of its many permutations: Eve DeVaro Fowler, Fred Evans, Charles Johnson, Farah Griffin, Timothy Chambers, Eleanore Holveck, John McClendon, Steve Martinot, Dan Watkins, Kathy Glass, Charles W. Mills, Clevis Headley, Janine Jones, Laurence M. Thomas, Lorraine Code, Shannon Sullivan, Bettina Bergo, Nancy Tuana, Clarence Shole Johnson, Maria Del Guadalupe Davidson, Robert Birt, Manomano M. M. Mukungurutse, Lisa Heldke, Cynthia Kaufman, Barbara Applebaum, John Warren, and Alison Bailey.

I would like to thank those individuals from the University of Pittsburgh at Bradford, Indiana University of Pennsylvania, Johns Hopkins University, Slippery Rock University, Wabash College, and Middle Tennessee State University, who attended talks I gave and who provided genuine dialogue that helped further shape the ideas within this text. Students from my "Race Matters" classes, my "Critical Race Theory" classes, and my "Race and Film" class at Duquesne are thanked for insightful lines of questioning that forced me to demand greater clarity of myself. Undergraduate and graduate students at my new home university, Emory University, are also to be thanked for their influence on the second edition of this text. Charles Johnson, Thomas S. Slaughter, Linda M. Alcoff, and Lewis R. Gordon are thanked for their complex philosophical analyses of racial embodiment.

I especially thank James G. Spady for his unwavering stand for excellence in scholarship and unmatched influence on my intellectual development. Lucius T. Outlaw, Jr., the late Joyce M. Cook, Charles Berlin, and William L. Banks are thanked for their abiding confidence. My mother, Ruth Yancy, and my late father, George D. Yancey, El, Artrice and Carson, and Lillian and Geoff are thanked for their support and love. The Yancy boys who are so loved. This work also speaks to them, to their bodies. And to Susan Hadley, my amiable consort, whose embodied presence is a mysterious gift, a source of profound love, joy, and creation.

In addition, I would like to thank various publishers for permission to use copyrighted material. Quotations from *The Bluest Eye* by Toni Morrison, copyright © 1970 and renewed 1998 by Toni Morrison. Afterword copyright © 1993 by Toni Morrison. Used by permission of Alfred A. Knopf, a division of Random House, Inc. Quotations from *Invisible Man* by Ralph

Ellison, copyright 1947, 1948, 1952 by Ralph Ellison. Copyright renewed 1975, 1976, 1980 by Ralph Ellison. Used by permission of Random House, Inc. Parts of this book previously have been published elsewhere. Chapter 1 is a slightly modified version of "White Suturing, Black Bodies, and the Myth of a Post-Racial America," in *ARTS/The Arts in Religion and Theological Studies*, 26(2), 2015, 5–14. Chapter 2 is a modified version of an article that appeared in *Philosophy & Social Criticism* in 2008 by SAGE publications Ltd. Chapter 3 is a modified version of "Whiteness and the Return of the Black Body," *The Journal of Speculative Philosophy*, 19(4), 2005, 215–41. Copyright 2005 by The Pennsylvania State University. Reproduced by permission of the publisher. Chapter 4 is an expanded and modified version of an article that appeared in *Western Journal of Black Studies*, 28(2) (Summer 2004), 337–53. Chapter 5 is an expanded and modified version of an article that appeared in *Philosophy & Social Criticism*, 28(3), 2002, 297–320. Chapter 8 is a slightly modified version of "White Embodied Gazing, the Black Body as Disgust, and the Aesthetics of Un-Suturing," in *Body Aesthetics*, ed. Sherri Irvin (Oxford University Press, 2016).

Introduction

I want my voice to be harsh, I don't want it to be beautiful, I don't want it to be pure.

—Frantz Fanon

In his much discussed speech on race, which was just given prior to the completion of this book in March 2008, Barack Obama provided personal testimony of his white grandmother as someone who loved him and sacrificed for him, but added that she was "a woman who once confessed her fear of black men who passed by her on the street, and who on more than one occasion has uttered racial or ethnic stereotypes that made me cringe."[1] Even as she no doubt affectionately looked into the eyes of her phenotypic dark grandson and taught him about duty and compassion, she feared Black male bodies that passed her on the street, perhaps characterizing them as "niggers" up to no good. Loving God while simultaneously hating those "niggers" is another contradiction that the history of white racism makes palatable, indeed, "rational," to many whites. Obama's white grandmother's loving gaze was weighed down by, riddled with, contradictions and tensions that reveal the insidious nature of whiteness and subtextually speak to the pain and suffering of Black bodies that have been stereotyped, criminalized, and rendered invisible by the white gaze. Social scientists will be long preoccupied with the fact that so many whites actually voted for Obama. After all, it is *not* incompatible for those whites who voted for him to be afraid of Black male bodies they see walking in their direction, who they prejudge as criminals. Given the historically distorted white gaze vis-à-vis Black male bodies, one can only wonder what it is that whites force themselves to see or not to see when they gaze upon the dark body of Obama.

Black Bodies, White Gazes is precisely a sustained effort to explore the Black body within the context of whiteness, a context replete with contradictions and mythopoetic constructions. To do this, I use multiple frames of reference from personal testimony, Black autobiography, and fiction, to critical whiteness studies, white antiracist forms of disarticulating and struggling against whiteness, and Black embodied sites of resistance. The use of these various frames allows for a multiplicity of perspectives on the Black body. Indeed, these frames capture the current and historical epistemic and habituated embodied orders that configure and sustain the white gaze and function to objectify the Black body as an entity that is to be feared, disciplined, and relegated to those marginalized, imprisoned, and segregated spaces that restrict Black bodies from "disturbing" the tranquility of white life, white comfort, white embodiment, and white being. The objectification of the Black body raises the issue of Black invisibility and hypervisibility as modes of further erasure of the integrity of the Black body. The Black body as objectified also raises issues around the constitutive and constructive semiotic, material, and sociopolitical processes that hail and fix the white body as normative, thus reinforcing the importance of the social "ontological space of white ego genesis [and maintenance] that requires the evading of the humanity" of Black people.[2] Against this backdrop, I wrote this text in the spirit of Frantz Fanon's critical explorations of the lived experiences of Blacks, experiences weighed down by the white imaginary, which has "woven me [and other Black bodies] out of a thousand details, anecdotes, stories," and to show whites that they are "at once the perpetrator[s] and the victims[s] of a delusion."[3]

The history of the Black body in North America is fundamentally linked to the history of whiteness, primarily as whiteness is expressed in the form of fear, sadism, hatred, brutality, terror, avoidance, desire, denial, solipsism, madness, policing, politics, and the production and projection of white fantasies. From the perspective of whiteness, the Black body *is* criminality itself. It *is* the monstrous; it is that which is to be feared and yet desired, sought out in forbidden white sexual adventures and fantasies; it is constructed as a source of white despair and anguish, an anomaly of nature, the essence of vulgarity and immorality. The Black body is deemed the quintessential object of the ethnographic gaze, the "strange," exotic, and fascinating object of anthropology. The Black body is constructed as antithetical within a binary logic that points to the white body's own "signifying [and material] forces to call attention to itself " as normative.[4] Indeed, whiteness is deemed the transcendental norm, the good, the innocent, and the pure, while Blackness is the diametrical opposite. This is the twisted fate of the Black body vis-à-vis white forms of disciplinary control, processes of white racist embodied habituation, and epistemic white world-making.

Lynched, castrated, raped, branded, mutilated, whipped, socially sequest-ered, profiled, harassed, policed, disproportionately arrested and incarcerated, the Black body has endured a history of more than symbolic white violence. One need not reach back into the remote past of American history—a history indelibly stained by the blood of Black bodies as a result of white power—to find whites tormenting Black bodies. As recently as September 2007, six whites held Megan Williams, a twenty-year-old Black woman, prisoner in a trailer in West Virginia. Williams' captors raped her, poured hot water and hot wax on her body, forced her to drink out of the toilet and to eat feces (possibly dog, rat, and human), cut off and yanked out her hair, forced her to lick their toes, taunted her with racial slurs, cut her ankle and stabbed her thigh, and forced her to perform oral sex on one of the white women.[5]

This violent scene replicates the history of whiteness as terror. The scene is one of spectacle. Gazing upon the despised and violated Black body—the historically marked "Black nigger bitch"—as it is forced to eat feces and drink from a toilet, is also a site of white racist pleasure, masochism, and dominance. It was not enough that the Black body was sexually violated. It had to be dehumanized and humiliated, reduced to an eater of shit and a drinker of urine, forced to mimic white fantasies of the Black body as animal-istic and infrahuman, fixed as a "thing" of teratology, a monster, something freakish, abnormal, and capable of the most disgraceful acts.

Many whites will read about Megan Williams and posit her situation as anomalous, something of which only "those racist whites" are capable. This form of moral distancing functions to allow many whites a sense of moral superiority over "those white racists," while obfuscating their own racism through the act of disavowing only a *particular form* of racism. This creates deep forms of self-deception.

Recall the Black students (2006) at Jena High School in Jena, Louisiana, who decided to exercise their right to sit under a tree that had been de facto segregated for whites only. The next day, the Black students were sent a definitive message: three nooses hanging in the tree's branches. Although apparently not the result of Klan activity, the message was clear: the only good nigger is a dead nigger. In response to the nooses found hanging in the so-called "white tree," a raced space of whiteness, a white woman in the area reported that there are no race problems in Jena. About the nooses, she said, "The nooses? I don't even know why they were there, what they were sup-posed to mean. There're pranks all the time, of one type or another, going on. And it just didn't seem to be racist to me."[6] This is the sort of response from someone who would argue that a large swastika painted on a synagogue is not anti-Semitic, but just an instance of boys being boys. It takes a massive form of self-deception not to see the nooses as racist vitriol. The board of education also seems to have believed that the hanging of the nooses was a youthful prank. The three white male students who were responsible for hanging the nooses were suspended from school for a few days, a form of reprimand indicative of habituated modes of white denial, structured ignorance, white bonding, and disrespect for Black people.

When white bodies affix nooses to trees that Black bodies have decided to sit under, in a public space that whites had literally appropriated for white bonding, the force of effective history informs the entire scene. The charge that the white students had performed a youthful prank is a form of gross disrespect for those Black bodies that were mutilated and dismembered during lynching spectacles and those Black families that had to live with the results of those horrors. The charge also involved a profound case of disgraceful ignorance of America's racist history. In fact, the very act of hanging the nooses was a form of violence, effectively communicating to the Black students that they are unwanted "niggers" who ought to know their place in a world where whiteness is supreme. The nooses signaled the historical specificity of the castration of Black bodies, broken necks, bulging eyes, flesh torn from the body, burned flesh, fingers and knuckles sold in local stores. The nooses signaled death for Black bodies who would dare to "transgress" white space.

On any given day in North America, the Black body vis-à-vis the white gaze—that performance of distortional "seeing" that evolves out of and is inextricably linked to various raced and racist myths, white discursive practices, and centripetal processes of white systemic power and white solipsism—undergoes processes of dehumanizing interpellation. The white gaze, given the power of the ocular metaphor in Western culture, is an important site of power and control, a site that is structured by white epistemic orders and that perpetuates such orders in turn.

Talk-show host Don Imus's "nappy-headed hos" comment about the Rutgers University women's basketball team in 2007 was not an isolated incident, but is a comment replicated within enduring epistemic orders of whiteness. Imus's comment was both a form of white "nation-building" that fosters a spoken and unspoken sense of white bonding, and is part and parcel of a larger white racist cartography that has always already mapped and overdetermined the Black body. I have heard many whites argue that there are also Blacks who say such things as "nappy-headed hos." Arguing that Blacks also use demeaning language toward other Blacks leads to the presumptive conclusion that whites who use such language ought to be exempt from the charge of racism. Hence, or so the logic goes, Blacks should not, in good conscience, accuse whites of racism when they also use such language. Besides committing the fallacy of *tu quoque*, this stratagem completely flattens out the differential histories between whites and Blacks. It attempts to mystify differential power relations between Blacks and whites and conceal the fact that whites deployed and continue to deploy a racist iconography to maintain power. Indeed, white discursive practices are inextricably linked to forms of political and social power.

Whites who use racist descriptions form part of a long racist history of those who have controlled, and continue to control, not only the power to denigrate Black bodies through language but also to murder and dismember those bodies. Within the context of white racist America, whites inherited the privileged status of being the "lookers" and gazers, with all the power that this entailed. As Jean-Paul Sartre noted, "For three thousand years, the white man has enjoyed the privilege of seeing without being seen; he was only a look—the light from his eyes drew each thing out of the shadow of its birth."[7] Whites also presumed the a priori right to nominate Black bodies as they saw fit. This is consistent with white hubris to define the "reality" of nonwhites in categorical terms, stipulations, conditions, and appellations predicated upon white power and privilege.[8]

As a white racist speech act, Imus's "nappy headed hos" expression carried the force of violence that attacked the integrity of Black female bodies, bodies that ought to be inviolable. The discourse reflects white social practices that constitute the fabric of white America and the enduring reality of anti-Black racism. Within this context, the production of the Black body is an effect of the discursive and epistemic structuring of white *gazing* and other white modes of anti-Black performance. And while these performances are not always enacted consciously but the result of years of white racism calcified and habituated within the bodily repertoire of whites, whites are not exempt from taking responsibility for the historical continuation of white racism.

While walking across the street, I have endured the sounds of car doors locking as whites secure themselves from the "outside world," a space that is raced as nonwhite. In fact, this outside world represents the inverted white self and "mark[s] the 'imaginary' relations that characterize the colonial encounter."[9] This "outside world" functions as a trope that renders Black bodies, *my* Black body, ostracized, different, and unwelcome. This outside world dialectically exists alongside a presumptive space of whiteness as unmarked, unraced, civilized, and normal. Those on the outside are rejected because they are deemed suspicious, vile, unclean, infestations of the (white) social body. Within the social context of white racist power, I do not traverse what I take to be an objective neutral space (walking through a white neighborhood at night, for example). Rather, the space of the white neighborhood has already been polarized into "inside and outside" in such a way that "curtails black people's inhabiting of [that] space."[10]

The sounds of car doors locking are deafening: *Click. Click. Click. Click. Click. Click. Click. ClickClickClickClickClickClickClick.* The *clicking* sounds are always accompanied by nervous gestures and eyes that want to look but are hesitant to do so. The *click* ensures their safety, effectively re-signifying their white bodies as in need of protection from *blackness*, that site of danger, death, and doom. In fact, the *clicks* begin to return me to myself—even as I continue to disrupt the constituting effects of the *clicks* that overdetermine me—as a dangerous beast. The *clicks* attempt to seal my identity as a dark savage. The *clicking* sounds mark me; they inscribe me, materializing my presence, as it were, in ways that I know to be untrue. Unable to stop the *clicking*, unable to stop white women from tightening the hold of their purses as I walk by, unable to stop white women from crossing to the other side of the street once they have seen me walking in their direction, unable to stop white men from looking several times over their shoulders as I walk behind them minding my own business, unable to establish a form of recognition that creates a space of trust and liminality, unable to give public talks without many whites feeling uncomfortable with the refusal of a Black man to engage in acts of self-censorship about *their* racism, there are times when one wants to become *their* fantasy, to become *their* Black monster, *their* bogeyman. For example, in the case of the *clicks*, one wants to pull open the car door: "Surprise. You've just been car-jacked by a ghost, a fantasy of *your own* creation. Now, get the fuck out of the car!"

The depiction of the Black body as the quintessence of *evil* has endured across historical space and time. Hence, *my* Black body is a site of enduring white semiotic constructions and historical power relations that inscribe and mark it as a particular *type* of body, an indistinguishable, threatening, evil pre-sence, the so-called black bugaboo.

News in 2007 of a video that allegedly depicts a German army instructor ordering a recruit who is training with a machine gun to imagine that he is firing at three African Americans who pull up in a van in the middle of the Bronx and begin to insult his mother is unsurprising.[11] To marshal the hatred and focus necessary to kill, one needs a powerful catalyst. The German instructor exploits the image of the Black body, reproducing the historical racist image of the Black body as dangerous, subhuman, despicable, and unruly. On this score, the Black body is deemed the real enemy, a cross-cultural icon, the *sort* or *type* of body that generates global hatred and fear through the marketing of white lies.

The normative construction of the Black body as evil had already begun as early as the fifth century. Gustav Jahoda writes about John Cassian, a monk, who wrote a series of spiritual *Conferences*. Some of these portrayed the devil "'in the shape of a hideous Negro,' or a demon 'like a Negro woman, ill-smelling and ugly.'" Saint Benedict, an admirer of Cassian, made sure that the *Conferences* were read in the monasteries and thus these images would have had a wide circulation.[12] An axiological frame of reference where blackness is identified with demons presupposes the identification of whiteness with "light," "divinity," and "goodness." As I endure those *clicking* sounds, I catch a glimpse of myself through the white person's gaze. I am constructed as evil and darkness. Like the night, I am to be avoided. After all, peril lurks in the dark. As I move along urban streets, the white imaginary projects upon my Black body all of its fears, rendering my Black body the instantiation of evil. The distinction between signifier and signified have collapsed. In Levinasian terms, my "face" does not appear in the form of the imperative "Thou shall not murder."

In the case of the German army recruit, my Black body does not solicit "the concrete requirement, the command, to support the life, to alleviate the pain and suffering, and to forestall the dying of the other."[13] There is no moment of postponement. After he tells the recruit to imagine the three African Americans insulting his mother, the German instructor says, "Now do something!" The recruit begins firing. The Black body appears in the form of the imperative: "Kill the nigger!" And because the Black bodies will inevitably disrupt the security of law and order—for they are said to be ruled by caprice—the imperative is to kill them all before they strike.

Angela Davis argues that there has been a failure to confront seriously and honestly the ways in which the "ideological power of the figure of the young black male as criminal" continues to circulate in the American imaginary. Pointing to California as one of the states that approved mandatory sentencing legislation, otherwise known as Three Strikes and You're Out, Davis notes that Governor Pete Wilson argued after the bill passed that there should be a "two strikes and you're out bill" as three was still too many. Davis argues that this sort of logical mathematical regression may very well lead to the position that even one crime is too much. According to Davis, their watchword will be, "Get them before the first strike!" And because certain populations have already been criminalized, there will be those who will say, "We know who the real criminals are—let's get them before they have a chance to act out their criminality."[14]

Here is a case where the Black body is condemned before it even acts; it has always already committed a crime. According to Davis's interpretation of those hardcore anticrime advocates, the Black body is not born free, but is imprisoned by ideological frames of reference that reduce the Black body *ontologically* to the level of the criminal. Even in the womb, the Black body is already *against the law*. While it is true that Bill Bennett, who was secretary of education under President Ronald Reagan, said he disbelieves the statistic that crime is down because abortion is up, thus disagreeing with "findings" in the book *Freakonomics*, he also says, "I do know that it's true that if you wanted to reduce crime you could, if that were your sole purpose, you could abort every black baby in this country, and your crime rate would go down."[15] He goes on to say how impossible, ridiculous, and morally reprehensible this would be—but still *true*. So, while he clearly disagrees with the statistic that crime is down because abortion is up, he has no problem using the epistemic operator *true* vis-à-vis the apparent necessary connection between aborting *black babies* and the decrease in crime rate. Note that he says, "I do *know*." In short, Bennett *knows* that it is *true* that Blacks who are still in the womb will necessarily commit crimes, and he knows this prior to their birth. Hence, in the name of a future we cannot possibly predict, little Jamal, let us say, has already received his death sentence, because Bennett knows that it is true that aborting him will make our crime rate go down. This is a case where Black *existence* constitutes the threat, leading to the conclusion that the nullification of Black *being* is the only sure prerequisite for white safety.

Given the above, it is clear that part of the meaning of Black embodiment is disclosed within the context of an anti-Black racist world. The disclosure of its meaning, while inextricably and *relationally* tied to the history of anti-Black racism, is not *reduced* to that history. The point here is that the meaning of the Black body *is* historical. And as historical, the Black body and the white body are explored not in terms of an ontology of essences, but in terms of a historical ontology that appreciates the fluidity of the historical formation of the meaning of, in this case, the Black body and the white body, even as the white body engages in bad-faith practices of stipulating its modes of being as sacrosanct, reified, and independent of meaning-bestowing human beings. As *historical*, the Black body does not have its meaning ontologically (qua essence) given or sealed in advance. The Black body is a historical project and as such is capable of taking up new historical meanings through struggle and affirmation. As affirmative, the Black body is not simply defined in its opposition to a racist episteme, but engages its meaning beyond the horizon of the Black imago in the white imaginary while always keeping track of whiteness's recuperative efforts, its institutional rigidity, material power, and various complex forms of insidious manifestation.

More generally, then, the body's meaning is a site of contestation. That the body is a site of contested meanings signifies the historicity of its "being" as *lived* and *meant* within the context of social semiotics, institutional forces, and various discursive frames of reference. Hence, the body is less of a thing or a being than a shifting or changing historical meaning that is subject to cultural configuration and reconfiguration. This assumption is in stream with a major aim of *Black Bodies, White Gazes*, that is, to interrogate the Black body as a "fixed and material truth" which is said to preexist "its relations with the world and with others." The body's meaning is fundamentally symbolic.[16] The body's meaning is congealed through symbolic repetition and iteration that emits certain signs and presupposes certain norms. Also, the body is a battlefield, one that is fought over continuously across particular historical moments. This does not mean that the body has no material force of its own, but how we interpret that force is through historical discourse, even as that discourse may falter.

As I hope to show throughout this text, it is not only the Black body that defies the fixed fantasies and distorted images projected upon it through the white gaze, and, hence, through the episteme of whiteness, but the white body is also fundamentally symbolic, requiring demystification and exposure of its status as the norm, the paragon of beauty, order, innocence, purity, restraint, and nobility. In other words, given the assumptions about the body stated above, both the Black body and the white body lend themselves to processes of interpretive fracture, moments of disarticulation.

Black Bodies, White Gazes consists of eight chapters that explore in various ways the concept of whiteness as the transcendental norm—where whiteness takes itself to be that which remains the *same* across a field of difference—in relationship to the social ontological implications of racial embodiment. In chapter 1, the tragic deaths of Eric Garner, Michael Brown, Eric Harris, Tamir Rice, and Travon Martin are framed through a critically engaging and insightful understanding of the violence of the white gaze and how Black embodiment is constructed as a site of disposability. In chapter 2, I theorize how the white body, within the quotidian space of an elevator, engages in profound acts of Negrophobia as a result of racist effective history and white ego maintenance. The white body's performance is interpreted as an act of interpellation whereby the Black body is deemed always already problematic. Moreover, my argument is that the white body also undergoes processes of hailing or interpellation through the larger white social imaginary and that this process of interpellation is linked to larger forms of white historical power. In chapter 3, I explore what I refer to as the "phenomenological return" of the Black body. This process of return is explored in terms of the structure of the white gaze, particularly in terms of its power to attempt to install the Black body as "inferior," as a "thing" fit for "comedy," as "hypersexual," as "animal-like," as "untouchable," and as an object of white racist caricature. These white modes of representation are theorized as instances of epistemic violence that fragment and traumatize Black embodiment. In chapter 4, I explore the issue of Black resistance within the context of an anti-Black racist world. It is not sufficient to detail the lived experience of Black people within this context without a critical discussion of the ways in which Black bodies have engaged in acts of taking a stand against racism. I explore the logic of resistance as an affirmative and dialectical act. It is here that the Black body as agential emerges as ontologically resistant and more than the white gaze is capable of nullifying through its power. I then complicate Black resistance by rethinking hope, which is presupposed in acts of resistance. In chapter 5, I explore how the Black body has undergone various disciplinary techniques deployed by whites, not only in order to discipline the Black body physically but also to "confirm" the existential and onto-logical ersatz status of the Black body. I philosophically explore Frederick Douglass's autobiographical self-reflections as a way of focusing on the power and mendacity of whiteness, and its brutal impact on the Black body, and the Black body's efforts at engaging in axiological and deep existential claims to freedom. In chapter 6, I offer an interpretation of Toni Morrison's text *The Bluest Eye*. The text demonstrates how the Black body, through the protagonist, Pecola Breedlove, is torn asunder through the internalization of the white gaze. This chapter reveals just how destructive the norms, values, and iconography of whiteness can be on the Black body within the context of an anti-Black racist world. In chapter 7, I explore how whiteness is a form of what I call "ambush." I further theorize the white body as habituated and as always already having undergone and undergoing processes of interpellation. Hence, I critique the performance metaphor of "undoing" whiteness, arguing that this process does not culminate in a white person's having "arrived" in the form of a static anti-racist identity. Rather, undoing whiteness is a *continuous* process of disarticulation, especially as the white self is profoundly ensconced within material, historical, institutional, and discursive forces that involve the citation and assertion of whiteness as privilege and power. I argue that disarticulating the white gaze involves a continuous effort on the part of whites to forge new ways of seeing, knowing, and being. I remain cognizant, though, of the reality that whiteness is a form of conscious and unconscious investment that many whites would rather die for than to call into question, let alone to "dismantle." In chapter 8, I engage the white gaze and its pro-crustean and violent impact on Renisha McBride, Jordan Davis, and Sandra Bland. I also engage ways in which the Black body, through the white gaze, appears, shows up, in the mode of disgust. I also return to Trayvon Martin. I explore in detail two powerful metaphors, suturing and un-suturing, that not only provide an indispensable vocabulary for understanding whiteness, but that provide important ways of rethinking the possibility for a radical rela-tional ontology, rethinking issues of white racial embodiment, and rethinking ways of what it means to be-with or dwell near.

NOTES

1. "Barack Obama's Speech on Race," transcript, *New York Times*, online, April 5, 2008, http://www.nytimes.com/2008/03/18/us/politics/18text-obama.html?_r=1&incamp=article_popular&oref=slogin

2. Paget Henry, "African-American Philosophy: A Caribbean Perspective," in *A Companion to African-American Philosophy*, ed. Tommy L. Lott and John P. Pittman (Malden, MA: Blackwell, 2003), 52.

3. Frantz Fanon, *Black Skin, White Masks*, trans. Charles Lam Markmann (New York: Grove Press, 1967), 112, 225.

4. Bryant Keith Alexander, "Black Skin/White Masks: The Performative Sustainability of Whiteness (With Apologies to Frantz Fanon)," *Qualitative Inquiry* 10, no. 5 (2004): 647–72, quotation on 655.

5. The reader should note that after the publication of this book, reports surfaced that Megan Williams would recant many of the statements regarding her testimony that she was kidnapped, sexually assaulted and tortured by six whites. As it stands, Bobby Ray Brewster, his mother, Frankie Lee, Danny Combs, George Messer, Karen Burton, and her daughter Alisha Burton were all charged with kidnapping. Karen Burton was given one ten-year sentence for violation of civil rights and two two to ten year sentences for assault. Frankie Brewster received ten to twenty-five years for second-degree sexual assault. They had both pleaded guilty in exchange for reduced sentences. Bobby Brewster pleaded guilty to second-degree sexual assault, conspiracy to commit kidnapping and malicious assault. He was sentenced to thirteen to forty years in prison. Danny Combs will serve twenty years for conspiracy to commit kidnapping. He pleaded guilty to sexual assault, assault during the commission of a felony, and conspiracy to commit kidnapping or holding hostage. Alisha Burton and George Messer both pleaded guilty to assault and kidnapping and were sentenced to ten years each. In 2009, Williams recanted her earlier charges, saying that she lied because she was angry with one of the defendants with whom she had a relationship. This is extremely baffling. I say this because all six of the accused pleaded guilty. Had they not pleaded guilty, one might understand Williams' change of heart. How do we make sense of the physical evidence used in the case and the confessions of all six in the light of Williams' claim that she lied? How can six individuals plead guilty for crimes that they did not commit—indeed, such horrible crimes? Surely, they could have said that Williams was fabricating the entire story given that she exaggerates and is apparently "mentally challenged." Could they have undergone processes of "collective harassment" or "collective bullying" to confess? Did they consciously exert an effort to get their stories right so that they would be certain to get lighter sentences? And what do we do with the physical evidence? Was it planted by Williams? Was the prosecutor in the case so disgusted by the presence of six *poor* whites that she wanted to see them imprisoned? Will the accused only now claim that they were pressured into pleading guilty? My sense is that Williams' new claim that she lied is deeply troubling, especially given the death of her adopted and supportive mother. The events that Williams initially said occurred are not inconsistent with the sheer degradation and de-humanization that racist whites have historically visited upon Black female bodies. As of this writing, all six whites are in prison because of the evidence in the case and because of their confessions, not simply because of what Williams said. For details regarding sentencing and coverage of Williams' reversal of her earlier claims, February 22, 2010, see: http://en.wikipedia.org/wiki/Megan_Williams_case.

6. Amy Goodman, "The Case of the Jena Six: Black High School Students Charged with Attempted Murder for Schoolyard Fight after Nooses Are Hung from Tree," *Democracy Now*, April 5, 2008, http://www.democracynow.org/article.pl?sid=07/07/10/1413220.

7. Jean-Paul Sartre, "Black Orpheus," in *Race*, ed. Robert Bernasconi (Malden, MA: Blackwell, 2001), 115.

8. In this text, white privilege denotes various ways in which whites are advantaged in virtue of being white within a larger systemic sociopolitical context that in general *protects* white people/makes them *immune* in ways that nonwhites are not.

9. Abdul R. JanMohamed, "The Economy of the Manichean Allegory: The Function of Racial Difference in Colonialist Literature," in *"Race," Writing, and Difference*, ed. Henry Louis Gates, Jr. (Chicago: University of Chicago Press, 1986), 87–88.

10. Shannon Sullivan, "The Racialization of Space," in *The Problems of Resistance: Studies in Alternate Political Cultures*, ed. Steve Martinot, with Joy James (Amherst, NY: Humanity Books, 2001), 91.

11. Reuters, "German Soldier Told To 'Shoot African Americans,'" News.com.au, April 5, 2008, http://www.news.com.au/story/0,23599,21560017-2,00.html

12. Gustav Jahoda, *Images of Savages: Ancient Roots of Modern Prejudice in Western Culture* (New York: Routledge, 1999), 26.

13. Richard A. Cohen, "Levinas: Thinking Least about Death—contra Heidegger," in *Self and Other: Essays in Continental Philosophy of Religion*, ed. Eugene Thomas Long (New York: Springer, 2007), 35.

14. Angela Y. Davis, "Race and Criminalization: Black Americans and the Punish-ment Industry," in *The Angela Y. Davis Reader*, ed. Joy James (Malden, MA: Blackwell, 1998), 66.

15. *"Media Matters* exposes Bennett: '[Y]ou Could Abort Every Black Baby in This Country, and Your Crime Rate Would Go Down,'" *Media Matters for America*, April 5, 2008, http://mediamatters.org/items/200509280006. See also Steven Levitt and Stephen J. Dubner, *Freakonomics: A Rogue Economist Explores the Hidden Side of Everything* (New York: William Morrow/HarperCollins, 2005).

16. For an elaboration on these three interpretive points regarding the body, see Deborah E. McDowell, "Recovering Missions: Imagining the Body Ideals," in *Recovering the Black Female Body: Self-Representations by African American Women*, ed. Michael Bennett and Vanessa D. Dickerson (New Brunswick, N.J.: Rutgers University Press, 2001), quotations on 301.

Chapter 1

Black Bodies and the Myth of a Post-Racial America

The condition of Black life is one of mourning.

—A friend of Claudia Rankine

"To be or Not to be." Hadn't he heard the whitefolks? We couldn't be, so the question was a waste of time.

—Maya Angelou

WHITE GAZES AS SITES OF BLACK ASPHYXIATION

Since the publication of this text in 2008, the Black body has continued to be confronted by the death-dealing impact of the white gaze. In the twenty-first century, Black Americans have had to proclaim, through expressed mass protest, resistance, and pain and suffering, that *Black lives matter*. There is something very peculiar about being *human* and having to demonstrate that humanity, to announce it, to fight for it to be recognized. There is not only the ridiculous redundancy of such a need but also the profound pathology of the conditions under which Black people find it necessary to proclaim, "Our lives matter!" The need to say this is to drive home Cornel West's observation that "the notion that black people are human beings is a relatively new discovery in the modern West."[1]

"I can't breathe. I can't breathe. I can't breathe. I can't breathe. I can't breathe. I can't breathe. I can't breathe. I can't breathe. I can't breathe. I can't breathe. I can't breathe"—these eleven iterative cries are from a forty-three-year-old Black male Eric Garner in Staten Island in 2014 after he was forced to the ground by New York police officers. Before he was thrown to the ground, he

1

was heard saying, "Don't touch me, please!" Then we see white police officer Daniel Pantaleo put his left arm around Garner's neck, bringing him down. While on the ground, Garner was heard, at one point with his right hand showing with his palm out, pleading for help: "I can't breathe," which was followed by ten additional cries. As we now know, Garner was pronounced DOA (dead on arrival) at the hospital on July 17, 2014. The medical examiner said that his death was a homicide caused by compression of the neck and of the chest. Garner's voice troubles my soul as I feel helpless, a form of helplessness that only increased after hearing that there would be no police indictment for his death. This sense of helplessness can have deep psychic and physiological effects. The feeling of helplessness left me in a state of stupor, powerless against white policing forces that felt inexorable—*like the coming of death*. In short, my life, the lives of my Black sons, and other Black sons and daughters, felt disposable, worthless, caught within an inexplicably larger, universal expression of a morose manifest destiny that I was resigned to watch, to witness, and to do so passively.

Each time that I listen to Garner's cries, I can't help but hear deep distress and existential anguish; I can feel his desperate attempt to hold tight to life. I wait to exhale. And when I see his body fall to the ground, I see violence used against his person. I witness the historical weight of the white gaze. I feel the urge, the obligation, to reach out to Garner. I feel the urge to shout at the white police officers: "This is a precious life here; this is somebody's son, somebody's child, somebody loves this man!" I can hear Garner calling out for recognition, an entreaty for his very existence. His cry, his call, is intelligible within the framework of a relational ontology. "I can't breathe" is a call for help, a crying out to others, a call that says, "Please *hear* me." It implicates the white Other. "I can't breathe" challenges white perceptual practices, ones that have become *sutured*, held intact, seemingly impregnable. They have seemingly closed off the possibility of entering into battle with their historically created white selves.[2] To "hear" Garner would take those white police officers great pains to do so. Bearing upon their white bodies is effective white history. James Baldwin argues that "it is with great pain and terror"[3] that one begins to realize that history has shaped what, in this case, those white police officers have created as their *white* frame of reference, but those white police officers avoided that pain and terror.

I hear Garner's voice through the prism of the history of Black-embodied suffering, which implies both a symbolic and literal *un-suturing*, where that un-suturing is profoundly *corporeal*, where the finite body profoundly suffers in anguish, a place perhaps where Jesus says, "I thirst."[4] Judith Butler writes, "The body implies mortality, vulnerability, agency: the skin and flesh expose us to the gaze of others, but also to touch, and to violence."[5] As Black, Garner's body is always already vulnerable to white gazes that fail or refuse to alleviate *his suffering*. His is a Black body that is rendered ersatz and is, collectively, one that has fought mightily to be included within a (white) body politic that is governed by an ontology that has been deeply shaped by whiteness as the transcendental norm, leaving whiteness unmarked, unraced, and as the human *simpliciter*. Yet, whiteness is not the site of an unconditioned (noncontingent) autonomous subject, one free of heteronomous forces. Rather, "whiteness is a product of time."[6] As the transcendental norm, the Black body is framed through white ontological assumptions about Black bodies. Butler writes, "It is not a matter of a simple entry of the excluded into an established ontology, but an insurrection at the level of ontology, a critical opening up of the questions, what is real? Whose lives are real? How might reality be remade?"[7]

Garner is crying because he feels his spirit (from the Latin *spiritus*, meaning "breath") slipping away. Yet, as a Black male body, for those white police officers, perhaps he has no spirit, no *Geist*. His crying does not lead to an insurrection at the level of white ontology. His cries are no doubt deemed acts of deception that he uses to leverage an opportunity to overpower the white police officers. Moreover, why should they listen to cries from the mouth of a criminal, a Black body believed devoid of value? For them, he really has nothing to lose. In the event of his death, he will not, in the eyes of those white police officers, "qualify as 'grievable.'"[8]

One can imagine that the police officers' brutality toward Garner is linked to an avoidance of recognizing the racialized Black specter that they themselves have created. In their refusal to act on Garner's behalf, to respond to his entreaty, to interrogate their white gazes, the actions of the white police officers were loud and clear: "Your life doesn't matter!" Recall that it was on April 2, 2015, in Tulsa County, Oklahoma, that forty-four-year-old Black male Eric Harris was shot in the back "by accident" by white male Robert Bates, a seventy-three-year-old reserve deputy. While a police officer's knee is on his head, which, like Garner's, is pressed to the ground, Harris is heard screaming, "Oh, my God, I'm losing my breath!" Like Garner's cry, the illocutionary force of the expression was a plea, a species of supplication. That plea was met with a ruthless response: "Fuck your breath!"[9] To hear Harris's screams, and the vitriol returned by the white police officer, only to know that he will later die from the gunshot wound on that same day, produces more than moral outrage; it leaves that potent and confusing sense of embodied powerlessness, emptiness, stress, fear, nausea.

If the cry, "I can't breathe," of Eric Garner in Staten Island constitutes a clarion call of the suffering Black male body in twenty-first-century America, then "Fuck your breath!" is the twenty-first-century response in 2015 and beyond. It is a response that positions Black male bodies in the mode of waiting, a temporary delay in the inevitability of violent death by complex forms of white hatred, white occlusion, white suturing, white embodied habits, white material and state power, and a perverse economy of white desires. "Fuck your breath!" is the callous and haunting articulation of a form of contempt, in this case, for Black male life. The materialization of this contempt has been witnessed over and over again as unarmed Black males, what might be called the zone of the "state of exception," have been and are being brutally killed by white police officers, those who have sworn to protect and serve.[10] In short, the Black body has been confiscated to serve the needs of whiteness. The white gaze has fixed the Black body within its own procrustean frame of reference.

One wonders if the white police officers *heard* Garner's cries. And if they did hear them, why didn't they respond responsibly? What is it about a Black male body, in this case pleading for help, that occludes a sympathetic response? Did they hear *his* suffering? Did they see *his* nonviolent resistance? Did they hear *his* effort to speak to *his* reality, what *he* said he was doing outside that store, that *he* was not selling illegal cigarettes? One might even ask, was he really *hearable* or *seeable*? Did they recognize *his* capacity of self-presentation, his agency? Part of the answer has to do with something that Frantz Fanon understood. Fanon knew that the Black body is made "out of a thousand [white racist] details, anecdotes, [and] stories."[11] It is these racist details that are part of the "visible epidermal terrain"[12] of the Black body that constituted/constitutes the site of otherness within the framework of a deeper, historically embedded, axiological, racial Manichean divide that goes back to Europe itself, an epidermal terrain that continues, even today, to signify "truths" regarding the entire cartography, as it were, of the Black body. Butler argues, "Racism pervades white perception, structuring what can and cannot appear within the horizon of white perception."[13] In the case of the white police officers' perceptions, it is not a passive process, but a process of interpellation, a process of hailing Garner's body as a problem body. It is a process of racist ascription through a visual technology that "knows" the Black body well in advance. Seeing Garner's body outside that store was "not a simple seeing, an act of direct perception, but the racial production of the visible, the workings of racial constraints on what it means to 'see.'"[14] Indeed, on this score, hearing is also not a passive site, but the racial production of what is hearable and worthy of response. So, "the visual [or audible] field is not neutral to the question of race; it is itself a racial formation, an episteme, hegemonic, and forceful."[15]

There is historical continuity here that speaks to the perpetuation of the white racist imago of the Black body, where there is an attempt to ontologically truncate the Black body into the very essence of criminality, danger, and suspicion. Hence, Black bodies must be *stopped*, frisked, imprisoned, suffocated, shot dead in the streets and left to rot in the hot sun, or lynched and left swinging like some strange fruit. For the assumption is that they are always already about to do something wrong. In short, the "Negro by nature [is] a criminal type."[16] Swedish scientist Carolus Linnaeus (1707–1778), who is considered the "Father of Taxonomy," argued that Black people (what he termed, *Africanus*) were "governed by caprice," which means that they are impulsive, unpredictable.[17] Khalil Gibran Muhammad writes, "Southern lawyer William Drayton . . . wrote in an anti-abolitionist pamphlet in 1836 that 'personal observation must convince every candid [white] man, that the negro is constitutionally indolent, voluptuous, and prone to vice.'"[18] White anthropologist Frederick Starr (1858–1933) maintained that because of Negroes' savagery and immorality, "they were naturally predisposed to criminal activity."[19] And Louisiana physician Samuel A. Cartwright (1703–1863) argued in 1861 that "the negro must, from necessity, be the slave of man or the slave of Satan."[20] These historical disclosures are not flattering to Black people. "On the other hand" as Baldwin argues, "[white people], who imagine that history flatters them (as it does, indeed, since they wrote it) are impaled on their history like a butterfly on a pin and become incapable of seeing or changing themselves, or the world."[21]

The white racist perception of Eric Garner is not an inaugural event, but the everyday historical practices of whiteness, a site of historical white racist sedimentation. Baldwin writes, "White man, hear me! History, as nearly no one seems to know, is not merely something to be read. And it does not refer merely, or even principally, to the past. On the contrary, the great force of history comes from the fact that [you] carry it within [you], are unconsciously controlled by it in many ways, and history is literally *present* in all that [you] do."[22] The white gaze, then, is a site of racist sedimentation that viciously operates in the present.

The above historical assumptions about Black bodies are what Butler might call racist phantasmatic productions that are projections from the white imaginary,[23] an imaginary that is linked to institutional and material hegemony. Think here of the death of Michael Brown, the Black unarmed teenager who was killed after a white police officer, Darren Wilson, shot him six times on August 9, 2014. White conservative pundit Ben Stein said of unarmed Brown that his Black body was a "weapon." According to Stein, Brown "wasn't unarmed. He was armed with his incredibly strong, scary self."[24] In other words, Brown's body was racially transmogrified, perceived as terrifying, bloodcurdling. His body was weaponized as it is perceived as incredibly strong, "scary," and dare I say—*Black.* In line with this, the racist narrative that Wilson tells is one that relationally positions him as a little white child vis-à-vis the big Black brute. For example, Wilson stated that as he was being "attacked" by Brown, Brown was like Hulk Hogan and he, Wilson, a five-year-old kid.[25] Wilson also said that Brown was so angry

that he looked like a "demon."[26] Why a demon? Surely, Wilson had not read
Samuel A. Cartwright's reference to the Black body as a "slave of Satan."
Yet, Brown became a malevolent being; an enemy of all that is good and
divine. Wilson's encounter with Brown was already conditioned by white
racist actions that exploited Black bodies, actions that reaped city revenue
in Ferguson, Missouri, as a result of targeting Black bodies. White violence
directed toward Black bodies preceded the actual encounter between Brown
and Wilson. Brown was already on the "wrong side" of the law. Police and
municipal leadership were already corrupted, and Black bodies were made to
suffer. [27] The white power structure in Ferguson is inextricably responsible
for creating the conditions for the violent encounter that ensued between
Wilson and Brown.

To understand Wilson's racist discourse, one must understand how a Black
body can show a wallet and that wallet can *become* a gun (as in the case of
Amadou Diallo in 1999) or how a toy gun *become*s a real gun when carried
by a twelve-year-old Black boy (as in the case of Tamir Rice in 2014). Within
this context, " 'seeing' and attributing are indissoluble"[28]; they are part and
parcel of the discursive power to name reality, which, again, is linked to institutional and material power. Amadou Diallo *had to* have a gun. And twelve-
year-old Tamir Rice *can't* be a child playing with a toy gun. According this
logic, Black boys are really Black men; they have forfeited their innocence
from birth, beginning in the "dysfunctional" wombs of their Black mothers.
In fact, one of the white officers thought that Rice was at least twenty years
old, not twelve. Black bodies are constituted through a racist episteme, a way
of "knowing" in advance. Black bodies are shot in exchange not necessarily
for what they do, but for what they *will do*. What they *will do* is based upon
racial and racist teleological assumptions about the Black body itself, a body
that is "criminal," "scary," "demonic."[29]

In stream with this racist epistemic power over what is "seen" (or "will
be seen"), Shamil Tarpischev, Russian president of the Tennis Federation,
referred to the Williams sisters as "The Williams brothers" and said that: "It's
frightening when you look at them."[30] So, as Black women they have become
masculinized as *Black men*, and, as formidable players, they are *frightening* (i.e., terrifying). They are deemed "monstrous." The process of mascu-
linization is consistent with the racist discourse that alleges that First Lady
Michelle Obama is really a man.[31] Undergirding this discourse implicates the
nineteenth-century assumptions of the Cult of True Womanhood, especially
with respect to the denial of any measure of "femininity" to Black women.
Within the larger context of these fictional constructions, I am reminded of
Francis Bacon's utopian text, *New Atlantis* (1627), where there is the story
of a holy hermit who wanted to see the very spirit of fornication. It is said
that a small nasty and frightful "Aethiop" appeared. Yet, had this same

hermit wanted to see the spirit of chastity, there would have appeared before him a fair, innocent, and beautiful cherub.[32] Within this context, the theological implications are complicit with a certain racist Manichean divide that demonizes the Black body as foul and unclean.

So, my Black body, one that is fungible vis-à-vis other Black bodies that are deemed criminal, scary, monstrous, demonic, has already undergone a process of racial interpellation that has done metaphysical violence, where, historically, the governing norms of white philosophical anthropology marked Black bodies as disgusting and occluded from the realm of the conceptually white *anthropos*. In short, my being Black is not a nominal phenotypic marker. Rather, my Black body is situated within history, a history that is racially oppressive and violent. It is part of a larger social integument—a social skin—that has claimed my body to be ontologically problematic. Within the context of this racist and violent semiotic field, how can any of us—Black bodies—truly breathe? How can we avoid both social-ontological and physical asphyxiation? After all, we are deemed the *dark* plague. It is as if I carry a *Black essence*, a type of infection that proceeded from "some natural infection of the first inhabitants . . . and so all the whole [progeny] of them descended, are still polluted with the same blot of infection."[33]

Through the white imaginary, I am fit for teratology, a thing from the remote past, simian-like. Think here of North Korea's state-run media KCNA that referred to President Obama as a "wicked black monkey"[34] or of the white police officer who was captured on video referring to Ferguson protesters as "Fucking animals."[35] I can hear Hegel's voice from the past: "The Negro is an example of animal man in all his savagery and lawlessness."[36] Yet, the Black body vis-à-vis the white body is a site of a peculiar paradox.[37] The Black body is both desirable and yet disgusting. Think here of white male enslavers and "slave masters" who raped Black women who were deemed subpersons, chattel, ugly, foul, and, no doubt, ungodly creatures. How does one rape such a "creature" with such intimate proximity without moral revulsion or even vomiting? How does one rape enslaved Black women without falsifying one's own assumptions about their status as "beasts of burden" or one's own white status as "civilized"? In other words, think about the lynching of Black male bodies and how white males hovered over those Black bodies, making sure that the nooses were fitted correctly, touching Black genitalia while castrating those intimate parts that were said to be nasty and despicable. These cases constitute forms of violent, racially perverse, intimacy that implicated white male desire, disgust, and hatred. Likewise, when Eric Garner, believed to be a criminal, had to be removed from that public space in Staten Island, New York, it took an act of violent proximity to remove him—forcefully grabbing his neck, bodies mounted upon his, his head held down, close to the ground. It was on the white police officers' terms that Garner's body became touchable, a site of violent intimacy.

On this score, Black bodies are profiled and policed according to a racist logic that is grounded in the fantastical necessity to protect white spaces from the Black body's criminal intrusion, an infringement that could easily be linked to revulsion. Dan Flory notes that "disgust possesses a clear if often problematic sociomoral dimension: our protective reactions to what we perceive as contaminants to our bodily integrity or endangerments to our survival shade into sociomoral categories. Threats to our bodies and threats to our social, moral, or political being often generate many of the same bodily responses, facial expressions, and linguistic utterances."[38] While I will explore both of the following situations in greater detail in chapter 3, think here of the young white boy in his mother's arms saying, when he "sees" Fanon on a train in France: "Look, a Negro!"[39] The boy becomes frightened and thinks that "the nigger's going to eat [him] up." [40] Fanon's body *appears* as an object of fear, curiosity, dread, surprise, and disgust. Similarly, as a small child, Audre Lorde remembers the disgust and hatred directed toward her by a white woman seated on the AA subway train to Harlem. As she sat next to this white woman, Lorde remembers this woman pulling her coat away from Lorde's snowsuit. Lorde talks about how she thought that perhaps there was a disgusting insect that the woman was trying to avoid. Yet, it was Lorde who was the perceived "problem." She writes, "When I look up the woman is still staring at me, her nose holes and eyes huge. And suddenly I realize there is nothing crawling up the seat between us; it is me she doesn't want her coat to touch." [41] This experience involves the meaning of Lorde's embodiment having been confiscated through the white gaze. Lorde undergoes a process of interpellation that marks her Black body as repulsive. The distance between Lorde's Black body and the white woman's body had been violated, leaving Lorde marked as an object to be avoided—untouchable.

WHITE SPACES AS SITES OF OCCLUSION

It is important to note that predominantly white monochromatic spaces, while oppressive vis-à-vis Black people and people of color, can and often do operate in ways that don't bring attention to their oppressive ways. For example, it is difficult to explain to white students at predominantly white universities that the socially constituted spaces that they inhabit are *white spaces*, especially as so many of them see such spaces as racially neutral. Their bodies move through such spaces with ease because those spaces constitute sites of affordances, ways of engaging those spaces successfully without bodily hassle or feelings of alienation. Such spaces are part and parcel of a long history of white domination. They are spaces of familiarity that are already given before the moment of an individual white person's arrival. "The [white] bodies and [white] spaces 'point' towards each other, as a 'point' that is not seen as it is also 'the point' from which [they] see."[42] I have the same trouble explaining to my white philosophy graduate students about why I find predominantly white philosophical conferences so alienating, how such spaces place oppressive stress on my body. Entering into those spaces is like entering into a strange house that has acquired the shape of those who inhabit it, a space that speaks to their modes of traversing it. Their habits, their movements, and their values are expressed through the configuration of the space within that house, and it is that configured space that, in turn, subsequently shapes their courses of action. In terms of predominantly white philosophical conferences, white philosophers *can* disappear as racialized. Their white bodies *can* move with ease, unraced, comfortable, and safe.

At predominantly white philosophical conferences, the white social and communicative space "calls" to white philosophers like my computer keys "call" to me to tap on them, to complete the operation of typing. My fingers are mobilized by my glance toward the keys. There is a smooth transaction that takes place uninterrupted vis-à-vis my computer. My body and the computer feel like they are made for each other. So, too, within the context of predominantly white philosophy conferences, white bodies move effortlessly, complementing each other. Their bodies are mobilized by the entire scene: white interviewers and white interviewees as candidates for jobs—sporting tweed jackets, bow ties, pipes; white bodies frantically eager to make impressions on other white bodies—white hair, white skin, contorted white faces deep in philosophical reflection, looks of perplexity, slight hints of wine and cheese breath, and strained eyes red with intensity.[43] The entire philosophical performance, with all of its props and accoutrement, constitutes a site of effective (white) history. The same process of white intellectual formation occurs within the context of other academic value-laden spaces where young white sociologists, psychologists, historians, religious studies scholars (men and women) come to inhabit such spaces without question, without critical self-reflexivity, without readjusting their white gazes, without noticing that something has gone awry. Yet, as a Black body, my body becomes stressed within such white conference spaces and such white academic spaces. White bodies move through those spaces habitually, and, as such, their bodies "trail behind actions."[44] Black bodies, however, are stressed and their appearance becomes hypermarked against the unmarked spaces of white intelligibility. In short, then, such philosophical spaces "do not 'extend' the surfaces of [Black bodies and bodies of color]."[45] My Black body becomes the racialized figure against the white ground. Within such spaces, one is hyperattentive to one's movements, to one's presence and collective absence.

Within the context of the white conference space, one feels the violence of objectification by the white gaze. This is confirmed in the rich and frightening current literature on anti-Black implicit biases and how self-described good and progressive white liberals exhibit such biases.[46] So, within that space, one wonders how one is really perceived, fashioned, and *imprisoned*. For example, after questioning various whites, Fanon found out that by inserting the word "Negro" into the conversation, stereotypical associations emerged: "*Negro* brought forth biology, penis, strong, athletic, potent, boxer, Joe Louis, Jesse Owens, Senegalese troops, savage, animal, devil, sin."[47] In white spaces, one notices that one is being *looked at*. One wonders if one has mastered all of the institutional normative assumptions about what it means to inhabit such a space, to move through such a space, to comingle. Is one using "proper" *academese*? As a Black philosopher, I wonder have I adopted the confident white male swagger—moving through space, god-like, with a sense of white confidence—that says that one *really* belongs? And even if one begins to doubt one's authenticity as a philosopher, one can be certain of at least something: "I know only one thing, which is the purity of my conscience and the whiteness of my soul."[48] With this, unfortunately, one enters within the space of the neurotic, as Fanon might say.[49] Alternatively, one might begin to feel engulfed by a nagging sense that the space at the conference does not extend one's body through that space successfully. There is the absence of that sense of being "ready for action" as one doesn't feel mobilized within that space. Within that white space where white bodies socialize, engage in scuttlebutt, talk of tenure and promotion, where the "goodies" to be gotten from doing philosophy appear to be overwhelmingly within their (white) reach, one feels as if one has been thrown into a colonial space. As Ahmed writes, "Colonialism makes the world 'white', which is of course a world 'ready' for certain kinds of bodies, as a world that puts certain objects within their reach."[50] Within the context of such white spaces, everything goes as planned. There are no major disruptions. In fact, many whites believe that instances of "real" white racist violence interrupt (or are deviations from) otherwise nonracist white modes of being. Yet, what about the everyday *white racist violence* (experienced by Black people and people of color) that has to be present in order for white "normal" functioning to continue in the ways that it does? It is a form of violence that many white people would rather not know about in order for their lives to continue to operate as they do.[51]

TRAYVON MARTIN AND OCCLUDED SPACE

Oscar Grant, Jordan Davis, Jonathan Ferrell, Renisha McBride, Eric Garner, Michael Brown, Tamir Rice, and so many more, all had dreams. Yet, their dreams were cut short by white police officers or their proxies. We will never know what Trayvon Martin was dreaming about as he left the convenience store in Sanford, Florida, on the night of February 26, 2012. Perhaps, on that very night, he was dreaming about becoming a pilot, something his parents knew he dreamed about becoming. Yet, any dreams that he had were severed from *any* chance of getting realized. Martin could have brought healing to our nation and to our world; he could have been a great spiritual leader, a philosopher of tremendous creativity and genius; perhaps he could have become the best and most skilled pilot the world has ever known. Yet, as a site of Black embodiment, within the context of anti-Black racism, Martin's being-toward-the-future was precarious, teetering on the precipice of existential nullification. And while it is true that we are all dispossessed by death, destined to die because of our finitude, not all of us are socially marked for death. It is imperative that the existential gravity of Martin's birth, his being, is appreciated and properly understood. Trayvon Martin will never come this way again. Martin is irreplaceable—a unique ontological opening onto the world that has been closed. His was a site of lived engagement where time, space, affection, beauty, love, play, family, friendship, wonder, and divinity *meant* something *to him*. It is that *meaning something to Trayvon Martin* that is not repeatable, that is irreplaceable.

The gravity of thinking about the loss of my Black sons, the tragic shattering of *their lived perspective on the world*, because systemic white racism/the white gaze has dictated that they look suspicious in virtue of being Black, is a weight I have no desire to bear. And while it is true that my sons are certainly not exempt from possibly being killed by someone not white, it is an entire white racist historical system that has marked, and continues to mark, Black male life as devalued and nugatory. In other words, although there are those who deploy a discourse of "Black-on-Black crime" as a way to obfuscate the magnitude and toxicity of white supremacy and its impact on Black people, "Black-on-Black crime" is not an *institutional system* based upon white racist assemblages of "knowledge" and an entire ideological apparatus underwritten by white hegemonic material power. While this does not make "Black-on-Black crime" any less important, such discourse renders Black people the cause of their own demise.

I wonder whether Zimmerman has come to terms with the violent destruction of Martin's existential uniqueness. Perhaps he will never come to recognize the profound mystery of that truth. By killing Martin, Zimmerman has cut off the very possibility of knowing himself differently through the eyes of Martin. Perhaps Martin could have conveyed to Zimmerman what it meant to look like a "creepy ass Cracker," especially given the latter's racist panoptic surveillance of Martin. Perhaps this knowledge would have enabled Zimmerman to understand the relational impact that his racist surveillance

can have on Black bodies that live under so much existential white supremacist duress. Given this knowledge, perhaps Zimmerman would have decided
against chasing one of those "assholes" (his term) who apparently always
get away. Zimmerman's *violent* world-making not only destroyed Martin but
destroyed an important access to his own meaning. Zimmerman has rendered
forever irretrievable a more multifaceted response, at least from Martin, to
the question of his own being: "Who am I?" Now that Martin is gone, part
of Zimmerman has also gone into permanent exile. Sutured and believed
closed off from Martin, having "nothing" in common, Zimmerman, through
white supremacist lies, thought Martin bereft of anything *to give*. Martin
was believed there *to take*. Hence, Zimmerman was there *to preserve* and to
do so in the name of law, order, cleanliness, civilization, safety, purity, and
territoriality—all powerful tropes of whiteness. To preserve, however, was
to remain sutured, making it almost impossible to be enlarged by Martin's
presence. The suturing process involved the reinforcement of effective white
history. For Zimmerman, there was no "attempt to achieve a level of personal
maturity and freedom which robs [white] history of its tyrannical power."[52]
    Martin was paradoxically rendered both invisible and hypervisible.
Zimmerman refused to tarry or linger with Martin's ontological depth and the
ways in which his Black body calls to him outside of his myopic perceptual
profiles. After all, even the cup of tea on my desk, *promises* more as I stare
at it from a particular angular perspective. My cup's virtual side, indeed, its
virtual multiplicity, has more to offer—indeed perhaps having indefinite profiles. All the more, then, one might think that Martin's embodied humanity
would usher in a flood of promises vis-à-vis Zimmerman. Martin's embodiment should have solicited Zimmerman to look again, to wonder and to stand
in awe of Martin's shared humanity. Yet, it is precisely his humanity that was
questioned and denied within white North America. As the "predator," the
"monster," or the "thug," Martin was the racial contaminant.
    Why didn't Zimmerman challenge his own perceptual practices? My sense
is that to let go of these practices, white people will experience loss; they will
undergo forms of trauma and crisis, especially as the process of un-suturing
will require the troubling of their own identities as the axiological standard in
terms of which Black people and people of color are negatively judged and
brutally treated. After writing "Dear White America,"[53] which I treated as a
gift to white America, I was inundated with white hatred, with messages that
were vile. I was called "nigger" hundreds of times. "Nigger" functioned as a
term that obfuscated the need for white self-interrogation. By calling me by
such a racist epithet, whites were able to overlook the source of the term's
origin, that is, as one that was/is created from their own distorted white imaginary, to distance themselves from their own brokenness. In other words, the
term "nigger" functioned, and functions, to provide for them a sense of white

"wholeness." To practice forms of epistemological humility vis-à-vis whiteness will be necessary for white people to challenge whiteness as the transcendental norm that actually conditions their perception of themselves as not needing to undo anything at all. As the transcendental norm, whiteness elides itself as a problem. Hence, the process of letting go must involve the capacity for vulnerability (to be wounded), which is another way of saying that whites must strive to be *un-sutured*. Being un-sutured is a powerful concept as it implies, especially for whites, the capacity to tarry with the multiple ways in which their whiteness is a problem, and to remain with the weight of that reality and the pain of that realization. Being un-sutured is a site of openness, loss, and great discomfort. It is a site of suffering, a form of suffering that is necessary for white people. This is linked to Baldwin's argument that an open and honest dialogue involving white people with Black people will, because white people are opaque to themselves, "become a personal confession—a cry for help and healing,"[54] one that, in my view, should not reinscribe whiteness qua pity. Baldwin also believed that Black people and people of color must have that dialogue with whites, but that it will involve "an accusation,"[55] which will require white courageous listening.

For white people to tarry within such a space is dangerous. It is dangerous because it is demanding; dangerous because it refuses to play it safe, which is another way of remaining sutured. Whites will find themselves in a process of alienation as they struggle to undo white racial parasitism. As they go in search of themselves, Black bodies will no longer function as props.[56] In my view, Zimmerman *needed* Travon Martin's Black body; he needed the chimera of Martin's "criminal essence" to authorize his "absolute right" to stop Martin's Black body for being in the "wrong" place. Sutured, Zimmerman failed/refused to be undone by Martin's presence. "To be undone by another," as Butler writes, "is a primary necessity, an anguish, to be sure, but also a chance—to be addressed, claimed, bound to what is not me, but also to be moved, to be prompted to act, to address myself elsewhere, and so to vacate the self-sufficient 'I' as a kind of possession."[57]

I have no illusions about the history of white supremacy, especially the kind that is uneventful, mundane, and every day—the kind that shows itself each Sunday morning where white bodies commune together, and bond together, where Black bodies are de facto absent through iterative white practices of exclusion. Within the context of how I think about the complexity of whiteness and white people engaging in the process of attempting to undo it, the concept of *arrival* has very little if any purchase. When white people stress arrival vis-à-vis their antiracism, this can function to keep them sutured, from lingering with the profound and intricate layers of white supremacy. *Kenosis* (or emptying) in relationship to white racism involves diligence and a constant process of return. There is no single and total kenotic moment or *emptying* of white racist sedimentations, assumptions, images, and affects. This is why I continue to stress the importance of nurturing a disposition to be un-sutured, a disposition to crack, re-crack, and crack again the calcified operations of the white gaze. While this practice sounds "absurdist" in nature, it is a disposition that *promises* so much more. Resistance to whiteness has within it its own end. And it is through this resistance that one takes a stand and confronts history, battles forms of historical creation that have gotten us to this place, a place where whiteness (and white people) refuse or fail to be undone, fail to lose themselves to an address that comes from outside of themselves, from outside of their white gazes.

NOTES

1. Cornel West, *The Cornel West Reader* (New York: Basic *Civitas* Books, 1999), 70.

2. James Baldwin, *The Fire Next Time* (New York: The Modern Library, 1995), 410.

3. Baldwin, *Fire Next Time*, 410.

4. John 19:28, New International Version.

5. Judith Butler, *Precarious Life: The Powers of Mourning and Violence* (New York: Verso, 2004), 26.

6. John Warren, "Performing Whiteness Differently: Rethinking the Abolitionist Project," *Educational Theory*, 51(4), 2001, 454, 451–66.

7. Butler, *Precarious Life*, 33.

8. Butler, *Precarious Life*, 32.

9. See http://thinkprogress.org/justice/2015/04/12/3646057/fuck-breath-officer-caught-video-mocking-unarmed-black-man-fatally-shot-police/

10. See http://www.borderlands.net.au/vol6no3_2007/chowdhury_once.htm

11. Frantz Fanon, *Black Skin, White Masks*, trans. Charles Lam Markmann (New York: Grove Press, 1967), 111.

12. Robyn Wiegman, *American Anatomies: Theorizing Race and Gender* (Durham, NC: Duke University Press, 1995), 31.

13. Judith Butler, "Endangered/Endangering: Schematic Racism and White Paranoia," in *Reading Rodney King, Reading Urban Uprising*, ed. Robert Gooding-Williams (New York: Routledge, 1993), 15–16.

14. Butler, "Endangered/Endangering," 16.

15. Butler, "Endangered/Endangering," 17.

16. George M. Fredrickson, *The Black Image in the White Mind: The Debate on Afro-American Character and Destiny, 1817–1914* (Hanover, NH: Wesleyan University Press, 1971), 281.

17. Audrey Smedley, *Race in North America: Origins and Evolution of a Worldview* (Boulder, CO: Westview Press, 1999), 161.

18. Khalil Gibran Muhammad, *The Condemnation of Blackness: Race, Crime, and the Making of Modern Urban America* (Cambridge, MA: Harvard University Press, 2010), 21.

19. Lee D. Baker, *From Savage to Negro: Anthropology and the Construction of Race, 1896–1954* (Berkeley: University of California Press, 1998), 59.

20. Fredrickson, *The Black Image in the White Mind*, 55.

21. James Baldwin, *The Price of the Ticket: Collected Nonfiction, 1948–1985* (New York: St. Martin's Press, 1985), 410.

22. Baldwin, *Price of the Ticket*, 410.

23. Butler, "Endangered/Endangering," 18.

24. Maranda Blue, "Ben Stein: Michael Brown Wasn't Unarmed. He Was Armed with His Incredibly Strong, Scary Self," August 27, 2014; see http://www.right-wingwatch.org/content/ben-stein-michael-brown-wasnt-unarmed-he-was-armed-his-incredibly-strong-scary-self (accessed on January 26, 2015)

25. Darren Wilson, "I Felt Like a five-Year-Old Holding onto Hulk Hogan," November 25, 2014; see http://www.cbsnews.com/news/ferguson-decision-darren-wilson-said-he-felt-like-a-5-year-old-holding-onto-hulk-hogan/ (accessed on January 26, 2015)

26. Jamelle Bouie, "Michael Brown Wasn't a Superhuman Demon, but Darren Wilson's Racial Prejudice Told Him Otherwise," November 26, 2014; see http://www.slate.com/articles/news_and_politics/politics/2014/11/darren_wilson_s_racial_portrayal_of_michael_brown_as_a_superhuman_demon.html (accessed on January 26, 2015)

27. Conor Friedersdorf, "Ferguson's Conspiracy against Black Citizens," March 5, 2015; see http://www.theatlantic.com/national/archive/2015/03/ferguson-as-a-criminal-conspiracy-against-its-black-residents-michael-brown-department-of-justice-report/386887/ (accessed on June 1, 2016)

28. Butler, "Endangered/Endangering," 20.

29. Butler, "Endangered/Endangering," 19.

30. Sneha Shankar, "Shamil Tarpischev, Russian Tennis Federation Head, Fined for Referring to Serena, Venus as 'Williams Brothers'," October 18, 2014; see http://www.ibtimes.com/shamil-tarpischev-russian-tennis-federation-head-fined-referring-serena-venus-williams-1707354 (accessed on January 26, 2015)

31. "More and More Americans Think Michelle Obama Is a man," August 10, 2014; see http://www.dcclothesline.com/2014/08/10/americans-think-michelle-obama-man/ (accessed on January 26, 2015)

32. http://www.mayanastro.freeservers.com/bacon1.html (accessed on January 26, 2015)

33. Winthrop D. Jordan, *White over Black: American Attitudes toward the Negro, 1550–1812* (Chapel: University of North Carolina Press, 1968), 15.

34. Madison Park, "North Korea Insults Obama with Racist Barbs, South Korea's Park with Sexist Ones," May 9, 2014; see http://www.cnn.com/2014/05/09/world/asia/north-korea-insults-obama/ (accessed November 16, 2014)

35. Amanda Terkel, "Police Officer Caught on Video Calling Michael Brown Protesters 'F***ing Animals'," August 24, 2016; see http://www.huffingtonpost.com/2014/08/12/michael-brown-protests_n_5672163.html.

36. Emmanuel Eze, *Race and the Enlightenment: A Reader* (Malden, MA: Blackwell, 1997), 127.

37. I would like to acknowledge Alex Gorman, my graduate teaching assistant, for raising a related question that led to questions about violence, intimacy, and race.

38. Dan Flory, "Imaginative Resistance, Racialized Disgust, and 12 Years a Slave," in *Film and Philosophy*, 19, 2015, 78–9, 75–95.

39. Fanon, *Black Skin, White Masks*, 112.

40. Fanon, *Black Skin, White Masks*, 114.

41. Audre Lorde, *Sister Outsider: Essays & Speeches*, News Foreword by Cheryl Clarke (Berkeley: Crossing Press, 1984), 47–148.

42. Sara Ahmed, "A Phenomenology of Whiteness," *Feminist Theory*, 8(2), 2007, 158.

43. For a more detailed exploration of the characterization of this sort of white performative philosophical context, see George Yancy, *Look, a White! Philosophical Essays on Whiteness* (Philadelphia, PA: Temple University Press, 2012), Chapter 5.

44. Ahmed, "A Phenomenology of Whiteness," 156.

45. Ahmed, "A Phenomenology of Whiteness," 163.

46. http://www.biasproject.org/ (accessed November 17, 2014)

47. Fanon, *Black Skin, White Masks*, 166.

48. Fanon, *Black Skin, White Masks*, 192–193.

49. Fanon, *Black Skin, White Masks*, 192.

50. Ahmed, "A Phenomenology of Whiteness," 153.

51. I would like to acknowledge Slavoj Žižek for his insights that led to this line of argument. See "Julian Assange in Conversation with Slavoj Žižek Moderated by Democracy Now's Amy Goodman," June 1, 2016; see https://www.youtube.com/watch?v=j1Xm08uTSDQ

52. Baldwin, *Price of the Ticket*, 410.

53. George Yancy, "Dear White America," December 24, 2015; see http://opinionator.blogs.nytimes.com/2015/12/24/dear-white-america/?_r=0 (accessed June 1, 2016)

54. Baldwin, *Price of the Ticket*, 412.

55. Baldwin, *Price of the Ticket*, 412.

56. After all, whites need Black bodies to be exactly what they imagine them to be—"Capricious," "Nigger," "Hulk Hogan," "Demonic," Vermin," "Disgusting." By learning to understand this need, whites can begin to undo their form of mass delusion of non-dependency and self-possession.

57. Judith Butler, *Giving an Account of Oneself* (New York: Fordham University Press, 2005), 136.

Chapter 2

The Elevator Effect

Black Bodies/White Bodies

> When invoking the term "body," we tend to think at first of its materiality—
> its composition as flesh and bone, its outline and contours, its outgrowth of
> nail and hair. But the body, as we well know, is never simply matter, for it
> is never divorced from perception and interpretation.
>
> —Carla L. Peterson

There is a form of writing that is not meant to be simply cerebral, but to impact the body and to weave a narrative that captures something that is profoundly familiar and intensely mundane. Writing about what has been called "the elevator effect" is an example of such a form of writing. I have noticed, and this has been acknowledged by colleagues, that this style of writing in the area of critical philosophy of race has now been adopted more frequently. I am more than delighted to have helped to push a discursive style that has helped to get at the lived experience of race.

From the perspective of whiteness, I am, contrary to the existentialist credo, an essence ("Blackness") that precedes my existence. Hence, my emergence upon the historical scene requires that I engage in a battle that is not only iconographic and semiotic but also existential. Indeed, the Black body, my Black body, is itself a battleground. The Black body has been historically marked, disciplined, and scripted and materially, psychologically, and morally invested in to ensure both white supremacy and the illusory construction of the white subject as a self-contained substance whose existence does not depend upon the construction of the Black qua "inferior". As a Black person, this is my existential standpoint, my inheritance. And it is this existential standpoint, this past inheritance, that informs my sense of agency.

The Black body has been confiscated. This confiscation occurred in the form of the past brutal enslavement of Black bodies, the cruel and sadistic

17

lynching of Black bodies, the sexual molestation of Black bodies on Southern plantations, the literal breeding of Black bodies for white exploitation, and the unethical experimentation on Black bodies during the horrific "Tuskegee Syphilis Study" (1932–72). This "Study," started by the U.S. Public Health Service, was designed to confirm, among other things, its belief in the differential (dimorphic) racial impact of syphilis. "Whereas the disease was thought to do its worst damage to the neurological systems and brains of whites, it was thought to wreak its worst havoc on the cardiovascular systems of blacks, sparing their relatively primitive and 'underdeveloped' brains."[1] Within the context of my analysis, however, confiscation also occurs at the quotidian, everyday level of social transaction, which includes the disproportionate incarceration of young Black bodies, and the construction of Black women's bodies as promiscuous by nature, reckless, and "purposely hav[ing] more and more children to manipulate taxpayers into giving them more money."[2] It is within such quotidian social spaces that *my Black body* has been confiscated.[3] When followed by white security personnel as I walk through department stores, when a white sales person avoids touching my hand, or when a white woman looks with suspicion as I enter the elevator, I feel that in their eyes I am this indistinguishable, amorphous, black seething mass, a token of danger, a threat, a criminal, a burden, a rapacious animal incapable of delayed gratification.[4]

Within such social spaces as these, the sheer cumulative impact of such racist actions can result in a form of self-alienation, where the integrity of one's Black body is profoundly shaken, though not necessarily shattered. Self-alienation can assume various forms, from self-doubt to self-hatred. Unlike the form of alienation a young Karl Marx described, where workers are alienated from their labor, Charles Mills states that "under white supremacy, one has an alienation far more fundamental; since while one can always come home from work, one cannot get out of one's skin."[5] While I agree with Mills, I realize that class standing and its role in alienation can also follow one home; it does not stop at the factory gates, as it were. Think here of real situations where low expectations constitute part of the lived normative framework of a lower-class white family. Within such families, it may not even occur to parents to imagine their children attending college or doing any other work than that characteristic of their lower-class standing. Indeed, lower-class whites (particularly, non-WASPs) in North America have also been characterologically described as shiftless, lazy, and worthless, and were even victims of systematic sterilization during the eugenics movement in the nineteenth and early twentieth centuries. However, despite this deplorable crime against poor white women and men, immigrants, and the physically and mentally disabled, such "innate" character traits attributed to poor whites were not conceptualized as resulting from a specifically *"Black* essence."

Anti-miscegenation laws and the so-called one-drop rule kept this "essence" firmly in place for Blacks, while for Irish or Italian immigrants their alleged "essence" might be said to dissipate eventually through intermarriage and assimilation.

The corporeal integrity of my Black body undergoes an onslaught as the white imaginary, which centuries of white hegemony have structured and shaped, ruminates over my dark flesh and vomits me out in a form not in accordance with how I see myself. From the context of my lived experience, I feel "external," as it were, to my body, delivered and scaled in white lies.[6] The reality is that I find myself within a normative space, a historically structured and *structuring* space, through which I am "seen" and judged guilty a priori. I find myself in the North American context, where the discourses of race and racism possess a shared intelligibility. Not only do I actively negotiate my course of action within this space but it is also a space within which I am part of an interpretive stream, which has configured my identity and shaped my course of action.

I am said to bear the pernicious mark of *dark* skin. My darkness is a signifier of negative values grounded within a racist, social, and historical matrix that predates my existential emergence. The meaning of my Blackness is not intrinsic to my natural pigment; it has *become* a value-laden "given," an object presumed untouched and unmediated by various contingent discursive practices, history, time, and context. My Blackness functions as a stipulatory axiom from which conclusions can be drawn: "Blackness is evil, not to be trusted, and guilty as such." This stipulatory axiom forms part of a white racist distal narrative that congeals narrative coherence and intelligibility, providing a framework according to which the Black body is rendered "meaningful." Whites "see" the Black body through the medium of historically structured forms of "knowledge" that regard it as an object of suspicion. This understanding of the white *gaze* vis-à-vis tacit forms of "knowledge" has a family resemblance to Michel Foucault's use of the term *positive unconscious*.[7] In other words, whiteness comes replete with its assumptions for what to expect of a Black body (or nonwhite body); how dangerous and unruly it is; how unlawful, criminal, and hypersexual it is. The discourse and comportment of whites are shaped through tacit racist scripts, calcified modes of being that enable them to sustain and perpetuate their whitely-being-in-the-world.[8]

Frantz Fanon observed that "not only must the black man be black; he must be black in relation to the white man."[9] This relational dimension is incredibly significant.[10] Hence, the meaning of my Blackness is constituted and configured (*relationally*) within a semiotic field of axiological difference, one that is structured vis-à-vis the construction of whiteness as the transcendental norm. To say that whiteness is deemed the transcendental norm is to say that whiteness takes itself to be that which remains the *same* across a field of

difference. Indeed, it determines what is deemed different without itself being
defined by that system of difference. Whiteness is that according to which
what is nonwhite is rendered other, marginal, ersatz, strange, native, inferior,
uncivilized, and ugly.

Poor whites are not simply possible instantiators of this kind of whiteness.
Rather, they have historically been and currently are invested psychologically
and morally in this kind of whiteness, dutifully juxtaposing themselves to
those inferior *Black* bodies, safeguarding the appellation "white" as a magical
category that names, fixes, and substantiates their ontological superiority and
special status within the Great Chain of Being (*scala naturae*). "Yassir, boss,"
accompanied by bending, heard from Black mouths was "proof" of who was
in charge. These words of "respect" could be "followed by sleazy laughter
that turned human dignity into a limp thing. But you liked it. And you felt
big, important, superior even, as you heard it, though you might not be able
to read or write."[11] In fact, the poor white body is invested in its whiteness in
ways that are precisely designed to offset the variable of poverty. Destitute
and without viable economic power, whiteness functions as an invaluable
asset. Historically, poor whites were fed on Jim Crow, even as their stomachs
went empty. As the transcendental norm, whiteness has tremendous value
within North America. The fact that poor whites shared their whiteness with
wealthy whites was enough to instill within the former a sense of "greatness,"
but this was to some extent based upon a false equivalence: Poor whites confused "You're *white* like us," with "You're one of us." However, being white
created a sense of solidarity that kept poor whites content even when it meant
their own political and economic demise.

As indicated above, unlike Black bodies *physically* confiscated from
Africa, my body is confiscated within social spaces of meaning construction and social spaces of transversal interaction that are buttressed by a
racist value-laden episteme. It is a peculiar experience to have one's body
confiscated without physically being placed in chains. Well-dressed, I enter
an elevator where a white woman waits to reach her floor. She "sees" my
Black body, though not the same one I have seen reflected back to me from
the mirror on any number of occasions. Buying into the myth that one's
dress says something about the person, one might think that the markers of
my dress (suit and tie) should ease her tension. What is it that makes the
markers of my dress inoperative? She sees a Black male body "supersatu-
rated with meaning, as they [Black bodies] have been relentlessly subjected
to [negative] characterization by newspapers, newscasters, popular film,
television programming, public officials, policy pundits and other agents of
representation."[12] Her body language signifies, "Look, *the* Black!" On this
score, though short of a performative locution, her body language functions
as an insult.

Over and above how my body is clothed, she "sees" a criminal, she sees me as a threat. Phenomenologically, she might be said to "see" a Black, fleeting expanse, a peripherally glimpsed vague presence of something dark, forbidden, and dreadful. She does not see a dynamic subjectivity, but a *sort*, something eviscerated of individuality, flattened, and rendered vacuous of genuine human feelings. However, she is one of the "walking dead," unaware of how the feeling of her white bodily upsurge and expansiveness is purchased at the expense of my Black body. Independently of any threatening action on my part, my Black body, my existence in Black, poses a threat. It is not necessary that I first perform a threatening action. The question of *deeds* is irrelevant. I need not *do* anything. After all, "the torturer is the black man, Satan is black, one talks of shadows, when one is dirty one is black—whether one is thinking of physical dirtiness or moral dirtiness."[13] It is as if my Black body has always already committed a criminal *deed*. As a result, my being as being-for-itself, my freedom, is fundamentally called into question. Who I have become as partly constituted through the history of my own actions is apparently nugatory. My dark body occludes the presumption of innocence. It is as if one's Blackness is a congenital defect, one that burdens the body with tremendous inherited guilt. On this reading, one might say that Blackness functions metaphorically as original sin. There is not anything as such that a Black body needs *to do* in order to be found blameworthy.

As such, the woman on the elevator does not really "see" me, and she makes no effort to challenge how she sees me. To begin to see me from a perspective that effectively challenges her racism, however, would involve more than a *cognitive* shift in her perspective. It would involve a continuous effort at performing her body's racialized interactions with the world differently. This additional shift resides at the somatic level as well. After all, she may come to judge her perception of the Black body as epistemologically false, but her racism may still have a hold on her lived-body. I walk onto the elevator and she feels apprehension. Her body shifts nervously and her heart beats more quickly as she clutches her purse more closely to her. She feels anxiety in the pit of her stomach. Her perception of time in the elevator may feel like an eternity. The space within the elevator is surrounded from all sides with my Black presence. It is as if I have become omnipresent within that space, ready to attack from all sides. Like choking black smoke, my Blackness permeates the enclosed space of the elevator. Her palms become clammy. She feels herself on the precipice of taking flight, the desperation to flee. There is panic, there is difficulty swallowing, and there is a slight trembling of her white torso, dry mouth, nausea. The point here is that deep-seated racist emotive responses may form part of the white *bodily* repertoire, which has become calcified through quotidian modes of bodily transaction in a racial and racist world.

Despite what I think about myself, how I am for-myself, her perspective, her third-person account, seeps into my consciousness. I catch a glimpse of myself through her eyes and just for that moment, I experience some form of double consciousness, although what I see does not shatter my identity or unglue my sense of moral decency. Despite how my harmless actions might be constructed within her white racialized framework of seeing the world, I remain capable of resisting the white gaze's entry into my own self-vision. I am angered. Indeed, I find her gaze disconcerting and despicable. As I undergo this double consciousness, my agency remains intact. My sense of who I am and how I am capable of being—that is, the various ways in which I am capable of deploying an oppositional form of representation— has not been eradicated. I know that I am not a criminal or a rapist. At no point do I either desire to be white or begin to hate my dark skin. And while I recognize the historical power of the white gaze, a perspective that carries the weight of white racist history and everyday encounters of spoken and unspoken anti-Black racism, I do not seek *white* recognition, that is, the white woman's recognition. Though I would prefer that she does not see me in terms of the Black imago in the white imaginary, I am not *dependent* upon her recognition. Indeed, to "prefer" that she see me differently does not bespeak a form of dependency. Rather, my preference is suggestive of my hope of a radically different world. On another day, for example, I might say, "To hell with it. I simply don't care if she changes or not." Today, I would rather that she stand and deliver. The subtext is a moral critique that she gets her shit together.

For me to seek white recognition as a stimulus to a healthy sense of self-understanding is a form of pathology.[14] This pathology is understandable given the history of white hegemony. After all, the white woman in the elevator might be said to possess the only real point of view. By "real," I mean the sense in which her perspective, her subjectivity, is deemed the only important perspective, the one that makes a difference, the one that has historically reaped the benefit of recognition within the context of white North America. Her perspective, her gaze, is grounded within past and present material forces that accord greater power to white people.

One important objection that might be raised at this juncture is that I have simply misread the white woman's intentions. I have read racism into a situation where it simply does not exist. This objection raises the issue of how it is that Blacks learn to read white gestures, gazes, and other forms of apparently racially benign behaviors. I want to avoid the claim that the white woman's response to me is simply a case of "direct" observation, as if any other person (even any other Black or white person) need only "observe" her behavior and will ipso facto come to justifiably believe what I do about her comportment. That is, it is not as if *any* knower can "see" this and claim,

"Yes, her gesture was racist." One colleague of mine once stated, "Perhaps your claim that her gesture was racist is an instance of epistemic privilege concerning which only *you* are aware." In his aim to recast my observation as epistemic privilege only, there is the sense in which he attempted to reduce my observation to something that has no basis in social reality. I am not claiming that having a justified belief about the white woman is just *my* epistemic privilege, but I am claiming to have a privileged take on things that is based both systemically and systematically.

The fact of the matter is that from the perspective of an oppressed and marginalized social position, Blacks do in fact possess a level of heightened sensitivity to recognizable and repeated occurrences that might very well slip beneath the radar of others who do not have such a place and history in a white dominant and hegemonic society. In other words, the claim that I have a justified belief that the white woman's gesture was racist is grounded within a social context that informs and supports this claim. I reject the claim that *all* knowers are "substitutable for one another" when it comes to something like recognizing that a particular gesture is a racist one.[15] There is no universal neutral knowing subject such that he or she can come to have the justifiable belief that a particular gesture from a white woman was racist *simpliciter*. To say that *any* knower can "know" what I do about the white woman's racist gesture would render my experiences and the similarly shared experiences that other Blacks have had under similar circumstances irrelevant. To argue that any and all knowers can simply open their eyes and "see" the white woman's gesture as racist is to flatten out significant differential histories.[16] Sure, when I look at her, I do have an experience, sensory receptors are firing, but this alone does not justify the claim that she has just performed a racist act. Rather, it is precisely those experiences, those shared bits of knowledge, which structure, render intelligible, and justify my belief that the white woman did indeed engage in a racist act. My judgment is fundamentally a social epistemological one, one that is rendered reasonable within the context of a shared history of Black people noting, critically discussing, suffering, and sharing with each other the traumatic experiential content and repeated acts of white racism. Within this context, one might say that Black people constitute a kind of "epistemological community" (a community of knowers). What justifiably allows me to maintain that a particular action is racist, what allows me to develop a coherent narrative of the event that took place within the elevator,[17] one that cements a powerful level of coherence in my knowledge base, are the background histories of oppression that Blacks have experienced vis-à-vis whites.

So, what is the evidence for my claim that the white woman's behavior in the elevator is racist? Her gestures cohere both with my knowledge of white racism and with past experiences I have had with whites performing racist gestures, and my experience is consistent with the shared experiences of other Blacks, who have a long history of having become adept at recognizing these gestures for purposes of resistance and survival. This form of knowledge speaks to a socially and behaviorally complex way in which Black people have had to organize the world and recognize how that world is organized in ways that systemically and systematically vitiate their dignity and literally reduce them to a state of nonbeing. One might say that claims about white people and their racist gestures have empirical content in relationship to the larger history within which they get their purchase, and they are underwritten by white racist brutality. The history of racism in the United States underwrites and supports my knowledge regarding the white woman's gestures. One might argue here in a Quinean fashion that each bit of racist information is supported by the other bits and pieces of racism.[18] My judgment is not whimsical or simply subjective; her gestures are interpreted within the context of cumulative cases, where the reasons I give are "like the legs of a chair, not the links of a chain," indicative of a gestalt-like assessment of the evidence.[19] So, my justifiable belief about the white woman's gesture is interdependent; the evidence for her having enacted a racist gesture is a form of commonsense knowledge among Black people. In other words, my claim is warranted in its compatibility with other "we-experiences" whose warrantability is determinable through intersubjectively shared experiences. Not only I but also others in my epistemological community have seen white women pull their purses close to them when in our presence. I, and others in my epistemological community, later came to learn that many of those tugs turned out to be based upon racist prejudices. What's more, the hypothesis that "pulling one's purse under such-and-such circumstances is an expression of racist prejudice" coheres with a number of other facts, for example, the racist portrayals of African Americans in the media, the effects of racist media on those viewing it, and the past and present circulating myth that the Black body is criminal and dangerous by nature. Given the above, my interpretation of the white woman's behavior is embedded in a coherent picture of the (social) world.

Given the above, it does not follow that my judgment about this particular white woman is epistemically incorrigible. After all, I could be incorrect. In fact, the requirement for infallibility quickly slips into skepticism. But this does not invalidate the warranted assertability of other claims regarding the racist actions of whites that I have made on so many other occasions. Again, this reasoning avoids the charge that the evidence I have is arbitrary or whimsical. The evidence is based on the *lived* experiences and histories of Black bodies in relation to the history of white racist brutality, white racist gazes, the ways whites have comported their bodies in the presence of Black bodies, and how whites have manifested their presumptive superiority or paternalistic proclivities. Rarely do I face the anonymous white woman within the elevator in isolation from an informed history of the mythical purity of white female bodies and the myth of the Black male rapist. Keep in mind that this is a history Black people have inherited. The history of the power of white bodies and how this power policed, insulted, humiliated, and murdered Black bodies informs me, critically shapes my subjectivity, providing me with a perspective from which I am able to see the "entrails" of whiteness, as W. E. B. Du Bois said.[20] To reject my having reliable knowledge about racist gestures because I got one wrong, or to say that I could theoretically be mistaken, does not thereby rule out the reliability or warranted assertability of my judgment upon future or past occasions. To do so is to reject the long history of complex brutal practices that whites have used to discipline Black bodies; it is to deny a collective memory critical to Black survival; and it is to engage in a process of elision regarding the asymmetrical social dynamics and power relations between whites and Blacks that have informed Black people about white terror. Indeed, it is to deny Black critical subjectivity and its capacity to discern correctly a racist action.[21]

To say that the woman in the elevator engaged in a white racist gesture is not to isolate a piece of data, a mythical given, from social history. Indeed, the confines of that small space within the elevator can certainly function as a replicative instance of the larger social macrocosm of problems in Black and white. In fact, my ability to read her gesture is never based upon an isolated datum, as it were, of experiential reality. Rather, broader social and historical dynamics informing how I justifiably read her body are at play. I would argue that the Black community of "we-knowers" is anterior to my encounter with *this* particular white woman on the elevator. These we-knowers construct, acquire, and negotiate knowledge and evidence regarding racism and racist practices. This collective effort is indicative of a communal sense of subjectivity, though many whites denied this sort of collective agency on the part of Blacks. Hence, these Black "communities that construct and acquire knowledge [regarding racist gestures] are not collections of independently knowing individuals; such communities are epistemologically prior to individuals who know."[22] This statement, by the way, does not deny that the white woman's racist gesture is any less stigmatizing and humiliating *to me*.

It is important to note that Black communities' perceptions are not in principle inaccessible to those not from them. In short, we can communicate the shared experiences, conceptual frameworks, and background assumptions to others if they are open to instruction and willing to take the time to listen. So even if all knowers are not intersubstitutable, it does not mean that non-Black knowers, once suitably instructed, cannot come to learn to cognize in ways that enable them to identify racist behavior readily. In this way, I avoid the "picture of monadic epistemic communities with divergent perceptions who are unable to have any kind of intersubjective dialogue."[23] Of course, this line of reasoning also allows for the possibility that even Blacks can disagree about what constitutes a racist form of behavior.

Returning to the context of the elevator, the history of racism shapes the dynamics of this dyadic relationship. Indeed, the elevator encounter is permeated with racist, semiotic, and mythopoeic constructions, constructions that are not only based upon historical precedent but also grounded within the current context of North American culture and life. Years ago, my penis could have been cut off and stuffed in my mouth because a white woman (or man) misread my intentions. It might be argued that I live in a bygone past, trapped in a Fanonian time loop, and that America is different now and that one's abundance of melanin is irrelevant. I do not deny the juridical progress that Blacks have made. This progress, however, has not eliminated the many ways in which Black bodies are stereotypically criminalized, physically harassed by white police officers, detained by white police officers while driving expensive cars that are believed to have been purchased with drug money, subjected to surveillance while shopping in stores, harassed and detained when it is announced that a Black man committed a certain crime, and pegged the so-called Willie-Horton type, lascivious and sexually irresponsible. White counterparts to these racist practices do not readily come to mind. The Black body is the dialectical staple of white bodily integrity.

Within the context of the elevator, one might say that the white woman's consciousness of the meaning of my Black body coincides with the meaning of the Black body *as such* and that from her perspective there is no meaning that the Black body possesses that is foreign to her, that is, a meaning that is capable of enlarging her field of consciousness or her "seeing." When she "sees" me, the symbolic order of "Blackness *as* evil" collapses: I *am* evil. My Blackness *is* the stimulus that triggers her response. "The Negro," as Fanon noted, "is a phobogenic object, a stimulus to anxiety."[24] On this score, I am invested with causal powers, while she is deemed passive and vulnerable. Her perceived sense of "passivity" is part of a complex form of denial. As "passive," she abdicates all responsibility for the ways in which she sustains the Black body as a stimulus to anxiety. Even as words may not come to her mind, as I have described, her body reacts—anxiety rises, sweat glands secrete—to the presence of the Black body, and at once, she is *certain* I will strike.

In the everyday world of encountering Black bodies, the meaning of my Black body is deemed immediate to her consciousness.[25] One might refer to this view as the "natural attitude" of her consciousness of my Black body. The meaning of my body is reduced to a transhistorical signification, an essence with a fixed teleology. Her perspective, however, is far from "direct" and "veridical." Her consciousness is far from transparent. Her gaze is "not a simple seeing, an act of direct perception, but the racial production of the visible, the workings of racial constraints on what it means to 'see.'"[26] As Black, I am the "looked at." As white, she is the bearer of the "white look." But note that it is against my will to have my body transformed, reshaped, and thrown back to me as something I am supposed to *own*. As described above, she grabs her purse, eagerly anticipating the arrival of her floor, "knowing" that this Black predator will soon strike. As she pulls her purse toward her, I am reminded of the sounds of whites locking their car doors as they catch a glimpse of my Black body as I walk by. Changes begin to occur in her brain, neurons begin to fire. The amygdala, which is that part of the brain that functions to alert the body, triggers the white body to protect itself.[27] Her muscles begin to tense, her facial expressions tighten, and her peripheral vision surveils my body as she makes an effort to look ahead. Perhaps she stands in fear of "a Mandingo sexual encounter."[28]

The tragedy of young Black Emmett Till flashes before my mind. Only fourteen years old, Till was murdered in 1955 by two white men for allegedly whistling at a white woman. Beaten beyond recognition and shot in the head, his murderers tied his body to a heavy metal fan and threw it into the Tallahatchie River in Mississippi. Given the long history of white racism in North America, it is not unusual to have specific memories that fail to fade, memories that associate the experience of whiteness with instances of lynching, castration, and terror, memories that justifiably push Black people to the precipice of existential fear and trembling. "Black men," as Ann DuCille notes, "have been lynched because someone said they looked at, spoke to, or thought about a white woman."[29]

The elevator example is far from uncontroversial, of course. For example, during an invited lecture that I gave on the Black body and whiteness, one white male student pointed out to me that it might be argued that the white woman in the elevator had been raped by a man a few months ago. She sees me step onto the elevator and feels my eyes size her up in a "predatory" fashion. Although she has been in intensive psychotherapy and has since learned how to defend herself more effectively, she feels trepidation because of my male presence, my physical proximity to her within the small space of the elevator, and the fact that we are alone. So, she clutches her purse, revealing her level of insecurity or perhaps as an act of self-protection. I agree that this example shows that one can provide a counter-reading of my scenario, that is, a counter-reading of how I read her grabbing her purse, the movement of her eyes, and her bodily posture. This counter-reading shows that it is possible for me to be incorrect in my interpretation of the situation. Indeed, I grant that one of the difficulties with racism is that it is not always obvious. It can be difficult to ascertain under particular circumstances whether someone is

simply having an awful day, is typically obnoxious, is preoccupied, or is racist. However, this does not make racism less of a problem. What this says is
that situations have layers of complexity.

Critical pedagogy theorist Audrey Thompson points out that if the white
male student's objective in the counter-reading is to use complexity to make
the problem of racism disappear, then this is an *invalid* use of complexity.
She also notes, and I agree, that what is interesting is that whites may worry
about whether someone is being obnoxious, having a bad day, and so on,
but they don't worry about racism when it comes to how they are addressed.
Moreover, within such a systemically racist context as North America, it is
reasonable to assume racism, even if one happens to be incorrect, though this
assumption can function as an easy way of not attending to greater layers of
hermeneutic complexity that may point beyond racism in any given situation.
Being incorrect or highlighting exceptions to acts of racism does not unseat
claims regarding racist patterns and proclivities, since being incorrect or
having exceptions are compatible with such racist patterns and proclivities.
Whiteness theorist Christine Sleeter notes that "what white students often
find it more difficult to understand is that generally people of color know that
they may over-interpret race, but can't afford not to because most of the time
the interpretation is correct."[30] I would add that it could also prove fatal for
people of color to respond to each situation as if it were sui generis. It would
be great to respond to white women in elevators, white state police officers
who pull Black males over, white Realtors who show Black people property,
bank lenders, and others, beyond the presumption of anti-Black racism, but it
would be a mistake born of an idealism that is belied by the reality of pervasive white racism in North America.

I recall an African American student of mine sharing the experience of
being really angry when a white academic counselor at one university, after
the student disclosed that he received a scholarship, asked him, "So, which
sport do you play?" Sharing the experience of having received a scholarship,
which was actually an academic one, was a disclosure of pride for the student,
but the counselor's racist response challenged this pride, attempting to reduce
the student's acquisition of a scholarship to one of *those* scholarships, the
ones that Black students receive. After all, as the racist reasoning goes, Black
bodies, given their unique physical stamina and athletic prowess, are guaranteed scholarships for playing sports. I once asked my students if they thought
that "race" is real, whether it cuts at the joints of reality, as opposed to a
social construction. One white male student confidently said: "Of course race
is real. Why do you think so many Blacks dominate the NBA?" There was
a kind of silent compliance throughout the room, until another white student
struggled—at least she dared to offer an alternative response—to articulate
how many Blacks who live in poverty treasure things like basketballs, and see

the sport as a route out of the ghetto, and who go on to develop a profound mastery of the sport, particularly as the space within which it is played is competitive, forcing a sense of learned excellence that has nothing to do with a racial causative substratum.

On another occasion, a white female student of mine stated that she would feel apprehensive in an elevator regardless of the race of the male. All that was necessary was a male present on the elevator, one that she presumably did not know. Within such a context, for her, gender was the primary lens through which she comprehended the potential danger of the situation. Given the power of male dominance, this view certainly gives credence to the argument that a fundamental part of women's existence is asking the question, "Are you going to rape me?"[31] This also points to the reality that the gaze is not simply raced, but gendered, and that many white women do not always feel comfortable in rooms or small spaces with men whom they do not know. While I certainly do not wish to marginalize the experiences of my student, there was something unsettling in the speed with which she responded. As the majority of other white female students nodded in agreement with her, her response effectively turned the discussion away from race to that of gender; somehow, we were now talking about males qua males. I began to think of how her response may have functioned as a way of obfuscating her own racism, as a way of eliding her whiteness. After all, the context of our discussion had to do with white racism, specifically how whites feel in the presence of *Black* males. Her response demonstrated how feminism and antiracism do not always go hand in hand, though one would think that they should/would.[32] Within this context, violence against women, a very real, enduring, and disturbing reality, functioned as the banner under which she was able to ignore or bracket her own whiteness/racism. Surprising me with her honesty, another white female student of mine said, "I actually feel afraid when I notice that Black males are walking on the same side of the street that I am." In this case, her disclosure pointed to the intersectional dynamics of her fear. It was about (non-additive) *Black maleness*. There was silence throughout the classroom. The fact of the matter is that there is no male qua male. Moreover, Black males still socially embody a lethal and threatening presence in the white imaginary. "Are you going to rape me?" is a question that gets inflected in ways profoundly differently in the presence of a Black man than in the presence of a white man. By flattening out the discussion and making it into one that deflects the importance of racism, patriarchy is elevated over the explanatory resources found in exploring the *white* (i.e., raced) imaginary in greater depth. This flattening not only avoids the subtle power of racism, and how it operates in the everyday lives of whites, but also impoverishes forms of social theory that highlight the complexity at the intersections between race and gender.

Created from the mire of the white imaginary, representations and fantasies of Black males as excessive, as "lusting murderously after innocent white women,"[33] as buffoons, or inferior animals, have been played out in the anti-Reconstruction filmic narratives and novels, such as D. W. Griffith's *Birth of a Nation* (1915) and Thomas Dixon's *The Leopard's Spots: A Romance of the White Man's Burden* (1902). Like the spots on a leopard, Black men are believed unable to change their lusting ways and inferior constitution. And Blacks, more generally, are unable to eradicate the "curse" of their darkness. Through the mouth of one of his characters, Dixon asks, "Can you change the color of his [the Ethiopian/the Black] skin, the kink of his hair, the bulge of his lips, the spread of his nose, or the beat of his heart with a spelling book?" The character answers, "The Negro is the human donkey. You can train him, but you can't make him a horse."[34] Of course, such racial representations of Black men helped create and sustain the rationalization to "protect" white women through the creation of such "law-abiding" groups as the Ku Klux Klan. Moreover, such representations helped sustain the white gaze. Of course, the white gaze continues to get its sustenance through various media representations of Black bodies.

Returning to the white woman in the elevator, she desires to look, but feels uncomfortable doing so. She fears that a direct look might incite the anger of the Black predator. She feels a strange combination of attraction, disgust, and trepidation. She fakes a smile in order to soothe what she "knows" to be moving through my savage breast. By her smile she hopes to elicit a spark of humanity from the dark savage. But I don't return the smile, fearing that she might interpret it as a sexual advance.[35] After all, within the social space of the elevator, which has become, to use Judith Butler's turn of phrase, "a racially saturated field of visibility," a hermeneutic transactional space within which my intended meanings get falsified, it is *as if* I am no longer in charge of what I mean/intend.[36] What she "sees" or "hears" is governed by a racist epistemology of certitude that places me under erasure; only through *not* seeing me am I visible; only through *not* hearing me am I audible. Within this space, she "controls" the "truth" of my intentions. Her alleged literacy regarding the semiotics of my Black body, however, is actually an instance of profound illiteracy. Her gaze upon my Black body might be said to function like a camera obscura. Her gaze consists of a racist socio-epistemic *aperture*, as it were, through which the (white) *light* of "truth" casts an inverted/distorted image of me upon the back walls, so to speak, of her mind. My meaning, in short, is flipped on its head.

I place particular emphasis upon this notion of the racist socio-epistemic *aperture*. Take the well-known *Plessy v. Ferguson* case (1896), which resulted in the U.S. Supreme Court's establishment of the separate-but-equal doctrine. Homer Plessy was 7/8 white and 1/8 Black. He argued that because of this he should be allowed to sit in the whites-only railroad car. This was a calculated effort on the part of Plessy and the Citizens Committee to Test the Constitutionality of the Separate Car Law to call into question the Louisiana statute (1890) that made it mandatory for Blacks and whites to ride in separate railroad cars. Plessy lost the case and had to pay a $25 fine. Apparently, just having 1/8 of "Black blood" was sufficient to make him Black.

Consider the following hypothetical scenario: Plessy enters the elevator. It is my assumption that the white woman would not automatically begin her ritual performance of anti-Black racist suspicion. On the contrary, she would probably perform her whiteness in ways that signify that she feels comfortable and safe around this "white" male. However, let's further assume that the *Plessy v. Ferguson* case was televised and that she had just watched the news, seeing pictures of Plessy. According to my argument, despite his phenotypic whiteness, she would come to react to him in ways that she would react to my *dark* body. There is an important qualification here. On prior encounters with the Black male body, she has reacted negatively; that is, her body is *habituated* to react to black skin. In the case of Plessy, however, she would first see white skin/male, then experience the moment of recognition, the man on TV, the Black man, and then experience the upwelling and flood of the racial imaginary reframing her response. There is a kind of "translating" process in this case that does not appear to take place with regard to black skin, where "the overt act of interpretation itself is skipped in an attenuated process of perceptual knowing."[37]

The point here is that the white gaze as a racist socio-epistemic aperture will "see" a threatening Black body in white. Noting the above qualification, her physical eyes may see white skin, but her gaze eventually overrides what is visual. Made accessible through those myths and tropes that constitute the socio-epistemic aperture of the white gaze, she comes to "see" a Black in whiteface, she discerns the "stained" Black body in white. Citing (though critical of) the racist assumptions propagated in R. W. Shufeldt's *The Negro, A Menace to American Civilization*, Charles Johnson notes how a single drop of Black blood is capable of causing "a white family to revert to Negroid characteristics even after a full century; the mulatto, though possessing white blood, is depicted as dangerous because his surface 'outside,' not being stained, betrays the criminality and animality of his interior."[38] Her gaze comes replete with an essentialist ontological perspective on Blackness, no matter the abundance of "white blood" or the miniscule amount of "Black blood."

Again, returning to my experience with the white woman on the elevator, it is through her gaze that I become hypervigilant of my own embodied spatiality. On previous occasions, particularly when alone, I have moved my body within the space of the elevator in a noncalculating fashion, paying no particular attention to my bodily comportment, the movement of my hands, my eyes, the position of my feet. I did not calculate the distance between my arm, hand, and my fingers in relationship to the buttons indicating the various floors. On such occasions, my "being-in" the space of the elevator is familiar; my bodily movements, my stance, are indicative of what it means to *inhabit* a space of familiarity. In short, it is a space within which I am meaningfully absorbed in the habitual everydayness of riding elevators. The elevator could break down, in which case I might experience the space within the elevator as too confining; I might panic as I perhaps only now, all of a sudden, begin to experience how stuffy the elevator is, how tiny it is, and how it does not have an operational phone. Under these circumstances, I become calcula-tive. I perceive the elevator as an object that represents a challenge to me, as something standing over and against me. What was previously a familiar space in the elevator, which I inhabited as an uncomplicated modality of my meaningful bodily comportment, has all of a sudden become "a something" that is threatening; my everyday mode of "being-in" has become a mode of *being-trapped-in*.

The movement from the familiar is what is also effected by the white woman's gaze. My movements become and remain stilted. I dare not move suddenly. The apparent racial neutrality of the space within the elevator (when I am standing alone) has become an axiological plenum, one filled with white normativity. As Shannon Sullivan would say, I no longer inhabit the space of the elevator "as a corporeal entitlement to spatiality."[39] I feel trapped. I no longer feel bodily expansiveness within the elevator, but corpo-really constrained, limited. I now begin to calculate, paying almost neurotic attention to my body movements, making sure that this "Black object," what now feels like an appendage, a weight, is not too close, not too tall, not too threatening. "Double layers of self-awareness must interrogate the likely meanings that will be attributed to every utterance, gesture, action one takes."[40] So, I genuflect, but only slightly, a movement that somewhat resembles an act of worship. I am reminded of how certain postures—"bow-ing and scraping"—were reenacted over generations, sometimes no doubt unconsciously. My lived-body comes back to me, as does the elevator in the example above, as something to be dealt with, as a challenge. The gaze of the woman disrupts my habituated bodily comportment and I am thrown into an uncomfortable awareness of my body. Where I am standing, the color of my skin and my posture are, in a moment, foregrounded and I am suddenly aware of how I am being perceived. Indeed, my lived-body begins to feel like some-thing ontologically *occurrent*, something merely *there* in its facticity. Notice that she need not speak a word (speech-acts are not necessary) to render my Black body "captive." She need not scream "Rape!" She need not call me "Nigger!" to my face. Indeed, although how she reacts to me is certainly not without its deeper moral implications, and must be called into question, it is not a necessary requirement that she hates me or is morally vicious in order for her to script my body in the negative way that she does. Her nonverbal movements construct me, creating their own socio-ontological effects on my body. Her negrophobia depicts me in a shockingly monstrous fashion. White America has bombarded me and other Black males with the "reality" of our dual hypersexualization: "you are a sexual trophy and a certain rapist."[41] Her gaze imposes upon me a certain form, albeit distorted.

Fanon, aware of the horrible narrative myths used to depict Black bodies, noted that the Negro *is* the genital and *is* the incarnation of evil, being that which is to be avoided and yet desired.[42] Face to face, the white woman "feels the need to recall the times of cannibalism."[43] Ritualistically enacting her racialized and racist consciousness, she reveals her racist narrative competence, a putative self-evident script vis-à-vis my "savage" Black body. After all, from her perspective, my Black body is reducible to the biological. And although "one cannot decently 'have a hard on' everywhere," within the white imaginary, I apparently fit the bill. To put a slight interpretive inflection on Fanon here, as the unquenchable Black penis, a walking, talking, hard-on, I am believed eager to introduce white women into a sexual universe for which the white male "does not have the key, the weapons, or the attributes."[44] But it is precisely this Black penis that is always already a site of violence. She deems that my passions are so out of control that I will not be able to control my lust for her. After all, it is the "beauty" and "purity" of her white skin that I can't seem to resist. Within the *lived* and consequential semiotic space of the elevator, might it be said that the white woman has "taken" my body from me, sending a fundamentally different meaning back to me, and thus forcing an ever-so-slight level of cognitive dissonance, a *lived* or phenomenologically given disparity, that I must now fight against?

The space within the elevator has become a microcosm of some of the dynamic processes of a larger, systemic form of colonial invasion within which its undesired incursions, pernicious acts of usurpation, and regulatory processes of white normativity are played out on the lived-body of the colonized. Just as the colonial presence attempts to deplete the power of the colonized to lay claim to their own subjectivity, I feel as if my power to communicate my own scripted identity and my agency to invalidate the constellations of meaning imposed from without are ineffective. My agency to act-in-the-world, to assert how I understand/narrate my own identity, appears reduced to a form of knowledge regarding my actions of which I am restricted to having privileged, epistemic access only. In other words, it is as if I am forced within an epistemic *solipsistic* position because her racist interpretive metanarrative chips away at my intended meanings. Thus, she challenges my act of pressing my meaning into service, which would function to counter her interpretations, even as I am cognizant of what I intend.

For once I act, my action enters into a hermeneutic traffic of semiotic distortion, my actions undergo a process of transvaluation. The meaning that I intend through a given action, which is the embodied correlate of that intention, becomes a threat to her. Within this racially saturated field of visibility, she "sees" me as this predator stereotype. Her embodied comportment is entangled within a web of habituated lies and distortions. It is as if with every attempt on my part to resist this racially saturated field of visibility, for example, when I think about smiling, she returns my good and harmless intentions back to me, interpreted, through the medium of this field of visibility, as "evidence" of my ulterior predatory or criminal motives. The white woman thinks that her act of "seeing" me is an act of "knowing" who I am, of knowing what I will do next; that is, her "seeing" is believed to be simply a process of unmediated or uninterpreted perception. However, her coming to "see" me as she does is actually a cultural achievement, a racist sociohistorical schematization, indeed, an act of epistemic violence.

Of course, I could always turn around and state contemptuously, "Frankly, I don't give a damn about you or your kind!" But this would only confirm her fears of the mythical raging, angry Black male. In other words, my action would only increase her feelings of trepidation. I could also strike up a conversation that would eventually lead to the disclosure of some personal information that might create a wedge between myth and reality. "I am a philosopher, a PhD, and I also attended Yale University." There is the possibility, though, that her white gaze is so fixed that this newly discovered information would not shake her framework. Her head would say yes, but her body would say no. After all, I am still *Black* and her fear of Blackness has become deeply corporeal and woven into the fabric of her unconscious.[45] But even as I made an effort to put her at ease through the disclosure of such personal information about myself, I feel that I would have placed inordinate pressure upon myself to convince her that I am a "good Black," a nonviolent Black. I wonder to what extent other Black men, under similar circumstances, have felt a certain rush of joy to announce, "I am not your typical Black male. I am better. In fact, if you look closely you will see that I'm not really Black" and in doing so reinforce the prevailing racist imaginary while attempting to "other" one's self.

In addition, should *she* not be the one doing the work to challenge *her* racism? As an alternative approach, as I reach my floor and before exiting, I could view this as a transgressive moment in which I could impact her habitual mode of embodied racism through the process of triggering a sense of shame: "Miss, I assure you that I am not interested in your trashy possessions. I especially have no desire to humiliate you through the violence of rape, nor are my sexual desires outside my control." *Naming* her fears, dispassionately bringing them into the open, I position my moral agentive subjectivity in such a way that she relationally comes to take up the position of a particular kind of subject, one who feels shame. In other words, this shame is "a constituted effect" produced through the effective positioning of myself as a moral actor within this dyad.[46] Having effectively reversed the gaze, her head and eyes would drop. There would be a distinct look of shame that would cover her face and body posture. Without uttering another word, I would turn and exit the elevator. The hope is that this shame is only the beginning of a new narrative, a new way of delving into and remaking her identity. Shame is no substitute for the real struggle ahead, the honesty to examine and reexamine the residual habits of racism, and the struggle to transcend these habits yet again and again and again. Perhaps as I leave that elevator I have gained a victory, "a livable space between the poles of other [white] people's imagination and the nice calm center of oneself where dignity resides."[47] Then, again, she could be thinking, " 'Nigger,' just who do you think you're talking to?" This would function as a way of eliding the truth that she felt threatened by what she and other whites daily construct and naturalize as the "Black monster," while still maintaining a sense of "superiority" by questioning that I spoke to her in such an "impudent" or "uppity" fashion.

As an example of how the Black body is concretized as ontologically problematic within a white racist hermeneutic traffic of semiotic distortion, Judith Butler provides an insightful analysis of the Rodney King beating and verdict that squares well with my interpretation of the interconnections between what is "seen," what is "not seen," racism, and the construction of the "Black body." Butler's analysis illustrates how white fear was projected onto King's body, as it is projected onto my Black body in my elevator example, to the point that his attempts to defend himself were seen as a threat. As Butler makes clear, "the video shows a man being beaten."[48] She asks, though, how the jury in Simi Valley came to "see" King's prone body as a dangerous and threatening object that the police had to further subdue over and over again with their batons? Like in the elevator, a contestation emerges within the visual field and a battle takes place over the meaning of the Black body's intentions.[49] According to Butler, King's Black body was schematized through "the inverted projections of white paranoia." In short, King's "threatening" Black body was produced within a white metanarrative that constitutes "the racial production of the visible."[50] She argues:

> The kind of "seeing" that the police enacted, and the kind of "seeing" that the jury reenacted, is one in which a further violence is performed by the disavowal and projection of that violent beating. The actual blows against Rodney King are understood to be fair recompense, indeed, defenses against, the dangers that are

"seen" to emanate from his body. Here "seeing" and attributing are indissoluble. Attributing violence to the object of violence is part of the very mechanism that recapitulates violence, and that makes the jury's "seeing" into a complicity with that police violence.[51]

This process translates into a site of phantasmagoria, according to Butler, and "in this sense, the circuit of violence attributed to Rodney King is itself the circuit of white racist violence which disavows itself only to brutalize the specter that embodies its own intention. This is the phantasm that it ritualistically produces at the site of the racialized other."[52]

Further theorizing this space of phantasmagoria, it is important to note that not only does the white woman in the elevator ontologically freeze my "dark" embodied identity but she also becomes ontologically frozen in her own embodied (white) identity. For she only "sees" a criminal, a predator, a phantasm. She too is a prisoner of her own historically inherited imaginary and the habitual racist performances that have become invisible to her. She "sees," but she does not necessarily reflect upon, herself as normative, "innocent", "pure". Her performances reiterate the myth of the proverbial white victim at the hands of the Black predator. Butler argues that reading of the video of the King beating is indeed a form of reenacting "the phantasmatic scene of the crime, reiterating and re-occupying the endangered status of the white person on the street."[53] Like Emmett Till, King's body, the "Black body," embodies all that is antithetical to "civilization" (read: white). Regarding the manner in which King's body was said to be a "self-evident threat" to the police officers, Robert Gooding-Williams, like Butler, challenges the positivist myth of "brute facts" when it comes to the process of "seeing" Black bodies within a white racist context of constituted social reality. He argues:

> After inviting the jurors to see events from the point of view of the police officers, the defense attorneys elicited testimony from King's assailants that depicted King repeatedly as a bear, and as emitting bear-like groans. In the eyes of the police, and then again in the eyes of the jurors, King's Black body became that of a wild "Hulk-like" and "wounded" animal, whose every gesture threatened the existence of civilized society. Not surprisingly, the defense attorneys portrayed the white bodies which assailed King as guardians against the wild, and as embodying a "thin blue line" that separates civil society from the dangerous chaos which is the essence of the wild.[54]

The woman in my elevator example, however, does not realize that she has come to see herself as pure, civilized, innocent, and an easy victim of untamed Black men, through a socially constructed and historically manufactured normative framework that has become inter- and intra-subjectively formative and stable through systemic social practices of white hegemony. Her whiteness is deemed "nonthreatening." Of course, it is through the historically sedimented centrality and weight of whiteness's ontology that these constructions appear at all. The Black body (in this case the Black *male* body) *is* by nature criminal, because the white body (in this case the white *female* body) *is* by nature innocent, pure, and good. There is nothing historically necessary about the fact that the Black body has been typified as criminal. "Yellow bodies" (Asian Americans) and "red bodies" (Native Americans) have also been criminalized and othered within contexts involving white racist hegemonic practices. Think here of the fact that Asians are referred to as "yellow Negroes" and Arab bodies are characterized as terroristic and swarthy "sand niggers." And Native Americans are depicted as savages and alcoholics.

In reference to what he refers to as the "average ordinary White Man," Gilles Deleuze notes that "the first divergence-types, are racial: yellow man, black man."[55] Note how he marks "divergence" as *racial*. In diverging or deviating from whiteness (the "nonracial" center), the yellow, the black, and the red are signifiers of inferior difference compared to whiteness as the same/ transcendental norm. According to Deleuze, "Racism never detects the particles of the other; it propagates waves of sameness."[56] While I agree with Deleuze that Blacks have been defined relative to their divergence from the historically constructed "standard" of whiteness, as a critical addendum to Deleuze's position, I would add that within the European imaginary Blacks have not only been conceptualized as divergent but that at times they have also been conceptualized as a different *kind*. For example, let x stand for the standard against which y and z are judged divergences. In this case, x, y, and z might still be said to be of the same kind, where y and z are said to diverge more or less in some fashion. In instances involving the European imaginary in terms of the "nature" of Blacks, however, Black people were not simply "divergent" from the standard (x), and hence were neither y nor z, but belonged to a fundamentally different *type*. On this score, then, not only does whiteness reserve the power to define others as "divergent" or "deviant" but it also has the power to define "differences" entirely outside the standard– divergence dialectic. Supporting my assumption that Black is not simply divergent, but, within the white imaginary, has been deemed a different type/ kind, Lewis Gordon notes:

But what the Black is, is the not-Other and not-self. To put it differently, in the Western framework the only way the Other can emerge is if there were some notion that the Other can be a human being. Racism, properly understood, reduces Blacks below the human. Speaking of what was also conquest, Fanon said, in *Les Damnes*, that when the French took Algeria they saw themselves as taking nothing more than the land. And in a context like that it is the Hegelian thesis that there is no *Geist* there, there is no human being there—and consequently no "experience." And literally if there is no *Geist*, then one cannot even get into the dialectics of recognition.[57]

Within the context of the long and arduous history of white racism in America, it is *the Black* that is deemed by nature the *Untermenschen*, because whites are by nature the *Übermenschen*. Whiteness sets itself up as the thesis. Within the dialectical logic of whiteness, Blackness *must* be the antithesis. Within the space of the elevator, the white woman clings to her identity *as* white, effecting thereby the necessary distance/difference between the white self (*her* white self) and the Black other (*my* Blackness as otherness). The space of our "confrontation" is governed by a dialectical representational logic, one that is tied to a long history of material forces, which can be "understood as the representational form wherein two terms are positioned in a diametrically opposed and hierarchical structure."[58] Within a larger context, getting her to examine and struggle against the historical fictions about her white identity is a call to challenge those conditions that require such historical fictions.[59]

On the elevator, my Black body is ontologically mapped, its coordinates lead to that which is always immediately visible: the Black surface. The point here is that the Black body in relation to the white gaze *appears* in the form of a sheer exteriority, implying that the Black body "shows up," makes itself known in terms of its Black surface. There is only the visible, the concrete, the seen, all there, all at once: a single Black *thing*, unindividuated, threatening, ominous, *Black*. The white woman thinks she takes no part in this construction; she acts "in the name of the serious."[60] She apparently fails to see how her identity is shot through in terms of how she constructs me. This failure is to be expected given how white privilege renders invisible, indeed, militates against the recognition of, various whitely ways of being-in-the-world. Sullivan notes that the "habits of white privilege do not merely go unnoticed. They actively thwart the process of conscious reflection on them, which allows them to seem non-existent even as they continue to function."[61]

When Rodney King was brutally beaten by the Los Angeles Police Department officers, he held up the palm of his hand, which was turned away from his body.[62] The construction of the "innocence" of the white police officers hinged upon a reversed interpretation of a show of the palm as an act of violence, and, hence, as further justification to subdue the "Hulk-like" powerful Black male body. Similarly, the woman in the elevator does not see that her identity is constructed and shaped through her negation of my humanity. She takes her identity to be full, a pure self-presence, unrelated, dialectically, to my distorted presence. While none of us are completely transparent to ourselves, her blinkers are specifically shaped through the power of whiteness as the transcendental norm. Within the context of the elevator, her ignorance is not simply a lacuna that results from her own epistemic complacency but is part of a larger systemic process whereby her ignorance is a dynamic social production. What is her "positive" whiteness apart from my "negative" Blackness? After all, the positive norms that govern her self-understanding as white are norms that govern her self-understanding of my Blackness as problematic and morally flawed. Perhaps this is partly what James Baldwin had in mind when he wrote about the paradox that "those [whites] who believed that they could control and define Black people divested themselves of the power to control and define themselves."[63] The point here is that the narrative intelligibility of her white identity is always already parasitic upon the narrative distortion of my Black identity. "To the extent that [white] identity always contains the specter of non-identity within it, the [white] subject is always divided and identity is always purchased at the price of the exclusion of the Other," in this case the Black other.[64]

Like the white police officers who brutally beat Rodney King, the white woman on the elevator sees herself as on the side of the law. Historically, white women have been protected under the law in relation to Black males. Their engendered whiteness guaranteed their innocence before the law; their authority to speak the truth concerning incidents involving the "lascivious" Black male body was granted a priori. The "law" functions here as a metonymic term for what it means to be white. Within the framework of a binary economy of racial metonymic opposites, Blackness is deemed "unlawful." Since the Black body is deemed unlawful, the act of "seeing" King or "seeing" my Black body in the elevator is linked to the issue of what a white racist episteme in fact produces as visible. My Blackness, for her, is a sufficient register used to substantiate/confirm the "veridicality" of her perception. My Blackness is sufficient evidence of my brutality. What is passed off as seeing, however, is really a form of *reading*.[65] Her "reading" of my Black body is characteristic of the epistemology of ignorance. More specifically, an epistemology of ignorance involves "a particular pattern of localized and global cognitive dysfunctions (which are psychologically and socially functional), producing the ironic outcome that whites will in general be unable to understand the world they themselves have made."[66] She suffers from a structured blindness, a sociopsychologically reinforcing opacity that obstructs the process of "seeing" beyond falsehoods and various modes of whitely bodily comportment that continue to reinforce and sustain white hegemony and mythos. While an epistemology of ignorance is certainly operative, this does not mean that in order to become an antiracist *all* that is needed is that she adopts the project of uprooting those beliefs that are false or filling in all of the epistemic blanks, and thereby creating a cognitively sound (non-dysfunctional) way of understanding how she has helped to create a racist world. My point here is that her racist actions are also habits of the body and not simply cognitively false beliefs. Recall that the white woman's body shifts nervously and her heart beats more quickly as she catches a glimpse of my Black body. Anxious, her palms become sweaty. There is an acute sense of panic. There is difficulty swallowing, dry mouth, nausea. All of this happens at the level of the somatic. In other words, this blindness is also embedded within her encrusted bodily ways of engaging-in-the-world; it is a form of blindness that involves bodily ways of traversing spaces within which Black bodies are present. Moreover, her constructed ignorance is *cultural*, and not just an individual act. She does not realize the subtle, habitual performances that she enacts in order to sustain the socially constructed nature of her gaze and, hence, to continue to perpetuate the distortion of my Black body as criminal.

The white woman is not simply influenced by racist practices, but she is the *vehicle* through which such practices get performed and sustained. Again, while she is cognitively dysfunctional through deep-seated racist socio-epistemological forms of belief, her racism involves habitual, somatically ingrained ways of whitely-being-in-the-world, and systemically racist institutional structures, of which she is partly a product. As a "product," this does not mean that she is simply an epiphenomenon of social conditioning, although such conditioning is formative. And yet, her performance of the white gaze is not reducible to an individual, isolated act. Moreover, she is not the "metaphysical originator," as it were, of the first white gaze. There is no white *Ur*-gaze. Rather, the intelligibility and effectiveness of the performative white gaze are always already fueled by a larger social imaginary, which is historically grounded in white institutional and brute power. More specifically, my sense is that against this institutional, habitual, and socio-epistemological backdrop, she maintains the potential for opposition, no matter how difficult, for "sliding into," as it were, an antiracist discourse with its counter-racist embodied practices and ways of knowing, even as this will involve a complex, continuous effort.

For the woman in the elevator, the white racist horizon has come to have greater saliency. However, it is the counter-racist horizon that must come to have greater saliency for the white woman. While there are no epistemological *foundational grounds* according to which I can appeal that would *incontrovertibly* convince her that it is immoral to be a racist, this does not negate my earlier discussion of shame. After all, the shift she underwent is not just a cognitive response, but a profound, affective *embodied* response. This does not mean, however, that arguments and counterarguments cannot be advanced against a particular horizon like white racism. Powerful arguments can still be marshaled in the form of various rhetorical strategies, persuasive techniques, and internal criticism. The assumption, of course, is that my interlocutor is at least open.

The white woman's gaze is reiterated within the context of power relations that not only help to sustain the larger social racist imaginary but also sanction her performance of the gaze in the first place, guaranteeing its performance with impunity and ensuring material effects on the gazed-upon Black body. Nevertheless, she engages in a form of evasion. While performing this gaze, while performing an act of "reading the surface" of my Black body, which is really an act of *constructing* my Black body, I feel the necessity to defend my identity. There are times, though, when "I [take] myself far off from my own presence, far indeed, and [make] myself an object," if only to examine critically the image of the monster that she has constructed.[67] Although I do not feel my body image slip away from me, pushing me toward the precipice of epistemic violence, ever closer to living in a state of self-hatred, it is precisely within the context of various racist social spaces that I feel as if I *become* "Black" (read: evil, sexually rapacious) anew within the context of each encounter with the generative dimensions of the white gaze/imaginary. I am, as it were, a phantom, indeed, a "spook," that lives between the interstices of my physical, phenotypically dark body and the white woman's gesticulatory performances. *She performs her white body, ergo I "become" the predatory Black.* These gesticulatory performances, ways of being toward me, provide evidence of the generative workings of the white imaginary. I am reduced to a racialized essence. This process of racial hypostatization manifests itself to the white woman in the form of my dark body's "intention" to do her harm. I become, for her, "the origin and potential instrument of all danger in the [elevator] scene." [68]

Within the dynamic racialized space of the elevator, I have undergone a process of what might be termed "misplaced concretion." From the abstract sphere of the white imaginary, my dark body is the concrete and particular instantiation of a racist abstraction: Blackness *is* dangerous. While I continue to resist this undesirable and unwanted identity relationship, the copula is designed to congeal me. I have become, as it were, the externalized figure, the fantasized object of the white woman's own white distortion.[69] Hence, her actions only further perpetuate the construction of racial boundaries that sustain her transactions with me on the elevator.

I think it is important to note that the range of racist behaviors performed by whites in response to the presence of Black bodies in elevators, for example, is not reducible to a single explanatory model that postulates that such racist behaviors are due to *consciously* held prejudices or beliefs that might be further said to be capable of being ameliorated through the mere process of encouraging more rigorous epistemic attentiveness to how whites intellectually assent to a given proposition (e.g., "Blacks *are* evil and not to be trusted"). For there are many whites who will reject being racists qua consciously assenting to a set of racist propositional beliefs about Blacks, and, yet, who might be said to perform "whitely" (i.e., distancing themselves physically, looking with suspicious eyes, feeling themselves physically threatened or repulsed by Blackness) in the presence of Black bodies. My point is that acting whitely is not limited to possessing *occurrent* racist beliefs or feeling hatred for (or having that hatred *directed* toward) a particular Black person encountered on an elevator. Acting whitely might be described as a form of orientation that comes replete with a set of sensibilities that unconsciously or pre-reflectively position or configure the white self vis-à-vis the nonwhite self.

Of course, simply reducing whiteness qua racism to a set of false beliefs can lead to the consequence of not acknowledging or even to rejecting the existence of larger *systemic* power relationships (that exist beyond the space of elevators) that form a *system* of white supremacist practices that are supported by white legal, material, socioeconomic, sociopolitical, and cultural power. The faulty reasoning might run something like this: "White racist beliefs are agent-centered.[70] Systems of power don't denote persons qua agents. Hence, systems of power relationships don't constitute white racism." Moreover, to reduce whiteness to a set of false beliefs overlooks the fact that many whites, those who have very honorable intentions, those who might be described as "goodwill" whites, who deny holding racist beliefs, benefit from acting whitely-in-the-world in ways that they themselves may not consciously intend. On this score, benefiting from acting whitely-in-the-world can have negative implications for nonwhites, even if whites are unaware of the consequences of their actions. I feel compelled to exclaim, "But he/she *ought* to have been aware! And where he/she *ought* to have been aware, he/she *can* indeed be aware."

In a sociopolitical and cultural structure where whiteness is privileged and normative, it is neither necessary nor sufficient that people designated as white cling to racist beliefs in order to benefit from whiteness. Hence, even though there are white bodies that do not possess what might be referred to as a "white supremacist subjectivity," they still reap benefits from being more highly valued within the larger white racist sociopolitical, cultural context. I am arguing that there is nothing intrinsically problematic about one's white phenotypic constitution. White racist supremacy is not a natural property that inheres within the skin of those classified as white; it does not result from an innate, genotypic disposition. There is indeed a *contingent* relationship between having "white skin" and being a white racist.[71] Then why not use the term *white supremacy* as opposed to *whiteness* to avoid giving the impression that the problem lies with phenotypic whiteness? *Whiteness* not only points to the ways in which colorism (*white* as believed to be supremely beautiful, untainted, moral, good, intelligent, civilized, and lawful) is the hallmark of North American racism but also points to those phenotypical whites who make every effort to guard against racist beliefs. In other words, as stated before, even these whites benefit unjustly from being white in their phenotypic constitution because of the larger social positioning and valuing of white bodies over other bodies. Hence, they play a role in constituting the Black body as "other" and in sustaining white racism.

The elevator example is designed to illustrate a slice of my lived reality. The space within the elevator is only a pale reminder of how the Black body has been historically marked and inscribed in derogatory terms, how it has been subjected to inhuman brutality and pernicious acts of violence, and how it has been marginalized and derailed within the space of the white body politic. This history of marginalization and derailment serves as an important reference point in terms of which I position and negotiate my identity. This history also partly *positions* me, constituting my identity and thus informing my *lived* standpoint. This history is the past and present threatening space within which I move and have my being.

On any given late evening, I *know* that white police officers might kill me as I reach for identifying information. As with Rodney King when he showed his palms, any intentional movement toward my wallet—which I struggle to produce so as to identify myself, attempting to cut through the historical layers of white lies that have pre-identified me—is interpreted as an act of violence. Such identifying information, though, is always relevant ex post facto. This is because *who* I am has already been determined. I am the Black who is present in his absence, whose genuine intentions arrive too late. I am a "seen absence." I am visible in my invisibility. What is seen is a stereotypical "object" devoid of nuance. Tautologically, "a Nigger is just a Nigger," one who is swallowed up in anonymity. White racist practices construct an iterable conception of the Black body: All Blacks are the same. Within the space of racist logic, "A nigger has always done something."[72] Let a Black commit a crime and it is said to have been predictable. Let a white commit a crime and it becomes anomalous, something that was off the map of expectation. When Timothy McVeigh bombed the Murrah Federal Building in Oklahoma City, white men, in virtue of their whiteness, were not profiled and hunted down. Tim Wise writes, "That's what it means to be white, and certainly what it meant for me: no matter what another white man does, I will not be thought of in the same light merely because I too am a white male."[73]

As *the* Black male body, I *am* Amadou Diallo (1999), who reached for his wallet and was shot at forty-one times by the NYPD and hit with nineteen bullets; I *am* Abner Louima (1997), who was sodomized with a plunger handle by white New York police officers; I *am* Garnett Paul Johnson (1997), who was burned alive and beheaded by two white men; I *am* James Byrd, Jr. (1998), who was dragged to death by three white men; I *am* Rodney King, who underwent a brutal beating by white police officers (1991); I am the fifteen-year-old Latasha Harlins, who, thirteen days after the brutalizing of Rodney King, was shot in the back of the head and killed in South Central Los Angeles by a Korean American woman who thought that Harlins was trying to steal orange juice; I am those "disposable" Black bodies floating in the streets of New Orleans after Hurricane Katrina (2005); and I am the Jena Six (2006), and I am all those young Black bodies who already know what it means to be the targets of racial injustice. I inhabit the same socially constructed space of being present in my absence, of being a token of danger beyond my control. I am that pre-marked Black *thing*, that site of historical white discursive markings that precede my birth, leaving my Black body typified and anonymous. I arrive on the scene already overdetermined. Within the context of white North America, before I am born, my body's meaning has been defined by those historically embedded racist practices, discourses, and institutional forces that often remain invisible. But even whites who do not profess to be racist and yet benefit from being embodied as "white" also have their bodies defined relative to racist practices, discourses, and institutional forces. White bodies, unlike Black bodies, however, are privileged by normative structures and institutional structures that protect them, that deem them "honorable" and "safe" bodies. And yet, while both Black and white bodies are constituted by various problematic discursive practices, such practices can and must be challenged and troubled.

NOTES

1. Harriet A. Washington, *Medical Apartheid: The Dark History of Medical Experimentation on Black Americans from Colonial Times to the Present* (New York: Doubleday, 2006), 157.

2. Dorothy Roberts, *Killing the Black Body: Race, Reproduction, and the Meaning of Liberty* (New York: Vintage Books, 1999), 17.

3. The following is a personal testimony, which functions as a pastiche of a variety of experiences in which my Black body has been marked in terms of the white gaze. The personal dimension, however, should not be reduced to a state of monadic isolationism. And while I hold no pretensions to speak for *all* Black bodies, a project that would constitute a false start, I do believe that my faithful telling of and theorizing about these experiences might resonate with the various ways in which many Blacks have felt the sting of white racism in their lives and in their bodies. As African sociologist Felly Nkweto Simmonds says, my aim is "to explore the relationship between my [Black] body as a social construct and my experience of it [or how it is *lived*]. I want to examine the relationship I have with my body and how I negotiate, daily," with those social contexts within which my body is negatively marked. See Simmonds, "My Body, Myself: How Does a Black Woman Do Sociology?" in *Feminist Theory and the Body: A Reader*, ed. Janet Price and Margrit Shildrick (New York: Routledge, 1999), 52.

4. My Black body is also a *gendered* Black body. On this score, it is also not the case that my aim is to speak for all Black *male* bodies (as I do not presume to speak for all Black bodies), but there is an effort to describe lived experiential dimensions of racism that speak to or resonate with other lived moments of racism as experienced by Black bodies, male or female, as they negotiate various racist terrains. Keep in mind that white lies that seal me will be inflected differently from white lies that seal Black female bodies. For example, Black male bodies, within the white imaginary, are deemed hypersexual and thereby are looked upon as uncontrollable rapists. Black women's hypersexual tendencies render their bodies impossible to rape, for they are always already sexually lascivious. Commenting on the sexual vulnerability of enslaved Black women, Roberts notes, "The law also fostered the sexual exploitation of slave women by allowing white men to commit these assaults with impunity. Slaves were at the disposal of their masters. Owners had the right to treat their property however they wished, so long as the abuse did not kill the chattel. Conversely, slave women had no recognizable interest in preserving their own bodily integrity. After all, female slaves legally could be stripped, beaten, mutilated, bred, and compelled to toil alongside men. Forcing a slave to have sex against her will simply followed the pattern. This lack of protection was reinforced by the prevailing belief among whites that Black women could not be raped because they were naturally lascivious"; Roberts, *Killing the Back Body*, 30–1. I thank Alison Bailey for encouraging me to make this distinction early on in this chapter.

5. For an explication of his early views on alienation, see Karl Marx's The *Economic and Philosophic Manuscripts of 1844* (New York: Dover Publications, 2007); and Charles Mills, *From Class to Race: Essays in White Marxism and Black Radicalism* (Lanham, MD: Rowman & Littlefield, 2003), 192. By using the term *skin*, my aim is not to imply (nor do I think that this is Mills's point) that the darkness of my skin is *intrinsically* problematic. My dark skin, which gets "read" *as* bestial or inferior, is not *given* at the level of perception alone. Rather, what the white gaze "sees" when it sees my darkness is what appears at the symbolic level. Hence, the white gaze is far more complicated than is conveyed by the process of just "looking." Although I elaborate upon this point later, the "seeing" of my darkness is always already mediated in terms of various symbols, affective associations, historical myths, and tropes. I thank John H. McClendon for pointing out the need to clarify this point early on so as to preempt the objection that the problem with Blackness can or should be reduced to the level of dark skin qua dark skin.

6. My attempt to grapple philosophically with racial embodiment, the dynamics of invisibility, alienation, and what I refer to as "the phenomenological return of the Black body," is similar in spirit to the work of Charles Johnson, Lewis Gordon, and Linda Alcoff.

7. Michel Foucault, *The Order of Things: An Archaeology of the Human Sciences*, trans. Alan Sheridan (New York: Random House, 1970), xi.

8. On the use of her terms *whitely* and *whiteliness*, see Marilyn Frye, "White Woman Feminist," in *Overcoming Racism and Sexism*, ed. Linda A. Bell and David Blumenfield (Lanham, MD: Rowman & Littlefield, 1995), 117–132.

9. Frantz Fanon, *Black Skin, White Masks*, trans. Charles Lam Markmann (New York: Grove Press, 1967), 110.

10. Although I do not explore this within the context of the elevator example I provide within this chapter, more unpacking can be done in such a case where the woman is Black and the man is white. How do Black women feel when traveling in elevators with white men, particularly given the historical molestation and oppression of Black women's bodies by white men, and where Black women's testimony against white men carried little if any weight?

11. Lillian Smith, *Killers of the Dream* (New York: W.W. Norton & Co., 1994), 97.

12. Robert Gooding-Williams, "Look, a Negro!" in *Reading Rodney King, Reading Urban Uprising*, ed. Robert Gooding-Williams (New York: Routledge, 1993), 158.

13. Fanon, *Black Skin, White Masks*, 189.

14. Fanon was well aware of this pathological phenomenon.

15. Lorraine Code, "Taking Subjectivity into Account," in *Feminist Epistemologies*, ed. Linda Alcoff and Elizabeth Potter (New York: Routledge, 1993), 16.

16. To flatten out significant differential histories is to erase the everyday *embodied* knowledge that I have come to feel from the various experiences of so many acts of white aggression across a variety of social encounters.

17. It was actually the site of an elevator that launched one of the biggest race conflagrations in American history. This happened in Tulsa, Oklahoma (1921). Dick Rowland, a Black man, entered an elevator operated by Sarah Page, a white woman. He accidentally tripped over her shoe or perhaps on the actual elevator. Grabbing her arm so as to protect himself from falling, she screamed and he fled. This led to accusations that he sexually assaulted her, which led to many whites calling for him to be lynched. The events that ensued resulted in the death of many Blacks and the destruction of the economically and professionally developed Black city of Greenwood, which was also known as "Black Wall Street," http://www.youtube.com/watch?v=pH900FGqwKs (accessed, April 5, 2008)

18. Linda Alcoff and Elizabeth Potter (Eds) *Feminist Epistemologies* (New York: Routledge, 1993), 121–159.

19. John Wisdom, "Gods," in *Contemporary Analytic and Linguistic Philosophies*, ed. E. D. Klemke (Buffalo, NY: Prometheus Books, 1983), 343.

20. Du Bois, "The Souls of White Folk," in *W. E. B. Du Bois: A Reader*, ed. David Levering Lewis (New York: Henry Holt and Company, 1995), 453.

21. I have given lectures at predominantly white universities concerning the elevator example. A typical response from audience members, though perhaps in good faith, is to create scenarios designed to cast doubt upon what I take to be a racist act. It is as if they refuse to concede that there is the possibility that I could be correct. But even if I were correct only sometimes, it would be important to explain such happenings. After one lecture, a person in the audience even suggested that perhaps the woman in the elevator is actually blind. While this is an interesting suggestion—the kind of abstract philosophical, "But what if?" question that is attention grabbing—it might be said to function as a way in which whites attempt to explain away what is far more implicative (and far more likely than blindness, I might add) of their character, namely. racism.

22. Nelson, "Epistemological Communities," 124.

23. I thank Charles Mills for his suggestion that I try to avoid the reduction of Black epistemic communities to monadic epistemic communities.

24. Fanon, *Black Skin, White Masks*, 151.

25. Paul Ricoeur, *Freud and Philosophy: An Essay on Interpretation*, trans. Denis Savage (New Haven, CT: Yale University Press, 1970), 32–6.

26. Judith Butler, "Endangered/Endangering: Schematic Racism and White Paranoia," in *Reading Rodney King, Reading Urban Uprising,* ed. Gooding-Williams, 16.

27. For a discussion on greater amygdala activity vis-à-vis photographs shown of African Americans as opposed to Caucasians, see Stuart Wolpert, "African-Americans and Caucasians Have Similar Emotional Brain Activity When Seeing African-Americans," *Medical News Today*, April 5, 2008, http://www.medicalnewstoday.com/medicalnews.php?newsid=24085. I recall coming across a fragment of this discussion at the Council of Conservative Citizens' official website. Next to rapper Tupac Shakur, who was photographed apparently spitting at the cameras, there was the caption announcing the research: "Sight of blacks trigger alarm in brain." Given the white conservatism, to say the least, of the Council of Conservative Citizens, I was very suspicious of the deployment of this research.

28. When approached by white female Highway Patrol Officer Melanie Singer, Rodney King is said to have shook his buttocks at her. In an effort to explain the potential danger that she faced, Sergeant Stacey Koon said she was afraid and that "the fear was of a Mandingo sexual encounter." See Kobena Mercer, "Fear of a Black Penis—White Males' Perceptions of Black Males—Man Trouble," *ArtForum*, April 5, 2008, http://www.findarticles.com/p/articles/mi_m0268/is_n8_v32/ai_16109614

29. Ann DuCille, *Skin Trade* (Cambridge, MA: Harvard University Press, 1996), 144.

30. Christine Sleeter, personal correspondence with author.

31. Ana Marie Cox, Freya Johnson, Annalee Newitz, and Jillian Sandell, "Masculinity without Men: Women Reconciling Feminism and Male-Identification," in *Third Wave Agenda: Being Feminist, Doing Feminism*, ed. Leslie Heywood and Jennifer Drake (Minneapolis: University of Minnesota Press, 1997), 189.

32. Shannon Sullivan made this astute observation in personal correspondence with author.

33. DuCille, *Skin Trade*, 144.

34. Thomas Dixon, *The Leopard's Spots: A Romance of the White Man's Burden* (New York: Grosset & Dunlap, 1902), 463–4.

35. Note that the white gaze in this example is a gendered female gaze. Given white supremacist myths about the predatory sexual nature of the Black male, it is not far-fetched that the gendered white male would also feel fear and anxiety about being sexually assaulted by the Black male in a similar situation. On this reading, the white female and the white male body are said to be sexually vulnerable to Black sexual rapaciousness. As Jessie Daniels notes, "While not eliminating the image of white women as sexual victims of Black men (this is still a central feature of white supremacist discourse), contemporary constructions have amended white men onto

this centuries-old racial iconography. Now, white men also see themselves as potential victims of sexual assault by brutish Black men. The extension of white supremacist ideology to include white men as potential victims illustrates the pervasive fear of Black sexuality which is fundamental to white supremacy." See Jessie Daniels, *White Lies: Race, Class, Gender, and Sexuality in White Supremacist Discourse* (New York: Routledge, 1997), 39.

36. Butler, "Endangered/Endangering," 15. I am not endorsing the view that one ever has *total* control or mastery over his or her meaning. In other words, we all have meaning thrust upon us by others. Hence, I am not operating with a standard of total control/mastery over oneself that white people come closer to, but to which Black people can and should aspire. This would not reflect my understanding of the social ontology of the human person.

37. Linda Martín Alcoff, "Toward a Phenomenology of Racial Embodiment," *Radical Philosophy: A Journal of Socialist and Feminist Philosophy* 95 (May/June 1999), 15–26, quotation on 21.

38. Charles Johnson, "A Phenomenology of the Black Body," *Michigan Quarterly Review* 32(4), 595–614, quotation on 605.

39. Shannon Sullivan, "The Racialization of Space: Toward a Phenomenological Account of Raced and Antiracist Spatiality," in *The Problems of Resistance: Studies in Alternate Political Cultures*, ed. Steve Martinot, with Joy James (New York: Humanity Books, 2001), 94.

40. Alcoff, "Toward a Phenomenology of Racial Embodiment," 24.

41. Jane Lazarre, *Beyond the Whiteness of Whiteness: Memoir of a White Mother of Black Sons* (Durham, NC: Duke University Press, 1999), 81.

42. Fanon, *Black Skin, White Masks*, 180.

43. Fanon, *Black Skin, White Masks*, 225.

44. Fanon, *Black Skin, White Masks*, 165.

45. Lillian Smith provides a powerful example of how white racism has a deep impact on the body itself. Describing a moment in Southern history where a few white women decided to break the taboo against eating with Black women, Smith writes, "One of these church women told me of her first eating experience with colored friends. Though her conscience was serene, and her enjoyment of this association was real, yet she was seized by an acute nausea which disappeared only when the meal was finished. She was too honest to attribute it to anything other than anxiety welling up from the 'bottom of her personality,' as she expressed it, creeping back from her childhood training." See Smith, *Killers of the Dream*, 148.

46. Wendy Drewery, "Why We Should Watch What We Say: Position Calls, Everyday Speech, and the Production of Relational Subjectivity," *Theory & Psychology* 15(4), 2005, 305–24, quotation on 312.

47. Patricia J. Williams, *Seeing a Color-Blind Future: The Paradox of Race* (New York: Farrar, Straus, and Giroux, 1997), 73.

48. Butler, "Endangered/Endangering," 16.

49. Here, one wonders to what extent white racist police officers actually reap satisfaction from the sight of a "whimpering" Black male. This point transcends the problem involving the battle over the meaning of the Black body's intentions.

50. Butler, "Endangered/Endangering," 16.

51. Butler, "Endangered/Endangering," 19–20.

52. Butler, "Endangered/Endangering," 20–1.

53. Butler, "Endangered/Endangering," 21.

54. Gooding-Williams, "Look, a Negro!" 166.

55. Gilles Deleuze and Felix Guattari, *A Thousand Plateaus: Capitalism and Schizophrenia*, trans. Brian Massumi (Minneapolis, MN: University of Minnesota Press, 1987), 178.

56. Deleuze and Guattari, *A Thousand Plateaus*, 178.

57. George Yancy, "Interview with Lewis Gordon," in *African-American Philosophers, 17 Conversations,* ed. George Yancy (New York: Routledge, 1998), 107.

58. K. E. Supriya, "White Difference: Cultural Constructions of White Identity," in *Whiteness: The Communication of Social Identity*, ed. Thomas K. Nakayama and Judith N. Martin (Thousand Oaks, CA: Sage Publications, 1999), 140.

59. My point here is in stream with Karl Marx's point regarding the importance that workers challenge the material conditions that require illusions that prevent them from correctly seeing the reality of their material condition.

60. Simone de Beauvoir, *The Ethics of Ambiguity*, trans. Bernard Frechtman (New York: Citadel Press, Kensington Publishing Corp., 1948), 96.

61. Shannon Sullivan, *Revealing Whiteness: The Unconscious Habits of Racial Privilege* (Bloomington: Indiana University Press, 2006), 5–6.

62. Butler, "Endangered/Endangering," 16.

63. James Baldwin, "On Being 'White' . . . and Other Lies," in *Black on White: Black Writers on What It Means to Be White*, ed. David R. Roediger (New York: Schocken Books, 1998), 180.

64. Diana Fuss, *Essentially Speaking: Feminism, Nature, and Difference* (New York: Routledge, 1989), 103.

65. Butler, "Endangered/Endangering," 16.

66. Charles W. Mills, *The Racial Contract* (Ithaca, NY: Cornell University Press, 1997), 18.

67. Fanon, *Black Skin, White Masks*, 112.

68. Butler, "Endangered/Endangering," 20.

69. Butler, "Endangered/Endangering," 20.

70. For an interesting discussion of belief-centered and act-centered conceptions of racism, see Katherine D. Witzig, "Philosophical Analyses of Individual Racism," *Radical Philosophy Review* 4(1–2), 2001, 78–94.

71. Frye, "White Woman Feminist," 117.

72. Lewis R. Gordon, *Bad Faith and Anti-Black Racism* (Amherst, NY: Humanity Books, 1995), 101.

73. Tim Wise, *White Like Me: Reflections on Race from a Privileged Son* (Brooklyn, NY: Soft Skull Press, 2005), 49.

Chapter 3

The Return of the Black Body

Nine Vignettes

It is sometimes advantageous to be unseen, although it is most often rather wearing on the nerves.

—Ralph Ellison

I write out of a personal existential context. This context is a profound source of knowledge connected to my "raced" body. I theorize from a place of lived embodied experience, a site of exposure. In fact, it is a double exposure. I am exposed because I am embodied and as such fragile. Yet, I am exposed because I am also raced as Black. In philosophy, the only thing we learn is to "expose" (and to do so brutally) is a weak argument, a fallacy, or someone's "inferior" reasoning power. The embodied self is bracketed and deemed irrelevant to theory, superfluous and cumbersome in one's search for truth. It is best, or so we are told, to reason from *nowhere*. I can't afford to do philosophy from "nowhere." The white racist world confronts me precisely from a *somewhere*, from a *here*. The white male philosopher/author presumes to speak for *all* of "us" without the slightest mention of his raced (or gendered) identity. Self-consciously writing as a white male philosopher, Crispin Sartwell observes:

Left to my own devices, I *disappear* as an author. That is the "whiteness" of my authorship. This whiteness of authorship is, for us, a form of authority; to speak (apparently) from nowhere, for everyone, is empowering, though one wields power here only by becoming lost to oneself. But such an authorship and authority is also pleasurable: it yields the pleasure of self-forgetting or apparent transcendence of the mundane and the particular, and the pleasure of power expressed in the "comprehension" of a range of materials.[1]

To theorize the Black body one must "turn to the [Black] body as the radix for interpreting racial experience."[2] This particular strategy also functions as a lens through which to theorize and critique whiteness, for the Black body's "racial" experience is fundamentally linked to the oppressive modalities of the raced white body. However, there is no denying that my own racial experiences or the social performances of whiteness can become objects of critical reflection. In this chapter, I describe and theorize a variety of instances in which the Black body is reduced to instantiations of the white imaginary, resulting in what I refer to as "the phenomenological return of the Black body." These instantiations are embedded within and evolve out of the complex social and historical sedimentation of whites' efforts at self-construction through complex acts of erasure and denigration of Black people. These acts of self-construction are myths or ideological constructions predicated upon maintaining white power. As James Snead explained, "Mythification is the replacement of history with a surrogate ideology of [white] elevation or [Black] demotion along a scale of human value."[3]

I do not hold the view that Blacks only offer *experiences* while whites provide the necessary *theoretical* framing of those experiences. Consistent with my own theorizations on the subject, Lewis Gordon recognizes the historical impetus of this move toward experience and how such a move as such is not problematic. "After all," as Gordon argues, "for a long time there was the denial of black inner life, of black subjectivity; the notion of a black person's point of view suggested consciousness of the world, which would call for dynamics of reciprocal recognition."[4] Of course, the objectives are (1) to avoid reducing Black people to experience and (2) to avoid making whites the oracle interpretative voices of Black experiences. By implication, it is important to avoid a relationship of dependency and to assert an agential Black exegetical role in rendering their experiences meaningful. Hence, the nine vignettes that follow provide a critical, interpretive framework for understanding the impact of the white gaze. The reader should note that Aiyana Stanley-Jones, Trayvon Martin, Eric Garner, Tamir Rice, Michael Brown, Renisha McBride, Sandra Bland, and others, can function as poignant scenes of white violence perpetrated upon their Black bodies. I have opted to use other examples in this chapter, which are just as powerful. In other chapters, 1 and 8, I provide critical reflections on these more contemporary examples.

JACQUELINE WOODSON

As she gave her acceptance speech after receiving the prestigious 2014 National Book Award (NBA) in the category of Young People's Literature on November 19, 2014, one could see on Jacqueline Woodson's face a sense of gratitude and jubilation. Her body language communicated a sense of being at home within that ceremonial space. With style and humility, she congratulated the other finalists and stressed just how important young adult and children's literature are to our world. Her embodied presence was marked by a sense of accomplishment, of having revealed to the world, through the literary creation of *Brown Girl Dreaming*, what it is like to grow up in the 1960s and 1970s vis-à-vis the vestiges of Jim Crow and the Civil Rights Movement. *Brown Girl Dreaming* is her existential odyssey, one explored through verse, a text that signifies to the literary world and beyond that she is part of a formative tradition that feeds the active imaginations of young adults and children regardless of race. Her dreams speak to universal themes that denote fungible relationships among all readers. She could have said with Frantz Fanon, "I wanted to come lithe and young into a [literary] world that was ours and to help to build it together."[5]

Woodson *dreamed* through the critical imaginary of a Black/Brown body, tracing her origins, and making meaning of life, of joy and pain. Yet, and without a moment's notice, there was set into motion a series of unfortunate *racist* events, ones that decentered Woodson's humanity and installed in its place an event of racist violence, an event of embodied malediction. Daniel Handler, host of the NBA, reminded Woodson (and all Black bodies by implication) that her most sublime moment of achievement was secondary to the true meaning of her racial epidermal surface, a surface that is woven "out of a thousand [white racist] details, anecdotes, stories,"[6] stereotypes, myths, and lies. She was transmogrified into an oddity, like Sarah Baartman's "primitive" backside. While there is no attempt to conflate the deep existential tragedy that happened to Baartman with Woodson's experience at the NBA ceremony, there is that sense in which Woodson became a *spectacle*, a wonder to behold, a racial and racist essence as Handler revealed that "Jackie Woodson is allergic to watermelon." Handler then asked the audience to "Just let that sink in your mind." By doing so, he drew on the collective white racist meme within the audience and effectively engaged in an act of discursive violence against Woodson's Black embodied integrity. "Let that sink in" is an invitation to the audience to join him in a collective act of affirming their racism through acknowledging the racist joke that implicates *all* Black bodies as bodies that love watermelon. After the audience allows it to sink in, there is laughter from the predominantly monochromatic (white) audience, revealing the active production of a form of racist knowledge that is distortive and dehumanizing. It's not simply that they understood the joke, but that they affirmed, through laughter (and not outrage) their sense of humor regarding the oxymoronic idea of a Black body allergic to watermelon. They think that they are hip and cool (racially neutral) literati who can laugh without being deeply implicated in the perpetuation of white racist injustice and anti-Black racism. Yet, the collective laughter further marked Woodson as an essence, as a Black body, with big eyes and oversized lips, which *naturally* and sloppily eats watermelon; she is gluttonous and lacks control, a racist trope that has deeper hypersexual implications.[7] The audience, along with Handler, forgot about the flesh and blood Black woman standing there before them, her feelings, and her sense of pride. They were more concerned about what they took to be humorous than Woodson's sense of dignity and elation in what was *her moment*. In other words, Handler, and the other white people who laughed, helped to install a racist value-laden colonial space at the NBA ceremony, creating a racist Manichean divide between "us" (whites) and "them" (Woodson and other ontologically "problematic" Black bodies). And as is typical within the colonial order of things, the colonizer assumes a position of definitional power.

Handler invited the audience to participate with him in the re-inscription of a form of racist essentialism that he endorsed. It is a form of racist essentialism where to be Black and to love watermelon is a tautology. For a Black body to be allergic to watermelon leaves us with just a few options: either Woodson is an oxymoron or Woodson isn't really Black. In either case, it is an abhorrent racist claim. And notice how this happened within the context of Woodson having been recognized for her achievement, an achievement that apparently only white people are supposed to garner. Handler's re-centering the white gaze on something far more palatable (a non–watermelon-eating "Nigger") places under erasure the significance of Woodson's achievement. The space of that ceremony was flooded with white racist history, calling forth a panoply of racist images/iconography: "Coons," "Sambos," "Picaninnies," "Mammies," and "Calibans." More specifically, Handler's invitation—his call and the response it received—revealed the racist logics always already at play just waiting to be tapped within such predominantly white spaces. The implication here is that white racism is not an anomaly or something extraordinary, but quotidian; white racism is a *normal* part of white American life. Moreover, "good" white people, progressive and liberal white people, demand that Black people or people of color underwrite both their racism and their "goodness" in one fell swoop.[8] This happens when Handler said to Woodson that he would write a book about a Black girl who is allergic to watermelon only if he received an endorsement from Woodson, Cornel West, Toni Morrison, and Barack Obama. As he says, their support would communicate, "This guy's ok! This guy's fine!" Yet, this is more essentialism. It assumes that "ordinary" Black people don't really understand the harm that is being done to Woodson, or know a racist when we see one, that we stand in need of being corrected regarding the ethical credentials of "good white" folk, those who mean no real harm.

There was so much racist toxicity in Handler's remarks. It was as poisonous as the racist ideology of the Klan. And yet, there is no pretending from the Klan. Hence, it is "good" white folk like Handler that I fear. Woodson no doubt saw Handler as a friend, one of the "good ones." After all, she had disclosed to him something personal about her medical history regarding a particular fruit. He threw that personal disclosure back at her within a public space. The act of throwing that back at her was a kind of social death blow. While not the kind of death blow experienced by Michael Brown at the hands of white Officer Darren Wilson, Woodson may have experienced a form of death—a nonphysical death by micro-aggression. It is the kind of death that Black people and people of color experience on a daily basis. For example, being followed while shopping or being pulled over while driving, Black bodies undergo forms of erasure/death. Handler attempted to subject Woodson's work to a certain kind of death, her winning the National Book Award was subjected to a certain kind of death, and her literary and imaginative creativity was subjected to a certain kind of death. At the height of validation vis-à-vis the award, Handler attempted to invalidate Woodson's moment. Handler effectively created a space where Woodson's "oxymoronic" racialized identity was returned to her as a *brown girl dreaming* of what it would be like to consume watermelon voraciously without having an allergic reaction. It wasn't about her dreams, but the dreams of Handler and those whites in the audience who laughed or who refused to call Handler on his racism.

It is fascinating that at the end of his racist insult, Handler says to Woodson, "Alright, we'll talk about it later." Again, there is laughter from the audience. It is as if Woodson is open to further conversation about the matter. He doesn't want to let it go; he refuses to let it go, perhaps convinced that Woodson will endorse his book about a Black body that defies the very *metaphysics* of race. *His decision* to postpone the conversation until later suggests that he is the one in control of how the racist narrative will play out.

It is important that we call Handler on his racism and that we unambiguously communicate to him (and the white audience) that what he said at the National Books Awards ceremony was *not* a mistake, a mere fluke in an otherwise racist-free life, but that what he said speaks to the logics of everyday white racism (*his white racism*) that does violence to Black people and people of color. Finally, I would argue that the racist violence that Handler perpetrated on Woodson can't be propitiated through acts of monetary charity. I would reject both his offer to donate US$10,000 to We Need Diverse Books and to match any donations of up to US$100,000. This is just another way of seeking white shelter, a form of easy redemption, from the gravity of the pervasive reality of white racism in America. It is also a form of redemption that positions Handler as a white Hollywood savior figure through a dialectics of an oppressed other.[9] Handler again attempts to control the narrative. This time as the "good" white who committed an awkward social *faux pas*, but one that can be easily fixed through grand gestures of monetary dispensation. "The messiah fantasies," as Vera and Gordon argue, "are essentially grandiose, exhibitionistic, and narcissistic."[10] On the one hand, Handler functions as the white oppressor, the one who hurls racist insults. On the other hand, he gets to be the white "liberator," to authorize his narcissistic role within a larger racist ideology of manifest destiny. In short, Handler continues to benefit from white power, hegemony, and privilege. I would rather Handler *tarry* with his racism and come to terms with how he and other "good whites" are complicit with more complex interpersonal and institutional forms of white supremacy that result in discursive forms of violence vis-à-vis Black and Brown bodies. I would rather Handler publish an engaged and critical analysis of how he thought that he knew the limits of his own white racism and how he was profoundly mistaken.

OSSIE DAVIS

To have one's dark body penetrated by the white gaze and then to have that body returned as distorted is a powerfully violating experience. The experience presupposes an anti-Black lived context, a context within which the lived experience of the Black unfolds. Late writer, actor, and activist Ossie Davis recalled that at age six or seven, two white police officers told him to get into their car and took him down to the precinct. They kept him there for an hour, laughing at him and eventually pouring cane syrup over his head. This humiliation only created the opportunity for more laughter, as they *looked* upon the "silly" little Black boy. If he was able to articulate his feelings at that moment, think of how the young Davis was returned to himself: "I am an object of white laughter, a buffoon, a clown, a nigger." Davis no doubt appeared to the white police officers in ways they had approved. They set the stage, created a site of Black buffoonery, and enjoyed their sadistic pleasure without blinking an eye. As Sartwell explains, "The [white] oppressor seeks to constrain the oppressed [Blacks] to certain approved modes of visibility (those set out in the template of stereotype) and then gazes obsessively on the spectacle he has created."[11] Davis noted that he "went along with the game of black emasculation, it seemed to come naturally"; after that, "the ritual was complete" and he was then sent home with some peanut brittle to eat.[12] Even at that early age and without the words to articulate what he felt, Davis knew he was an innocent victim of vicious white supremacy. He referred to the ritual as the process of "niggerization" and noted that America had already told him what his response "should be: not to be surprised; to expect it; to accommodate it; to live with it. I didn't know how deeply I was scarred or affected by that, but it was a part of who I was."[13]

Davis, in other words, was made to feel that he had to accept who he was, that "niggerized" little Black boy, an insignificant plaything within a system of ontological racial differences. The trick of white ideology is operative in this context, giving the appearance of fixity, where the "look of the white subject interpellates the black subject as inferior, which, in turn, bars the black subject from seeing him/herself without the internalization of the white gaze."[14] On this score, white bodies are deemed agential, configuring "passive" Black bodies according to their will. But it is no mystery, for "the Negro is interpreted in the terms of the white man. White-man psychology is applied and it is no wonder that the result often shows the Negro in a ludicrous light."[15] While walking across the street, I have endured the sounds of locking car doors. I have endured white women clutching their purses or walking across the street as they catch a glimpse of my approaching Black body. During such moments, my body is given back to me in a ludicrous light, where I *live* the meaning of my body as confiscated. Davis also had the meaning of his young Black body stolen. One might argue that Davis (like me) is "called on for more";[16] called on to be the superlative instantiation of the *raced Black* body. The surpluses whites gain in each case are not *economic*. Rather, the surpluses extracted can be said to be ontological through *existential* exploitation; they are "semblances of determined presence, of full positivity, to provide a sense of secure being."[17]

PERSONAL EXPERIENCE

When I was seventeen or eighteen, my white math teacher initiated such an invasion, pulling it off with complete calm and presumably self-transparency. Given the historical construction of whiteness as the norm, his own raced subject position was rendered invisible. After all, he lived in the real world, the world of the serious man, where values are believed anterior to their existential founding. As I recall, we were discussing my plans for the future. I told him I wanted to be a pilot. I was earnest about this choice and had spent a great deal of time not only reading about aerodynamic lift and drag but also the requirements involved in becoming a pilot, such as accumulating flying hours. After taking note of my firm commitment, he *looked* at me and implied that I should be *realistic* (a code word for me to *realize* that I am Black) about my goals. He said I should become a carpenter or a bricklayer. I was *exposing* myself, telling a trusted teacher what I wanted to be, and he *returned* me to myself as something I did not recognize. I did not intend to be a carpenter or a bricklayer (or a janitor or elevator operator for that matter).

The situation, though, is more complex. The teacher did not simply return me to myself as a carpenter or a bricklayer when all along I had had this image of myself as a pilot. Rather, he returned me to myself as a *fixed entity*, a "niggerized" Black body whose epidermal logic had already foreclosed the possibility of being anything other than what befitted its lowly station. He was the voice of a larger anti-Black racist society that "whispers mixed messages in our ears," the ears of Black people who struggle to think of themselves as a *possibility*.[18] He mentioned that there were only a few Black pilots and again implied that I ought to face reality. (One can only imagine what his response would have been had I said that I wanted to be a philosopher, particularly given the statistic that Blacks constitute about 1.1 percent of philosophers in the United States.) Keep in mind that this event did not occur in the 1930s or 1940s, but around 1979. The message was clear: because I am Black, I had to settle for an occupation suitable for my Black body, unlike the white body that likely would have been encouraged to become a pilot. As with Davis, having one's Black body returned as ontologically problematic, one begins to think, to feel, to emote, even if unconsciously: "Am I a nigger?" The internalization of the white gaze creates a doubleness within the Black psyche, leading to a destructive process of superfluous self-surveillance and self-interrogation.

This moment was indeed a time when I felt ontologically locked into my body. My body was indelibly marked with this stain of darkness. After all, he was the white mind, the mathematical mind, calculating my future by factoring in my Blackness. He did not "see" me, though. Like Ralph Ellison's invisible man, I occupied that paradoxical status of "visible invisibility." Within this dyadic space, my Black body phenomenologically returned to me as inferior. To describe the phenomenological return of the Black body is to disclose how it is returned as an appearance to consciousness, *my consciousness*. The (negatively) raced manner in which my body underwent a phenomenological return, however, presupposes a thick social reality that has always already been structured by the ideology and history of whiteness. More specifically, when my body is returned to me, the white body has already been constituted over centuries as the norm, both in European and Anglo-American culture, and at several discursive levels from science to philosophy to religion.[19] My math teacher's whiteness was invisible to him, just as my Blackness was hypervisible to us both. We should keep in mind that white Americans, more generally, define themselves around the "gravitational pull," as it were, of the Black.[20] The *not* of white America is the Black of white America. This *not* is essential, as is the invisibility of the negative relation through which whites are constituted. All embodied beings have their own "here." My white math teacher's racist social performances (e.g., his "advice" to me), within the context of a white racist historical imaginary and asymmetric power relations, suspends and effectively disqualifies my embodied *here*. What was the message communicated? Expressing my desire *to be*, to take advantage of the opportunities for which Black bodies had died in order to secure, my ambition "was flung back in my face like a slap."[21] Frantz Fanon wrote that within the lived context of the white world he "was expected to behave like a black man—or at least like a nigger. I shouted a greeting to the world and the world slashed away my joy. I was told to stay within bounds, to go back where I belonged."[22]

According to Bettina Bergo, drawing from the thought of Emmanuel Levinas, "Perception and discourse—what we see and the symbols and meanings of our social imaginaries—prove inextricable the one from the other."[23] Hence, the white math teacher's perception, what he "saw," was inextricably linked to social meanings and semiotic constructions and constrictions that opened up a "field of appearances" regarding my dark body. There is nothing passive about the white gaze. There are *racist* sociohistorical and epistemic conditions of emergence that construct not only the Black body but the white body as well. So, what is "seen" when the white gaze "sees" "my body" and it becomes something alien to me?

In stream with phenomenology, consciousness is always "consciousness-of." What was my white math teacher "conscious-of"? The answer to this question, to which I already alluded, can only be given through the acknowledgment of a culturally and historically sedimented "racialized" consciousness-of structure. Hence, white racist acts of consciousness in regard to the Black body are meaning giving in ways that specifically distort the Black body. After all, they are acts of meaning giving structured through the white imaginary. Indeed, the construction of the "manners-of-givenness" of the Black body as inferior, for example, is contingent upon white racialized consciousness—of a socially ordered, and, by phantasmatic extension, "naturally" ordered world. Conversely, the construction of the "manners-of-givenness" of the white body is contingent upon the distortion or negation of the Black through whites' reactionary value-creating force. Instead of my white teacher self-consciously admitting (to the extent that was possible) the role he played (and continues to play) in the perpetuation of this white social imaginary (and the racist way in which he was conscious-of my body) in his everyday social performances, ideologically he "apprehended" the Black body, *my* Black body, as pregiven in its constitution as inferior. Of course, he cannot claim responsibility for the entire stream of white racist consciousness given the fact that these constructions are part of a larger historical imaginary, a social universe of white racist discourse that comes replete with long, enduring myths, perversions, distorted profiles, and imaginings of all sorts regarding the nonwhite body.

Charles Johnson has noted that one can become blind to seeing "other 'meanings' or profiles presented by the object if the perceiver is locked within the 'Natural Attitude', as [Edmund] Husserl calls it, and has been conditioned culturally or racially to fix himself upon certain 'meanings.'"[24] On my reading, within the framework of an anti-Black racist world, the meaning of the Black body is a synthesis formed through racist distal narratives that ideologically inform whites of their "natural superiority," that enable whites to flee their part in constructing a "racial regional ontology" fit for Blacks only. Phenomenologically, I experience myself as "the profile that their frozen intentionality brings forth."[25] After all, whiteness is deemed the horizon of all horizons, unable to recognize the imaginary "racial" dualism that it has created. The white gaze has constructed the Black body "as the specular negative images of itself and that hence, abstracts the white person into an abstract knower."[26] The meaning of my lived body is phenomenologically skewed when white consciousness negatively intends me as my Black (read: inferior, evil) body. I become alienated, thrown outward, and assigned a meaning not of my intending. In my everydayness, I live my body from an existential *here*. Wherever I go, I go embodied. As Gordon writes, "*Here* is where I am located. That place, if you will, is an embodied one: it is consciousness in the flesh. In the flesh, I am not only a point of view, but I am also a point that is viewed."[27] In my phenomenological return, however, I am reduced to a point that is viewed. My *here* is experienced as a *there*. The experience of being reduced to one's "Black exteriority," rendered thing-like, through processes of meaning-intending acts of white racist intentional consciousness, is insightfully described by Charles Johnson:

> I am walking down Broadway in Manhattan, platform shoes clicking on the hot pavement, thinking as I stroll of, say, Boolean expansions. I turn, thirsty, into a bar. The dimly-lit room, obscured by shadows, is occupied by whites. Goodbye, Boolean expansions. I am *seen*. But, as black, seen as stained body, as physicality, basically opaque to others . . . . Their look, an intending beam focusing my way, suddenly realizes something larva in me. My world is epidermalized, collapsed like a house of cards into the stained casement of my skin. My subjectivity is turned inside out like a shirtcuff.[28]

In the face of my white teacher's racism, I could have decided to lose myself in laughter, but, like Fanon, I was aware "that there were legends, stories, histories, and above all *historicity*."[29] My dark embodied existence, my lived historical being, became a chain of signifiers: inferior, nigger, evil, dirty, sullen, immoral, lascivious. As Fanon wrote, "In the unconscious, black = ugliness, sin, darkness, immorality."[30] When phenomenologically returned to myself, I appeared no longer to possess *my* body, but a "surrogate" body whose meaning did not exist anterior to the performance of white spectatorship.

FRANTZ FANON

"The Black has no ontological resistance in the eyes of the white man."[31] Again, this involves the asymmetry of representational power. From the perspective of the somatic regulatory epistemic regime of whiteness, the Black body appears to have no resistance. The Black body becomes ontologically pliable, just a thing to be scripted in the inverse image of whiteness. Cutting away at the Black body, the Black person becomes resigned no longer to aspire to his or her own emergence or upheaval.[32] Blacks undergo processes of ontological stagnation and epistemological violence while standing before the one "true" gaze. In a very powerful discourse describing how he was "unmercifully imprisoned," how the white gaze forced upon him an unfamiliar weight, Fanon asked, "What else could it be for me but an amputation, an excision, a hemorrhage that spattered my whole body with black blood?"[33]

The burden of the white gaze and the insidious reality of anti-Black racism were responsible for Fanon's "difficulties in the development of my bodily schema," where his embodiment was no longer "a definitive structuring of the self and the world."[34] Rather, his body was thrown back, returned, as an object *occupying* space. "Below the corporeal schema," Fanon wrote, "I had sketched a historico-racial schema. The elements that I used had been provided for me not by 'residual sensations and perceptions of a primarily tactile, vestibular, kinesthetic, and visual character,' but by the other, the white man [or woman]."[35] In other words, Fanon saw himself through the lens, as it were, of a historico-racial schema. Fanon had become the threatening "him" of the Negro kind/type. Under pressure from and assailed by anti-Black racism, the corporeal schema was collapsing. It was giving way to a racial epidermal schema. The white gaze constructed the Black body into "an object in the midst of other objects."[36] Furthermore, Fanon noted, "I took myself far off from my presence, far indeed, and made myself an object."[37] Note that there was nothing intrinsic to his physiology that forced his corporeal schema to collapse; it was the "Black body" as always already *named* and made sense of within the context of a larger semiotics of white bodies that provided him with the tools for self-hatred. His "darkness," a naturally occurring phenomenon, became historicized, residing within the purview of the white gaze, a phenomenal space created and sustained by socio-epistemic and semiotic communal constitutionality. The Black body evolves from within a space of constitutionality, that is, the space of the racist white *same*, the *one*. Against the backdrop of the sketched historico-racial (racist) scheme,

Fanon's "darkness" returned to him, signifying a new genus, a new category of man: A Negro![38] He inhabited a space of anonymity (he is *every* Negro), and yet he felt a strange personal responsibility for his body. "I was responsible at the same time for my body, for my race, for my ancestors," Fanon explained. "I subjected myself to an objective examination, I discovered my blackness, my ethnic characteristics; and I was battered down by tom-toms, cannibalism, intellectual deficiency, fetishism, racial defects, slave-ships, and above all else, above all: "sho' good eaten.'"[39]

Fanon wrote about the Black body and how it can be changed, deformed, and made into an ontological problem in relation to the white gaze. Describing an encounter with a white woman and her son, Fanon narrated how the young boy screamed, "Look at the nigger! . . . Mama, a Negro!"[40] Fanon:

> My body was given back to me sprawled out, distorted, recolored, clad in mourning in that white winter day. The Negro is an animal, the Negro is bad, the Negro is mean, the Negro is ugly; look, a Negro, it's cold, the Negro is shivering because he is cold, the little boy is trembling because he is afraid of the nigger, the nigger is shivering with cold, that cold that goes through your bones, the handsome boy is trembling because he thinks that the nigger is quivering with rage, the little white boy throws himself into his mother's arms: Mama, the nigger's going to eat me up.[41]

The white imagery of the Black as a savage beast, a primitive and uncivilized animal, was clearly expressed in the boy's fear that the "cannibalistic" Negro would eat him. "The more that Europeans dominated Africans, the more 'savage' Africans came to seem; cannibalism represented the nadir of savagery."[42] Of course, the boy may someday come to "confirm" his fears through reading an "authoritative" voice such as Georg Hegel, who linked the supposed contempt Africans/Negroes held for man to their failure to make historical progress. "To the sensuous Negro," Hegel argued, "human flesh is purely an object of the senses, like all other flesh."[43] To Hegel, Africans/Negroes apparently lacked the capacity of representation that tells them that human flesh, though identical with animal nature, is distinctive and identical with our own bodies, which are bodies of beings capable of representation and self-consciousness. African/Negro bodies are tethered to the immediate, the arbitrary, and the sensuous and have not "reached the stage of knowing anything universal."[44]

Presumably, the young boy did not know his words would (or how they would) negatively affect Fanon. However, for Fanon, the young white boy represented white society's larger perception of Blacks. The boy turned to his white mother for protection from impending Black doom. The young white boy, however, was not simply operating at the affective level; he was not simply haunted, semiconsciously, by a vague feeling of anxiety. Rather, he was operating at both the affective and the *discursive* level. He said, "Mama, the nigger's going to eat me up." This locutionary act carries a perlocutionary force of *effecting* the phenomenological return of Fanon to himself as a cannibalistic threat, as an object to be feared. Fanon, of course, did not "want this revision, this thematization."[45]

One is tempted to say that the young white boy saw Fanon's Black body "as if" it were cannibal-like. The "seeing as if," however, was collapsed into a *"seeing as is."* In Fanon's example, within the lived phenomenological transversal context of white racist behavior, the "as if" reads too much like a process of "conscious effort." On my reading, what appears in the uninterrupted lived or phenomenological flow of the young white boy's racist experience is "young-white-boy-experiences-nigger-dark-body-cannibal-evokes-trepidation." There is no experience of the "as if." Indeed, the young white boy's linguistic and nonlinguistic performance indicates a definitive structuring of his own self-invisibility as "white-innocent-self-in-relationship-to-the-dark-nigger-self." This definitive structuring is not so much remembered or recollected as it is always present as the constitutive imaginary background within which the white boy is both the effect and the vehicle of white racism; indeed, he *is the orientation* of white epistemic practices, ways of "knowing" about one's (white) identity vis-à-vis the Black other. The "cultural white orientation" is not an "entity" whose origin the white boy needs to grasp or recollect before he performs whiteness. He is not a tabula rasa, one who sees the Black body for the first time and instinctively says, "Mama, the nigger's going to eat me up."

The boy *did* indeed undergo an *experience* of the dark body as frightening, but there is no concealed meaning, as it were, inherent in the experience qua experience of Fanon's body as such. Rather, the fright that he experienced regarding Fanon's dark body was always already "constructed out of . . . social narratives and ideologies."[46] The boy was already discursively and affectively acculturated through microprocesses of "racialized" learning (short stories, lullabies, children's games,[47] prelinguistic experiences, etc.) to respond "appropriately" in the presence of a Black body. His racist actions were not simply dictated by what was going on in his head, as it were. His racism, though he is young, was "'in' the nose that smells, the back, neck, and other muscles that imperceptibly tighten with anxiety, and eyes that see some but not all physical differences as significant."[48] The gap that opened up within the young white boy's perceptual field as he "saw" Fanon's Black body had already been created while innocently sitting on his mother's lap.[49] His habituated perceptions were "so attenuated as to skip the stage of conscious interpretation and intent."[50] His mother's lap constituted a raced zone of security, a maternal site of racist pedagogy.

Learning about taboos against masturbation and associating with Negroes, and how both of these taboos were associated with sin, guilt, and a sense of deserved punishment, Lillian Smith has described these forbidden acts as the first lessons she learned as a young white girl raised in Southern society. Such taboos were "ideological pabulum," as it were, fed to Smith as a young child. She notes that such lessons "were taught us by our mother's voice, memorized with her love, patted into our lives as she rocked us to sleep or fed us."[51] Smith's father also played a formative role in this process of racist tutelage. Her father scolded her for her sense "of superiority toward schoolmates from the mill and rounded out his rebuke by gravely reminding me that 'all men are brothers,' [but] trained me in the steel-rigid decorums I must demand of every colored male."[52] This point acknowledges the fundamental "ways the transactions between a raced world and those who live in it racially constitute the very being of those beings."[53] In the case of the young white boy in Fanon's situation, the association of Blackness with "nigger" and cannibalism is no mean feat. Hence, the young white boy is already attending to the world in a particular fashion; his affective and discursive performances bespeak the (ready-to-hand) inherited white racist background according to which he is able to make "sense" of the world. Smith knows that how she came to see the world, to make sense of her place within it, was based upon lies about skin color, and lies about white adults' "own fantasies, of their secret deviations— forcing decayed pieces of their and the region's obscenities into the minds of the young and leaving them there to fester."[54]

Like moving my body in the direction of home, or only slightly looking as I reach my hand to retrieve my cup of hot tea that is to the left of my computer screen, the young white boy dwells within/experiences/engages the world of white racist practices in such a way that the practices qua racist practices have become invisible. The young boy's response is part and parcel of an implicit knowledge of how he gets around in a Manichean world. *Being-in* a racist world, a *lived* context of historicity, the young boy does not "see" the dark body as "dark" and then thematically proceed to apply negative value predicates to it, where conceivably the young boy would say, "Yes, I 'see' the dark body as existing in space, and I recognize the fact that it is through my own actions and intentions that I predicate evil of it." "In order even to act deliberately," as Hubert L. Dreyfus maintains, "we must orient ourselves in a familiar world."[55]

My point here is that the young white boy is situated within a familiar white racist world of intelligibility, one that has already "accepted" whiteness as "superior" and Blackness as "inferior" and "savage." *Involved* within the white racist Manichean world, the young boy has found his orientation, he has already become part and parcel of a constituted and constituting force within a constellation of modes of being that are deemed natural. However, he is oblivious to the *historicity* and cultural conditionedness of these modes of being. Despite the fact that "race" neither exists as a naturally occurring kind within the world nor cuts at the joints of reality, notice the evocative power of "being Black," which actually points to the evocative power of being white. The dark body, after all, would not have evoked the response it did from the young white boy were it not for the historical mythos of the white body and the power of white normativity through which the white body has been pre-reflectively structured, resulting in forms of action that are as familiar and as quotidian as my reaching for my cup of tea. His white racist performance is a form of everyday coping within the larger unthematized world of white social coping. The socio-ontological structure that gives intelligibility to the young white boy's racist performance is prior to a set of beliefs of which he is reflectively aware.

Fanon underwent the experience of having his body "given back to him." Thus, he experienced a profound phenomenological experience of being disconnected from his body schema. Fanon felt his body as flattened out or sprawled out before him. And yet his "body," its corporeality, was forever with him. It never left. So, how can it be "given back"? The physical body that Fanon had/was remained in space and time. It did not somehow disappear and make a return. But there is a profound sense in which his "corporeality" was interwoven with particular discursive practices. Under the white gaze, Fanon's body was not simply the *res extensa* of Cartesian dualism. Within the context of white racist practices toward the Black body, there is a blurring of boundaries between what was "there" as opposed to what had been "*placed* there." Hence, the body's corporeality, within the context of lived history, is shaped through powerful cultural schemata. The above line of reasoning does not mean that somehow the body does not exist. After all, my body forms the site of white oppression. To jettison all discourse regarding the body as "real," being subject to material forces, and such, in the name of the "post-modern body," is an idealism that would belie my own philosophical move to theorize from the position of my real *lived embodiment*. The point here is that *the* body is never given as such, but always "appears there" within the context of some set of conditions of emergence.[56] The conditions of emergence for the phenomenological return of Fanon's body qua inferior or bestial were grounded in the white social imaginary, its discursive and nondiscursive manifestations. Having undergone a gestalt-switch in his body image, his knowledge/consciousness of his body had become "solely a negating activity. . . . a third-person consciousness. The body is surrounded by an atmosphere of certain uncertainty."[57]

Linda Alcoff discusses this phenomenological sense of being disjointed as a form of "near-incommensurability between first-person experience and historico-racial schema that disenables equilibrium."[58] Here, Alcoff emphasizes Fanon's notion of the "sociogenic" basis of the "corporeal malediction" Blacks experience.[59] On this score, "the black man's [and woman's] alienation is not an individual question."[60] In other words, the distorted historico-racial schema that occludes equilibrium takes place within the realm of sociality, a larger complex space of white social intersubjective constitutionality "of phenomena that human beings have come to regard as 'natural' in the physicalist sense of depending on physical nature."[61] Of course, within the context of colonial or neocolonial white power, the objective is to pass off what is historically contingent as that which is *ahistorically* given.

AUDRE LORDE

Kyeong Hwangbo writes, "Trauma is a liminal experience of radical deracination and calamity that brings about a violent rupture of the order on both the personal and the social level. It annihilates the sense of continuity in our lives and our self-narratives, bringing to the fore the contingency of our lives."[62] Of course, as Black, the contingency of Fanon's life, my life, Jacqueline Woodson's life, and Ossie Davis's life, and how they are brought to the fore, is through the violence of white normative assumptions that destabilize and traumatize our Black embodiment. Sara Ahmed writes, "For bodies that are not extended by the skin of the social, bodily movement is not so easy. Such bodies are stopped, where the stopping is an action that creates its own impressions. Who are you? Why are you here? What are you doing? Each question, when asked, is a kind of stopping device: you are stopped by being asked the question, just as asking the question requires that you be stopped. A phenomenology of 'being stopped' might take us in a different direction than one that begins with motility, with a body that 'can do' by flowing into space."[63] Interpellation, then, is by no means inconsequential in an anti-Black world. The hail impacts the Black body through the skin of the social. The hail is the site of a social ontological and sonic material vector. The NYPD's racial profiling practice of stop-and-frisk disproportionately targets both Black and Brown bodies; a racial hailing that stresses and traumatizes hundreds of thousands of innocent people, especially as many of those individuals have been stopped at least more than once. Imagine the impact on one's body integrity to undergo stop-and-frisk based upon "reasonable suspicion" where the "reasonableness" is governed by a racial and racist logic that has already constructed certain bodies as "criminals" and "urban savages."

Adding to Ahmed's concept of a phenomenology of being stopped, I emphasize that a phenomenology of traumatization in virtue of being specifically Black in an anti-Black world (which does not exclude other bodies of color) can also take us in a different direction, one that theorizes specific forms of Black trauma that don't occur for white people. Within the context of a white normatively structured world, there is no *racialized* radical deracination and calamity for whites. It is this absence, for whites, of a *racialized* traumatic and dehumanizing deracination that also speaks to the absence of forms of white racialized grieving that helps us to understand the limits of white empathy and the ways in which these absences are underwritten by an unspoken philosophical anthropological norm that guarantees that white lives *really* matter.

That unspoken white norm frames the experience, for example, that Audre Lorde remembers in terms of the disgust and hatred directed toward her, as a young Black girl, by a white woman seated on the AA subway train to Harlem. "I clutch my mother's sleeve, her arms full of shopping bags, Christmas-heavy. The wet smell of winter clothes, the train's lurching. My mother spots an almost seat [next to a white woman], pushes my little snow-suited body down." As she sat next to the white woman, Lorde remembers this woman pulling her coat away from Lorde's snowsuit. The white woman is staring at the young Lorde. She writes, "Her mouth twitches as she stares and then her gaze drops down, pulling mine with it."[64] Lorde talks about how she thought that perhaps there was a disgusting insect that the woman was trying to avoid. This "thing" that has created such a visceral repugnance on the part of the white woman "must be something very bad from the way she's looking."[65] So, it is the white gaze that Lorde recognizes. After all, she knows the white gaze, its penetrating hatred, its impact upon her body. In fact, she says, "I don't like to talk about hate. I don't like to remember the cancellation and hatred . . . seen in the eyes of so many white people from the time I could see."[66] Lorde's use of the term cancellation suggests a sense of existential annulment and personal invalidation. Lorde says that she has seen this hatred since the time she could see. "From the time that I could see" speaks painfully and insightfully to the fact that Lorde has undergone the trauma of the hatred of the white gaze very early on. But was it literally from the time that she could see or from the time that she could recognize the white gaze, that is, see with insight its problematic machinations? Either way, Lorde makes it clear that she has been confronted by white people in ways that sent a clear and deliberate message: "You are a Nigger!" As Lorde soon discovers, it was her body that the white woman perceived as vermin. She writes, "When I look up the woman is still staring at me, her nose holes and eyes huge. And suddenly I realize there is nothing crawling up the seat between us; it is me she doesn't want her coat to touch."[67] This experience leaves Lorde with the impression that she has done something wrong—that *she is embodied as wrong*. Lorde came too close to the "purity" of white embodiment, to white "scared" occupied space. As a result, her Black body underwent a powerful manifestation of white perceptual violence, a racialized regulatory surveillance. The white woman's disgust communicates: as an embodied contaminant, you are too close.[68]

INVISIBLE MAN

In *Invisible Man*, Ralph Ellison's "thinker-tinker," his "Jack-the-Bear," his invisible man, also experiences the phenomenological "return of his Black body." Although he tries to live the life of an individualist, he soon finds that individualism is an illusion, particularly given the fact that at every turn he learns that whites threaten his efforts at "autonomy." After all, he is constantly under erasure, unable to stand out as an individual. In an anti-Black racist context, it is difficult for Blacks to be "just me." His Blackness prevents a mode of living according to liberal ideals. More accurately, whites are able to enact a "just me" status because of their normative status. However, they prevent Blacks from hiding in a fictive world where race ceases to matter. Society whispers, "Don't forget. Don't think that you're above race, that you're one of us. After all, you *are* Black!"

The invisible man knows himself as embodied flesh and blood, and yet he is invisible. His body is, and yet he is not. The invisible man observes, "I am an invisible man. No, I am not a spook like those who haunted Edgar Allan Poe; nor am I one of your Hollywood-movie ectoplasms. I am a man of substance, of flesh and bone, fiber and liquids—and I might even be said to possess a mind. I am invisible, understand, simply because people [in this case white people] refuse to see me."[69]

In Fanon's example, the Black body is *seen* as hypervisible; for Ellison, the Black body is *seen* as invisible. In the case of hypervisibility, the Black body becomes excessive. Within this racially saturated field of hypervisibility, the Black body still functions as the unseen as it does in the case of its invisibility. Perhaps in the case of invisibility, though, one has a greater opportunity of not being seen while taking advantage of this invisibility. Think here of those whites who may have disclosed pertinent information in the company of Blacks who had been rendered invisible, information that may have functioned to empower them in some way. The ocular frame of reference in both cases is central. "Seen invisibility" suggests the paradoxical sense in which the Black body is a "seen absence." In either case, the Black body "returns" distorted.

A fundamental phenomenological slippage occurs between one's *own* felt experience of the Black body and how others (whites) understand/construct/ experience/see that "same" Black body. Ellison also raised the issue of how the Black *other* is a reflection of the white *same*. Ellison says in *Invisible Man* that when whites "see him" they see "themselves, or fragments of their imagination—indeed, everything and anything except me."[70] The invisible man's invisibility is a racialized invisibility. The white one sees everything and anything vis-à-vis the Black other, but not the Black. Fanon asked, "A feeling of inferiority? No, a feeling of nonexistence."[71] Felt invisibility is a form of ontological and epistemological violence resulting from "the construction of their *inner* eyes with which they [whites] look through their physical eyes upon reality."[72]

Ellison's reference to inner eyes that look through physical eyes suggests that the "inner eyes" are precisely those white racist, epistemic perspectives, interlocked with various social and material forces, from which whites "see" the world and violate Black subjectivity. The "inner eyes" that Ellison refers to as "a matter of construction" raise the issue of the sociogenic. Ellison's invisible man is "seen" against the unthematized backdrop of everyday forms of white coping. To be "seen" in this way is not to be seen at all. Gordon writes, "The black is invisible because of how the black is 'seen'. The black is not heard because of how the black is 'heard'. The black is not felt because of how the black 'feels.'"[73] Within this context, Blacks are trapped, always already ontologically closed. In each case, the totalizing power of whiteness holds Blacks captive. When Blacks speak or do not speak, such behavior is codified in the white imaginary. To be silent "confirms" passivity and docility. To speak, to want to be heard, "confirms" brazen contempt and Black rage. The point here is that no matter the response, Black emergence outside of whiteness's *scopic* power is foreclosed. Ellison's invisible man knows the frustration of being "seen" and yet "not seen." There is an upsurge of protestation whereby the Black body begins to make itself felt. "You ache with the need to convince yourself that you do exist in the real world, that you're a part of all the sound and anguish, and you strike out with your fists, you curse and you swear to make them recognize you. And, alas, it's seldom successful."[74] Again, note that even as the invisible man protests, he is "seldom successful," which may be partly why he decides to "walk softly so as not to awaken the sleeping ones. Sometimes it is best not to awaken them; there are few things in the world as dangerous as sleepwalkers."[75]

Throughout the text, the invisible man finds himself objectified/distorted by the white gaze. Hence, like Fanon, he has difficulties in the development of his bodily schema. Consider the Black men who are made to participate in the battle royal—a site constructed for white men only, indeed, for white *eyes*. During the fight, the Blacks are all blindfolded. Symbolically, the blindfolds replicate the larger socioeconomic powerlessness of Blacks in relation to whites. The Black body is *looked at*. The Black body does not return the gaze. The white body *looks at*. The battle royal is a spectacle, a visual (or ocular) power zone within which Black male bodies are mere surfaces. Before they are instructed to fight like animals for the pleasure of *the lookers*, however, a naked blond white woman, with a small American flag tattooed on her abdomen, sensuously dances before them. One might say that she is "dangled" before them like a piece of white flesh they dare not touch or look at. Indeed, "some of the boys stood with lowered heads, trembling."[76] Some of the white men threatened them if they actually looked, while others were threatened if they did not look. After all, she is a white woman and therefore taboo. She is not to be looked at by Black males, and yet some of the white men forced them to look, creating a psychosexual "complex fusion of desire and aversion." [77]

The battle royal is a site of pain, pleasure, hatred, misogyny, and white myths interwoven into a sadistic and erotic spectacle. It is a site of white male terror, anxiety, and desire. The white men—the "bankers, lawyers, judges, doctors, fire chiefs, teachers, merchants" [78]—create a context of sexual intensification through the unthinkable juxtaposition of Black male bodies with white female bodies, creating an erotic space in which the white male imaginary is able to "get off" at the thought of watching a Black male desire a white woman. The erotic ritual is designed to intensify white men's pleasure as they imagine one of the Black men having sex with the blond white woman. Referring to the early days of Malcolm X's career as a hustler, Sartwell notes, "Thus interracial sex has a very intense and particular erotic/specular power, an erotic power that draws the white men . . . to stare obsessively at black men fucking white women."[79]

Black men are also rendered invisible through the eyes (inner eyes) of white women. Ellison explores this theme through the female character, Sybil, who never really sees Ellison's protagonist. All that she sees is her own distorted and sexually perverse projections upon the Black male body. The invisible man describes himself as "Brother Taboo-with-whom-all-things-are-possible."[80] Sybil is interested in literally playing the role of the white innocent victim in relation to the myth of the "Black rapist." Indeed, the invisible man jokingly references D. W. Griffith's film *Birth of a Nation*, invoking the memory of the filmic narrative construction and semiotics of the Black male as rapist. He asks, "What's happening here . . . a new birth of a nation?"[81] Sybil wants him to take her against her will, to play at being raped by a Black "buck." "But I need it," she says, uncrossing her thighs and sitting up eagerly. "You can do it, it'll be easy for *you*, beautiful. Threaten to kill me if I don't give in. You know, talk rough to me beautiful."[82] She describes him as "ebony against pure snow."[83] She describes her husband as "forty minutes of brag and ten of bustle."[84] She describes the protagonist, however, as having unbelievable sexual endurance, whom she wants "to tear [her] apart."[85] Playing into her fantasies, and playing within his own invisibility, he says, "I rapes real good when I'm drunk." She replies, "Ooooh, then pour me another."[86] In a state of mythopoetic (and masochistic) frenzy she says, "Come on, beat me, daddy—you—you big black bruiser. What's taking you so long?" she said. "Hurry up, knock me down! Don't you want me?" Annoyed, he slaps her, but this only leaves her "aggressively receptive." He never rapes her, but constructs the moment with a different semiotic spin, writing on her belly with lipstick: "SYBIL, YOU WERE RAPED BY SANTA CLAUS, SURPRISE."[87] The invisible man has unveiled the core of Sybil's projections. What she wants is a *fantasy* that does not exist. The point here, though, is that Ellison provides a rich narrative portrayal of the psychosexual dynamics involved in the *erasure* of Black male identity in relationship to white female desire for the Black body as phantasmatic object.

Throughout the text, Ellison's protagonist is never really in charge of who he is, which is another manifestation of his invisibility and powerlessness. When he joins the Brotherhood, which is where he thinks he will finally gain recognition, he is still treated as amorphous, invisible.[88] During a moment in the text where he is *used* to give a speech at a rally, the invisible man notes, "The light was so strong that I could no longer see the audience, the bowl of human faces. It was as though a semitransparent curtain had dropped between us, but through which they could see me—for they were applauding—without themselves being seen."[89] The influx of light is significant here. In one way or another throughout the text, the protagonist has had to contend with the blinding light of whiteness, its power to see, to gaze, to control. Here again, the protagonist cannot return the gaze; he is seen, but cannot see. Indeed, he cannot see that he is being tricked by the Brotherhood. Beneath the façade of an intrinsic interest in the invisible man, the Brotherhood wants him as a political and ideological *speaking* Black body, a mere verbal Black surface. For example, a character named Emma asks, "But don't you think he should be a little blacker?"[90] His subjectivity and humanity are not valued. Rather, it is his *Blackness* that functions as a site of political semiosis; he is a manipulated political tool. The invisible man notes, "Maybe she wants to see me sweat coal tar, ink, shoe polish, graphite. What was I, a man or a natural resource?"[91] Perhaps the history of American slavery offers the answer: he is a means to a larger *white* purpose, a "natural resource" to be exploited.

Ellison explores the dialectics of how whiteness is constructed through the reconstruction/negation of Blackness in a brilliant example where the protagonist gets a job working for a paint plant. As the invisible man arrives at the plant, he sees a large sign that reads: "Keep America Pure with Liberty Paints."[92] Working under Mr. Kimbro, the invisible man learns how to make the paint. He is instructed to open each bucket of paint and put in ten drops of a liquid that is black. To his surprise, as the black liquid disappears, the pure white paint appears. After the invisible man completes a few buckets, Mr. Kimbro exclaims, "That's it, as white as George Washington's Sunday-go-to-meetin wig and as sound as the all mighty dollar! That's paint!" he said proudly. "That's paint that'll cover just about anything!"[93] Another white employee, Lucius Brockway, later describes the pure white paint as "Optic White." Describing how he helped create the slogan for optic white paint, Brockway says, "If It's Optic White, It's the Right White."[94]

The symbolism regarding the black liquid raises the dynamics of Black erasure in relation to whiteness. Just as the paint's quality of pure white needs the black drops, "racialized" whiteness as normative, moral, good, and pure is dependent upon the projection of the Black body as "inferior," "stained," and "impure." Of course, by the time the paint has become pure white, there is no trace of Blackness. This symbolism is characteristic of white America's denial that its very existence is inextricably linked to the presence of Black people. The large sign rings true, America must be kept pure. The pure whiteness of the paint can "cover just about anything." Hence whiteness "covers" that which is sullen, dirty, evil. It does away with the unclean. As demonstrated in chapter 6, the tragic character Pecola Breedlove in Toni Morrison's *The Bluest Eye* believes that whiteness can "cover" over her Black ugly features, permanently washing from her the stain of Blackness. Think here too of how white America "covers" the cultural productions by Black people. To acknowledge Blackness, after all, might lead to the uncovering of whiteness. It might also be said that the power and normative structure of whiteness, through the denial of its own history, "covers" over its acts of injustice and brutality through an ideological structure that gives the appearance of all things proceeding as normal.

Optic white literally can be translated as "eye white" or "seeing white" or figuratively as "I white," where the verb is deleted. Of course, the term *optic* raises the issue of the gaze. Optically, the protagonist is rendered invisible. Optically, whites either refuse to see him or see him as if he was the reflected image given back as a result of being "surrounded by mirrors of hard, distorting glass."[95] As optic white is "*Right* White," the white gaze, as it renders the protagonist invisible/distorted, is exempt from critique because white is always right. Moreover, since optics is the science that deals with the propagation of light, which Europeans historically brought to so-called backward cultures of "darkness," optic white *is* "Right White." Consistent with this symbolism, Africa *became* "dark" as "explorers, missionaries, and scientists flooded it with light, because the light was refracted through an imperialist ideology that urged the abolition of 'savage customs' in the name of civilization."[96]

MALCOLM X

Felt invisibility is a form of ontological and epistemic violence, a form of violence initiated through white spectatorship, a generative gazing that attempts to violate the integrity of the Black body. The white gaze is capable of seeping into my consciousness, skewing the way I see myself. But the gaze does not "see" me, it "sees" itself. This experience is similar to what happened early in Malcolm X's life with his English teacher, Mr. Ostrowski.[97] At Mason Junior High School, Malcolm was the only Black student in the eighth grade. Although Malcolm mentioned in his autobiography that he had not given thought to it before, he said that he disclosed to Mr. Ostrowski that he wanted to be a lawyer. Malcolm made it clear that Ostrowski always provided encouragement to white students when asked for his advice regarding their future careers. But to Malcolm, Ostrowski replied:

> Malcolm, one of life's first needs is for us to be realistic. Don't misunderstand me, now. We all here like you, you know that. But you've got to be realistic about being a nigger. A Lawyer—that's no realistic goal for a nigger. You need to think about something that you *can* be. You're good with your hands— making things. Everybody admires your carpentry shop work. Why don't you plan on carpentry? People like you as a person—you'd get all kinds of work.[98]

Note the perverse construction of "We all here *like* you." Ostrowski was attempting to obfuscate the fact that he was a racist. He wanted to clear his conscience by stating upfront his "affections" for Malcolm right before he violated Malcolm's body integrity, reducing him to a *nigger*, as someone who must learn to live with mediocrity and accept his place within the "natural" order of things. The young Malcolm was returned to himself qua *nigger*. "To forcibly strip someone of their self-image," as Drucilla Cornell argues, "is a violation, not just an offense."[99] At this time, Malcolm had already been elected class president and was receiving grades among the highest in the school. Yet all that Ostrowski "saw" was a *nigger*. Despite the countervailing empirical evidence, Ostrowski "saw" more of whiteness's *same*. As Malcolm noted, "I was still not intelligent enough, in their eyes, to become whatever *I* wanted to be."[100] Malcolm's point is consistent with what has been theorized thus far. First, within a white racist order of things, for the Black, there is apparently no being-as-possibility beyond the totalizing white gaze. As argued above, it is here that perception, epistemology, and ontology are collapsed. Second, Malcolm's first-person perspective ("I desire," or "I have my own perspective on the world") is disrupted and rendered void in relation to the third-person (white) perspective that has negatively overdetermined his Blackness.

Malcolm also described his history teacher, Mr. Williams, as one who was fond of "nigger jokes."[101] Of course, such "nigger jokes" were told at Malcolm's expense and no doubt "confirmed" many of the circulating myths white students consciously or unconsciously held. Malcolm noted:

> We came to the textbook section on Negro history. It was exactly one paragraph long. Mr. Williams laughed through it practically in a single breath, reading aloud how the Negroes had been slaves and then were freed, and how they were usually lazy and dumb and shiftless. He added, I remember, an anthropological footnote of his own, telling us between laughs how Negroes' feet were "so big that when they walk, they don't leave tracks, they leave a hole in the ground."[102]

Although Malcolm *heard* these racist jokes, one might say, in keeping with Alexander Weheliye, that "the white subject's vocal apparatus merely serves to repeat and solidify racial difference as it is inscribed in the field of vision."[103] Whether through the ritualistic practice of Ostrowski putting Blacks in their "natural" place or through the racist jokes Mr. Williams told, whites "adjusted their microtomes" and objectively cut away at Malcolm's reality.[104] After such racist acts, Malcolm later admitted, "I just gave up."[105] Along the same lines, Fanon wrote, "I slip into corners, and my long antennae pick up the catch-phrases strewn over the surface of things—nigger underwear smells of nigger—nigger teeth are white—nigger feet are big—the nigger's barrel chest—I slip into corners, I remain silent, I strive for anonymity, for invisibility. Look, I will accept the lot, as long as no one notices me."[106] Malcolm was reduced to the anonymous Black other. He was returned to himself as an absence. Although "accepted" by whites, he was accepted only on their terms. "We [whites] will sweep you up into significance; we offer you a name: *our* name. But as we inscribe ourselves on you, we erase you."[107] Hence, there was no genuine acceptance, only further distancing from the Black body. Only as a mascot did Malcolm come to experience his "acceptance" (erasure) by whites.

> They all liked my attitude, and it was out of their liking for me that I soon became accepted by them—as a mascot, I know now. They would talk about anything and everything with me standing right there hearing them, the same way people would talk freely in front of a pet canary. They would even talk about me, or about "niggers," as though I wasn't there, as if I wouldn't understand what the word meant. A hundred times a day, they used the word "nigger."[108]

Malcolm was cognizant of the hidden questions residing at the heart of white acceptance: To what extent are you (the Black) willing to erase yourself? To what extent are you willing to conform to our (white) stereotype of you? How much can you hate yourself, while forgetting that it came from us?

Within the context of an anti-Black racist context, white acceptance comes at an existential ontological price for Black people: a mode of nonbeing.

Critiquing the "good-will" white, Malcolm noted, "I don't care how nice one is to you; the thing you must always remember is that almost never does he really see you as he sees himself, as he sees his own kind." Expounding upon the Ellisonian theme of invisibility, he wrote:

> What I am trying to say is that it just never dawned upon them that I could understand, that I wasn't a pet, but a human being. They didn't give me credit for having the same sensitivity, intellect, and understanding that they would have been ready and willing to recognize in a white boy in my position. But it has historically been the case with white people, in their regard for black people, that even though we might be *with* them, we weren't considered *of* them. Even though they appeared to have opened the door, it was still closed. Thus they never did really see *me*.[109]

When one thinks about the long-term negative impact of Ostrowski's and Mr. Williams's racism on young Malcolm, one better understands the dynamic of Black self-hatred. Self-surveillance or getting the Black body to regulate itself in the physical absence of the white gaze is a significant strategy of white racist ideology. Malcolm had internalized the white gaze. Through the act of conking his hair, he policed his Black body in the image of whiteness:

> This was my first really big step toward self-degradation: when I endured all of that pain, literally burning my flesh to have it look like a white man's hair. I had joined that multitude of Negro men and women in America who are brainwashed into believing that the black people are "inferior"—and white people "superior"—that they will even violate and mutilate their God-created bodies to try to look "pretty" by white standards.[110]

The powerful appeal the Nation of Islam had for Malcolm as he got older is not difficult to comprehend. Given the murder of Malcolm's father, Earl Little, who was believed to have been killed by white racists because of his affiliation with Marcus Garvey's Universal Negro Improvement Association; given that the Ku Klux Klan had surrounded Malcolm's house and threatened his family while his mother, Louise, was pregnant with him; given that the white state social service system had broken his family apart; and given that his mother was declared insane by white doctors, the Nation of Islam's narrative of Yacub's history would certainly have helped Malcolm make sense of white America. According to this narrative, a Black mad scientist named Yacub rebelled against Allah and created, along with 59,999 of his followers, evil white people.[111]

W. E. B. DU BOIS

In his seminal work, *The Souls of Black Folk* (1903), W. E. B. Du Bois, on my reading, also located the problem of white *racism* within the realm of the sociogenic. As I will show, Du Bois's conceptualization of double consciousness attests to the significance of the *lived* experience of race. Du Bois's work provides a revealingly profound example of how "Blackness" gets negatively configured within a (white) gestural, semiotic space. In the following example, there is a phenomenological moment of slippage resulting from the white gaze/glance, between how he may have understood himself and how he suddenly experienced himself as different from the other (white) children. "In a wee wooden schoolhouse," Du Bois wrote, "something put it into the boys' and girls' heads to buy gorgeous visiting cards—ten cents a package—and exchange. The exchange was merry, till one girl, a tall newcomer, refused my card—refused it peremptorily, with a glance. Then it dawned upon me with a certain suddenness that I was different from the others; or like, mayhap in heart and life and longing, but shut out from their world by a vast veil."[112]

When I've taught this part of Du Bois's work, I have had many white students immediately jump to the conclusion that Du Bois was mistaken, that he was just a child. Indeed, they typically argue that the newcomer's refusal is simply an example of the way in which children react to each other, how little girls generally treat little boys. However, the tall newcomer did not apparently negatively react to any of the other (white) boys. This refusal was not about Du Bois's gender. Even if we grant that as a newcomer she felt uncomfortable around the new students, she apparently only expressed this toward Du Bois. Hence, it is obvious that there is a fundamental link between racial reification of the young Du Bois and the girl's callous rejection. As for my students, one could argue that they failed to show empathy toward Du Bois because of the more general ways in which contemporary American society has become profoundly atomized, where social actors' imaginative capacities have become dulled. While this explanation may very well help account for why my students rarely see any problem with the newcomer's response to Du Bois, perhaps there is something that they also refuse to face or are afraid to face. I am thinking here of what one white male student of mine, Andrew Thomas, pointed out. After hearing so many responses that aimed to reinterpret Du Bois's experience for him, Thomas introduced a very significant point: "I think that many whites might feel the need to reject what Du Bois is saying because they are perhaps reminded of situations where they've treated a Black person in the way that the newcomer treated Du Bois. The Du Bois example reminds them of something that they don't want to see in themselves. They don't want to admit that they too harbor such racism."

Du Bois's example suggests that he was in some sense similar to the other (white) children. In "heart," "life," and "longing" he appears to have felt a kindred relationship. Indeed, the pain and trauma of rejection was probably all the more intense because he thought that he shared certain similarities. But something went awry. There was a sudden annoying feeling of difference, which presumably did not exist prior to this encounter. Hence, Du Bois underwent a distinctive phenomenological process of coming to *appear* to himself differently as one who is expelled. He moved from a sense of the familiar to the unfamiliar. A slippage occurred in his corporeal schema. In this example, Du Bois's body schema has become problematic. He is forced to deal with the *meaning* of a racial epidermal schema as a result of (or introduced by) the meaning-constituting activities of the young girl's racialized consciousness. As with Fanon, Ellison's invisible man, and Malcolm X, Du Bois was "taken outside" of himself and *returned*. Surely, Du Bois is the same self he was prior to the gestured glance the tall white girl performed. Surely, he was classified "Black" prior to his encounter that day with the tall newcomer, though he may not have experienced this classificatory designation as something problematic or as a mark of disdain. But is he the same? As the tall white girl refused him, she sent a semiotic message, a message whose constructive meaning was immediately registered in the consciousness of the young Du Bois. Her body language, her refusal, involved a ritual that had tremendous power. The *ritual* glance/refusal took place within a pre-interpreted space of racial meaning. This precondition formed the basis upon which the glance's meaning registered for Du Bois that something had become problematic at the level of his epidermis. In order for Du Bois to have understood the specific racial meaning of the glance he had to have a certain level of racial narrative competence. In short, part of his horizon involved an awareness of difference, but also an awareness of difference in an exclusionary sense.

The ritual glance is both a product of this space and a vehicle through which racial and racist performances are perpetuated. Du Bois wrote that the tall white girl "refused it peremptorily, with a glance." This refusal involves the arrogance and self-centeredness of whiteness, a form of white narcissism articulated through a look. The performance of whiteness, then, is not restricted to a set of articulated propositional beliefs or in the deployment of various rhetorical strategies. White racism can be expressed through the modality of physical comportment, a way of inhabiting physical space, a way of glancing/not glancing. "Seen" through the eyes of the newcomer, Du Bois's Black body was already *coded* as different, as a problem, as that which should be avoided. Though young, the tall white newcomer had already learned complex ways of white coping, ways of seeing the Black body as a site of avoidance, ways of not seeing her body as raced, different. Her whiteness as norm is reinforced through this exclusionary act. Her racial status as white remains paradoxically unmarked and yet marked in this communicational space, though she never spoke.

The unspoken power of whiteness reflects the effective transmission of racism, not only through words but also through subtle actions. "We learned far more from acts than words, more from a raised eyebrow, a joke, a shocked voice, a withdrawing movement of the body, a long silence, than from long sentences," Smith notes.[113] Within the context of this highly racial and racist communicational space, Du Bois's body came to matter. He was the materialization of darkness with all its normative and typological associations, "the colored kid, monkeychild, different."[114] Indeed, the newcomer's ritual glance "produced bodily effects through immediate [non]verbal acts that reify racial difference."[115] Through her refusal to exchange with Du Bois, he returns to himself as excluded. The white girl, however, returns to herself as the center; her glance policed her whiteness as a privileged (unspoken) site.[116] She never says in a declarative voice, "I'm white!" Du Bois did not say in the indicative, *"You're white!"* Williams writes, in America "whiteness is rarely marked in the indicative there! there! sense of my bracketed blackness. And the majoritarian privilege [of whites] of never noticing themselves was the beginning of an imbalance from which so much, so much else flowed."[117] The newcomer's whiteness is interpellated, performed, claimed, through a nonverbal gesture of negation. Although young and "innocent," her actions reflect larger political hallmarks of white racism: the audacity and power to relegate nonwhites to the margins, to segregate them, to instill in them the sense of existing outside the space of white normalcy and normativity.

The tall white newcomer has been situated (and situates her own identity) in the role of a member of a "superior" group. Describing the importance placed upon whiteness as a symbol of group purity and superiority, Smith observes, "There, in the land of Epidermis, every one of us was a little king."[118] As within a dramaturgical narrative (as *homo histrio*), she plays her assigned role well. One might say she has been given a role to play from within a *distal* narrative (an influential narrative of white supremacy that extends back into her past) that comes replete with assumptions regarding how to act in the presence of a dark body qua other. In other words, she has become a prisoner, so to speak, of a distal anti-Black racist hermeneutic that informs her actions in relation to differentially raced bodies. Through the performative act of refusal, though words were presumably never spoken, Du Bois became, even if unknowingly, "a damn nigger." Through her glance and her refusal, she reduced Du Bois to his Blackness, a mere surface, *a thing of no particular importance*, though important enough to reject and avoid. Du Bois was no longer within the group, but outside it, left looking upon himself through the newcomer's eyes. One might say the meaning-giving acts of his own consciousness in terms of his own dark body for all intents and purposes functioned as an instantiation of white racist consciousness intending the Black body as other. Hence, he became, if only momentarily, other to himself.

Like Fanon, who described the phenomenological dimensions of corporeal malediction, Du Bois underwent a similar process, one that he termed *double consciousness*:

> It is a peculiar sensation, this double-consciousness, this sense of always look-ing at one's self through the eyes of others, of measuring one's soul by the tape of a world that looks on in amused contempt and pity. One ever feels his twoness—an American, a Negro; two souls, two thoughts, two unreconciled strivings; two warring ideals in one dark body, whose dogged strength alone keeps it from being torn asunder.[119]

Du Bois began to experience a disjointed relationship with his body. In this process of disjointedness, one ceases to experience one's identity from a locus of self-definition and begins to experience one's identity from a locus of externally imposed meaning. In short, Du Bois was forced into a state of doubleness, *seeing* himself as other (the inferior Black) through the gaze of the young girl as the one (the superior white). This white scopically imposed meaning of Blackness as dirty, immoral, and inferior interpellates the Black body as a prescopic essence. The tall white newcomer's glance marked Du Bois as absent, as different. Her white glance possessed the power to con-fiscate the Black body, only to have it returned to Du Bois as a burden and a curse.

At the heart of each of the aforementioned experiences emerges a ques-tion. The question is posed from within what Du Bois calls "the veil." Whether interpreted as symbolic of systemic racism/structural segregation or as that which "indicates, rhetorically, a knowledge of difference that is itself discursively based," the veil is fundamentally linked to the hegemonic performances of whiteness, performances that can lead to deep societal fissures or to profound levels of existential phenomenological fracture.[120] I emphasize the latter here. So what is this question? It is not a question born of solitude, but of racist discriminatory practices, oppression, white lies and white myths, embodied struggle and sustained existential and onto-logical tension, a struggle that emerges within the context of a powerful racializing white regime. It is not born of hyperbolic doubt, a questioning of all things that fail the test of epistemological indubitability, though it may involve, as Du Bois wrote, "incessant self-questioning and the hesitation that arises from it."[121] The question is: "What, after all, am I?"[122] Aware of the systematic negation of Black humanity under colonialism, Fanon argued that "colonialism forces the people it dominates to ask themselves the ques-tion constantly: 'In reality, who am I?'"[123] Similarly, theorizing what he refers to as the "Negroes greatest dilemma," which he sees as the ambivalence regarding an identity that is both African and American, Martin Luther King, Jr., wrote, "Every man must ultimately confront the question 'Who am I?' and seek to answer it honestly."[124] Unlike René Descartes, who asked a similar question—"But what then am I?"—after arriving at the indubitable *cogito* argument and who reached the eventual conclusion that he was a *thing* that thinks, Du Bois's question is linked to his having been racially marked and relegated to the domain of the wretched.[125] Far from a *disembodied* thing that thinks (*res cogitans*), Du Bois is cursed precisely in terms of his racially epidermalized embodiment. The internalization of this cursed wretchedness helps mystify the various ways in which white racism systematically encourages this form of pathology. Stuart Hall writes, "It is one thing to position a subject or set of peoples as the Other of a dominant discourse. It is quite another thing to subject them to that 'knowledge', not only as a matter of imposed will and domination, by the power of inner compulsion and subjective conformation to the norm."[126] Hence, one plausible answer to the question might be: "I am a problem! Who I am as an embodied Black body *is* a problem!" This response to the question would indicate Hall's conceptualization of the "inner compulsion and subjective conformation to the [white] norm."

The connection between Blackness and the concept of "being a problem" is central to Du Bois's understanding of what it means to be Black in white America. Du Bois revealed how whites engage in a process of duplicity while speaking to Blacks. They often approach Blacks in a hesitant fashion, saying "I know an excellent coloured man in my town; or, I fought at Mechanicsville; or, Do not these Southern outrages make your blood boil?"[127] Du Bois maintained that the real question whites want to ask is: "How does it feel to be a problem?"[128] Du Bois also pointed out that some whites greet Blacks with a certain amicable comportment. They talk with you about the weather, while all along performing hidden white racists scripts: "My poor, unwhite thing! Weep not nor rage. I know, too well, that the curse of God lies heavy on you. Why? That is not for me to say, but be brave! Do your work in your lowly sphere, praying the good Lord that into heaven above, where all is love, you may, one day, be born—white!"[129] With regard to the notion of being a problem, whites do not ask, "How does it feel to *have* problems?" The question is raised to the level of the ontological: "How does it feel *to be* a problem?"

As a problem from the perspective of white mythopoetic constructions, Du Bois was aware that it is the "stained" Black body at both the phenotypic and the consanguineous level that is deemed criminal. "Murder may swagger, theft may rule and prostitution may flourish and the nation gives but spasmodic, intermittent and lukewarm attention," he noted. "But let the murderer be black or the thief brown or the violator of womanhood have a drop of Negro blood, and the righteousness of the indignation sweeps the world."[130] The question regarding how it feels to be a problem does not apply to people who have at some point in their lives felt themselves to be a problem. In such cases, feeling like a problem is a contingent disposition that is relatively finite and transitory. When whites ask the same question of Blacks, the relationship between being Black and being a problem is noncontingent. It is a necessary relation. Outgrowing this ontological state of being a problem is believed impossible. Hence, when regarding one's "existence as problematic," temporality is frozen. One is a problem *forever*, fixed, permanent. However, it is important to note that it is from within the white imaginary that the question "How does it feel to be a problem?" is given birth. To be human is to be *thrown-in-the-world*.

To be human not only means to be thrown within a context of facticity but also *to be* in the mode of the subjunctive. The etymology of the word *problem* suggests the sense of being "thrown forward," as if being thrown in front of something, as an obstacle. Within the white imaginary, to be Black means to be born an obstacle at the very core of one's being. To exist as Black is *not* "to stand out" facing an ontological horizon filled with future possibilities of being other than what one is. Rather, being Black negates the "ex" of existence. Being Black is reduced to facticity. For example, it is not only within the light of my freely chosen projects that things are *experienced* as obstacles, as Sartre might say; as Black, by definition, I *am* an obstacle. As Black, I am the very obstacle to my own metastability and transphenomenal being. As Black, I am not a project at all. Hence, within the framework of the white imaginary, to be Black and to be human are contradictory terms.

Du Bois, like Toni Morrison after him, was aware of the strategic significance of averting the critical gaze from the racial "object" (the Black) to the racial "subject" (the white). In 1920, in his powerful and engaging essay entitled "The Souls of White Folk," Du Bois wrote:

> I see these souls [of white folk] undressed and from the back and side. I see the working of their entrails. I know their thoughts and they know that I know. This knowledge makes them now embarrassed, now furious! They deny my right to live and be and call me misbirth! My word is to them mere bitterness and my soul, pessimism. And yet as they preach and strut and shout and threaten, crouching as they clutch at rags of facts and fancies to hide their nakedness, they go twisting, flying by my tired eyes and I see them ever stripped—ugly, human.[131]

At this juncture, I will delineate what Du Bois's "tired eyes" saw of whiteness "ever stripped." As stated earlier, in my view, critical whiteness theorists have not given the attention to this pivotal essay that it deserves. Du Bois said of whites that he was "singularly clairvoyant."[132] He claimed to be able to see the working of their entrails. In short, Du Bois was claiming that he could see their psychological "innards" or the unconscious operations of whiteness. Du Bois's project was to *demystify* whiteness, to reveal "the mechanisms by which whiteness has reproduced its foundational myths."[133] Hence, Du Bois might be said to have been working within the critical space of ideology exposure, revealing that which is hidden. Historically situating the whiteness of Pan-Europeanism, Du Bois wrote, "Today . . . the world in a sudden, emotional conversion has discovered that it is white and by token, wonderful!"[134] Blacks, under this "religion of whiteness," as Du Bois said, come to see themselves as inferior, often resulting in a powerful form of psychological deformation.[135] Within the context of white power and brutality, Black people have come to internalize negative images of themselves, thus resulting in what I have previously referred to as epistemic violence.

Aware of how myths harden into "empirical truths," Du Bois wrote, "How easy, then, by emphasis and omission to make children believe that every great soul the world ever saw was a white man's soul; that every great thought the world ever knew was a white man's thought; that every great dream the world ever sang was a white man's dream."[136] Many Blacks, through white "emphasis and omission," have come to internalize the myth, at their own psychological peril, that whiteness is supreme. This raises the larger issue of how whites exclude nonwhites from playing significant roles in the movement of human history. Through the deployment of "metanarrative" historical constructions, white (read: Western) civilization is unified across space and time to represent the apex of human genius, scientific thought, political organization, philosophical speculation, and ethical behavior. As Du Bois noted, though, this is achieved through "emphasis and omission," which points to the interest-laden, self-referential dynamics of whiteness. Black children are taught to believe that "Blackness" is an aberration, that Black people, those who carry *the human stain*, are stupid by nature, uncivilized, and uneducable. Blackness is said to be that which sullies the "purity" of whiteness. Indeed, all is beautiful without Blackness; all is rational without Blackness; all, indeed, is perfect without Blackness. "In fact," Du Bois wrote, "that if from the world were dropped everything that could not fairly be attributed to White Folk, the world would, if anything, be even greater, truer, better than now."[137]

Du Bois's "tired eyes" saw even more. As long as Blacks resign themselves to "naturally" assigned stations in life, whites are content to provide them with gifts for minimal sustainability. As long as Blacks remain docile and thankful for "barrels of old clothes from lordly and generous whites, there is much mental peace and moral satisfaction."[138] However, as soon as Blacks begin to question the entitlement of whites to the best things that life has to offer, and when their "attitude toward charity is sullen anger rather than humble jollity," whites charge Blacks with impudence. They say "that the South is right, and that Japan wants to fight America."[139] Du Bois internationalized the rationalizations of whiteness with regard to the Japanese, the so-called Yellow Negro. Whiteness, within this context, functions as a trope of capitalist domination, exploitation, and cultural imperialism.

Du Bois noted that as whites began to think Blacks were insisting upon their right to human dignity, as John Jones did, and as whites subsequently began an unapologetic wage of brutality and oppression against Black people, "the descent to Hell is easy."[140] This "descent to Hell" is a powerful image. Du Bois saw whiteness as a form of misanthropy, a form of hatred and evil that lusts for Black blood. Du Bois:

> I have seen a man—an educated gentleman—grow livid with anger because a little, silent, black woman was sitting by herself in a Pullman car. He was a white man. I have seen a great, grown man curse a little child, who had wandered into the wrong waiting-room, searching for its mother: "Here, you damned black —." He was white. In Central Park I have seen the upper lip of a quiet, peaceful man curl back in a tigerish snarl of rage because black folk rode by in a motor car. He was a white man.[141]

Notice the refrain, "He was a white man." Du Bois used this refrain to establish a deepening and deafening portrayal of anti-Black racist hatred.

One tragic way in which this hatred has historically expressed itself is in the form of lynching, that spectacle of white fear, anxiety, desire, and sexual psychopathology, with its attendant pleasure reserved for the white racist scopophiliac. "These lynchings, then, formed a crucial part of the black subject's ecology both as physical threats and media representations," according to Weheliye, "making them subject to the look of white folks, yet unable to return the look."[142] Within this context, Du Bois spoke of the "lust of blood" that fueled the madness of lynching Black bodies, that "strange fruit" about which Billie Holiday sang. Du Bois was aware of how it really did not matter whether the Black person who was lynched had actually done anything wrong. All that mattered was that some Black, any Black, had to pay. Blood must be spilled to satisfy and appease the white demigods. With deep psychological insight into the "entrails" of whiteness, Du Bois observed:

> We have seen, you and I, city after city drunk and furious with ungovernable lust of blood; mad with murder, destroying, killing, and cursing; torturing human victims because somebody accused of crime happened to be of the same color as the mob's innocent victims and because that color was not white! We have seen—Merciful God! in these wild days and in the name of Civilization, Justice,

and Motherhood—what have we not seen, right here in America, of orgy, cruelty, barbarism, and murder done to men and women of Negro descent.[143]

Du Bois placed a level of responsibility on whites to be honest about their anti-Black racism. He wrote, "Ask your own soul what it would say if the next census were to report that half of black America was dead and the other half dying." Du Bois's response, a clear indictment of the misanthropy that appears to reside in the souls of white folk, indicates that he was aware that whites are prisoners of something deeper than false beliefs. "I suffer," he responded, "And yet, somehow, above the suffering, above the shackled anger that beats the bars, above the hurt that crazes there surges in me a vast pity—pity for a people imprisoned and enthralled, hampered and made miserable for such a cause, for such a phantasy!"[144] Du Bois pitied whites because they live with the mythos of being "greater" than nonwhites by virtue of "natural design"; they live their whiteness in bad faith, covering over the truth that whiteness is not beyond interrogation. They are imprisoned by years of performing whiteness and having whiteness performed on them to the point that "it is a matter of conditioned reflexes; of long followed habits, customs and folkways; of subconscious trains of reasoning and unconscious nervous reflexes."[145] Substituting the historical constructedness of whiteness for "manifest destiny," hence obfuscating the contingency of whiteness, whites remain imprisoned within a space of white ethical solipsism (only whites possess needs and desires that are truly worthy of respect[146]). It would seem that many whites would rather remain imprisoned within the ontology of *sameness*, refusing to call into question the ideological structure of their identities as "superior." The call of the other qua other remains unheard within the space of whiteness's sameness. Locked within their self-enthralled structure of whiteness, whites occlude—both consciously and unconsciously—the possibility of developing new forms of ethical relationality to themselves and to nonwhites. Partly through the process of interrogating their hegemonic, monologistic discourse (functioning as the "oracle voice") whites might reach across the chasm of (nonhierarchical) difference and embrace the nonwhite other in his or her otherness. Du Bois did not romanticize the tremendous amount of work involved in working through the anti-Black racism of whites. In short, given the rigidity of whiteness as an embodied, politically, institutionally, and economically rewarding site of identity and power, Du Bois realized that whiteness is not simply an issue of atomistic agency. More is required; "not sudden assault but long siege."[147] The etymology of the word *siege* suggests actively waiting and deploying careful analyses and theorizing and diligent work with regard to the insidious nature of whiteness. "A true and worthy ideal," as Du Bois wrote, "frees and uplifts a people." He adds, "But say to a people: 'The one virtue is to be white,' and people rush to the inevitable conclusion, "Kill the 'nigger'!" On this score, the presumed inextricable link between whiteness and virtue is structurally misanthropic vis-à-vis Blacks. Of course, the idea that "the one virtue is white" is a false ideal, for it "imprisons and lowers."[148]

Du Bois wrote of the arrogance of white power mongers: "These supermen and world-mastering demi-gods listened, however, to no low tongues of ours, even when we pointed silently to their feet of clay."[149] Whiteness takes itself as that universality that is beyond the realm of *particularity*. Black people embody particularity, have "feet of clay." Whiteness, however, embodies *all* that is good, moral, beautiful, and supreme. Du Bois noted:

> This theory of human culture and its aims has worked itself through warp and woof of our daily thought with a thoroughness that few realize. Everything great, good, efficient, fair, and honorable is "white"; everything mean, bad, blundering, cheating, and dishonorable is "yellow"; a bad taste is "brown"; and the devil is "black." The changes of this theme are continually rung in picture and story, in newspaper heading and movie-picture, in sermon and school book, until, of course, the King can do no wrong—a White Man is always right and a Black Man has no rights which a white man is bound to respect.[150]

The last line in this quotation is an explicit reference to the famous *Dred Scott* decision in which (white) Chief Justice Roger B. Taney declared that Dred Scott and his wife, Harriet, who had petitioned for freedom, would remain enslaved. How could it have been otherwise when whiteness proves "its own incontestable superiority by appointing both judge and jury and summoning only its own witnesses."[151]

SARA(H) BA(A)RTMAN(N)[152]

Whiteness is a "particular social and historical [formation] that [is] reproduced through specific discursive and material processes and circuits of desire and power."[153] Reproduced through circuits of desire and power, and through embodied, habituated forms of racism, whiteness, as Du Bois's writings suggest above, strives for totalization; it desires to claim the entire world for itself and has the misanthropic effrontery to territorialize the very meaning of the human.

Within the specific context of colonial desire, power, and knowledge production regarding the colonized Black body, Sara(h) Ba(a)rtma(n) was a tragic figure as the colonial gaze constructed her body against the backdrop of a racist discursive regime of "truth." The white colonialist gaze was invested in a racist regime of classificatory "truth." Theorizing the specular/ocular

dimensions of colonialist power and knowledge is a significant point of entry
into the racist colonialist *Weltanschauung*. Indeed, "the hegemony of vision
in Western modernity, its ocularcentric discourse, has been subjected to much
scrutiny, and Afro-diasporic thinkers, in particular, have stressed the centrality of the scopic in constructions of race and racism."[154]

The so-called Hottentot Venus was the product of the colonial white gaze
that had woven Sara(h) Ba(a)rtman(n) "out of a thousand details, anecdotes,
[and] stories," which thereby imprisoned her.[155] To theorize the so-called
Hottentot Venus is to theorize the French *male* imaginary as expressed
through monopolizing *desire* and power. Indeed, Hottentot Venus was a
mirror through which nineteenth-century French male desire and power are
reflected. Speaking more generally regarding how Black women are marked,
Hortense Spillers argues:

> Let's face it. I am a marked woman, but not everybody knows my name.
> "Peaches" and "Brown Sugar," "Sapphire" and "Earth Mother," "Aunty,"
> "Granny," God's "Holy Fool," a "Miss Ebony First," or "Black Woman at
> the Podium": I describe a locus of confounded identities, a meeting ground of
> investments and privations in the national treasury of rhetorical wealth. My
> country needs me, and if I were not here, I would have to be invented.[156]

Functioning as a site of rhetorical wealth, the Black female body inhabits a
social and discursive universe within which she is constantly *named*, always
already interpellated. As a "sexual abnormality," Ba(a)rtman(n)'s Black body
is a site of discursive formation that is structured through a larger historical
a priori that constitutes a white epistemic orientation to the Black (female)
body. In short, the Black female body as marked other is "trapped" within an
"essence" that functions as an important ontological register that constitutes
the Anglo-American/European as same/one. She is the exotic phantasm of
the white imaginary. Like the French colonial postcards depicting Algerian
women, a phenomenon that was created between 1900 and 1930, Ba(a)
rtman(n)'s Black body became the fantasized object of the Frenchman's
desire and power. In *The Colonial Harem*, Malik Alloula argues that it is
through the aperture of the French photographer's camera, which is actually
an extension of his voyeurism, that the Algerian, Oriental female became a
sexualized object, an effect of a "vast operation of systematic distortion."[157]
The postcard became a cheap opening (a form of penetrating) into the unveil-
ing (stripteasing) of the Orient. It became "the poor man's phantasm: for a
few pennies, display racks full of dreams. The postcard is everywhere, covering all the colonial space, immediately available to the tourist, the soldier, the
colonist."[158] The construction of Ba(a)rtman(n)'s body was quintessentially
the effect of a vast operation of distortion and discursive and nondiscursive

disciplinary power. Her body became the phantasm of French scopophilia. The perverse gaze directed at Ba(a)rtman(n) was a violent act of reduction and mutilation.

Not only is the Black female body deemed exotic, it is a site of contradictory investments, at once desirable and undesirable, known and unknown. It was important that Ba(a)rtman(n) was both an object of sexual interest and degraded. In short, to reconfigure her into "an object of derision, 'a spectacle, a clown', is to strip away her sexual appeal, albeit perverse and objectified, to the French male spectator, to reinforce and reinscribe Ba(a)rtman(n)'s position in the Manichaean social world as a primitive savage."[159] Hence, one consistent theme in the European imaginary has been that the Black female body is not "normal" (read: white, civilized). Indeed, it "represents the abnormal in Euro-centric discourse."[160]

Given the connections between anthropology and European expansionism, it is no wonder that the Black female body, and the Black body more generally, would come to signify the "abnormal," the "bizarre." V. Y. Mudimbe has described how the development of European anthropology was "a visible power-knowledge political system" that led to the "reification of the 'primitive.'"[161] As Jan Pieterse argues, "Anthropology, as the study of 'otherness,' never disengaged itself from Eurocentric narcissism."[162]

Capturing the gendered, racial, and sexual dimensions at stake in the production of the "truth" of Hottentot Venus, Tracy Sharpley-Whiting notes that Black women embodied "racial/sexual alterity, historically invoking *primal fears* and desire in European (French) men, represent ultimate difference (the *sexualized savage*) and inspire repulsion, attraction, and anxiety, which gave rise to the nineteenth-century collective French male imagination of Black Venus (*primitive narratives*)."[163] The production of the "truth" of Hottentot Venus is fundamentally linked to the white French gaze, which possesses the power "to unveil, 'to dissect', 'to lay bare' the unknown, in this case the black female. The gaze 'fixes' the black female in her place, steadies her, in order to decode and comfortably recode her into its own system of representations."[164] Sara(h) Ba(a)rtman(n) as Hottentot Venus is always already constrained within the anthropological text of a chain of signifiers. The chain of signifiers point back to their source: the white racist and racialized episteme. Ba(a)rtman(n) is caught within the dialectical structure of the same-other. "Anthropology, as well as missionary studies of primitive philosophies, are then concerned with the study of the distance from the Same to the Other."[165] One can only imagine the pain felt as Ba(a)rtman(n) measured her body by the constructions projected upon her from the unconscious/conscious European imaginary.

Within the context of early nineteenth-century French society, where Ba(a)rtman(n) was put on display for five years (which includes time in London[166])

for the French public to gaze upon, to gaze upon her big butt, French spectatorship was an active, constructive process that transmogrified Ba(a)
rtman(n)'s body. One might argue, "But they were only looking." However,
as I will continue to argue throughout this book, "the white racist gaze" is
itself a performance, an intervention, a violent form of marking, labeling
as different, freakish, animal-like. While in London (where her name was
changed from Sara[h] Baartman, which was given to her under Dutch colonial
rule in South Africa, to Sarah Bartmann), Ba(a)rtman(n), who was of African
Khoisan cultural identity, and who stood four feet six inches high, became the
"grotesque" prized object to be "seen" by parties of five and upward at 225
Piccadilly.[167] Ba(a)rtman(n) later found herself in Paris. Having parted with
her previous "guardians" (Alexander Dunlop and Hendrik Cezar) in London,
her new "guardian" was "a showman of wild animals named Réaux." Like a
monkey, Ba(a)rt-man(n) was fed small treats in order to entice her to dance
and sing, probably moving in such a way as to clearly exhibit her "large
cauldron pot."[168] For three francs one could either "see" the Hottentot Venus
or "at rue de Castiglione and for the same admission price, Réaux was also
exhibiting a five-year-old male rhinoceros."[169] One had a choice between two
wild and exotic animals. Both were oddities, placed on specular display, waiting to be visually dissected by the curious French onlookers.[170] Clearly, Ba(a)
rtman(n) was being violated despite her right to inviolability. Then, again,
"animals" would not have had such rights to inviolability.

Hottentot Venus became the other through which French gazers could
measure their own humanity and superiority. Echoing Spillers, the French
needed Ba(a)rtman(n). Similar to the empire or colonial French films of
the 1930s, Ba(a)rtman(n) was an outlet for the greatness of French national
identity. Sharpley-Whiting writes, "Like travelogues and documentary films,
elaborate feature films, depicting 'happy savages' and exotic and lush land-
scapes ripe for the taking, helped to garner support for continued colonial
expansion among the French spectators at home."[171] Indeed, countries such
as "Holland and Germany actually had government bureaus controlling and
directing the output and distribution of colonial propaganda films."[172] Thus,
the creation of Ba(a)rtman(n) and the colonial other is inherent in empire
building and imperialist domination. The sense of national failure (given
"France's defeat in the Franco-Prussian War and a not-so-stellar performance
during World War I"[173]), weakness, and overall fear regarding its status, the
"savage other" writ large (on the screen) became the medium in terms of
which France could eject all of its historico-psychodynamic crises. The very
act of gazing (even if sitting in the dark watching a film[174]) is itself a form
of visual penetration by the phallocentric hegemony of the colonizing gaze.
"The gaze is always bound up with power, domination, and eroticisation; it is
eroticizing, sexualized, and sexualizing."[175]

Sharpley-Whiting demonstrates how "seeing" Ba(a)rtman(n) is inextricably linked to discourses of power, dominance, and hierarchies. She is aware of the dialectical relationship between whiteness (as pure, good, innocent) compared to Blackness (as impure, bad, freakish, guilty). French Africanism was tied to the perception of the French as racially superior. This dialectic is clear where Sharpley-Whiting argues that "geographically, linguistically, culturally, and aesthetically, France, the French language, French culture, and Frenchwomen are privileged sites against which Ba(a)rtman(n), and hence Africa, are measured as primitive, savage, and grotesque."[176] Within the context of the French imaginary (a site where race, gender, and class intersect), "truth" about Black women, and Ba(a)rtman(n) in particular, was manufactured to foreclose any possibility of knowing Black women other than as prostitutes, sexually dangerous, diseased, and primitive. Historically, and I think this speaks to the pervasiveness of white male hegemony, late nineteenth-century science constructed *all women* as pathological (where this is linked to their sexuality), and that they could easily be "seen" as possessing the bestial characteristics of the Black female Hottentot. Within this context, it is also indicative that Sigmund Freud referred to adult white female sexuality as the "dark continent" of psychology.[177] Nevertheless, white women (read: civilized) were still superior to nonwhite women (read: savage).

Although she was not writing about the colonial context, it is difficult to resist referring to Toni Morrison's examination of a passage from Ernest Hemingway's *To Have and To Have Not*. The point that she raises speaks to the way in which white women, though historically oppressed by white men, receive an "existential wage," as it were, in virtue of being white when compared to Black/nonwhite women. The ideological significance of this example in relationship to Ba(a)rtman(n) is powerful. In a particular scene in the novel, the character Harry is making love to his wife, Marie, who asks:

"Listen, did you ever do it with a nigger wench?"
"Sure."
"What's it like?"
"Like nurse shark."

Morrison notes:

The strong notion here is that of a black female as the furthest thing from human, so far away as to be not even mammal but fish. The figure evokes a predatory, devouring eroticism and signals the antithesis to femininity, to nurturing, to nursing, to replenishment. In short, Harry's words mark something so brutal, contrary, and alien in its figuration that it does not belong to its own species and cannot be spoken of in language, in metaphor or metonmy, evocative of anything resembling the woman to whom Harry is speaking—his wife Marie.

The kindness he has done Marie is palpable. His projection of black female sexuality has provided her with solace, for which she is properly grateful. She responds to the kindness and giggles, "You're funny."[178]

"Hottentot maidens and Indian squaws are beautiful because of their comparability to Frenchwomen, the embodiment of beauty itself."[179] Prima facie, it would appear that to refer to Ba(a)rtman(n) as "Venus" might function as a term of praise. As Sharpley-Whiting points out, however, the use of the term "Venus" to describe the Black female body simply reinscribed the power of the *sameness* of European superiority.

> The Roman deity of beauty, Venus, was also revered as the protectress of Roman prostitutes, who in her honor erected Venus temples of worship. Within these temples, instruction in the arts of love was given to aspiring courtesans. It is the latter image of prostitution, sexuality, and danger that reproduced itself in narrative and was projected onto black female bodies. The projection of the Venus image, of prostitute proclivities, onto black female bodies, allows the French writer to maintain a position of moral, sexual, and racial superiority.[180]

To reiterate, the European has created a Manichaean world to buttress his/her own sense of who he/she is. The construction and deployment of essentialist discourse justified what the French "knew" to be true about Ba(a)rtman(n), and, hence, true about themselves. She was reduced to a wild animal. Just as the Black man was constructed as a walking penis, "most nineteenth-century French spectators did not view her as a person or even a human, but rather as a titillating curiosity, a collage of buttocks and genitalia."[181] During a three-day examination of Ba(a)rtman(n), with "a team of zoologists, anatomists, and physiologists," prominent naturalist Georges Cuvier also wanted to do a painting of Ba(a)rtman(n), just as a naturalist would want to get a better picture of the physiology and physiognomy of any other wild and exotic animal.[182] The idea here was to create a kind of physiological cartography of Ba(a)rtman(n), to map her primitive differences against the backdrop of the European subject.

"To see" her "big butt" (what was called steatopygia) and her other alleged hypertrophies (enlarged and "primitive" labia minoria) was *not* to "see" her at all. Concerning the labia minoria or the so-called Hottentot apron, "investigators of racial differences would spend the eighteenth century debating its anatomical specifications, producing in the absence of actual evidence a variety of phantasmatic representations."[183] Having the opportunity to examine Ba(a)rtman(n)'s body after she died, Cuvier's "objective scientific gaze" revealed the "truth" about her Black body. "As he reads and simultaneously writes a text on Ba(a)rt-man(n), the mystery of the dark continent unfolds."[184] In short, Ba(a)rtman(n)'s body "came into being" through the existence of categories that were ideologically fashioned. As John Bird and Simon Clarke note, "White people's phantasies about black sexuality, about bodies and biology in general, are fears that center around otherness, otherness that they themselves have created and brought into being."[185] Commenting specifically on the "objective" sketches made of Ba(a)rtman(n), Sharpley-Whiting argues that these "sketches allow the viewer to observe, document, and compare her various physiognomic and physiological differences, differences that vastly differentiate the Other from the European self."[186]

Ba(a)rtman(n)'s body *became* the distorted sexual *thing* that "it was" in terms of the paradigm/the epistemic regime through which she was "seen." Hence, the European power/knowledge position of spectatorship—mediated by certain atavistic assumptions, fears, and theories regarding polygenetic evolutionary development—gave rise to a historical accretion, making for the epistemic conditions under which Ba(a)rtman(n) "appeared." If we think of Ba(a)rtman(n) as the "referent" of the colonial gaze and colonial discourse, she might be said to have become Hottentot Venus qua phantasm, located within the discursive field of white representational power. Concerning the power of discursivity, Robert Young notes, "[Edward] Said's most significant argument about the discursive conditions of knowledge is that the texts of Orientalism 'can create not only knowledge but also the very reality they appear to describe.'"[187] The white colonist helped maintain and perpetuate the epistemic conditions according to which Hottentot Venus *became* an ideological emergent phenomenon, while maintaining distance as a mere observer. It is this distance that also implies a temporal rupture. As Fatimah Tobing Rony notes, "Johannes Fabian explains that anthropology is premised on the notions of time which deny the contemporaneity—what he calls coevalness—of the anthropologists and the people that he or she studies."[188]

In reference to Hottentot Venus, French male knowledge production and the perception of "reality" was negotiated within a context that ensured immunity to its own vested interests and desires. For this elaborate colonial form of vision to take place, cognitive agents operated under unacknowledged presuppositions that guaranteed the "veridicality" of their perception of the projected object of *spec*ulation. One might say that the use of the term "truth" when describing Hottentot Venus was not an epistemic indicator of correspondence, but a way of ideologically fixing belief within the entire colonial form of orientation with respect to the dark other. If the truth of one's beliefs were determined simply by stimulation from the external world,[189] then by simply opening one's eyes one could immediately "see" Hottentot Venus. However, to "see" Hottentot Venus requires nothing short of having lived within a particular language-game, a form of life that always already runs ahead, as it were, creating conditions of intelligibility that have already reconfigured the meaning of some *x*, for example, as that "dark continent." In this way, because

Hottentot Venus was not simply given, the construction of the phantasmatic object must involve a constant process of maintenance, not only at the level of projecting new information onto Ba(a)rtman(n), providing ad hoc explanations to sustain conceptual coherence but also to maintain ignorance regarding the role that one plays in the construction. As David Bloor reminds us, "Nature has power over us, but only [we] have authority."[190] Such authority signifies "the ways in which seemingly impartial, objective academic disciplines had in fact colluded with, and indeed been instrumental in, the production of actual forms of colonial subjugation and administration."[191]

To the extent that Ba(a)rtman(n) did not approximate the norm of European identity, which was also always already "seen" and "always constituted within, not outside, representation," she became ersatz, the *femme fatale*.[192] Drawing from the antagonistic, binary logic of Prospero/Caliban, A. R. JanMohamed notes:

> If . . . African natives can be collapsed into African animals and mystified still further as some magical essence of the continent, then clearly there can be no meeting ground, no identity, between the social, historical creatures of Europe and the metaphysical alterity of the Calibans and Ariels of Africa. If the differences between the Europeans and the natives are so vast, then clearly . . . the process of civilizing the natives can continue indefinitely. The ideological function of this mechanism, in addition to prolonging colonialism, is to dehistoricize and desocialize the conquered world, to present it as a meta-physical "fact of life," before which those who have fashioned the colonial world are themselves reduced to the role of passive spectators in a mystery not of their making.[193]

Sander Gilman asks, "How do we organize our perceptions of the world?"[194] This question is particularly important when it comes to my efforts to articulate the structure of the white gaze. Gilman, too, is concerned with the issue of how the world is "seen" from the perspective of the white gaze. Gilman ties perception, historical convention, and iconography together in relationship to the science of medicine, that science that helped "uncover" the "reality" of Ba(a)rtman(n)'s "inferiority"/"primitiveness" in the first place. Gilman writes:

> Medicine offers an especially interesting source of conventions since we do tend to give medical conventions special "scientific" status as opposed to the "subjective" status of the aesthetic conventions. But medical icons are no more "real" than "aesthetic" one's. Like aesthetic icons, medical icons may (or may not) be rooted in some observed reality. Like them, they are iconographic in that they represent these realities in a manner determined by the historical position of the observers, their relationship to their own time, and to the history of the conventions which they deploy.[195]

The (iconic) ideologically "seen" difference in the buttocks and genitalia of the Hottentot was very important "evidence" to justify drawing the distinction between lines of evolutionary development. Autopsies were performed, differences were "seen," and "facts" and "realities" suddenly "appeared." Gilman argues that the various vivisections performed on these women were ideologically linked to arguments for polygenesis. "If their sexual parts could be shown to be inherently different, this would be a sufficient sign that the blacks were a separate (and, needless to say, lower) race, as different from the European as the proverbial orangutan."[196]

Within a larger context, Africa was deemed that mysterious exotic dark continent, which "the light of white maleness illumines." This same light (read: reason) illuminated Ba(a)rtman(n)'s dark body, creating a historico-racial schematized body through which her alleged simian origins were "recognized." Sharpley-Whiting:

> Cuvier's description abounds with associations of black femaleness with bestiality and primitivism. Further, by way of contemplating Ba(a)rtman(n) as a learned, domesticated beast—comparing her to an orangutan—he reduces her facility with languages, her good memory, and musical inclinations to a sort of simian-like mimicry of the European race. By the nineteenth century, the ape, the monkey, and orangutan had become the interchangeable counterparts, the next of kin, to blacks in pseudoscientific and literary texts.[197]

The comparison of Ba(a)rtman(n) to an ape was central to the French imaginary concerning the bestial nature of Black women. The sexual appetites of Black people, more generally, were believed to have no end. Some French theorists even claimed that Black women copulated with apes.[198] Robyn Wiegman examines Edward Long's *History of Jamaica* (1774), which proposed a sexual compatibility between Hottentot women and apes. Long noted, "Ludicrous as the opinion may seem, I do not think that an oran-outang husband would be any dishonour to an Hottentot female."[199] After all, or so the myth goes, the Black female body is insatiable. The point here is that Ba(a)rtman(n) became the site for an entire range of sexual "perversions." Ba(a)rtman(n)'s "anomalous" labia were linked to the overdevelopment of the clitoris, which was linked to lesbian love. Hence, "the concupiscence of the black is thus associated also with the sexuality of the lesbian."[200]

The "truth" of the Black body is not outside the domain of white colonial *power*. White colonial power is exercised through its representational practices that actually *constrain* the Black body, passing over its embodied integrity and creating a chimera from its own imaginary. *Mythopoetic* constructions of Ba(a)rtman(n) were designed to "discover" the hidden "truths" about Blacks in general and Black women in particular. It was this "knowledge" that enabled Europeans/Anglo-Americans to repress many of their fears. "Sexual and racial differences," as Sharpley-Whiting argues with psychoanalytic insight, "inspires acute fears in the French male psyche. Fear is sublimated or screened through the desire to master or know this difference, resulting in the production of eroticized/exoticized narratives of truth."[201] Ba(a)rtman(n) was *codified* as the very epitome of unrestrained sexuality. Through various *rituals* (medically mapping her body while dead or alive, voyeuristically peeping and peering), Ba(a)rtman(n) was further "seen" as strange, a throwback to some earlier moment in evolutionary history. Ba(a)rtman(n) "became" what her gazers, operating in bad faith, wanted to "see." She was the victim of "a totalizing system of representation that allows the seen body to become the known body."[202] Through the process of "looking," which I have argued is a powerful act of construction, Ba(a)rtman(n) was *ontologized* into the Hottentot Venus. In "becoming" Hottentot Venus, Ba(a)rtman(n) underwent a process of dehumanization.

One can only imagine how Ba(a)rtman(n) felt as she learned to re-inhabit her body, to re-relate to it, as her consciousness of her body was shaped through the lens of a historico-racial schema. After all, everywhere she looked she found herself reconfigured by (heteronomous) gazes that returned her to herself, distorted and animal-like, imprisoned in a primitive essence. Within the semiotic social field of whiteness, she became an ontological cipher, waiting to be assigned meaning and identity from without, perhaps forever estranged from her African Khoisan identity. One can only imagine her traumatic experience of double consciousness, how she underwent the psychological duress of seeing herself through white symbols that ontologized her into the epitome of grotesqueness. Even at times when she found herself alone, the white gaze was no doubt operative. As she measured her soul by the tape of a white French world that gazed at/looked on her in amused contempt, desire, and pity, one wonders whether she had the dogged strength to keep herself from being torn asunder.[203] Possessing the dogged strength to avoid being torn asunder is an indispensable existential theme within the life of twenty-first-century Black America. We continue to fight against the violence of the white gaze. When Ba(a)rtman(n)'s remains returned to her home of South Africa, a place where she could find rest, she ceased to be a prisoner of that dehumanizing gaze.[204] In a beautifully written homecoming poem, "A Poem for Sarah Baartman," Diana Ferrus is clear that she engages in a poetics of intervention, re-presentation, combat, and freedom:

> I have come to wrench you away—away from the poking eyes of the man-made
> monster who lives in the dark with his racist clutches of imperialism,
> who dissects your body bit by bit, who likens your soul to that of satan
> and declared himself the ultimate God![205]

NOTES

1. Crispin Sartwell, *Act Like You Know: African-American Autobiography and White Identity* (Chicago: University of Chicago Press, 1998), 6.

2. Charles Johnson, "A Phenomenology of the Black Body," *Michigan Quarterly Review*, 32(4), 1993, 595–614, quotation on 600.

3. James Snead, *White Screens, Black Images: Hollywood from the Dark Side*, ed. Colin MacCabe and Cornel West (New York: Routledge, 1994), 4.

4. Lewis Gordon, "Africana Thought and African Diasporic Studies," *The Black Scholar*, 30(3–4), 2000–2001, 25–30, quotation on 25.

5. Frantz Fanon, *Black Skin, White Masks*, trans. by Charles Lam Markmann (New York: Grove Press, Inc., 1967), 112–13.

6. Fanon, *Black Skin, White Masks*, 111.

7. Jan Nederveen Pieterse, *White on Black: Images of Africa and Blacks in Western Popular Culture* (New Haven, CT: Yale University Press, 1992), 199.

8. I would like to thank philosopher Janine Jones for this concept.

9. Katy P. Sian, "Sara Ahmed," in *Conversations in Postcolonial Thought*, ed. Katy P. Sian (New York: Palgrave Macmillan, 2014), 25.

10. Hernan Vera and Andrew M. Gordon, *Screen Saviors: Hollywood Fictions of Whiteness* (Lanham, MD: Rowman & Littlefield Publishers, Inc., 2003), 3.

11. Sartwell, *Act Like You Know*, 11.

12. Manning Marable, "A Conversation with Ossie Davis," *Souls: A Critical Journal of Black Politics, Culture, and Society*, 2(3), 2000, 6–16, quotation on 9.

13. Marable, "Ossie Davis," 9.

14. Alexander G. Weheliye, *Phonographies: Grooves in Sonic Afro-Modernity* (Durham, NC: Duke University Press, 2005), 42.

15. William Stanley Braithwaite, "The Negro in American Literature," in *The New Negro: Voices of the Harlem Renaissance*, ed. Alain Locke (New York: Simon & Schuster, 1992), 36.

16. Fanon, *Black Skin, White Masks*, 111.

17. Paget Henry, "African and Afro-Caribbean Existential Philosophies," in *Existence in Black: An Anthology of Black Existential Philosophy*, ed. Lewis R. Gordon (New York: Routledge, 1997), 33.

18. Marable, "Ossie Davis," 9.

19. I delineate some of these discursive levels in Chapter 5.

20. I would like to thank Bettina Bergo for our conversation regarding this point.

21. Fanon, *Black Skin, White Masks*, 114.

22. Fanon, *Black Skin, White Masks*, 114–15.

23. Bettina G. Bergo, "'Circulez! Il n'y a rien à voir,' or, 'Seeing White': From Phenomenology to Psychoanalysis and Back," in *White on White/Black on Black*, ed. George Yancy (Lanham, MD: Rowman & Littlefield, 2005), 131.

24. Johnson, "A Phenomenology of the Black Body," 603.

25. Johnson, "A Phenomenology of the Black Body," 607.

26. Sartwell, *Act Like You Know*, 45.

27. Lewis R. Gordon, *Existentia Africana: Understanding Africana Existential Thought* (New York: Routledge, 2000), 76.

28. Johnson, "A Phenomenology of the Black Body," 606. Within the context of the history of African American philosophy, Johnson's article exploring a phenomenology of the Black body is an early and formative piece in the tradition of what is now termed Africana philosophy of existence. The article was written as early as 1975 and was subsequently published in the winter 1976 issue of *Ju-Ju: Research Papers in Afro-American Studies*. Johnson's article actually appeared prior to Thomas F. Slaughter Jr.'s "Epidermalizing the World: A Basic Mode of Being Black," which was included as a chapter in Leonard Harris' groundbreaking edited volume, *Philosophy Born of Struggle: Afro-American Philosophy from 1917* (Dubuque, IA: Kendall/Hunt, 1983).

29. Fanon, *Black Skin, White Masks*, 112.

30. Fanon, *Black Skin, White Masks*, 192.

31. Fanon, *Black Skin, White Masks*, 110.

32. Fanon, *Black Skin, White Masks*, 116.

33. Fanon, *Black Skin, White Masks*, 112.

34. Fanon, *Black Skin, White Masks*, 110, 111.

35. Fanon, *Black Skin, White Masks*, 111.

36. Fanon, *Black Skin, White Masks*, 109.

37. Fanon, *Black Skin, White Masks*, 112.

38. Fanon, *Black Skin, White Masks*, 116.

39. Fanon, *Black Skin, White Masks*, 112. Note that the expression "sho' good eaten'" is an English translation of the so-called African French "Y a bon banania." "Y a bon" stands for "C'est bon." In this quote, Fanon is making an important reference to the ways in which Blacks were caricatured not only in the French imaginary, but for purposes of selling French products. "Sho' good eaten'" refers to Bonhomme Banania, a French breakfast food consisting of sugar, banana flour, and cocoa. The caption consisted of a picture of a Senegalese, with a broad smile, eating the Banania. Whether or not the image was originally intended for purposes of caricature, it is impossible to miss the "smiling, contented darky" that the image depicts. The Senegalese man appears nonthreatening and exemplifies the close association of Blacks with the process of serving (whites) food. Think here of the image of Uncle Ben used in the United States to sell rice. Political acts often come in the form of very small quotidian decisions. When I'm shopping for syrup, I consciously decide against purchasing the bottle of syrup that is constructed in the image of the so-called Aunt Jemima figure. Although her frozen smile is inviting and sweet, it belies the material and ideological conditions that positioned Black women in subservient roles. *Her smile is not for me!*

40. Fanon, *Black Skin, White Masks*, 113. Lewis Gordon insightfully points out that Fanon deliberately uses the ambiguous French word *nègre*, which means both "Negro" and "nigger." See Lewis Gordon, "Through the Zone of Nonbeing: A Reading of *Black Skin, White Masks* in Celebration of Fanon's Eightieth Birthday," *CLR James Journal: A Special Issue: Frantz Fanon's 80th Birthday*, 11(1) (Summer 2005), 1–43, quotation on 22.

41. Fanon, *Black Skin, White Masks*, 113–14.

42. Patrick Brantlinger, "Victorians and Africans: The Genealogy of the Myth of the Dark Continent," in *"Race," Writing, and Difference*, ed. Henry Louis Gates, Jr. (Chicago: University of Chicago Press, 1985), 203.

43. Georg Wilhelm Friedrich Hegel, "Geographical Basis of World History," in *Race and the Enlightenment: A Reader*, ed. Emmanuel Chukwudi Eze (Malden, MA: Blackwell Publishers, 1997), 134.

44. Hegel, "Geographical Basis of World History," 133.

45. Fanon, *Black Skin, White Masks*, 112.

46. Brent R. Henze, "Who Says Who Says? The Epistemological Grounds for Agency in Liberatory Projects," in *Reclaiming Identity: Realist Theory and the Predicament of Postmodernism*, ed. Paula M. L. Moya and Michael R. Hames-García (Berkeley: University of California Press, 2000), 238.

47. David R. Roediger reveals how something as "benign" as playing a child's game is shaped through the white racist imaginary. Though he did not know any Blacks personally and lived in an all-white town, he notes: "I learned absolutely no lore of my German ancestry and no more than a few meaningless snatches of Irish songs, but missed little of racist folklore. Kids came to know the exigencies of chance by chanting 'Eeny, meany, miney, mo/Catch a nigger by the toe' to decide teams and first batters in sport. We learned that life—and fights—were not always fair: 'Two against one, nigger's fun.' We learned not to loaf: 'Last one in is a nigger baby.' We learned to save, for to buy ostentatious or too quickly was to be 'nigger rich'. We learned not to buy clothes that were a bright 'nigger green'. Sexuality and blackness were of course thoroughly confused." See David R Roediger, *The Wages of Whiteness: Race and the Making of the American Working Class*, rev. ed. (New York: Verso, 1999), 3. I recently learned that white children as far away as Australia still use the chant, "Eeny, meany, miney, mo/Catch a nigger by the toe."

48. Shannon Sullivan, *Revealing Whiteness: The Unconscious Habits of Racial Privilege* (Bloomington: Indiana University Press, 2006), 188.

49. While it is true that the young boy has come to internalize a form of negrophobia, I would not claim that he is in bad faith.

50. Linda Martín Alcoff, "Toward a Phenomenology of Racial Embodiment," *Radical Philosophy: A Journal of Socialist and Feminist Philosophy*, 95 (May/June 1999), 15–26, quotation on 21.

51. Lillian Smith, *Killers of the Dream* (New York: W. W. Norton & Company, 1994), 84.

52. Smith, *Killers of the Dream*, 27.

53. Shannon Sullivan, "The Racialization of Space: Toward a Phenomenological Account of Raced and Antiracist Spatiality," in *The Problems of Resistance: Studies in Alternate Political Cultures*, ed. Steve Martinot and Joy James (Amherst, NY: Humanity Books, 2001), 89.

54. Smith, *Killers of the Dream*, 12–13. Edmund Burke would have us believe that Blackness intrinsically causes some level of terror in the perceiver. Based upon a story given by the English surgeon William Cheselden (1666–1709) of a fourteen-year-old boy who gains sight for the very first time and experiences horror at the sight of a Black woman, Burke maintains that blackness and darkness *naturally* cause pain and horror in the perceiver (see http://www.bartleby.com/24/2/415.html). According to Elizabeth A. Bohls, "The boy's fear was not caused by association, Burke argues—since he had no time to accumulate visual

associations—but by human physiology, nature itself. For Burke as for [Comte de] Buffon, a non-European becomes an aesthetic object, while the subject who sets the standards and judges aesthetic value is white and European. Burke's negro woman, like Frankenstein's creature, 'naturally' inspires a negative aesthetic response in a 'standard' subject. The doctrine of the standard of tastes forms part of an aesthetic ideology that extrapolates the viewpoint of an educated white European man to a universal standard and contributes to justifying colonialism and slavery." See Elizabeth A. Bohls' "Standards of Taste, Discourses of 'Race', and the Aesthetic Education of a Monster: Critique of Empire in *Frankenstein*," http://www.english. upenn.edu/Projects/knarf/Articles/bohls.html (assessed, May 17, 2016)

55. Hubert L. Dreyfus, *Being-in-the-World: A Commentary on Heidegger's* Being and Time, *Division I* (Cambridge, MA: MIT Press, 1991), 85.

56. Ernesto Laclau and Chautal Mouffe, *Hegemony and Socialist Strategy* (London: Verso, 1985), 108.

57. Fanon, *Black Skin, White Masks*, 110–11.

58. Alcoff, "Toward a Phenomenology of Racial Embodiment," 20.

59. Fanon, *Black Skin, White Masks*, 111.

60. Fanon, *Black Skin, White Masks*, 11.

61. Lewis Gordon, *Her Majesty's Other Children: Sketches of Racism from a Neocolonial Age* (Lanham, MD: Rowman & Littlefield, 1997), 38.

62. See   http://ufdcimages.uflib.ufl.edu/UF/E0/00/73/02/00001/hwangbo_ k.pdf, p. 1 (assessed, May 17, 2016)

63. Sara Ahmed, "A Phenomenology of Whiteness," *Feminist Theory*, 8(2), 2007, 149–68, quote on 161; http://fty.sagepub.com/content/8/2/149 (assessed, May 17, 2016)

64. Audre Lorde, *Sister Outsider: Essays & Speeches*, News Foreword by Cheryl Clarke (Berkeley, CA: Crossing Press, 1984), 147.

65. Lorde, *Sister Outsider*, 147.

66. Lorde, *Sister Outsider*, 147.

67. Lorde, *Sister Outsider*, 147–8.

68. I would like to thank Eric Boynton and Peter Capretto for allowing me to reuse the Lorde example. I theorize the experience that Lorde undergoes within a larger chapter for their edited book on trauma.

69. Ralph Ellison, *Invisible Man* (1947; reprint, New York: Vintage Books, 1995), 3.

70. Ellison, *Invisible Man*, 3.

71. Fanon, *Black Skin, White Masks*, 139.

72. Ellison, *Invisible Man*, 3.

73. Gordon, *Her Majesty's Other Children*, 37.

74. Ellison, *Invisible Man*, 4.

75. Ellison, *Invisible Man*, 5.

76. Ellison, *Invisible Man*, 19.

77. Clyde Taylor, "The Re-birth of the Aesthetic Cinema," in *The Birth of whiteness: Race and the Emergence of U.S. Cinema*, ed. Daniel Bernardi (New Brunswick, NJ: Rutgers University Press, 1996), 27.

78. Ellison, *Invisible Man*, 18.
79. Sartwell, *Act Like You Know*, 109.
80. Ellison, *Invisible Man*, 517.
81. Ellison, *Invisible Man*, 522.
82. Ellison, *Invisible Man*, 518.
83. Ellison, *Invisible Man*, 520.
84. Ellison, *Invisible Man*, 521.
85. Ellison, *Invisible Man*, 520.
86. Ellison, *Invisible Man*, 521.
87. Ellison, *Invisible Man*, 522.
88. Given the Brotherhood's pro-proletarian emphasis, and its stress upon a classless society, one might argue that Ellison's invisible man's inner contradictions and existential plight within the context of his "raced" invisibility transcends the history of class conflict. I say this with some hesitation given my understanding of Ellison's ambivalent "involvement" with the Communist Party (CP).
89. Ellison, *Invisible Man*, 341.
90. Ellison, *Invisible Man*, 303.
91. Ellison, *Invisible Man*, 303.
92. Ellison, *Invisible Man*, 196.
93. Ellison, *Invisible Man*, 202.
94. Ellison, *Invisible Man*, 217.
95. Ellison, *Invisible Man*, 3.
96. Brantlinger, "Victorians and Africans," 185.
97. In his controversial book, Bruce Perry notes that his real name was Richard Kaminska. See Perry's *Malcolm: The Life of a Man Who Changed Black America* (Barrytown, NY: Station Hill Press, 1991), 42.
98. Malcolm X, with Alex Haley, *The Autobiography of Malcolm X* (New York: Ballantine Books, 1965), 36.
99. Drucilla Cornell, *Transformations: Recollective Imagination and Sexual Difference* (New York: Routledge, 1993), 125.
100. Malcolm X, *Autobiography*, 37.
101. Malcolm X, *Autobiography*, 29.
102. Malcolm X, *Autobiography*, 29.
103. Weheliye, *Phonographies*, 42.
104. The quotation is from Fanon, *Black Skin, White Masks*, 116.
105. Perry, *Malcolm*, 42.
106. Fanon, *Black Skin, White Masks*, 116.
107. Sartwell, *Act Like You Know*, 90.
108. Malcolm X, *Autobiography*, 26.
109. Malcolm X, *Autobiography*, 27.
110. Malcolm X, *Autobiography*, 54.
111. Imam Benjamin Karim, ed., *The End of White World Supremacy: Four Speeches by Malcolm X* (New York: Arcade Publishing, 1971), 54.
112. W. E. B. Du Bois, *The Souls of Black Folk* (1903; reprint, New York: New American Library, 1982), 44.

113. Smith, *Killers of the Dream*, 90.

114. Patricia J. Williams, *Seeing a Color-Blind Future: The Paradox of Race* (New York: Farrar, Straus and Giroux, 1997), 7.

115. John T. Warren, "The Social Drama of a 'Rice Burner': A (Re)Constitution of Whiteness," in *Western Journal of Communication*, 65(20), 2001, 184–205, quotation on 190.

116. Keep in mind that this act should not be deemed an aberration, a single, isolated incident. It is the result of a larger process, no matter how subtle the forms of acculturation. Hence the newcomer's performance of the glance is an instantiation of a larger system of white forms of policing Black bodies that secure white power and privilege.

117. Williams, *Seeing a Color-Blind Future*, 7.

118. Smith, *Killers of the Dream*, 90.

119. Du Bois, *Souls of Black Folk*, 45.

120. Quotation from Kirt H. Wilson, "Towards a Discursive Theory of Racial Identity: *The Souls of Black Folk* as a Response to Nineteenth-Century Biological Determinism," *Western Journal of Communication*, 63(2), 1999, 193–215, quotation on 205.

121. Du Bois, "Conservation of the Races," in *W.E.B. Du Bois: A Reader*, ed. David Levering Lewis (New York: Henry Holt and Company, 1995), 24.

122. Du Bois, "Conservation of the Races," 24.

123. Frantz Fanon, *The Wretched of the Earth* (New York: Grove Press, 1963), 250.

124. Martin Luther King, Jr., "Where Do We Go from Here," in *A Testament of Hope: The Essential Writings and Speeches of Martin Luther King, Jr.*, ed. James M. Washington (New York: HarperSanFrancisco, 1986), 588. Although King says "every man," within the overall context of this quote, he is, as with Du Bois and Fanon, specifically pointing to the profound sense of self-interrogation that Black people undergo within a life-world saturated with anti-Black racism.

125. Rene Descartes, *Meditations on First Philosophy* (1641; reprint, Indianapolis: Hackett Publishing Company, 1993), 20.

126. Stuart Hall, "Cultural Identity and Diaspora," in *Colonial Discourse and Post-Colonial Theory: A Reader*, ed. Patrick Williams and Laura Chrisman (New York: Columbia University Press, 1994), 395.

127. Du Bois, *Souls of Black Folk*, 43–4.

128. Du Bois, *Souls of Black Folk*, 43.

129. W. E. B. Du Bois, "The Souls of White Folk," in *W. E. B. Du Bois: A Reader*, ed. David Levering Lewis (New York: Henry Holt and Company, 1995), 454.

130. Du Bois, "Souls of White Folk," 456.

131. Du Bois, "Souls of White Folk," 453.

132. Du Bois, "Souls of White Folk," 453.

133. Ronald E. Chennault, "Giving Whiteness a Black Eye: An Interview with Michael Eric Dyson," in *White Reign: Deploying Whiteness in America*, ed. Joe L. Kincheloe, Shirley R. Steinberg, Nelson, M. Rodriguez, and Ronald E. Chennault (New York: St. Martin's Press, 1998), 305.

134. Du Bois, "Souls of White Folk," 453.

135. Du Bois, "Souls of White Folk," 454.
136. Du Bois, "Souls of White Folk," 454.
137. Du Bois, "Souls of White Folk," 454.
138. Du Bois, "Souls of White Folk," 454.
139. Du Bois, "Souls of White Folk," 455.
140. "The Coming of John," which is an important chapter in Du Bois's *The Souls of Black Folk*, is a story of John Jones who left his hometown in Altamaha, Georgia, to be educated. He was always known as an excellent worker in the fields. His mother, Peggy, wanted him to be educated. He went away to school and passionately embraced the areas of astronomy, history, and ethics. Upon his return home, he wanted to open a school for Black folk, but was told that he must only teach them how to be submissive. John had higher aspirations. He taught them about the French Revolution. Whites in the small town were furious, particularly a white racist magistrate, Judge Henderson. The school was closed and the children forced to leave. As the story progresses, Judge Henderson's son, whose name is also John, attempts to force himself physically upon John Jones' sister, Jennie. John sees this and kills Judge Henderson's son. The story ends with John looking bravely toward the sea, as the Judge and a white lynch mob ride toward him. Du Bois appears to define the notion of double consciousness in positive terms here. Had John remained ignorant of his situation, he would not have realized there was a world of white oppression and how that world functioned to keep him ignorant and oppressed. Thus developing a double consciousness, although resulting in unhappiness and ultimately death, John is empowered. Du Bois appears to be defining the state of unhappiness felt within the "veil" in terms that are empowering (Du Bois, "Souls of White Folk," 455).
141. Du Bois, "Souls of White Folk," 455.
142. Weheliye, *Phonographies*, 43.
143. Du Bois, "Souls of White Folk," 455.
144. Du Bois, "Souls of White Folk," 455.
145. Quoted in Shannon Sullivan's "Remembering the Gift: W. E. B. Du Bois on the Unconscious and Economic Operations of Racism," *Transactions of the Charles S. Peirce Society*, 39(2), 2003, 205–25, quotation on 218. Sullivan argues convincingly that Du Bois's thinking regarding racism underwent a radical transformation from an Enlightenment, liberal approach to one sensitive to Freud's understanding of the unconscious and a pragmatist understanding of habit.
146. Sullivan, "Racialization of Space," 100.
147. Quoted in Sullivan, "Remembering the Gift," 218.
148. Du Bois, "Souls of White Folk," 456.
149. Du Bois, "Souls of White Folk," 456.
150. Du Bois, "Souls of White Folk," 461.
151. Du Bois, "The Superior Race," in Lewis, *W. E. B. Du Bois: A Reader*, 472.
152. My decision to fragment her name thus functions visually to represent the various ways in which Bartmann's identity and body became a site of fragmentation and mutilation. To some extent, this form of nomination avoids the many visual representations of the so-called Venus Hottentot that reinscribe her body as the "looked at" by the

objectifying gaze. When I share these visual images with my students, I am often filled with the desire to demand that my students rip up the images as an act of deflecting the gaze or putting the gaze out of play to the extent to which that might be possible. I thank Laura Callanan for the deployment of this strategy, which she uses in her important book *Deciphering Race: White Anxiety, Racial Conflict, and the Turn to Fiction in Mid-Victorian English Prose* (Columbus: The Ohio University Press, 2006), 142–71.

153. Peter McLaren, "Whiteness is . . . : The Struggle for Postcolonial Hybridity," in Kincheloe et al., *White Reign*, 66.

154. Weheliye, *Phonographies*, 40.

155. Fanon, *Black Skin, White Masks*, 111.

156. Hortense J. Spillers, "Mama's Baby, Papa's Maybe: An American Grammar Book," *Diacritics* (Summer 1987), 65–81, quotation on 65.

157. Malek Alloula, *The Colonial Harem*, trans. Myrna Godzich and Wlad Godzich (Minneapolis: University of Minnesota Press, 1986), 4.

158. Alloula, *Colonial Harem*, 4.

159. T. Denean Sharpley-Whiting, *Black Venus: Sexualized Savages, Primal Fears, and Primitive Narratives in French* (Durham, NC: Duke University Press, 1999).

160. Sharpley-Whiting, *Black Venus*, 7.

161. V. Y. Mudimbe, *The Invention of Africa, Gnosis, Philosophy, and the Order of Knowledge* (Bloomington: Indiana University Press, 1988), 16–17.

162. Pieterse, *White on Black*, 221.

163. Sharpley-Whiting, *Black Venus*, 6.

164. Sharpley-Whiting, *Black Venus*, 5–6.

165. Mudimbe, *Invention of Africa*, 81.

166. She was displayed from 1810 to 1815.

167. Saartjie literally means "little Sarah" and Baartman "bearded man." Sharpley-Whiting, *Black Venus*, 18.

168. Sharpley-Whiting, *Black Venus*, 18.

169. Sharpley-Whiting, *Black Venus*, 19.

170. Robyn Wiegman, *American Anatomies: Theorizing Race and Gender* (Durham, NC: Duke University Press, 1995), 59.

171. Sharpley-Whiting, *Black Venus*, 4.

172. Fatimah Tobing Rony, *The Third Eye: Race, Cinema, and Ethnographic Spectacle* (Durham, NC: Duke University Press, 1996), 85.

173. Sharpley-Whiting, *Black Venus*, 4.

174. Think here of filmic pornography.

175. Sharpley-Whiting, *Black Venus*, 34.

176. Sharpley-Whiting, *Black Venus*, 37.

177. Sander L. Gilman, "Black Bodies, White Bodies: Toward an Iconography of Female Sexuality in Late Nineteenth-Century Art, Medicine, and Literature," *Critical Inquiry*, 12 (Autumn 1985), 204–242, quotation on 237.

178. Toni Morrison, *Playing in the Dark: Whiteness and the Literary Imagination* (New York: Vintage Books, 1993), 85.

179. Sharpley-Whiting, *Black Venus*, 35.

180. Sharpley-Whiting, *Black Venus*, 7.

181. Pieterse, *White on Black*, 175; Sharpley-Whiting, *Black Venus*, 17.

182. Sharpley-Whiting, *Black Venus*, 22.

183. Wiegman, *American Anatomies*, 58.

184. Sharpley-Whiting, *Black Venus*, 28–9.

185. John Bird and Simon Clarke, "Racism, Hatred, and Discrimination through the Lens of Projective Identification," *Journal for the Psychoanalysis of Culture & Society*, 4(2), 1999, 332–5, quotation on 333.

186. Sharpley-Whiting, *Black Venus*, 23.

187. Robert J. C. Young, *White Mythologies* (New York: Routledge, 2004), 168.

188. Rony, *Third Eye*, 10.

189. Peter T. Manicas refers to this position as "epistemological individualism." See his *A History and Philosophy of the Social Sciences* (New York: Basil Blackwell, 1987), 263.

190. David Bloor, *Knowledge of Social Imagery* (London: Routledge and Kegan Paul, 1976), 36.

191. Robert J. C. Young, *Colonial Desire: Hybridity in Theory, Culture and Race* (New York: Routledge, 1995), 159–160.

192. Stuart Hall, "Cultural Identity and Diaspora," 392.

193. Abdul R. JanMohamed, "The Economy of the Manichean Allegory: The Function of Racial Difference in Colonialist Literature," in *"Race," Writing, and Difference*, ed. Henry Louis Gates, Jr. (Chicago: The University of Chicago Press, 1986), 87.

194. Gilman, "Black Bodies, White Bodies," 223.

195. Gilman, "Black Bodies, White Bodies," 224.

196. Gilman, "Black Bodies, White Bodies," 235.

197. Sharpley-Whiting, *Black Venus*, 24.

198. Gilman, "Black Bodies, White Bodies," 231.

199. Edward Long, quoted in Wiegman, *American Anatomies*, 57.

200. Gilman, "Black Bodies, White Bodies," 237.

201. Sharpley-Whiting, *Black Venus*, 7.

202. Sharpley-Whiting, *Black Venus*, 22.

203. T. Denean Sharpley-Whiting noted in personal correspondence (March 2005) that there is some evidence that Ba(a)rtman(n) did enact a form of agency when she did not want to pose for the assembly at the Museum of Man. Apparently, she resisted removing the apron/tablier that covered her. Sharpley-Whiting also notes that Ba(a)rtman(n) then hid her genitalia between her thighs, avoiding having to lay herself bare before the white gaze. Rather than equate this with Ba(a)rtman(n)'s feelings of modesty, Georges Cuvier, given the racist paradigm that depicted African women as always already immodest, interprets her behavior as indicative of shame rather than pride.

204. The reader will note that Ba(a)rtman(n)'s skeleton, genitalia, and other body parts were still on display in 1974 at the Museum of Man in Paris. Through political protest and years of negotiation, in 2002 Ba(a)rtman(n)'s remains were brought back

to South Africa where she was born. The government of South Africa, after strongly criticizing England and France for its role in dehumanizing Ba(a)rtman(n) as an evolutionary anomaly, provided Ba(a)rtman(n) with a proper burial.

205. South African Government Information, "Sarah Bartmann Interment Ceremony," April 5, 2008, http://www.info.gov.za/events/2002/sarah.htm#tribute

Chapter 4

The Agential Black Body

Resisting the Black Imago in the White Imaginary

Disalienation will come into being [for Blacks] through their refusal to accept the present as definitive.

—Frantz Fanon

The history of Black resistance is a complex narrative, particularly as this history is tied to the context of a white racist episteme, which is a way of organizing the world politically, economically, and metaphysically. After all, it is the dominant white culture's view that Black people have no role to play in "the world of meaning as meaning-makers."[1] That is not a claim that has only political implications, but one that has metaphysical implications; it is a claim that speaks to the Black body's "nature" as being ontologically "insignificant," "subhuman," removed from the realm of semiotic and symbolic. Frantz Fanon was painfully aware of the hegemony and misanthropy of white racist ideology with regard to the denial of Black peoples' subjectivity and humanity. "All I wanted was to be a man among other men," he noted. "I wanted to come lithe and young into the world that was ours and to help to build it together."[2] However, within the lived or phenomenological domain of anti-Black racism, Fanon was expected to live, to think, to feel, to exist, *to be* "like a nigger."[3] Within the context of an anti-Black racist world, the lived experience of the Black is under the constant threat of being collapsed into the phenomenological or lived experience of the nigger. Once collapsed into the one-dimensional mode of niggerhood, as it were, it is easy to undergo a certain ontological resignation, a capitulation in the face of a reality whose past, present, and future seem fixed and stacked against any possibility of historical breach. For Fanon, "transformation . . . requires some-thing like a critical resistance to the dominating [white] episteme—an active denial of the mythos that intervenes in the formation of body-images."[4]

Historically, "the imago of the [Black] in the European mind" has involved a process of discursive and material violence.[5] Whether discursive or extra-discursive, this violence was designed originally to aid in breaking the Black body's claim to dignity and humanity. The background of this violence was shaped by the metaphysical assumption that whiteness signified humanity as such. As I have argued, the Black body, through the hegemony of the white gaze, undergoes a phenomenological return that leaves it distorted and fixed as a preexisting essence. The Black body becomes a "prisoner" of an imago—an elaborate distorted image of the Black, an image whose reality is held together through white bad faith and projection—that is ideologically orchestrated to leave no trace of its social and historical construction. The aim is to foreclose any possibility of slippage between the historically imposed imago and how the Black body lives its reality as fixed. But like the white body, the Black body is never simply pregiven. While "history has been terribly unkind to the African body," the Black body has, within the context of its tortuous sojourn through the crucible of American and European history, been a site of discursive, symbolic, ontological, and existential battle.[6] If the Black body's metastability had reached a point of ontological closure as a result of the power of the distorted imago projected from the white imaginary, there would have been no history of the Black body engaged in struggle and transformation. Blacks have struggled mightily to disrupt, redefine, and transcend white fictions. They have struggled with profound issues around identity and place. Yet Black people have always struggled to make a way out of no way, using the resources they had available. Although I will return to a discussion of the Middle Passage in chapter 5, one might look at the movement through the Middle Passage to the so-called New World as a medium through which an especially dynamic and difficult challenge to define and redefine a narrative of Black identity emerged. This narrative tells a complex story of the Black experience, one that is shaped through syncretism, bricolage, and the blending of cultural, epistemological, and ontological retentions with ever-new horrific and challenging experiences. There is no aim here to celebrate or recuperate an "authentic" identity qua essence or to ground a sense of identity in fixed metanarratives. There is the effort, however, to make sense of one's existence within the context of lived history, one that recognizes and acknowledges the reality of fissures in collective and individual identity formation and refuses to romanticize origins or points of historical continuity. Nevertheless, it is my sense that Black identity-talk within the context of North America must begin from below; that is, one must begin with the existential terror of whiteness faced by Black people and realize that Black people continue to define and redefine themselves through the deployment of conceptual and affective resources that are themselves *historical*.

In *A Tempest*, which is Aimé Césaire's version of Shakespeare's *The Tempest*, the Black body's resistance is captured through the voice of a transformed Caliban as he refuses to live by the dehumanizing imago constructed through ontological, epistemological, and aesthetic orders that privilege Prospero. Césaire's Caliban has become cognizant of the source of his double consciousness; he is now able to nihilate the given of Prospero's world and to resist the existential phenomenological problem of corporeal malediction. At the level of the gaze, he challenges the relational asymmetry of which he has been a victim.

> Prospero, you're a great magician:
> you're an old hand at deception.
> And you lied to me so much,
> about the world, about myself
> that you ended up by imposing on me
> an image of myself:
> underdeveloped, in your words, undercompetent
> that's how you made me see myself !
> And I hate that image . . .
> But now I know you, you old cancer,
> And I also know myself !
> And I know that one day
> my bare fist, just that,
> will be enough to crush your world!
> The old world is crumbling down![7]

The significant point here is that the needed slippage did occur; indeed, the Black body's history in the "New World" has been a history of resistance against whiteness as a lie. But what if the very structure of whiteness is a lie? What would telling the truth do to its "integrity"? Wouldn't the truth about whiteness shatter its being? And if Black bodies are conveyors of this truth, doesn't this mean that the Black body threatens whiteness in ways that white people would rather fictionalize?

We should keep in mind that even as it is important to telescope and valorize the significance of the history of Black resistance, this history does not deny the Black body's history of self-hatred, its passing for white, and its history of accommodation.[8] In other words, "resistance is cardinal and crucial to any description, definition, and interpretation of African American culture. . . . [That culture] in its full substance and scope is more complex than a singular thrust in the monodirection of resistance."[9] Keeping this caveat in mind, despite the power of white discursive disciplinary control and physical brutality, the Black body has historically disrupted the reduction of its being to that of a *thing*. To comprehend the Black body as a site of resistance, it is important to understand that the body "is not what it is and it is not yet what it will become."[10] In short, the Black body (as with the white body) is a *process*. It might be argued that the Black body/embodied Black existence in relation to the white gaze is ontologically excessive, something more than the white gaze is capable of nullifying through its power. Of course, to refer to the Black body as a site of resistance, I am referring to Black *embodied* existence as *socially situated*, that perspective from which the embodied self is capable of recognizing the possibility of reconfiguring or overcoming a set of circumstances. Resistance is linked to a level of comprehension of one's social conditions and not simply a question of psychological renewal. Resistance involves seeing through the "impersonal" discursive practices of whites, rejecting the "nature-like" constructions of social reality that threaten Blacks' lives, and transforming the debilitating psyche and the physical conditions in terms of which they have been imprisoned.[11] As Paget Henry notes, "Agency against these normative and institutional structures require[s] the decoding of their impersonal, nature-like appearance and their rewriting in codes that reveal their roots in ordinary communication and social action."[12] Indeed, Black resistance is a form of decoding of the ideological prison house of racist discourse, a discourse that "operates in the name of values" that valorize whiteness and dehumanize Black people.[13] Of course, such values assume the status of neutrality so as to appear natural.

I argue that Black resistance, as a mode of decoding, is simultaneously a process of recoding Black embodied existence through processes of opposition and *affirmation*. According to bell hooks, "Opposition is not enough. In that vacant space after one has resisted there is still the necessity to become—to make oneself anew."[14] While I agree with hooks's claim that opposition is certainly not enough, I question her thesis that there is a "vacant space after one has resisted." Indeed, I argue that resistance can occupy that "vacant space" and that the process of becoming and making oneself anew has already been enacted, though time is certainly needed to nourish and further develop the process of becoming and remaking the self anew. Rather than asking what exists on the other side of resistance, one might explore the affirmative dimensions of what is already embedded within resistance itself. The moment of *resistance*, in other words, *is* the moment of *becoming*, of being made *anew*. And while "human transcendence always involves becoming . . . , self-creation for an oppressed people whose transcendence is denied often finds its founding moments in resistance."[15]

Within a context where Black bodies are constantly under discursive and physical erasure, to resist (*re-sistere*), "to take a stand," is linked, existentially, to taking up a different *project*, that is, not settling for an anti-Black project superimposed by the white other. Resisting is not simply limited to saying, "No, I refuse!" It is not simply a negative process. Resistance is an instantiation of affirmation. Within the context of white mythmaking regarding the "docility" and "subhumanity" of the Black body and the refusal to grant the Black body a perspective on the world, taking a stand demonstrates and affirms the existential and ontological force of having a perspective, a subjectivity. Indeed, the moment of Black resistance calls into question the philosophical anthropological assumptions of white racism, assumptions that deny the reality and complexity of Black self-determination, self-reflexivity, and interiority. Black resistance, then, is a profoundly embodied *human* act of epistemological re-cognition, an affirmation that carries with it an ontological repositioning of the being of Black embodiment as a significant site of discursive (and material) self-possession.[16]

We typically think of resistance in terms of opposing an external force, which suggests a reaction couched in negation. On my interpretation, under colonial/neocolonial conditions or enslavement, when Black bodies resist, they affirm. Resistance embodies onto existential resources that might be articulated in the following forms: *I am*, *I exist*, I recognize myself as taking a stand against the white racist episteme that has attempted to render void my capacity to imagine other/alternative possibilities of being. However, it is not as if the Black body opposes, or resists, and then passively waits around, as it were, for an inventory of possible values to affirm. To take this interpretation of resistance even further, I argue that at the moment of resistance there is an instantiation of an axiological moment that grounds the Black body with value—a value that whites have historically denied.

It is not through resistance that the Black body "founds" a new set of values *ex nihilo*. Rather, even if Blacks "lean into," "take up," Anglo-American and European values of freedom, for example, the Black body affirms itself through a set of values historically denied to it. Of course, it is important to note that as Blacks take up those values of freedom, such values must be dislodged from various misanthropic racist presumptions. For example, Blacks must reject a form of freedom predicated upon the denial of the freedom of others, that is, where the social expression of freedom of whites, for instance, is structurally dependent upon the oppression of the Black body or defined parasitically in relationship to the oppression of the Black body. After all, "these values are still the 'values secreted by his masters.'"[17] The very embryonic moment of "leaning into" a set of values already presupposes that a certain level of agency is operating in the name of a set of affirmative values. Within the white colonial context, however, affirming values must not reinscribe white colonial values that are symptomatic of "the pathology of colonization."[18] Though I will not explore this issue within this text, it is important to engage the issue of whether it is possible to affirm values of

Black freedom that do not mimic white neoliberal conceptions of freedom. What if neoliberal conceptions of freedom are inextricably linked to a certain conception of political economy and an implicit social metaphysics that, at the end of the day, reinscribe forms of un-freedom? Is it possible that the freedom we seek as Black people is a form of freedom that allows us to "succeed" within a global political context that has deep negative implications for others, say, those in the Global South? Surely, on the other end, as it were, of Black resistance there must be something more than being white.

Within the conceptual space of existentialism, through resistance, the Black body denies its being as pure facticity. In affirming themselves as individual and collective sites of possibility, sites of value, Blacks realize that values are for the claiming/taking, that values are founded through human practices, and that as a lack, as an ontological excess,[19] as it were, new modes of being, new ways of valuing can be explicitly taken up. Besides the axiological moment, there is a moment of renarrating the self at the moment of resistance, which also involves a disruption of the historical force of the white *same*; for to resist is to re-story one's identity, even if that story is fragmented and replete with tensions and is only short-lived and the systemic material conditions of oppression have not been completely removed. The point here is that at the moment of resistance, a counternarrative, perhaps even a countermemory, has been performed.[20] One might argue that resistance, according to this construal, has built into it its own end. Hence, from the moment that resistance is executed, in one sense, it is complete. Even if one is physically beaten or killed after the moment of resistance, the act remains "complete" qua an act of resistance. This, of course, should not be confused with the valid point that there have been historical instances of Black resistance that have been terminated before the larger aims and goals of those resisting were accomplished. There is no attempt here to propound an idealist, ahistorical conception of agency/resistance or one grounded in a mere fleeting private moment of joyous transgression while the social and material conditions of oppression go unchallenged. My point is that there is something powerful to be said about the initial moment the Black self proposes, reflectively generates, other ways of being-in-the-world, especially within the context of those white iconographic frameworks that perpetuate distorted and dehumanizing depictions of the Black self. That initial moment points to the power of the Black self to interpellate itself and to respond to the call to *affirm* itself ("I am somebody!") against a history of denigration and Black nonbeing. The call to affirm oneself is always already situated; it is an affirmation grounded within history yet resisting the force of various racist historical interpellations and oppressive material conditions.

At the moment of resistance, I argue that a process of epistemic intervention also occurs. When called, when interpellated as "nigger," Blacks may *knowingly* refuse to answer, refusing this form of "recognition," preparing for an epistemic challenge. For example, I may opt to say, "I am not the one!" Through this act of resistance, from the perspective of the white gaze, I become a living contradiction, an anomaly. I become *more* than whites can measure within the horizon of their limited understandings of the Black body. "I am not the one!" throws whites into a state of cognitive dissonance. After all, the Black imago has served them well. They know that they are being *seen* and exposed. But I now return whites to themselves, which is a place of reaction. It is a place of bad faith, a place where I am *needed* to be what they say I am. By rejecting their need, I force whites into a state of anxiety. For they are forced to see the emptiness of a self dialectically predicated on a lie. Of course, refusing to face their freedom, they may continue to flee, which could cost me my very life. This raises the issue of how whites achieve and perpetuate power through the invisibility of whiteness while this paradoxically veils "from view the very vulnerability of whiteness and white folk. The presumptive invisibility of whites could be turned against them, their spoiled nature revealing a fragility at the heart of whiteness, its decadence a powerlessness possible to be challenged."[21] Of course, one may also resist through an ironic and exaggerated locutionary act. That is, one may respond to an instance of white interpellation with, "Yas suh, Boss?" In doing so, one consciously rejects a form of servility and retains an epistemologically privileged position regarding the mimicry one intends.

The concept of resistance is inextricably linked to the concept of identity. As one resists, one affirms a reconfigured identity; for in the act of resistance, the Black subject has already achieved a level of separation from the Black imago bounded by the white imaginary. However, transcending the Black imago is not a case of archeologically removing all white racist/colonialist distortions in order to uncover an *essential* Black self. Clevis Headley argues that when we claim an identity, the process need not involve essentialist, dogmatic, or objectivist conceptualizations of the self. He notes, "Realist portraits of identity often-times dissipate in the face of the fluidity of identity. The realist begins with the assumption of a specific ontology, namely a totality of objectivist entities that are discourse-independent; these entities are called identities."[22]

At the moment of challenging white racist hegemonic discourse—which does not mean one will be free of additional discursive and nondiscursive racist somatic attacks—one does not uncover a prediscursive self that is believed to be "prior to all identities."[23] The rejection of a prediscursive self does not imply that one should abandon Black identity discourse for some form of empty and abstract humanism. Forms of abstract humanism often obfuscate their ties to socially embedded and value-laden configurations of power. Moreover, abstract forms of humanism actually stand to misidentify Black identity as they place under erasure the location, specificity, and complexity of Black identity as embedded in history.

Identity discourse does not necessarily lead to bad faith. There are ways of claiming identity without the assumption that all identities are metaphysically fixed. This does not mean, however, that the only alternative open to Blacks is strategic essentialism. The subtext of strategic essentialism appears to presuppose that there is something fundamentally or intrinsically problematic about identities as such.[24] The expansion of embodied Black subjectivity/identity must move beyond white oppressors' representations, but not beyond all representations, not beyond all forms of discursive constructivity.[25] I reject the view that there is a history-less "Black essence" or "Black self" existing *simpliciter*, waiting for accurate representation, *true* representation that will establish a one-to-one correspondence as formulated in realist philosophical and scientific parlance. And while white racist hegemonic and distorted representations do create profound levels of corporeal malediction in Black people, this process does not obtain because there is a lack of corresponding fit, as it were, between the Black imago in the white imaginary and some sort of interior Blackness as such.

In realist parlance, one would say that white representations of Black people are *false*, because they fail to correspond to a Black essence; whereas those representations that do not create profound levels of ego instability in Black people would be said to be *true,* because they do correspond to a Black essence. This apparent *aporia* is due to the use of certain epistemic operators. Suspension of the use of true and false epistemic operators resolves this problem. When Blacks reject and move beyond white oppressors' representations of them, we can think of this in terms of moving beyond an unworkable set of categories or narratives. In other words, the white oppressors' narrative is not faithful to Blacks' hermeneutic self-understanding. There is the need for a set of categories or narratives (which are not fixed) that illuminates Blacks' being-in-the-world, their historicity. In this way, the discourse of *workable* and *unworkable* narratives replaces the logic of metaphysical essentialism regarding racial identities and dispenses with the correspondence theory of truth.[26]

One advantage of the narrative perspective is that questions regarding Black identity are not couched in ahistorical terms that necessitate a monolithic descriptive vocabulary. Instead, multiple vocabularies regarding Black identity and Black-being-in-the-world abound. Black identity is theorized as a dynamic core of narrative gravity that is sustained through historical and imaginative Black agency.[27] As Linda Alcoff argues:

> To self-identify even by a racial . . . designation [is to] understand one's relationship to a historical community, to recognize one's objective social location, and

to participate in the negotiation of the meaning and implications of one's identity. The word *real* here is not meant to signify an identity that is nondynamic, noncontingent, or not the product of social practices and modes of description. Rather, the word *real* works to counter a view that interpellations of social identity are always chimeras foisted on us from the outside or misrepresentations.[28]

"Taking a stand," renarrating one's Black identity, takes place from a historical location, a location within which one is always already *constituted* and yet within which one *constitutes* one's identity.

We can read Black identity as a site of meaning formation, one that avoids the totalizing tendencies of whiteness. Within the context of anti-Black racism, whites affirm themselves through negating Black existence. By "negating Black existence," my aim is not to suggest that all whites literally desire to negate qua kill Black people. To "negate" (*negare*, "to say no") suggests the sense in which whites affirm (or make firm) their identities through the discursive or nondiscursive act of *negating* the reality of full Black humanity, saying *no* to Black worth and *no* to Black critical subjectivity. After all, white identity needs Black existence in order to aggrandize its own. This need does not deny those moments where negating Black existence does in fact mean killing Black bodies. Even in such cases as these, killing the Black body is an act that functions to provide the white body with an "omnipotent" consciousness, giving whites the illusion of absolute power to take a Black life, which, according to racist ideology, is no more problematic than taking the life of a subhuman animal. In this way, although the Black body is negated qua killed, the dead Black body, the burned, castrated, and lynched Black body, is still needed in order to magnify white existence. Black identity, however, does not have as its ontological aim the negation of white people, though Blacks must negate the ideological structure of whiteness. Black embodied subjectivity is a dynamic process that is historically ensconced and engaged in the complex fusion of renarrating, rearticulating, and re-creating its being-in-the-world, creating ways of combating anti-Black racist effects, and making sense of what it means to be Black-in-the-world. Black identity is both a historically *narrated* and *narrating* process, a process that speaks to Black facticity and transcendence, respectively. In other words, Black identity is not to be sought in the realm of universal abstraction. "Nor is there a question of wrapping ourselves in a delusional shroud of 'ontological blackness.'" As Robert Birt argues:

Such essentialist methods create a new prison in which the many and often *enriching* complexities and perplexities of black consciousness and identity are concealed and denied. We do not wish to make of blackness a tomb within which to bury ourselves. But to abandon our common identity as blacks, to forget the common history, struggles and experiences which make us a people, is to deny our situated existence. And by denying our situation we undermine the prospects of actualizing our transcendence. Transcendence is also situated, or is realizable only within a given situation. That is why the flight toward an abstract humanity is vain. It forsakes our concrete, lived humanity for a metaphysical phantom.[29]

Black people have had to struggle and proactively create themselves in order to survive. Within this context, identity discourse is not to be feared but embraced as a constant process that is shaped within historical boundaries, shaped by coefficients of adversity, and shaped through imaginative and critical consciousness. Blacks ground their identities in a complex history that is constantly unfolding and rearticulated because Blackness is a *lived* existential project, the affirmative content of which is fundamentally shaped by (but need not be reduced to) that complex history.

The content of that lived existential project has indeed been shaped through acts of resistance and accommodation. It has involved solidarity and conflict. What is important to note, however, is that the content of that existential project is protean; it involves and should continue to involve a continual hermeneutic reassessment of who and what Black identity means and what the social, political, cultural, and existential implications are. Black homogeneity does not and should not define the content of that lived project. And while heterogeneity is important to our survival, a profound sense of inclusive solidarity should not be feared and need not be limited to that which is *politically* expedient.

Given the multiplicity of audible voices in our history—a history that has been shaped by contending political philosophies, power struggles, deeply conflicting recommendations for political praxis, aesthetic clashes concerning how best to represent the Black body, cultural difference, color, class, sex, religious, and gender complexities—does not mean that we should forget what we have in common and abandon ourselves to a "postmodern playground," to use Susan Bordo's turn of phrase. Of course, one of the salient features that Black people have in common is the complex historical reality of Black bodies in pain within the context of anti-Black racism. And, of course, that pain is storied through a complex labyrinth of discursive strategies, desires and hopes, fears and fortitude, and a healthy dose of fallibalism. Like a single life, there are aspects of that lived experience that can be centered or marginalized depending upon the plot. But this does not mean we create narrative plots willy-nilly. Black bodies, after all, historically suffered, sustained tremendous physical and psychological pain, and were subject to centuries of oppression—major experiences with profound somatic narrative implications.

We are linked to our shared history, and existentially and politically we continue to endure it. Of course, as we renarrate that history, as we define ourselves through a collective memory of it, as we penetrate and expand its meaning, we are in turn expanded by it. The pulling together and weaving of diverse aspects of that history need not lead to a Black metanarrative that is oppressive and hegemonic. But who says we can't struggle in the name of our Blackness, even as its meaning is protean? This need not mean that we struggle in the name of a Black racial essence, or without any cognizance of our class, sex, and gender differences. Nor does this mean that we should struggle in the name of an abstract "proletarian" identity at the exclusion of how our racialized and gendered identities impact and interpenetrate our identities as workers. Contrary to Jean-Paul Sartre's observations in "Black Orpheus," although he is referring to the Negritude Movement, Blackness need not function as an antithesis, a mere antithetical value to white supremacy, the resolution of which is to be achieved in the realization of a raceless society. To possess a collective sense of Black identity, while realizing its heterogeneous complexity, need not represent a minor moment of a larger dialectical progression. The rejection of the category of race does not entail the rejection of an identity interpreted through the historical struggle and affirmation of our dark bodies. To think Black people are capable of willing for only one aspect of their being-in-the-world smacks of a misguided conception of identity politics. To embody (discursively and nondiscursively) our Blackness as an existential project is not an enclosed limit, but a source of expansion, one open to renarration within the context of the contingency of lived history. As bell hooks argues:

> The unwillingness to critique essentialism on the part of many African-Americans is rooted in the fear that it will cause folks to lose sight of the specific history and experience of African-Americans and the unique sensibilities and culture that arise from that experience. An adequate response to this concern is to critique essentialism while emphasizing the significance of "The authority of experience." There is a radical difference between a repudiation of the idea that there is a black "essence" and recognition of the way black identity has been specifically constituted in the experience of exile and struggle.[30]

Though the history of Black people is inextricably linked to experiences of exile and struggle—indeed, such experiences constitute a fundamental matrix out of which Black identity has been shaped—Black identity should not be defined simply in reactionary terms. While no one will deny that aspects of Black identity are formations of recoil against white power and hegemony, Black identity is not a fragile cultural and historical structure waiting for the white other's *action* in order to establish the *reactionary* trajectory of its identity. Given the continued nature of white racism, Black identity must remain attentive to and resist against oppressive modes of being whitely-in-the-world. This is not the same as saying Black identity is to be defined in solely reactionary terms.

"Black is beautiful!" whose illocutionary function is one of *affirmation* of intent to celebrate and value the vivacity of Black embodied existence, should not be reduced to an inverted value response to the white claim that "Black is ugly," even if the affirmation takes place within the historical ideological force of whiteness and its aesthetic and moral frames of reference that conceptualize and enforce the notion that Blackness (and, by extension, Black people) are vile and ugly. Indeed, the aesthetics of whiteness is linked to norms of morality (whiteness *is* goodness, virtue, nobility). Of course, "Black is beautiful!" marks an identificatory mode of being-in-the-world grounded within social ontological and epistemological orders that involve assertive and agential modes of identity narrative formation. Historically, this affirmation has had a powerful perlocutionary impact on Blacks in terms of how they have affirmed their Black embodiment, creating a collective celebration of Black embodiment that functions as a powerful source of pleasure. "Black is beautiful!" can, must, and does occupy that Black existential space—a space within which Blacks responsibly affirm socio-ontologically who they are—where whiteness has ceased to matter, where it has ceased to be a point of reference. Within this context, it is possible to celebrate the specifically social ontological reality of one's identity as Black without the problematic signification of the self as transhistorical, while also avoiding the purely pragmatic adoption (or utility function) of one's identity as Black. In short, Black identity can be lived through an act of interpretive agency that is fully cognizant of the historical variability of various forms of nomination, but this awareness need not diminish the sense in which one grounds one's identity or significant aspects thereof in terms of a larger Black historical community and through which one rejoices in one's identity.[31] In an effort to avoid an essentialist reading of Blackness, so-called tactical Blackness elides, and in some ways places under erasure, the various ways in which Black identity speaks to a sense of abiding fullness, richness, and joy. Moreover, this sense of joy need not deteriorate into a form of smug hubris. And even as Blackness is a site of collective pride, this sense of shared collectivity ought not function as a normative (moral or otherwise) indicator of what defines "real kinds of persons." In this way, Black collectivity-talk, while predicated upon history and narrative retellings, avoids investing in "metaphysical seriousness."[32]

Adelbert Jenkins's conceptualization of Black agency provides a further theoretical framework that contests the imago of the Black as passive and without an embodied subjectivity from which to negotiate the conditions of white oppression.[33] I briefly draw from Jenkins's work because his project specifically grounds Black agency and resistance within a theoretical framework opposed to a behavioral or mechanistic model that sees behavior as the result of independent push and pull variables. The behavioral or mechanistic view of human behavior resonates with the way in which whites have conceptualized Black people.[34] According to Jenkins, to comprehend Black people, particularly within the context of white hegemony, one must come to terms with the "telic" element involved in Black agency.[35] By "telic," Jenkins means the teleological aspects of Black embodied subjectivity, particularly regarding the concept of human *intent*.[36]

By theorizing the concept of intent with regard to Black people under conditions of oppression, Jenkins elaborates a hermeneutic framework within which to describe modalities of Black agency. For example, whites believed that Blacks were meek and obsequious by nature. According to Jenkins, "Although Blacks showed humble and meek behavior in interracial situations historically, the intent of such behavior was often quite at variance with such a demeanor. Thus, at times Blacks intended in their meekness to act out of a conception of personal (Christian) dignity ("turn the other cheek") and/or moral superiority." Where whites could only see meek or obsequious forms of comportment, Blacks *intended* the very opposite of such constructions. Jenkins cites an example from Ralph Ellison's *Invisible Man*. In the example, a dying elderly Black man advises his son: "I want you to overcome 'em with yeses, undermine 'em with grins, agree 'em to death and destruction."[37] Ellison, as this example shows, was cognizant of the various ways Blacks enacted agency through processes of ironic signification. Although more will be said about this, Robin Kelley, drawing from the work of political anthropologist James Scott, maintains that Black working-class people were able to resist those in power by developing a "hidden transcript." In short, Black people engaged in acts of resistance from a hidden transcript that was beyond the cognitive range of white oppressors.

Although addressing white expectations outwardly, Blacks were able to resignify the meaning of their modes of embodied comportment that created an important slippage between white a priori assumptions, mythical self-serving beliefs, racist expectations, and Black agential reality. Take "thievery." Enslaved Blacks living on plantations would often steal food and tools. Rather than see agency, and, thus, recognize the possibility that enslaved Blacks envisioned alternative ways of survival, white oppressors rationalized such behavior as the result of a natural proclivity toward criminal behavior. Acts of stealing, however, were not only indicative of the capacity of Blacks to negotiate their circumstances and think beyond the veil of white control but we can also conceive of such acts as a means of maintaining a sense of dignity. The point here is that Black people had to imagine *alternative* ways of securing things (both material and nonmaterial) that whites denied them. To steal, under circumstances of tremendous oppression, can function as an act of self-assertion, an act of rethinking the possibilities inherent within a given context. Hence, an act of stealing, within the context of oppression, can function to reinforce and confirm one's self-worth.

Enslaved Black people also broke tools as a form of resistance, and no doubt as a form of gaining some sense of themselves as empowered, but given the magnitude of whites' denial of Black agency, they rationalized such behavior as indicative of clumsiness and stupidity. Relentless in his belief that Blacks were *agent-less*, a white Louisiana doctor, Samuel Cartwright, claimed that some work habits of Negroes were the direct result of what he termed *Dysaethesia Aethiopica.* Concerning this disease, and commenting on Cartwright's medical rationalizations, Kenneth Stampp explained:

> An African who suffered from this exotic affliction was "apt to do much mischief" which appeared "as if intentional." He destroyed or wasted every-thing he touched, abused the livestock, and injured the crops. When he was driven to his labor he performed his tasks "in a headlong, careless manner, treading down with his feet or cutting with his hoe the plants" he was supposed to cultivate, breaking his tools, and "spoiling everything." This, wrote the doctor soberly, was entirely due to "the stupidness of mind and insensibility of the nerves induced by the disease.[38]

Note Cartwright's phrase, "as if intentional." Since *intention* is a key feature of resistance and agency, saying this served Cartwright's racist aims, by allowing him to acknowledge a possible subtext of Black intentionality and, hence, agential behavior, only to nullify any such possibility by describing the behavior as the result of stupidity and insensibility of the nerves caused by a "Nigger disease." In short, Cartwright, along with other whites who bought into such white myths, was able to distance himself from his own activity and pretend as if he had no connection to the Black body's "natural" diseased dispositions.

Along with his understanding of teleological aspects of embodied subjectivity, Jenkins argues that Blacks engage in processes of "dialectical" thinking, "that quality in which every specific meaning is seen to suggest either its opposite or any number of other alternatives."[39] Disalienation is crucially dependent upon dialectical thinking. To see beyond the imago requires the capacity to imagine a form of Black humanity that has been denied. If "basic to identity, self-image, and being in the physical world is the body," then Blacks had to envision alternatives to the corporeal distortions projected from the white imaginary. Dialectically, Blacks were able to live their bodies, to perform their bodies, in ways that transformed their identities and self-images. Césaire's Caliban projected dialectically an alternative to his colonial situation. He *took a stand* against the myths of colonial whiteness, demonstrating not only to Prospero, but to himself, that he was capable of transgressing and transforming the distorted body-image into which he had been made. Jenkins is worth quoting in full:

> The human individual brings an actively structuring mind to the world, one capable of seeing alternative meanings in any given object or event. This enables the individual in principle to rise above the environment and to create or at least imagine something new and different. Since any one event can be interpreted in different ways, one must know how the individual conceives that event. Looked at this way, the survival of Black Americans can be understood as depending to a significant degree on their capacities to imagine a dignified sense of their humanity in spite of external circumstances.[40]

Black resistance in America is a powerful and historically rich narrative journey of individual efforts and mass movements. It is a history that is variegated, that has assumed various strategies and trajectories, and has led to defeats and incredible victories, to say nothing of the history of resistance throughout the Diaspora by people of African descent.

In the first edition of this book, I explored a variety of instances of Black resistance and agency within the context of everyday work activities during the antebellum period and later within the Black working class in the Jim Crow South. It was my attempt to deal with the existential quotidian experiences of Black people. I interpreted the insights of social historians through the lens of how I theorize Black resistance and agency vis-à-vis the white gaze/imaginary. As agential, I demonstrated how Black people confronted the world and constructed the world from unique perspectives. I argued for how they take up their *existence* within the framework of a given set of circumstances. And despite the horrible conditions that came with being forced to live and to work on plantations, I demonstrated how many Black people were able to reconfigure what was given. They were able to *take a stand* against white dehumanization and negotiate ways of achieving a sense of dignity. Moreover, I demonstrated how this had to be done while making whites think that they had succeeded in producing the most obedient and docile enslaved Black bodies around. In short, many Blacks had to "conform" to white myths while undermining those myths simultaneously. Such complex negotiations between myth and reality took place within a variety of work activities.

In this second edition, I end this chapter by raising a few pertinent ideas, ones that don't deny Black resistance, but complicate the sense of hope that undergirds that resistance. When I give public talks on whiteness, I begin with the qualification that I don't want white people to leave my talks with hope. Granted, it is a claim that sounds counterintuitive. The objective, though, is to get white people to see that hope can function as a site of obfuscation. I desire white people to tarry with my reflections on whiteness and the ways in which they are complicit with forms of white power. I encourage them to linger with the gravitas of their own whiteness and the history of whiteness. I want them to feel the weight of their responsibility for the perpetuation of white power, hegemony, and privilege. Hope, within this context, can be too easy. Hope can function as a distraction.

Recently, I have begun to rethink the conception of Black hope. Obviously, I don't mean to suggest that Black people ought to relinquish hope, that is, that they should abandon that powerful sense of deep existential openness toward the future, even as that future may mean merely staying alive for yet another day. To rethink hope within this context is not about hopelessness. But what if to be Black in North America is to be duped by the very structure of a certain kind of hope? I recall *feeling* the weight of this question as the nation witnessed one after another unarmed Black body killed by the state or proxies for the state. It was a powerful feeling, one that involved a tremendous affective intensity. There was an affective shudder that communicated: what if there is no way out of this nightmare, this cycle of death? What if Black bodies are *just waiting* to be slaughtered? What if I'm already dead within a white society within which I am always already disposable? The deaths of unarmed Black bodies by the hands of the state, especially during President Obama's tenure in the twenty-first century, made me feel a deep existential angst of being Black, being an *ontological problem*, in a white supremacist society, one predicated upon white power and privilege. What if white America is only willing to provide pity and charity, but not justice? As Lerone Bennett, Jr., argues, "It is impossible to be just in a situation of injustice. One can be kind, perhaps, or even charitable; but neither kindliness nor charity is justice."[41] What if the best for which Black people can hope is an endless piecemeal divvying out of glimmers of perfunctory recognition? And what if such recognition will never include a genuine commitment to the humanity of Black people? What if the hope that Black people possess is itself part of the very structure of white hegemony? Indeed, what if this hegemony actually fuels Black hope? Even as I believe in Black resistance, what if it will never free us politically? What if on the other side of resistance, as it were, is more resistance—resistance ad nauseam? What if full citizenship is like a carrot that is forever dangled before Black people, but used just to keep them hoping? I have come to think of these questions in terms of what Lauren Berlant has called "cruel optimism." She writes, " 'Cruel optimism' names a relation of attachment to compromised conditions of possibility."[42] So, one might say that there is a desire for robust democratic inclusion, the desire for the recognition of Black humanity, but such desires take place within the relational context of a form of white concession that these will never be achieved or achievable. On this score, whiteness "gives," but only enough to keep hope in place. What if Black humanity is a continual *almost* within the context of whiteness? Is this not a malicious state of affairs? Perhaps Black humanity, robust democratic inclusion, and the rights of Black people are always already problematic objects within a society whose logic is governed by whiteness as the transcendental norm. And what if Black life vis-à-vis the logics of whiteness is always already a process of loss? And what if we are left with a certain species of Black nihilism, the sort that expresses a certain abandonment of a certain political ordering that is underwritten by cruel optimism? As Calvin L. Warren argues, "Black nihilism resists emancipatory rhetoric that assumes it is possible to purge the Political of anti-black violence and advances *political apostasy* as the only 'ethical' response to black suffering."[43] While I continue to argue that resistance, taking a stand, is essential to Black survival, in the face of an existential predicament where Black existence is politically structurally nullified against the backdrop of whiteness as *the site of white sanctity*, perhaps the best that we have as Black people is a marronage existence where every day we must fight, we must take a stand; an existence where we return to those spaces of Black love and marginality where we gain sustenance for another day of battle. Perhaps, on this score, what is needed is a post-hope mode of social existence, one that nullifies the illusions of a post-racist America.

Black people are indeed not what they seem. We continue to renarrate ourselves and renegotiate our identities as human beings, as a people who have a need for their own cultural space of identity and pleasure, a space that is free from the tyranny of the white gaze. To understand Black people in relationship to their protean dynamism is to understand the humanity of Black people; it is to come to terms with Black resistance; it is to understand how Black people defy the myths of whites that depict the Black body as an ontological plenum and static by nature. Such an understanding disrupts forms of knowledge where many have only seen an ersatz and problematic form of Black embodiment—criminal, idle, pathological, agentless.

To see Black people through this white imago is to distort what it means to be Black in America. As Jenkins concludes, "Any conception of African Americans that fails to see them as engaged in exercising their human agency—sometimes successfully, sometimes not—cannot hope to grasp what they are about."[44] Hence, to recognize the historical reality of Black resistance is to affirm dynamic forms of Black embodiment that belie the historical legacy of white lies and the Black imago in the white imaginary.

NOTES

1. Kelly Oliver, "Alienation and Its Double; or, the Secretion of Race," in *Race and Racism in Continental Philosophy*, ed. Robert Bernasconi and Sybil Cook (Bloomington: Indiana University Press, 2003), 189.

2. Frantz Fanon, *Black Skin, White Masks*, trans. Charles Lam Markmann (New York: Grove Press, Inc., 1967), 112.

3. Fanon, *Black Skin, White Masks*, 114.

4. Jeremy Weate, "Fanon, Merleau-Ponty, and the Difference of Phenomenology," in *Race*, ed. Robert Bernasconi (Malden, MA: Blackwell Publishers, 2001), 179.

5. Paget Henry, "African and Afro-Caribbean Existential Philosophies," in *Existence in Black: An Anthology of Black Existential Philosophy*, ed. Lewis R. Gordon (New York: Routledge, 1997), 28.

6. Bibi Bakare-Yusuf, "The Economy of Violence: Black Bodies and the Unspeakable Terror," in *Feminist Theory and the Body: A Reader*, ed. Janet Price and Margrit Shildrick (New York: Routledge, 1999), 321.

7. Aimé Césaire, *A Tempest*, trans. Richard Miller (New York: Theatre Communications Group, 2002), 61–2.

8. "Passing for white" can function as a form of resistance. For example, take Walter White, who was from 1931 until his death in 1955 executive secretary of the NAACP. As an effort to gather empirical evidence of the horrible practice of lynching Black bodies so as to more forcefully make a case for creating federal laws against lynching, he would blend in with lynch mobs. Undetected as a Black man, he would use this evidence to strengthen the case for the NAACP's anti-lynching efforts.

9. John H. McClendon, III, "Philosophy of Language and the African American Experience: Are There Metaphilosophical Implications?" *Journal of Speculative Philosophy*, 18(4), 2004, 305–10, quotation on 309.

10. Bakare-Yusuf, "Economy of Violence," 321.

11. I am aware of the historical reality that Black bodies were, and continue to be, torn asunder as they cope with the sheer madness endured within the context of the encrusted institutional legacy of whiteness. Hence, I am aware of the danger of romanticizing Black resistance and thereby failing to comprehend the sheer existential weight of so many Black Americans who daily deal with issues of crack, unemployment, infant mortality, joblessness, police brutality, and the ever-implosive realities of ghetto life. Even as I conceptualize the Black body as a profound site of resistance and draw attention to its metastability, there is the recognition that the Black body is always situated within an anti-Black context where Black bodies are indeed torn asunder and where the capacity to imagine otherwise is seriously truncated by ideological and material forces that are systemically linked to the history of white racism.

12. Henry, "African and Afro-Caribbean Existential Philosophies," 16.

13. Fred Evans, "Genealogy and the Problem of Affirmation in Nietzsche, Foucault, and Bakhtin," *Philosophy and Social Criticism*, 27(3), 2001, 41–65, quotation on 42.

14. bell hooks, *Yearning: Race, Gender, and Cultural Politics* (Boston: South End Press, 1990), 15.

15. Robert Birt, "Blackness and the Quest for Authenticity," *White on White/Black on Black*, ed. George Yancy (Lanham, MD: Rowman & Littlefield, 2005), 273, n30.

16. I use the term *re-cognition* because it conveys the epistemological and ontological dimensions of disrupting, of refusing to accept, the stereotypes projected from the white imaginary that have attempted to hold the Black body prisoner, to freeze it in time.

17. Oliver, "Alienation and Its Double," 177.

18. Oliver, "Alienation and Its Double," 178.

19. Excess here suggests that one is always already more than something static.

20. According to Bakare-Yusuf ("Economy of Violence," 321), "Counter-memory enabled the slaves and their descendants to construct a different kind of history, a different kind of knowledge, a different kind of body that is outside the control of the dominant history and knowledge production."

21. David Theo Goldberg, "In/Visibility and Super/Vision: Fanon on Race, Veils, and Discourse of Resistance," in *Fanon: A Critical Reader*, ed. Lewis R. Gordon, T. Denean Sharpley-Whiting, and Renée T. White (Malden, MA: Blackwell Publishers, 1996), 199.

22. Clevis Headley, "Postmodernism, Narrative, and the Question of Black Identity," in *The Quest for Community and Identity*, ed. Robert E. Birt (Lanham, MD: Rowman & Littlefield, 2002), 45–6.

23. Linda Martín Alcoff, "Who's Afraid of Identity Politics?" in *Reclaiming Identity: Realist Theory and the Predicament of Postmodernism*, ed. Paula M. L. Moya and Michael R. Hames-Garcia (Berkley: University of California Press, 2000), 340.

24. Alcoff, "Who's Afraid of Identity Politics?" 322–5.

25. Alcoff, "Who's Afraid of Identity Politics?" 334.

26. The sense of "workable" and "unworkable" explicitly moves one away from a correspondence theory of truth to a language steeped in narrativity where the emphasis is placed upon whether or not a particular narrative actually works or not. Whether or not it works depends upon various presuppositions, aims, values, norms, and so on. Indeed, the criterion of what is workable and unworkable is linked to a certain level of comprehension regarding how one always already understands one's identity, how that identity has been damaged, uplifted, and so on. That a certain narrative is workable dispenses with the conception of a fixed identity. Moreover, it also dispenses with a fixed goal, as it were. While I might find a particular narrative workable, this does not mean that that narrative is forever fixed qua metanarrative goal. Sure, there is a sense in which it has a structure within which I make decisions, critical judgments, and within which I critique anti-Black narratives, but the goal is not fixed, that is, as if there is a single and unchangeable telos that directs my life. In short, the framework, which is already composed of diversity-cum-unity, can shift and accommodate other elements, which then become part of a narrative gravitational core, but, again, not a metanarrative with a fixed end.

27. I thank Clevis Headley for his insights regarding the relationship between identity and narrative as a philosophical approach that avoids the problems associated with conceptualizing identity as a fixed entity having a one-to-one correspondence to a "true" representation.

28. Alcoff, "Who's Afraid of Identity Politics?" 341.

29. Birt, "Blackness and the Quest for Authenticity," 270.

30. bell hooks, "Postmodern Blackness," in *The Truth about the Truth: Deconfusing and Re-constructing a Postmodern World*, ed. Walter Truett Anderson (New York: G. P. Putnam's Sons, 1995), 122. hooks' emphasis on Black identity as being constituted in the experience of exile and struggle points to what that identity can become. The history points beyond itself to "strands of possibility," as opposed to a new essence.

31. Alcoff, "Who's Afraid of Identity Politics?" 341.

32. Jason D. Hill, *Becoming a Cosmopolitan: What It Means to Be a Human Being in the New Millennium* (Lanham, MD: Rowman & Littlefield, 2000), 115.

33. Adelbert H. Jenkins, *Turning Corners: The Psychology of African Americans* (Needham Heights, MA: Allyn & Bacon, 1995).

34. This by no means suggests that behavioral or mechanistic views of human behavior are racist.

35. Jenkins, *Turning Corners*, 7.

36. Jenkins does not philosophically engage in a discussion of the ontological status of intention. For example, as a mental act ("I intend to do x"), how does Jenkins understand the ontological and epistemological status of first-person psychological attitudes? Given the importance that he attributes to the subjective sphere, it would follow that first-person psychological attitudes are not reducible to third-person psychological descriptions. This reductionism is a fundamental philosophical move of Skinnerian behaviorism and one that is supported by traditional logical empiricists. My point is that it would be interesting to get a sense of how Jenkins conceptualizes his form of humanism, aspects of which I find philosophically significant, within the context of a broader discussion of some of the salient philosophical issues in the area of philosophy of mind.

37. Jenkins, *Turning Corners*, 9.

38. Kenneth M. Stampp, *The Peculiar Institution: Slavery in the Ante-Bellum South* (New York: Vantage Books, 1956), 102.

39. Jenkins, *Turning Corners*, 10. Jenkins draws upon Joseph F. Rychlak, *The Psychology of Rigorous Humanism*, 2nd ed. (New York: New York University Press, 1988).

40. Jenkins, *Turning Corners*, 16.

41. Lerone Bennett, Jr., *The Negro Mood and Other Essays* (Chicago: Johnson Publishing, 1964), 92.

42. Lauren Berlant, "Cruel Optimism," *Differences: A Journal of Feminist Cultural Studies*, 17(3), 2006, 20–36, quotation on 21.

43. Calvin L. Warren, "Black Nihilism and the Politics of Hope," *CR: The New Continental Review*, 15(1), 2015, 215–48, quotation on 218.

44. Jenkins, *Turning Corners*, 279.

Chapter 5

Exposing the *Serious* World of Whiteness through Frederick Douglass's Autobiographical Reflections

> Trained from the cradle up, to think and feel that their masters are superior, and invested with a sort of sacredness, there are few [enslaved Blacks] who can outgrow or rise above the control which that sentiment exercises.
>
> —Frederick Douglass

> Blacks are often confronted, in American life, with such devastating examples of the white descent from dignity; devastating not only because of the enormity of white pretensions, but because this swift and graceless descent would seem to indicate that white people have no principles whatever.
>
> —James Baldwin

I am often amazed and frustrated that so many white students have not read anything by Frederick Douglass. When I teach Douglass, I often feel as if I am peeling back, for the first time, the many lies that they have been taught about the enslavement of Black bodies. This chapter, then, is important as a process of demythologization, of getting white students to tarry in that space of "danger" where they get to understand aspects of their own whiteness. It is a dangerous space as it encourages white students to become deeply unsettled, troubled, and thereby dangerous to the normative order of whiteness.

Through the lens of his *lived* embodied experience of white oppression, Frederick Douglass's sociopolitically and existentially rich autobiographical narratives, *Narrative of the Life of Frederick Douglass, An American Slave, Written by Himself,* and *My Bondage and My Freedom,* not only expose the discursive and nondiscursive impact of whiteness upon the Black body, but expose the *perniciousness of the ideology of whiteness to whites themselves.* To get a sense of the Black body as undergoing processes of white racist disciplinary control, in this chapter, I discuss how the Black body was subjected to what I call a "technology of docility" during the Middle Passage, a modality of shaping the dark body to internalize its being as fixed. Of course, this technology of docility was inextricably linked to the American slave system's bourgeois material interests and investment in methods of material productivity. Continuing with this theme of racist disciplinary control, I will show how the Black body became marked and mapped by various "authoritative" voices (philosophical and scientific) that functioned to discipline the Black body even further. These authoritative voices are ideological constructions that worked to sustain the *serious* world of whiteness. Hence, rather than immediately focusing on Douglass's lived experience of the serious world of whiteness, and how he challenged this serious world, my larger aim is to provide a sketch of the Middle Passage and a delineation of some of the powerful philosophical and scientific discourses that have been deployed to "justify" the so-called inferiority of Black bodies. In other words, this broader framework reveals that the oppressive social reality that Douglass inherited was always already in the process of being constructed to give the appearance of *necessity* and, hence, to perpetuate the illusion that racist values are *not* existentially founded but ahistorically given.

This propaedeutic move to consider the process of white mystification before turning to Douglass's *lived* experience of white oppression is similar in spirit to Simone de Beauvoir's strategy in *The Second Sex*, which takes the reader on a historical, scientific, and philosophical journey, in volume 1, revealing how women have become who they are through men's discursive practices. In conceptualizing the serious world of whiteness, I draw from what de Beauvoir terms in *The Ethics of Ambiguity* "the serious man." I argue that whiteness is fundamentally predicated upon a world within which whites understand their being white (and the ethical, aesthetic, and legal benefits that accrue) as an "unconditioned" state of being. Acts of performing whiteness are interpreted both as forms of flight from agency or alternative ways of conceptualizing or narrating one's being-in-the-world and as ways that whites construct themselves as subjects in relation to those (in this case, Black bodies) who are thereby constructed as "things." I also draw from Beauvoir's *The Second Sex*, pointing to some insightful parallels between how she conceptualized women under androcentric hegemony and the ways in which the Black body is denigrated under white hegemony. Important to my argument is the fact that Beauvoir was influenced by the phenomenological and politico-praxic work of Black novelist Richard Wright.[1] The issue that immediately arises here is the relevance of Beauvoir's work to understanding Douglass's existential situation and, indeed, its relevance to the Black experience, more generally. The rich historical and interpretative insights of Margaret Simons's work, who takes up Paul Gilroy's challenge to read Wright intertextually with Beauvoir, demonstrate the ways in which Beauvoir was philosophically indebted to Wright. Hence I at times read Douglass's existential situatedness through the philosophical lens of Beauvoir, who was reading sexism on the model of racism as theorized by Wright.

Simons's interpretation of Beauvoir demonstrates how Wright was an important figure who helped move Beauvoir from an exclusive concern with metaphysical problems to issues involving concrete political concerns. Simons aims to "uncover evidence of Wright's influence on . . . Beauvoir's philosophy, specifically in providing her with a theory of racial oppression and liberation that she utilized as a model in constructing the theoretical foundations of radical feminism in *The Second Sex*."[2] In *America Day by Day*,[3] Beauvoir described how Wright influenced the development of her thinking about race, mythopoetic images of Blacks that satisfy the needs of whites, and Black self-definitional agency as a means toward sociopolitical praxis. "The narrative portrays Wright as Beauvoir's teacher," as Simons writes, "guiding her understanding of race as a social construct."[4] Pointing to three major conceptual influences on Beauvoir, Simons argues:

> Wright, as the intellectual heir to W. E. B. DuBois, introduces Beauvoir to the concept of the "double consciousness" of blacks under racism, which serves as a model for Beauvoir's concept of woman as the Other in *The Second Sex*. Wright's phenomenological descriptions of black experience of oppression provide a methodological alternative to both [Gunnar] Myrdal's objectifying social science methodology and the economic reductionism of Marxist orthodoxy. Finally, Wright's rejection of white-defined essentialist views of racial difference allied with an affirmation of the salience of race in the lived experience of blacks under oppression, and its strategic usefulness when defined by blacks in the interests of liberation, provide Beauvoir with a model for an anti-essentialist but militant liberation politics.[5]

When Beauvoir discussed in *The Second Sex* how women have come to accept a form of epistemic violence, coming *to know* themselves as inferior, she referenced Wright's work:

> What Bigger Thomas, in Richard Wright's *Native Son*, feels with bitterness at the dawn of his life is this definitive inferiority, this accursed alterity, which is written in the color of his skin: he sees airplanes flying by and he knows that because he is black the sky is forbidden to him. Because she is a woman, the little girl knows that she is forbidden the sea and the polar regions, a thousand adventures, a thousand joys.[6]

As Simons points out, Beauvoir, when describing difficulties confronted by young girls under the metanarrative voice of androcentricity, relied on an analogy with racism. Pointing to the psychological phenomenon of young girls coming to discover that their "inferiority" is deemed an *essential* property, Beauvoir wrote:

> It is a strange experience for whoever regards [herself] as the One to be revealed to [herself] as otherness, alterity. This is what happens to the little girl when, during her apprenticeship for life in the world, she grasps what it means to be a woman therein. The sphere to which she belongs is everywhere enclosed, limited, dominated, by the male universe. . . . This situation is not unique. The American Negroes know it, being partially integrated in a civilization that nevertheless regards them as constituting an inferior caste.[7]

THE MIDDLE PASSAGE

At this juncture, I will provide a larger historical framework within which to conceptualize the white epistemic regime into which Douglass was born and through which his Black body (and the Black body, more generally) was discursively and nondiscursively marked. In the name of early European capitalist modes of production, its cultural assumptions, and its elaborate moral, scientific, and philosophical rationalizations, African bodies were torn from their land, family ties were severed, and their bodies were confiscated and brutalized.[8] During the triangular trade of human flesh,[9] Africans (Ashantis, Mandingoes, Ibos, Fulanis, and others) were subjected to tight forms of spatialization. Although Michel Foucault did not have Black bodies in mind when he wrote that "discipline proceeds from the distribution of individuals in space," this statement applies well to the experience of Africans who endured the Middle Passage.[10]

The African body was subjected to white power relations that seized it, invested in it, marked it, tortured it, and forced it to carry out various tasks, perform various rituals, and emit certain signs.[11] Bibi Bakare-Yusuf notes that "the history of the middle passage and slavery is a history of endless assaults on bodies; of bodies forcibly subjected, in order to be transformed into productive and reproductive bodies,"[12] but also to be transformed into subhuman animals and hypersexual savages. The point is that the subjugation of African bodies for material profit is inextricably tied to their "representation and regulation in discursive fields."[13] The Middle Passage was itself a regime of "truth," a regime that involved the *production* of the Black body's "truth" as chattel, bodies to be herded into suffocating spaces of confinement. This was not an issue of how many people could be comfortably accommodated, but how many *things*, owned property, could be stuffed into spaces of confinement. With its pernicious by-product of grammar (breeder, chattel, etc.), the terrible journey through the Middle Passage helped shape Africans into "objects" perceived as allegedly devoid of spirit, self-consciousness, and internal reflection. Because they were born within torrid regions, they also could not have been provided a foundation for human freedom or for the African to become part of a world-historical nation.[14] After all, besides the natural riches of the land, which included the African body as wild fauna, "Africa has no historical interest of its own, for we find its inhabitants living in barbarism and savagery in a land which has not furnished them with any integral ingredient of culture."[15]

There is nothing *ontologically* mutually exclusive about Africans and Europeans. Unlike Jean-Paul Sartre, I do not read the self-other problem as ontological, that is, that conflict must inevitably emerge between the self and the other in virtue of the fact that one solipsistic consciousness is seen as confronting another solipsistic consciousness and that both are engaged in a mutual dance of sadism and masochism.[16] However, I do not deny the phenomenon of xenophobia. Even here, though, fear of others, or suspicion of others, presupposes some type of differential *social* grouping such that one inhabits a (non-solipsistic) social space from within which another, who properly does not have a social standing within that same social group, is "seen" as other. Even within the same social group, the self is certainly purchased as a result of some form of differentiation and the recognition of difference. This differentiation and the recognition of difference, however, need not take the specific form of a mutual attempt to hold the other in my gaze as the other attempts to hold me in his/her gaze, a dynamic process resulting in violent conflict.

With regard to whiteness, as I have argued throughout this text, my view is that the (white) self and (Black) other problem is sociohistorically contingent in its origin. The Black body *became* the very site of evil. Hence, as Fanon notes, "Jean-Paul Sartre has forgotten that the Negro suffers in his body quite differently from the white man."[17] The Black does not simply suffer on the basis of a self-other conflict. Indeed, violent acts linked to material forces, which are further linked to exclusionary tactics that call into question the existential, ontological, aesthetic, and cultural legitimacy of Black people, create the problems. Moreover, the white gaze or "look" must be historicized within a racialized context in order to grasp its capacity to pose a violent threat to Black embodied subjectivity. "The experience of the black-as-body becomes," according to Charles Johnson, "not merely a Self-Other conflict, nor simply Hegel's torturous Master-Slave dialectic, but a variation on both these conditions, intensified by the particularity of the body's appearance as black, as 'stained', [and] lacking interiority."[18]

Moreover, there was nothing ontologically problematic about the epidermis of Africans that would have led to the historical necessity of their enslavement/colonization. The color of the epidermis does not found values.

Rather, the "Blackness" of African bodies in relation to white bodies assumed the historical character that they did (as savage or as stained) because white European values were conferred upon both groups. On my view, some material-cum-axiological/epistemological framework first must exist that "justifies" the valorization and sovereignty of whiteness, and, by extension, the denigration of Blackness. The so-called ontology of deep racial differences is actually a sociohistorical ontology of differences, though deployed as natural through an ideology of whiteness. Creating such differences as natural functions to conceal the *reactive* value-creating hegemony of whites. In other words, whites are able to assess the differences between themselves and Blacks based upon "objective" criteria that are believed to be independent of anything they do, as existing outside their sphere of responsibility. What in reality has become a phantasmatically constructed African body, a fantasized object, whites "see" instead as *given*, and thus not the result of any processes of rationalization, projection, ejection, or denial on the part of themselves. Hence, whites are able to mask or deny their dependency upon the fabrication of the phantasmatic object. As Bakare-Yusuf also notes, referencing the work of Michael Taussig, the white enslaver and victimizer desperately "needs the victim to create truth, objectifying fantasy in the discourse of the other."[19]

Theorizing the Middle Passage as a space of rupture and trauma, Hortense Spillers notes that "African persons in the 'Middle Passage' were literally suspended in the 'oceanic', if we think of the latter in its Freudian orientation as an analogy for undifferentiated identity: removed from the indigenous land and culture, and not-yet 'American' either." Furthermore, she argues that, "Inasmuch as, on any given day, we might imagine, the captive personality did not know where s/he was, we could say that they were the culturally 'unmade', thrown in the midst of a figurative darkness that 'exposed' their destinies to an unknown course."[20] If one thinks of subjectivity as a transversal relationship constituted through familiar and familial connections, then the Middle Passage was designed to throw into disarray any sense of subjectivity and destroy any sense of cultural teleology. The objective was to create a cultureless *thing*, an object that was defined within the same context as other commodities. In this way, the very process of positioning Black bodies within the slave ship functioned as a disciplinary technique to produce an obedient, *docile* Black body. This technology of docility not only had the effect of fashioning a strong workforce, fashioning Black bodies whose telos it was to labor, but it also reinforced the status of the enslaver as an active force, a driver of animal flesh.

As the human face of the enslaver was reinforced through his/her dominion over the African body qua animal of the field, working in tandem with the power to *name* the African, the humanity of the African was placed under constant erasure. Chained together like subhuman animals, the African body, as early as the Middle Passage, was being marked and defined, disciplined to begin the process of seeing itself as thing-like, of undergoing the phenomenological process of returning to itself as that which is not free, but owned by another. The process was not simply to enforce the cruel practices of physical subjugation, but to get the enslaved to appear to himself/herself as an object, to embody and instantiate those projections created by white racists themselves. Hence, the subjection of Africans was also an act of desubjectification.[21]

In the eyes of the enslaver, the captured African became a tool devoid of reason, human feeling, and will. The "will of the captured" was the will of the white captor. Soon, this African body would become subjected to white legalese that sanctioned its status as chattel. Whiteness as law vis-à-vis the African body would become whiteness as *divine* law and whiteness as the law of destiny, theology, and evolutionary science intertwining to create an "objective" discourse designed to mask the horrors perpetrated upon other human beings by white enslavers. Keep in mind that it was not the objective of enslavers to kill the enslaved, though more than a million Africans died en route to the New World due to the diseased conditions of the enslaver ships, to say nothing of those Africans who threw themselves overboard,[22] who would rather die than to be enslaved or eaten by the ghost-like strangers.[23] As Bakare-Yusuf notes, "To destroy the body in pain would have been tantamount to economic and ideological suicide. For how could the slave system perpetuate itself if the enslaved population was destroyed?" Bakare-Yusuf goes on to note, "The violent subjection of the slaves was a way of transforming their bodies into an entity that could produce and reproduce the property necessary for accumulating wealth."[24]

There was a great deal of dissonance, doubleness, as the African body was *returned* to itself as an unfamiliar thing chained deep down in the belly of slave ships, undergoing processes of redefinition by its brutal treatment, its spatial confinement. Within the framework of the equation (or regulatory and disciplinary economy) where humans became reduced to cargo, gender differentiation was redefined in terms of quantity and spatiality. "The female in 'Middle Passage', as the apparently smaller physical mass, occupies 'less room' in a directly translatable money economy," Spillers says.[25] The dispassionate reduction of Africans to cargo or merchandise is illustrated in Fred D'Aguiar's *Feeding the Ghosts*, which is a powerful fictional narration of an event that actually took place in 1781. For example, Captain Cunningham, who is in charge of the *Zong*, which is heading back to England, makes the purely calculative decision to throw 131 physically ill Africans (men, women, and children) into the ocean to die. He figures if he throws one-third of the infirm Africans overboard he will earn a profit from the remaining Africans who are not (as yet) sick. Cunningham asks his crew, "Are we to make a loss or a profit?"[26] Although his crew initially hesitates, with his first mate Kelsal finding the magnitude of his Captain's plan difficult to absorb, they decide profit is most desirable. Referring to the enslaved Africans as "cargo," they begin throwing them overboard. As men, women, and children plunge into the ocean, "Captain Cunningham marked the strokes in his ledger and nodded with satisfaction."[27] As the children are drowned for profit, angry and heartrending screams come from the deck below:

> Mothers shouted to children to show the evil men that they were not sick but healthy; to struggle and scream. Men banged their chains on the decks and shouted in Yoruba, Ewe, Ibo, Fanti, Ashanti, Mandingo, Fetu, Foulah, at the crew to leave the children and take them instead. Mothers pulled out their hair, fell into dead faints, wished for death to take them now, now, now, since life could never mean a thing after this. And cried with dry eyes and hardly a breath left in them.[28]

Note the contrast between Captain Cunningham, who marks in his ledger and nods with satisfaction, as if he were tallying up discarded inanimate objects, and the *lived* African bodies that wailed with sorrow, angst, pain, horror, and powerlessness. These bodies were not just sites of white *re*-presentations or discursive distortions, but sites of powerful trauma, torn flesh, broken hearts, and psychological madness. Each time that I read the above passage, I suffer. When I think of my children being thrown overboard, I feel that overpowering sense of profound horror. I want to scream. I feel helpless; I'm overcome with a sense of madness and desperation. I think of how their Black lives would not matter, reduced to profit or lack thereof. In our contemporary moment, Black parents and parents of children of color continue to shout to the world that their sons and daughters are human beings and not fictions created in the minds of whites who see them as disposable.

Further illustrating Foucault's understanding that discipline proceeds from individuals' spatial distribution, Africans were packed into very tight spaces on slave ships. On the slave ship *Pongas*, for example, 250 women, many of whom were pregnant, occupied a space just 16 by 18 feet. bell hooks writes that "the women who survived the initial stages of pregnancy gave birth aboard the ship with their bodies exposed to either the scorching sun or the freezing cold." Furthermore, "Black women with children on board the slave ships were ridiculed, mocked, and treated contemptuously by the slaver crew. Often the slavers brutalized children to watch the anguish of their mothers."[29] Not just scorching sun and freezing rain, but Black female bodies were also exposed to vicious acts of rape by white enslavers.

One white slave trader told of 108 boys and girls under age fifteen packed into a small hold: "As I crawled between decks, I confess I could not imagine how this little army was to be packed or draw breath in a hold but twenty-two inches high!"[30] Molefi Asante also captures the terror of the Middle Passage where he writes:

> Imagine crossing the ocean aboard a small ship made to hold 200 people but packed with 1,000 weeping and crying men, women, and children. Each African was forced to fit into a space no more than 55.9 centimeters (22 inches) high, roughly the height of a single gym locker, and 61 centimeters (24 inches) wide, scarcely an arm's length. There were no lights aboard the ships, little food, and no toilet facilities.[31]

Remember that the trip lasted thirty-five to ninety days, contingent upon weather. Moreover, the decks where Blacks were held were infested with lice, fleas, and rats. Diseased, dead, and dying Black bodies were chained together. My point here is that the sheer nondiscursive confinement of Black bodies/ selves within these tight spaces, filled with the putrid smell of death, sickness, blood, urine, and feces, was an exercise in discipline. The "Black body" in relation to the European imaginary was being created and produced, a docile and self-hating body. Whiteness as a site of concentrated power was *productive*. Foucault maintained that the effects of power are not simply manifested in terms of that which excludes, represses, and censors. Rather, "power produces; it produces reality; it produces domains of objects and rituals of truth. The individual and the knowledge that may be gained of him belong to this production.[32]

MYTHMAKING AND THE MAINTENANCE OF WHITE NORMATIVITY

Upon their arrival in the New World, Black people were sold from auction blocks, defined and treated like chattel. Standing naked, witnessed by both white men and white women, the Black body was *gazed* upon, checked, and assessed like an animal whose sole value rested in his/her fitness to work the land. This form of examination and the objectifying dimensions of the white gaze are part of the overall function of the white episteme. The white gazer "sees" what he/she is not. It is not that the physiology of the eye does not send proper neurological and chemical signals. Rather, between the white "seer" and the Black "seen" or the Black "unseen," there is an invisible/ imperceptible construction that occurs simultaneously with the process of white gazing. This construction does not involve "seeing" the dark body and then extrapolating that it is inferior. The drama and spectacle of the auction itself, the commodity exchange dynamics of the context, the bidding, the physical turning of the naked bodies, checking the teeth, the asymmetrical power relations embedded within the physical context of separating the gazers from the gazed upon, the unquestioned power to separate children from their parents, the ideological norms informing the *white* self as all seeing and all knowing, forms the larger, unthematized, sociovisual epistemology that militates against slippages between "seeing" and "knowing," at least with respect to the enslaved African body.

In *The History of Mary Prince: A West Indian Slave Related by Herself,* Prince described the process of being sold from an auction block as involving a white ritual performance in terms of which the Black body, in this case, her Black female body, became discursively marked as that which was merely usable, expendable, and sexually exploitable.[33] At the auction block, for example, Prince noted, "I was soon surrounded by strange men, who examined and handled me in the same manner that a butcher would a calf or a lamb he was about to purchase, and who talked about my shape and size in like words—as if I could no more understand their meaning than the dumb beasts."[34]

Gazing upon the Black naked body, the white gazer assumes the position of *knowing* subject. The Black naked body becomes the gazed upon *known* object. Within the white buyers' racially saturated field of visibility, Blacks do not *appear* fully human. The entire economic, cultural, epistemological, and anthropological apparatus of white domination collapses into a narrow aperture through which the Black body and the white body emerge as taxonomic differences. Hence, the Black body became a flesh-and-blood text upon which whites could project all of their fears, desires, and fantasies without the agony of guilt. Through the creation of the Black phantasmatic object, whites were able to conceal their historical practices that created the phantasmatic object. Blacks as inferior, ugly, bestial are *ejecta*, that is, negative material thrown out from the white body onto the Black body. To justify and sustain the enslavement of Blacks, one need only manufacture the Black body as an "objective state of affairs."

Theorizing whiteness in ways that are consistent with what I take to be a form of ideology exposure, Crispin Sartwell notes that "oppression is released by the oppressor into an 'objective' realm, where it is not anyone's doing in particular, but just a feature of the external facts."[35] Sartwell understands, I think correctly, that whites have been able to deal effectively with their white lies regarding themselves and the Black body in what he terms "ejected asceticism."[36] Whites created/create fantasies regarding the Black body as sullen and immoral so as to stabilize dialectically their own fantasized identity as clean and moral. Whites project "their hate [of Blacks and other nonwhites] into the 'objective' realm of laws and institutions (and 'values' and 'sciences') and then [fail] to experience themselves as haters. This movement into the objective displays the ghost-white self writ large."[37]

What becomes clear is that not only are Blacks ghosts, fantasies, but whites are also ghosts, fantasies. What we have is the unique case of a "white spook" manufacturing a "Black spook." "Whiteness," after all, "is the color of ghosts."[38]

With the advent of white racist biological theories in the nineteenth century, the Black body was further discursively marked and produced. Whites were fascinated by the alleged large and "exotic" genitalia of Black people. The objective was to confirm "scientific truths" both about the ("normative") white body and ("deviant" and ape-like) Black body. Again, such "truths" about white and Black bodies were deemed discovered, not constructed. To argue that so-called sexual deviances regarding the Black body were "discovered" also provided whites with psychological mechanisms with which to bury their own feelings of guilt, lust, insecurity, and fear. My point is that such "objective" scientific truths were propagated within the context of a powerful white imaginary infused with a complex of sexual desires and sexual repressions; indeed, such scientific "truths" about the Black body were formulated against the historical backdrop of white enslavers who sexually molested Black female bodies. Hence, white power networks, consisting of norms, "knowledge-claims," and so on, helped produce the myth of the "Negro rapist." According to Smith:

> It was of course inevitable for him [the white male enslaver] to suspect her [the white woman] of the sins he had committed so pleasantly and often. *What if,* he whispered, and the words were never finished. *What if.* . . . Too often white woman could only smile bleakly in reply to the unasked question. But white man mistook this empty smile for one of cryptic satisfaction and in jealous panic began to project his own sins on to the Negro male.[39]

Smith continues:

> Pictorially, the Klan presents this Return of the Repressed in a stunning manner. White pillow case and sheet . . . the face covered . . . identity disappears and with it the conscience . . . a group stalks in silence through the 'darkness' . . . a sudden abrupt appearance before the victim according to this paranoid fantasy, has 'raped' a 'sacred' white woman. It is a complete acting out of the white man's internal guilt and his hatred of colored man and white woman.[40]

In 1903, white physician William Lee Howard argued that Negro males attacked innocent white women because of "racial instincts that are about as amenable to ethical culture as is the inherent odor of the race."[41] The physiological basis of the problem of the "Negro rapist" had to do with the enormous size of his penis and "'the African's birthright' was 'sexual madness and excess.'"[42] Indeed, or so it was maintained, Negroes, by their very nature, are morally retrogressive, physically dirty (a trope of Blackness), and morally unclean. In 1900, Charles Carroll supported the pre-Adamite beliefs of physician Samuel Cartwright by describing the Negro as an ape and the actual "tempter of Eve."[43] Stuart Hall notes:

> The ways in which black people, black experiences, were positioned and sub- jected in the dominant regimes of representation were the effects of a critical exercise of cultural power and normalization. Not only, in [Edward] Said's "Orientalist" sense, were we constructed as different and other within catego- ries of knowledge of the West by those regimes. They had the power to make us see and experience ourselves as "Other." Every regime of representation is a regime of power formed, as Foucault reminds us, by the fatal couplet "power/ knowledge."[44]

The sciences of physiognomy and phrenology, with their emphasis on the prognathous jaw of Negroes, were said clearly to support the primitive nature of African people. Examining the so-called Negro anatomy, French physician Franz Ignace Pruner-Bey observed:

> The intestinal mucus is very thick, viscid, and fatty in appearance. All the abdominal glands are of large size, especially the liver and the supra renal cap- sules; a venous hyperaemia seems the ordinary condition of these organs. The position of the bladder is higher than in the European. I find the seminal vesicles very large, always gorged with a turbid liquid of a slightly greyish colour, even in cases where the autopsy took place shortly after death. The penis is always of unusually large size, and I found in all bodies a small conical gland on each side at the base of the fraenum.[45]

The Black body was also believed to be a site of disease, and, hence, some- thing to avoid. Again, Howard argued: "There is every prospect of checking and reducing these diseases in the white race, if the race is socially—in every aspect of the term—quarantined from the African."[46] In addition, Blacks were believed prone to moral and sexual retrogression. White evolutionary theo- rists held such beliefs to be true. Paul B. Barringer, for example, drew from the Darwinian stress on heredity. According to George Fredrickson, Barringer argued that Blacks' innate characteristics "had been formed by natural selec- tion during 'ages of degradation' in Africa and his savage traits could not have been altered in any significant way by a mere two centuries of proximity to Caucasian civilization in America."[47]

Even Charles Darwin, while aware and critical of whites who inflicted cruel pain upon Black bodies, "wrote about a future time when the gap between human and ape will increase by the anticipated extinction of such intermediates as chimpanzees and Hottentots."[48] Also theorizing within a

Darwinian framework, historian Joseph A. Tillinghast states: "The Negro character had been formed in Africa, a region which supposedly showed an uninterrupted history of stagnation, inefficiency, ignorance, cannibalism, sexual licence, and superstition."[49] Due to the perceived superiority of Egyptian culture, Egypt, while in Africa, was deemed separate from Africa. Through craniological investigations, the Egyptian skull was found to differ from that of the Negro, providing the needed rationalization for the so-called immutable primitive culture of Negroes. By 1840, physician Samuel George Morton "was confident that the brains of the five races he had classified (Caucasian, Mongolian, Malay, [Native] American, and Negro) were successively smaller, thereby proving the general superiority in intelligence (and hence civilization) of the Caucasian race."[50] Furthermore, speaking to the American Social Science Association in 1899, Walter F. Willcox maintained "that the liability of an American Negro to commit crime is several times as great as the liability of the whites."[51] As has been shown, constructing the Black body involved the deployment of scientific "truths" designed to regulate and discipline the Black body, stigmatizing the Black body with certain predictable patterns such as uncontrollable sexual and criminal habits. In this way, the "truth" about the Black body was a function of the white gaze and the procrustean episteme that informed it. In doing so, however, the alterity of Black people was eradicated.

Adding to the list of "authoritative" discourses regarding the inferiority of the Black body were those made by prominent European philosophers and intellectuals. With Emmanuel Levinas, I think it is plausible to argue that "Western philosophy [at least with Hume, Kant, Hegel, and so on] coincides with the disclosure of the other where the other, in manifesting itself as a being, loses its alterity."[52] In "Of National Characters," David Hume maintained:

> I am apt to suspect the negroes, and in general all other species of men (for there are four or five different kinds) to be naturally inferior to the whites. There never was a civilized nation of any other complexion than white, nor even any individual eminent either in action or speculation. No ingenious manufactures amongst them, no arts, no sciences. . . . In Jamaica, indeed, they talk of one negro as a man of learning; but it is likely he is admired for very slender accomplishments, like a parrot who speaks a few words plainly.[53]

Hume stated that this fundamental distinction between the inferior Blacks and the superior whites "could not happen . . . if nature had not made an original distinction between these breeds of men."[54] Given Hume's empiricism, his assertion of the existence of an "original distinction" between Blacks and whites is unempirical. His claim is inconsistent with his account of causality as constant conjunction. In fact, there is no a priori reason in his theory of causality that rules out that Blackness will be conjoined with rationality and whiteness conjoined with stupidity.[55] What is interesting is that Hume appears willing to "commit to the flames" *any* views that challenge his view regarding the superiority of whites over nonwhites. Hume was not simply speculating out of sheer ignorance, as some philosophers have argued. Hume's contemporary, Scottish poet and essayist James Beattie, argued against Hume's views regarding the inferiority of nonwhites:

> The empires of Peru and Mexico could not have been governed, nor the metropolis of the latter built after so singular a manner, in the middle of a lake, without men eminent both for action and speculation. Everybody has heard of the magnificence, good government, and ingenuity, of the ancient Peruvians. The Africans and [Native] Americans are known to have many ingenious manufactures and arts among them, which even Europeans would find it no easy matter to imitate.[56]

Although Beattie implied a certain privileging of Europeans when he said, "even Europeans would find it no easy matter to imitate," his view empirically challenged Hume's. Given Hume's response to Beattie, he appears not to have thought that Beattie's counterevidence was sufficient to undermine his belief in the superiority of whites. Hume simply made a minor change in phrasing. Instead of saying there "never" was a civilized nation other than white, Hume deleted never and replaced it with "scarcely ever."[57]

Although Kant credited Hume with his awakening from dogmatic slumber, on the issue of whiteness vis-à-vis the Black, Hume seems to have lulled Kant back to sleep. In his *Observations on the Feeling of the Beautiful and Sublime*, Kant wrote:

> The Negroes of Africa have by nature no feeling that rises above the trifling. Mr. Hume challenges anyone to cite a single example in which a Negro has shown talents, and asserts that among the hundreds of thousands of blacks who are transported elsewhere from their countries, although many of them have even been set free, still not a single one was ever found who presented anything great in art or science or any other praiseworthy quality, even though among the whites some continually rise aloft from the lowest rabble, and through superior gifts earn respect in the world. So fundamental is the difference between these two races of man, and it appears to be as great in regard to mental capacities as in color. The religion of fetishes so wide spread among them is perhaps a sort of idolatry that sinks as deeply into the trifling as appears to be possible to human nature. A bird feather, a cow's horn, a conch shell, or any other common object, as soon as it becomes consecrated by a few words, is an object of veneration and invocation in swearing oaths. The Blacks are very vain but in the Negro's way, and so talkative that they must be driven apart from each other with thrashing.[58]

Moreover, in reply to advice that a Negro carpenter gave to Father Labat, Kant commented, "And it might be that there was something in this which perhaps deserved to be considered; but in short, this fellow was quite black from head to foot, a clear proof that what he said was stupid."[59] Kant deduced the Black man's stupidity from the fact that a *Black* person ipso facto meant a stupid person.[60] Also, Kant said that the man's Blackness functioned as "proof" of his stupidity. Kant's use of the concept "proof" complicates the familiar line that Kant was simply a product of his time. Proof suggests the establishment of the validity of a claim based upon reasoning, not simply upon the uncritical acceptance of cultural prejudices.

Kant, like Hume, was also not philosophizing about the inferiority of Blacks in a cultural vacuum that did not challenge his racist beliefs. Tsenay Serequeberhan argues that "Kant was well aware of the faulty character of the empirical travel literature and information about non-European peoples that was available to him."[61] Indeed, as Serequeberhan notes in his review of Johann Gottfried Herder's "Ideas for a Philosophy of the History of Mankind" (1785), Kant acknowledged:

Working with a mass of descriptions dealing with different lands, it is possible to prove, if one cares to do so . . . that [indigenous] Americans and Negroes are relatively inferior races in their intellectual capacities, but on the other hand, according to reports just as plausible, that their potentialities are on the same level as those of any other inhabitants of the planet.[62]

So, why would Kant continue to maintain his racism in the face of "reports just as plausible"? Serequeberhan suggests that Kant turned a blind eye because of the importance he attributed to the making of "natural distinctions" and "classifications based on hereditary coloration . . . [and] the notion of race."[63] This view only served the colonial adventures of Occidental hegemony. Serequeberhan concludes, "It is calculative 'rational control' that, unlike the Tahitians' pursuit of 'mere pleasure', is the true and proper embodiment of 'the values of existence itself.'"[64] The point here is that Kant claimed whites were the most superior of the races. In fact, Kant postulated the existence of an original stem genus that he thought was either extinct or could be discerned through comparing extant races. Unsurprisingly, the stem genus was the original human form and whiteness was closest to it.[65] Kant said that the first race was "very blond (northern Europe), of damp cold."[66] While Kant would certainly argue that the white race is a deviation from the original stem genus, he sometimes implied a level of proximity so close as to be identical to the original stem genus.[67] According to Kant's classification, the copper-reds (Native Americans), Blacks (Senegambia), and yellows (Indians) were more deviant in comparison with the original stem genus, though he does maintain that Indians and Native Americans in that order are even "lower" than Blacks.

John Locke's racism is also evident. Indeed, his racism, when it came to Blacks, triumphed over his philosophy of natural rights and liberalism. Ironically though, Douglass used Locke's theories to declare his self-ownership. With cutting irony, Charles Mills notes that this was "the same John Locke who was an investor in the Atlantic slave trade and author of the Carolina Constitution which—in seeming contradiction to his later prescriptions in the *Second Treatise*—enshrined hereditary slavery."[68]

Although Thomas Jefferson waxed and waned on the issue of Black enslavement, "owning" Black bodies of his own, in his *Notes on Virginia*, written in 1782 and 1783, his belief in the superiority of whiteness is evident. Jefferson was respected as a learned man and scientific in his outlook. Despite his famous five words, "All men are created equal," Jefferson perpetuated myths regarding the Negro *type*. In addition to reducing Blacks' capacity to express genuine love to some form of base animal desire, Jefferson argued that the Black body is more predisposed to sensation than reflection. He wrote, "To this must be ascribed their disposition to sleep when abstracted from their diversions and unemployed in labor. An animal whose body is at rest, and who does not reflect must be disposed to sleep of course."[69]

Jefferson also thought that "in imagination they [Negroes] are dull, tasteless and anomalous."[70] Black astronomer and mathematician Benjamin Banneker (1731–1806) sent to Jefferson, then Secretary of State, a copy of his *Banneker's Almanac* as evidence to counter the myth that Negroes lacked intelligence. Jefferson sent Banneker's ephemeris to the Marquis de Condorcet with an enthusiastic letter.[71] According to Earl Conrad, however, "Later, in private correspondence, he belittled the mathematical and intellectual gifts of the almanac-maker."[72]

And we must not forget Hegel's distortion of Africa, when he wrote:

> Negroes are to be regarded as a race of children who remain immersed in their state of uninterested *naïveté*. They are sold, and let themselves be sold, without any reflection on the rights or wrongs of the matter. . . . They do not show an inherent striving for culture. . . . There [in Africa] they do not attain to the feeling of human personality, their mentality is quite dormant, remaining sunk within itself and making no progress, and thus corresponding to the compact, differenceless mass of the African continent.[73]

On this score, Africa is a site devoid of any Geist. Emmanuel Chukwudi Eze writes:

> It is clear, then, that nowhere is the *direct* conjunction/intersection of the philosophical and the political and economic interests in the European denigration

and exploitation of Africans so evident and shameless as in Hegel. Since Africa, for Hegel, "is the Gold-land compressed within itself," the continent *and* its peoples become, all at once, a treasure island and a *terra nulla*, a virgin territory brimming with natural and human raw material passively waiting for Europe to exploit and turn it into mini-European territories.[74]

Moreover, certain that there was a correlation between beauty and the power of intelligence, German philosopher Christoph Meiners maintained that light-complexioned people were superior and beautiful. Darker people were "deemed both 'ugly' and at best 'semi-civilized.'"[75] Charles White, a British surgeon who argued for the aesthetic superiority of white women, deemed blushing to be a mark of beauty (which he believed to be a feature exclusive to white women).[76] In a similar manner, White asked, "where, except on the bosom of the European woman, [shall we find] two such plump and snowy white hemispheres, tipt with vermilion?"[77] Enlightenment thinker Johann Friedrich Blumenbach, known as the father of physical anthropology, Swedish naturalist Carl Linnaeus, Arthur de Gobineau, French naturalist Comte de Buffon, Robert Knox, and others, further developed and shaped the discourse through which Black bodies came to be "known"/"seen." Blumenbach reiterated the "universal" dimensions of white beauty. He linked the universality of white beauty to his belief that whites were the progenitors of humanity, occupying the apex on the great chain of being. As Fredrickson notes, "He was the first to trace the white race to the Caucasus, and he did so because of the reputed beauty of its inhabitants." Blumenbach hypothesized that "those he dubbed 'Caucasians' were the original human race from which the others had diverged or degenerated. They were, he affirmed, 'the most handsome and becoming', having 'the most beautiful form of the skull.'"[78]

Although they differed at times in details, these thinkers believed their claims to be true and descriptive of the Black body as such. Claims differentiating Black bodies from white bodies were deemed unconditioned, natural distinctions waiting to be "discovered" and "accurately" described. These thinkers, after all, represented some of the "best" minds in Europe. How could they be incorrect? Europe was the "all seeing-eye of truth," disinterested and objective. However, the Black body qua docile, perverse, and inferior, *is* a product of the white imaginary. In stream with Simone de Beauvoir, I would argue that from a historical, discursive perspective, one is not born, but rather *becomes* "Black," that is, where "Black" denotes and connotes that which is impure, savage, immoral, stupid, dull in imagination, ugly, the white man's burden, evil, simian, childlike, and naturally fit to serve whites.

BLACK EMBODIMENT WITHIN THE
SERIOUS WORLD OF WHITENESS

The power of Frederick Douglass's narrative voice is grounded in his lived, embodied experiences under the American institution of slavery. While I recognize philosophically that "experience" is never simply and purely *there*, this does not negate the fact that the oppressed are capable of speaking from the authority of their own experiences. While it is true that Douglass interprets his experiences under slavery, his experiences cannot simply be "reduced to linguistic effects."[79] Douglass's experiences under slavery exceed their "various possible and actual discursive representations."[80] To reject the metaphysics of presence does not negate the significance of how the (non-discursive) lived experiential physicality and materiality of white oppression inform the interpretive dimensions of Douglass's enslavement. Although Douglass pre-dated the requiem sung to the "death" of the modern subject, the viability of metanarratives, and the metaphysics of presence, it is ironic that when Blacks and other minority and subaltern voices begin to speak that they often find themselves in the midst of some new "post-paradigm" that appears to undercut their efforts at self-authorship and self-voicing based upon *lived* experience.

Through the process of narrating his existence, Douglass challenged the racist assumption that Black people have no perspective on the world. By speaking out against the brutality of American slavery, he fought against the distorted view of the Black body and its history of subjection to a technology of docility; he defied and challenged the caricatured myths and normativity of whiteness. He did not begin with the abstract Cartesian "I think," but with a rich description of an embodied *here* of subjectivity whose historicity was linked to the Middle Passage and shaped by a racist discursive vortex. When Douglass wrote about himself from his own perspective, he was engaged in a larger political project that had existential implications in terms of resisting the state of being an object-for-white-others. His aim was to defend the humanity and the being-for-itself of Black people. He wrote, "I see, too, that there are special reasons why I should write my own biography, in preference to employing another to do it. Not only is slavery on trial, but unfortunately, the enslaved people are also on trial. It is alleged that they are, naturally, inferior; that they are *so low* in the scale of humanity, and so utterly stupid, that they are unconscious of their wrongs, and do not apprehend their rights."[81]

As the earliest form of Black protestational autobiography, Douglass attacked the inhumanity of whites through the modality of the slave narrative. Douglass wrote to reveal his pain and the collective pain of Black people.

He engaged in self-representation, one that countered white representation, exposing to the world structures of power within a particular domain that often go unrecognized, demonstrating his humanity and the humanity of Black people, and revealing the hypocrisy of whites. He also exposed both the mechanisms deployed to attempt to dupe enslaved Blacks into thinking they were fit for oppression and how white oppressors constructed ways of rendering their acts of oppression invisible.

Under the epistemic regime of whiteness, many Blacks no doubt came to think of whiteness as the property of great souls and great minds. Beauvoir argued that women have come to think, under the epistemic regime of androcentricity, that only *men* have great souls, thoughts, dreams, and perform great deeds. Whiteness, like androcentricity, is a specific historical position that masquerades as universal, as that which exists external to a set of embodied practices. For Beauvoir, "The serious man gets rid of his freedom by claiming to subordinate it to values which would be unconditioned."[82] One strategy used to maintain the veneer of unconditionedness is that whiteness does not speak its own name. As Russell Ferguson writes, "In our society dominant discourse never tries to speak its own name. Its authority is based on absence. The absence is not just that of the various groups classified as 'other', although members of these groups are routinely denied power. It is also the lack of any overt acknowledgment of the specificity of the dominant culture, which is simply assumed to be the all-encompassing norm. This is the basis of its power."[83]

Constituting itself as the site of universality and absolute presence, whiteness functions as an epistemological and ontological anchorage. As such, whiteness assumes the authority to marginalize other identities, discourses, perspectives, and voices. Raising the issue of white identity as a form of *ressentiment* directed toward the Black as other, indeed, as the negated other, Lewis Gordon observes, "perhaps the world would have been more just if [whites'] identity had not emerged since their identity is fundamentally conditioned by hating mine. And why should anyone continue to defend any identity that is premised upon being the primary agent of hate?"[84]

Given the above constructions of the Black body as framed within the metanarrative sovereignty of white ideology, with its procrustean tendencies, it is clear that African people (the other in this case) were constructed as things "trapped" within an economy of exchange value, alienated from themselves and from the rest of the civilized world, that is, "civilized" as defined by whiteness. Within this sociohistorical theater of whiteness, Douglass's body became an essential thing of nature. Beauvoir insightfully noted that "one of the ruses of oppression is to camouflage itself behind a natural situation since, after all, one cannot revolt against nature."[85]

As he began to narrate his own experiences within the context of his historical facticity, Douglass was always already coded and narrated, deeply scripted by preexisting racist assumptions. He was born into a social reality where everything, as Beauvoir might have said, confirmed him in his belief in white superiority.[86] "By far the larger part of the slaves know as little of their age as horses know of theirs, and it is the wish of most masters within my knowledge to keep their slaves thus ignorant," Douglass wrote.[87] To inquire about one's age was judged an act of "impudent curiosity."[88] For the system of enslavement to function, the enslaved should be focused only on the role for which nature made them: to serve, not to ask questions of their own existence. This strategy of avoiding such questions allowed the white enslaver to flee his responsibility for treating the enslaved with at least a modicum of dignity.

Parents were also torn away, prohibiting any sense of connectedness. As Douglass said, "Genealogical trees do not flourish among slaves."[89] Douglass realized that the practice of separating children from their mothers and fathers "is in harmony with the grand aim of slavery, which, always and everywhere, is to reduce man to a level with the brute."[90] White power relations shape the Black body into that which is *history-less*. Terms like *sister, brother, father,* and *mother* are nominal only. According to Douglass, slavery obliterated the structure of family life among the enslaved, and, thereby, robbed "these terms of their true meaning."[91] On the plantation, "the order of civilization was reversed here."[92] Within the context of the slave system, it was not motherly affection that mattered. What was important was that the enslaved mother "adds another name to a master's ledger."[93] As Bakare-Yusuf notes:

> Therefore, the reproduction of mothering has radically different meanings for free white women and enslaved black women. For white women reproduction enables them to define themselves as human subjects since they are able to birth the next generation of the human subject even though they are excluded from full participation in the public realm of citizenship. For the enslaved woman, constituted as property, her reproductive capacity did not free her, in fact it reinstated her role as property. In this instance reproduction is not a reproduction of mothering but of property, because she transmits her unfreedom to her offspring.[94]

This was Douglass's situation, his objectivity, which involved "the quality or state of being an object."[95] Beauvoir noted that women have been reduced to a womb, an ovary.[96] Blacks have been reduced to animals, to their genitalia. Douglass mentioned horses, deemed to be brutes of the field. Time or meaningfully lived existential temporality, seizing one's life as a protensive project, a felt movement of historical *becoming*, is irrelevant to horses. Comparable to a horse, Douglass's existence was assigned a purpose by another, a white oppressor. With horror and dread, Douglass was aware of the ontological chain of being within which he was assigned an inferior role. He wrote, "We were all ranked together at the valuation. Men and women, old and young, married and single, were ranked with horses, sheep, and swine. There were horses and men, cattle and women, pigs and children, all holding the same rank in the scale of being, and were all subjected to the same narrow examination."[97] Ranked on the same ontological scale as other subhuman animals, the objective was to get Blacks to "see" themselves as naturally occupying the same rung as beasts of burden. The more Blacks were able to so identify with this racist categorization, the more they became the mimetic reflection of white projections. Beauvoir compared this type of existence to a state of vegetation and maintained that "life justifies itself only if its effort to perpetuate itself is integrated into its surpassing and if this surpassing has no other limits than those which the subject assigns himself."[98]

Through this method of keeping enslaved Black people ignorant of their birth dates, parents, and so on, many came to experience their lives as purely given without any sense of historical movement marked by deep existential significance. One's birthday was not marked and recalled as a significant existential emergence in-the-world. Douglass described this entire process of keeping him ignorant as leaving him "without an intelligible beginning in the world."[99] On a phenomenological or lived level, the Black body was returned as that which has always been, always is, and always will be fit for slavery. Within such a context, Blacks internalized their identities along a temporally truncated axis. They and their enslavers are presumed locked in an eternal dominated–dominator dynamic. "'The eternal feminine' corresponds to 'the black soul' and to 'the Jewish character'," according to Beauvoir.[100] In other words, the eternal feminine, like the Black soul, is deemed an immutable thing, an essence. But unlike Blacks, at least white women were shown levels of respect by virtue of being the mothers, wives, and sisters of white men.[101]

Within the narrative, it is clear that Douglass has a sense of himself as dejected, a brute, a thing, and as an abomination before God. His knowledge that his father was possibly a white man further solidified his identity as a dejected thing, a reminder of his owner's lust for (and possible rape of) the female Black body that was deemed subhuman and lascivious. Douglass noted that the biological father "may be white, glorying in the purity of his Anglo-Saxon blood; and his child may be ranked with the blackest slaves." The presence of the mulatto on a plantation was clear evidence of the powerful ideological workings of the slave system. After all, the enslaved mulatto was white in phenotype, and, yet, deemed "Black." All that was necessary is that "the child be by a woman in whose veins courses one thirty-second part of African blood."[102] By the one-drop rule, no matter how light, the child was still "tainted"/"stained" Black and therefore less than human.

The ideology of the one-drop rule no doubt made it easy for white men to ignore their children, to flee from the anxiety possibly caused by the blatant contradiction of enslaving their own children. Moreover, ideologically framing the Black female body as always sexually available, indeed, hypersexed, served to obscure the fact that the "hypersexed" Black female body was a fantasy whites themselves created. In short, as argued, the Black body became the phantasmatic object of the white imaginary. In this way, the white enslaver was able to disclaim responsibility for his actions, maintaining that the Black female body was the site of seductive dark mystery, a seductiveness of which white men were incapable, because of Black female seductive power and trickery, of resisting. Thus, the white enslaver was able to objectify his own perverse practices to be outside of his control, trying to push out of his consciousness the tension around the mixture of sexual attraction and guilt.

Given the construction of the Black as a brute of the field, having sex with Black women had all of the perversity of having sex with a cow. "Surely," as Lillian Smith writes, "something akin to the dread felt by one who indulges in zoophilic practices must have nagged at their minds on a level rarely admitted to consciousness." Exploring the deep contradictory elements involved in the pathology of white male desire, Smith writes, "And succumbing to desire, they mated with these dark women whom they had dehumanized in their minds, and fathered by them children who, according to their race philosophy, were 'without souls'—a strange exotic new kind of creature, whom they made slaves of and sometimes sold on the auction block."[103] Black women were the objects of what Saidiya Hartman refers to as the "erotics of terror."[104] The sexually terrorized Black female body, then, was a distorted object projected out from the inner workings of the sexual rapaciousness of the white enslaver himself. She was deemed the seductive "Jezebel Negress," the Black insatiable vagina, while the white enslaver became the "honorable" white Southern gentleman. In Gayl Jones's *Corregidora*, Portuguese slave master Corregidora refers to his Black female slaves' genitalia as "his pussy."[105] He feels entitled to fuck them or have them fucked by other white men. This served the function of both "justifying" the brutal rape of Black female bodies and providing a moral basis upon which to privilege the civilized sexual modesty of white women. In a powerful observation, Douglass wrote, "Women—white women, I mean—are IDOLS at the south, not WIVES, for the slave women are preferred in many instances."[106] An idol is a mere object of enchantment; it is lifeless. Smith notes that as white men made more and more trips to the cabins where Black women could be taken and fucked at will, the more elevated they raised their white wives on "a pedestal when he returned to the big house. The higher the pedestal, the less he enjoyed her whom he had put there, for statues after all are only nice things to look at."[107] Keep in mind, though, that the projection of the Black female body as hypersexual was also fundamentally tied to economic ends. As Joane Nagel notes:

> Ideological hegemonies do not exist in a material vacuum . . . . Enslaved women were especially likely targets of sexual abuse since their rape was rewarded by the possibility of pregnancy, and thus could increase a slaveowner's hold-ings. This incentive increased in importance after 1808 when the *importation*, but not the *reproduction* of slaves was outlawed in the United States. For the next fifty-seven years until slavery was ended in 1865 with the passage of the Thirteenth Amendment to the U.S. Constitution, a slaveowner's holdings could only be increased by "breeding" slaves. Enslaved black women thus labored for slave owners in all senses of the word—as productive workers in slaveowners' houses, businesses, and fields, and as reproductive workers whose pregnancy, childbearing, and childrearing increased slaveowners' "stock" of slaves.[108]

Douglass witnessed the sadistic sexual practices of white male enslavers as a young boy. He mentioned an enslaved woman named Esther who lived with his old master. Douglass noted that "this was a young woman who possessed that which is ever a curse to the slave-girl; namely,—personal beauty."[109] Douglass's old master clearly wanted her for himself; for he forbade her to see Ned Roberts, another enslaved Black whom she loved. Upon finding out that she disobeyed his orders, he tied her wrists and stood her on a bench with her shoulders and back exposed. "Behind her stood old master," Douglass related, "with cowskin in hand, preparing his barbarous work with all man-ner of harsh, coarse, and tantalizing epithets. The screams of his victim were most piercing. He was cruelly deliberate, and protracted the torture, *as one who was delighted with the scene.* Again and again he drew the hateful whip through his hand, adjusting it with a view of dealing the most pain-giving blow."[110]

The process of lynching Black male bodies comes to mind here.[111] The entire scene is *serious*. As Beauvoir might say, during a lynching of a Black body, whites are "led to take refuge in the ready-made values of the serious [white] world."[112] There is the spectacle of the scene, its public nature, its consumerism in the form of the exchange of images of the mutilated Black body and indeed actual body parts, the ritualism of getting dressed for the occasion, bringing children as if it were a family picnic.[113] Then of course, there is the slow hanging, and the heightened sadistic and frenzied moment of castration, of severing the fantasized, hypertrophied Black penis. Within the context of this "den of horrors," what is it about the smiling white faces as they gaze upon the mutilated Black body?[114] Clyde Taylor suggests that the smiling faces are indicative of people having experienced an event that was pleasurable.[115] One should not overlook the homoerotic elements played out in the spectacle. In removing the Black penis, in "white men embracing . . . the same penis they were so over-determinedly driven to destroy, one encounters a sadistic enactment of the homoerotic at the very moment of its most extreme disavowal."[116] Consistent with this theme of perverse eroticization, Sartwell notes:

> First of all, perhaps the dirtiest secret of white racism is its eroticisation of dominance: its sexual sadism. If we cannot acknowledge the fact that we get off on brutalization, and that our ancestors associated orgasm with the whip and the threat of the whip, then we cannot penetrate to the heart of whiteness. Very few people will acknowledge to themselves, much less to others, still less to their victims, that cruelty is pleasurable, but the whole history of American race relations is incomprehensible without that acknowledgment. [117]

The white enslaver was invested in an ideological world-picture or what Sartwell refers to as "the technology of appearance."[118] The point here is that the ideological world-picture was necessary; for it provided whites with a powerful means for moral elision. If this technology of appearance was not in place, whites would realize their inhumanity, their brutality toward those whom they deemed inferior others. However, the ideological framework was needed to maintain their understanding of themselves as superior. As Sartwell notes, "We [whites] construct our pure moral agency by the exclusion of what we construct you [Blacks] to be: particular, appetitive, passionate, incapable of reason, incoherent."[119] However, it is precisely Douglass's stories like the one about Esther, the spectacle of lynching, and the rape of Black female bodies by white men who were protected under laws that denied Blacks the legal right to testify against them in a court of law that reveal unreason, incoherence, and perverse appetite at their worst.

There are family resemblances between the dynamics of white ideology that I expose, Sartwell's conceptualization of the technology of appearance, and Beauvoir's conceptualization of the serious world. All three approaches aim to reveal a form of profound dishonesty, a form of eliding one's responsibility through the establishment of values deemed fixed and universal. As Beauvoir would have said, white enslavers have become blind and deaf, sub-men, hiding behind a world that they take to be readymade. In this way, as Douglass said, they can be "indecent without shame, cruel without shuddering."[120] Characterizing the serious man, Beauvoir is worth quoting in full:

> Dishonestly ignoring the subjectivity of his choice, he pretends that the unconditioned value of the object is being asserted through him; and by the same token

he also ignores the value of the subjectivity and the freedom of others, to such an extent that, sacrificing them to the thing, he persuades himself that what he sacrifices is nothing. The colonial administrator who has raised the highway to the stature of an idol will have no scruple about assuring its construction at the price of a great number of lives of the natives; for, what value has the life of a native who is incompetent, lazy, and clumsy when it comes to building highways? The serious leads to a fanaticism which is as formidable as the fanaticism of passion. It is the fanaticism of the Inquisition which does not hesitate to impose a credo, that is, an internal movement, by means of external constraints. It is the fanaticism of the Vigilantes of America who defend morality by means of lynchings.[121]

Douglass did know his mother but only for a brief time. He wrote of the time she walked twelve miles to see him despite the threat of being whipped like a beast of the field if caught. This encounter disrupted his state of "atemporality." She commuted his condemnation "to mark time hopelessly," providing him with a sense of heritage and a consciousness of history.[122] Douglass noted that he was "not only a child, but *somebody's* child."[123] The recognition that he was *somebody's* child militated against his simply being somebody's *property*. No longer just a homogeneous thing, undifferentiated from other disposable Black bodies at white hands, Douglass was differentiated in his being as somebody's child. Being somebody's child, in Douglass's situation, created the conditions necessary for self-recognition as someone who was loved. Being loved opens up a dynamic self-reflective moment: *I am* valued in my person; I am other than how I have been depicted in comparison with whiteness. As such, a dynamic *subjective* world opened to Douglass through the recognition of the other, love from the other. In this case, the other, his mother, did not collapse his world, but expanded it. Indeed, there was a mutual "we-expanding" between mother and child, an expansion constantly being erased under enslavement.

Having no doubt received hostile and cold gazes from whites, his being-for-his mother could be "a comfort and encouragement to the self."[124] This process set in motion a phenomenological return of Douglass's dark body as that which was admired in the eyes of another. Her presence, her embodied acts of love and sacrifice, validated Douglass's sense of self and his historical and genealogical continuity. After all, as Beauvoir stated, "it is not as single individuals that human beings are to be defined in the first place."[125] Douglass's mother provided a sense, though brief, of parental fellowship (*Mitsein*). Douglass's mother was willing to die to show him love, to lie down with him until he fell asleep at night. Indeed, her willingness to risk death to see her son undermined the "absolute" anti-Black value system that attempted to define her identity as a nonmaternal, nonnurturing breeder. The irony, of course, is that enslaved Black women were used precisely for purposes of nurturing white infants, serving as wet nurses, allowing white infants to suckle from Black breasts, taking in the "white" milk. Reflecting on her southern roots, Smith recalls that it was not unusual "to see a black woman with a dark baby at one breast and a white one at the other, rocking them both in her wide lap, shushing them to sleep as she hummed her old songs."[126] The overall point here is that Douglass's mother enacted a form of existential resistance that spoke to the power of whiteness as a regime that was a sociohistorical creation capable of disruption.[127]

In many ways, in the above context, Douglass was treated as less than an animal. At least an adult animal would have been allowed to raise its young. Not long after a few brief encounters with his mother, she fell ill and died. He wrote, "The heartless and ghastly form of *slavery* rises between mother and child, even at the bed of death. The mother, at the verge of the grave, may not gather her children, to impart to them her holy admonitions, and invoke for them her dying benediction. The bondwoman lives as a slave, and is left to die as a beast; often with fewer attentions than are paid to a favorite horse."[128]

As argued throughout this project, whiteness is deemed absolute, the essential, and the center. According to Beauvoir, however, "universal, absolute man exists nowhere."[129] Whiteness deems Blackness inessential. While young and enslaved on the plantation, Douglass was almost naked, suffered from hunger, and whipped by his so-called white master. According to Douglass, "The great difficulty was, to keep warm during the night. I had no bed. The pigs in the pen had leaves, and the horses in the stable had straw, but the children had no beds."[130] Through sheer neglect, Douglass was being taught to "see" himself as lower than an animal. He began to recognize in his situation "several points of similarity with that of the oxen. They were property, so was I."[131] Douglass revealed that he was so often "pinched with hunger, that I have fought with the dog—'Old Nep'—for the smallest crumbs that fell from the kitchen table, and have been glad when I won a single crumb in the combat."[132] The objective of the plantation was to stabilize Douglass, and other enslaved Blacks, as objects, to relegate him to a state of immanence. As Beauvoir says, "Every time transcendence falls back into immanence, stagnation, there is a degradation of existence into the '*en-soi*'—the brutish life of subjection."[133] Pertinent here is Sartre's description of an object. He wrote, "An object is what my consciousness is not and what has in itself no trace of consciousness." [134] From the perspective of whiteness, one might say, "Blackness is what my consciousness is not and what has in itself no trace of consciousness." If "*Being-for-itself* (Être pour-soi) is coextensive with the realm of consciousness, and the nature of consciousness is that it is perpetually beyond itself," then enslaved Blacks were no doubt considered sentient (like a pig or a cow), but deemed not to possess a dynamic form of consciousness, one capable of projecting toward the future and always ahead of itself.[135]

The point here is that Blacks were not believed to be frustrated in their transcendence. Many whites were convinced that Blacks were happy in their state of servitude. They saw what they wanted to see: genuine "happy darkies" fixed in their being and satisfied with their lot. "What we want is grinning, dancing idiots, so we simply manufacture them. We then notice that these folks seem to be grinning, dancing idiots, and justify our racism out of our own invention."[136]

Douglass's narrative repudiated this myth and clearly demonstrated what it meant for Blacks to be profoundly frustrated in their transcendence. In existentialist terms, whites saw Blacks as ontological plenums, they were deemed simply *there*—an essential thing that does not grasp itself through a process of being and nothingness. Sartre wrote that transcendence was "the process through which the for-itself goes beyond or surpasses the given in pursuing its project."[137] Black reality was not deemed a projective reality; Blacks were beings whose essence preceded their existence. Blacks were born into the world readymade and devoid of "the metaphysical risk of a liberty in which ends and aims must be contrived without assistance."[138] Freedom is a form of distance that the for-itself (*pour-soi*) takes toward its own being. Under slavery, Blacks were defined as an ontological positivity without any value except for that conferred upon a "thing." For Sartre and Beauvoir, at the heart of being human was nothingness. Human being "is a lack of being, but this lack has a way of being which is precisely existence."[139] For Sartre, " 'Nothingness' does not itself have Being, yet it is supported by Being. It comes into the world by the For-itself and is the recoil from fullness of self-contained Being which allows consciousness to exist as such."[140] To ex-ist (*ex-sistere*), which is a mode of *Ekstasis*, means to stand out, to be distant from one's being. One might say that to ex-ist is to take a stand regarding one's being, its direction and destiny. "It means that, first of all, man [woman] exists, turns up, appears on the scene, and, only afterwards, defines himself [herself]."[141] This does not mean, however, that human reality transcends situational embodiment. A *thing*, however, is confined to "its pure facticity."[142] Of course, Blacks were not literally regarded as rocks, but they were treated as thing-like. Reduced to their corporeality, relegated to the realm of nature, made to feel that they were to be slaves for life, many Blacks no doubt came to see themselves as static and fixed, incapable of transcending toward an open future of possibilities.

Although I have touched upon this briefly, it is important to bear in mind that slavery was also reinforced through the use of nondiscursive forms of brutality and oppression. The Black body fell prey to the white gaze and the physical disciplinary techniques of "human flesh-mongers," those that are concerned with mere surfaces.[143] Douglass told the story of Colonel Lloyd meting out 30 lashes on old Barney's dark flesh.[144] He told of Demby, who disobeyed an order given by Mr. Gore and was shot in the head as a result: "his mangled body sank out of sight, and blood and brains marked the water where he had stood."[145] From the perspective of those whites in power, Demby would not have been missed, though he was probably erased from the ledger. After all, one must keep abreast of one's financial accounts. Beauvoir aptly described Demby's situation: "Reduced to pure facticity, congealed in his immanence, cut off from his future, deprived of his transcendence and of the world which that transcendence discloses, a man no longer appears as anything more than a thing among things which can be subtracted from the collectivity of other things without its leaving upon the earth any trace of its absence."[146]

Douglass, while living in Baltimore, observed a young girl of fourteen, Mary, who was the object, along with her older sister, Henrietta, of the capricious will of her white mistress. Mary's "head, neck, and shoulders . . . were literally cut to pieces. I have frequently felt her head, and found it nearly covered with festering sores, caused by the lash of her cruel mistress."[147] Another story was of Douglass's wife's cousin, who had fallen asleep while watching a white baby and been killed as a result. The child's mother, Mrs. Hick, "jumped from her bed, seized an oak stick of wood by the fireplace, and with it broke the girl's nose and breastbone, and thus ended her life."[148] Such brutal treatment further reinforced the epistemic regime of whiteness: to be Black is to be an object of white physical aggression and vituperation; it is to have your teeth knocked out, to be hunted by dogs, to be beaten with sticks, shackled, lynched, and burned.[149] Douglass's "brother" Perry, for example, was violently attacked by the white enslaver Andrew Anthony. Because Perry was off playing when Anthony wanted him for something of little significance, he grabbed Perry by the throat, "dashed him on the ground, and with the heel of his boot stamped him on the head, until the blood gushed from his nose and ears."[150]

Black bodies were continuously subjected to trauma and many Blacks suffered from some form of post-traumatic stress disorder (PTSD). As Susan Brison notes, "A traumatic event is one in which a person feels utterly helpless in the face of a force that is perceived to be life-threatening. The immediate psychological responses to such trauma include terror, loss of control, and intense fear of annihilation."[151]

In *The History of Mary Prince*, Prince narrated how two young boys, Cyrus and Jack, often endured beatings until their flesh was ragged and raw. "They were never secure one moment from a blow, and their lives were passed in continual fear."[152] Prince described being stripped naked, tied to a tree branch by her wrists, and beaten with cow-skin. She also related the story of an enslaved Black man known as Old Daniel who, because he was lame in the hip and thereby slow, was stripped and had his flesh beaten with rough briar. Prince's white master "would then call for a bucket of salt, and fling upon the raw flesh till the man writhed on the ground like a worm, and screamed aloud with agony."[153] What more could the white enslaver desire than to make the Black body feel helpless, forever standing in fear of nonbeing, and lacking self-control. After all, they *had* to be subdued. All savage beasts must be controlled, and through such acts of violence, white enslavers were able to rest knowing they were simply doing their jobs, training animals how to behave. This allowed them to avoid the recognition of their own animality and vicious brutality. "It is the flesh, so horribly lacerated," according to Bakare-Yusuf, "that is marked for enslavement, for raw violence and objectification, that serves others' will-to-power and their becoming beings."[154]

From the above acts of brutality, I would argue that the white racist "loses himself in the object [whiteness] in order to annihilate his subjectivity."[155] For Beauvoir, "The serious man's dishonesty issues from his being obliged ceaselessly to renew the denial of this freedom."[156] The white racist attempts to deny the truth of his/her existence: freedom. The ideology of whiteness, as a species of the serious man, is a lie. Colonel Lloyd, Mr. Gore, and Mrs. Hick lost themselves in the lie of whiteness. Each was in a state of flight, creating complex distortions that functioned to blind them to their pernicious role in constructing the Black body as slavish. They avoided the recognition of the degree of choice that they had *to refuse* to cooperate (no matter how difficult or what the consequences were) with the practices of white hatred toward Black bodies. Keep in mind, though, that this does free them from moral critique and responsibility.

The process of becoming a white racist is linked to larger racially embedded sociohistorical practices of intelligibility. Yet, within the context of America's racist history, there was always already the counter-white racist position, the counter-anti-Black voice, to be taken up, and pursued, even as various social forces militated against the taking up of such a counter-white racist position/voice. Whites were not *determined* by the fixity of a racist axiological framework. There was still the freedom to challenge the "rigid training, long persisted in" that reinforces the fixity of values.[157] Hence, there is always the possibility of troubling one subject position and "leaning" into another. Along with heteronomy, then, there is autonomy. Without the concept of autonomy, we would be forced to claim that the self is no more than the plaything of external forces, a constantly shifting "voice" with absolutely no agency. There is thus the sense that the human subject is not a plenum, but always already incomplete, capable of claiming a counter-racist voice, though not one created ex nihilo. For the white racist to admit that one is always already becoming what one is not yet calls into question whiteness as an essential category of identity and mode of being. The consequence of this admittance is coming face-to-face with a profound sense of anguish. Even as whites are interpellated within a racist social structure, there is the reality of a reflective apprehension of themselves as freedom and the realization that they can continually engage in the action of choosing themselves[158] as antiracists over and over again.

Within the context of his narrative, Douglass began to face aspects of his "nothingness" qua freedom after hearing Mr. Auld scold his own wife for attempting to teach Douglass to read. According to Mr. Auld, "if you give a nigger an inch, he will take an ell. A nigger should know nothing but to obey his master—to do as he is told."[159] In other words, Douglass should not seek self-fulfillment in transcendence; rather, he should seek fulfillment in blindly executing the desires embedded within another's project. What did Mr. Auld fear? After all, Blacks were believed to be "inferior" by nature. As the serious man, Mr. Auld hid from his freedom. He believed that Douglass was by nature a slave and inferior, and, yet, his fear of Douglass learning how to read belied this assumption. This created epistemic slippage, though "hidden" from Mr. Auld through an elaborate ideological framework. Mr. Auld was fleeing his own freedom by grounding his decision—that is, not to allow Douglass to read—in the law, religion, tradition. In short, Mr. Auld circumnavigated his choice in the matter of perpetuating American slavery by rendering invisible his "membership" in a (white racist) community of intelligibility that created the very conditions that "justified" the inhuman treatment of Black bodies. His fear reveals to us his knowledge that Blacks were "slaves" (or enslaved) not by nature, but because of the actions of whites. Or, in my own preferred discourse, Mr. Auld reveals that the *lived* semiotics of whiteness (not white skin) does involve a level of choice, an act of performance sustained and justified by individual and institutional prac- tices. While this is true, it is also important to note that the serious world of whiteness is such that it actually thwarts various efforts to see through it and that Mr. Auld, while certainly the for-itself, was ensconced within a histori- cal and situational context of facticity that molded and limited him. Being in the situational reality of racism, Mr. Auld came to define himself and to be defined by the racist values of the serious world of whiteness. As such, he came to inherit the embodied weight of the formation of racist habits and modes of racist comportment.

Douglass was aware that Southern laws forbade the teaching of enslaved Blacks to read or write. Were Blacks really animals, why would there be such fines and penalties? After all, there was no law or statutes forbidding the teaching of cows to read. Douglass saw through Mr. Auld's hypocrisy where he wrote that "the manhood of the slave is conceded."[160] Douglass was resolved to learn how to read.[161] In short, Douglass underwent a process of existential conversion. "To convert the absence into presence, to convert my flight into will, I must assume my project positively."[162] He had begun to challenge his existential enslavement, his immanence. Douglass said, "You have seen how a man was made a slave; you shall see how a slave was made a man."[163] Within this context, the process of "becoming a man," for Douglass, involved the process of challenging the serious world of whiteness that had assigned him a mode of being comparable to that of a pig or a dog. Indeed, it involved the process of disrupting the passive, fixed role in terms of which white myths had depicted him.

Douglass's fight with Covey also exemplified his existential conversion; he negated the "unconditioned" values that depicted him as a passive. Covey's job was to break the so-called recalcitrant Negroes (like one would break a stubborn animal), to make them devoid of any recognition of their transcendence and their capacity to imagine alternative ways of being. Covey's tactics were designed to instill in Douglass a set of oppressive norms that would continue to work in Covey's absence. For example, Covey was always on the prowl, the quintessential overseer/overgazer. Covey became the faceless gaze, symbolic of "thousands of eyes posted everywhere."[164] As with Jeremy Bentham's panopticon, which was proposed as an effective means of imprisonment and control, Covey's white gaze was everywhere. The dynamics of seeing occurred without being seen. "Covey used techniques of manipulation and camouflage to create a sense of his omnipresence."[165] The objective was to get the Black body to internalize the white oppressive gaze. "For even the internal life of the slave could, finally, be contaminated by seeing, so that one became the watcher of oneself."[166] In this way, the enslaved Black body would behave in subservient ways in the absence of actual surveillance by the white oppressor. This technique created an effective form of double consciousness where the enslaved began to discipline his/her own Black body under the internalized regime of the power of the white gaze. The theological implications here are fascinating. The white gaze became god-like, which no doubt forced many Blacks to believe there was no place to hide from the all-seeing eye, perhaps eliciting feelings of guilt and fear in those Blacks who contemplated freedom or escape. Douglass was aware that whites deployed this strategy to break the enslaved Black body. "One half of his proficiency in the art of Negro breaking consisted, I should think, in this species of cunning. We were never secure. He could see or hear us nearly all the time. He was, to us, behind every stump, tree, bush and fence on the plantation."[167] Under Covey's gaze and brutal treatment, Douglass underwent epistemic violence. He suffered both in body and in spirit. He became the victim of the constant defeating thought: "*I am a slave—a slave for life—a slave with no rational ground to hope for freedom.*"[168]

One day in the field, Douglass became sick, felt dizzy, and could not stand. Covey kicked him in the side commanding him to stand. He could not. Covey then picked up a hickory slab, hitting Douglass in the head, "which caused a large gash, and caused the blood to run freely."[169] Douglass managed to escape to Master Thomas's place, who had given Douglass over to Covey to be broken in the first place. Douglass thought that if he could not be protected as a man, then perhaps Master Thomas would be willing to protect his own property from the abuses of Covey.[170] Unfortunately for Douglass, "the guilt of a slave is always, and everywhere, presumed; and the innocence of the slaveholder or the slave employer, is always asserted."[171] Master Thomas believed Douglass was trying to get out of work by feigning sickness. "The charge of laziness against the slaves is ever on their lips, and is the standing apology for every species of cruelty and brutality."[172] Hence, the power of the stereotype cancelled out any lenience that Master Thomas, a religious man, was capable of showing. In the end, he believed Covey was justified in beating Douglass. After all, Covey too was a religious man. Douglass referred to Master Thomas's response to him as "fairly annihilating me."[173] From the perspective of Covey's "justified" actions, Douglass had no voice, no position, no perspective, no interiority; he was annihilated.

Douglass was highly critical of white slavers' religious practices. Sartwell points out, however, that the epistemic structure of this situation was more than simply hypocrisy. "For the master not only claims to be what he is not; he claims the slave to be what he (the master) actually is." In other words, the "master" was claiming to be truly merciful, respecting the lives of others, and compassionate, but his actual behavior belied this claim. Whites accused slaves of being what the "masters" really were, hateful, brutal, and godless, which allowed whites to hide behind false religiosity, particularly given the fact that they were convinced they had a divine right to protect the savage Black body from itself, the same savage Black body that they had constructed/ projected. Whites were saviors whose duty it was, as argued earlier, to bring light where there was darkness.[174] The enslavers thereby masked their guilt in the name of the "divine father," allowing them to construct what happened to Blacks under slavery as something foreign to their (white) agency. On this score, beating and brutalizing a Black body was not an act of freedom or choice, but deemed an act of necessity.

Africans were deemed savages and their dark bodies were considered evil. On my interpretation, the act of constructing (and investing in) fantasized Black bodies, which was really the act of constructing (and investing in) fantasized white bodies, led to acts of savagery and evil. Through the process of rendering the Black body hypervisible, white bodies became invisible. "The master was civilized, Christian, and so forth, precisely in relation to the slave."[175] Douglass was aware of the sham of prevailing religious practices.[176] He wrote that between the Christianity white enslavers practiced "and the Christianity of Christ, I recognize the widest possible difference—so wide, that to receive the one as good, pure, and holy, is of necessity to reject the other as bad, corrupt, and wicked." Douglass is worth quoting in full:

> I am filled with unutterable loathing when I contemplate the religious pomp and show, together with the horrible inconsistencies, which everywhere surround me. We have men-stealers for ministers, women-whippers for missionaries, and cradle-plunderers for church members. The man who robs me of my earnings at the end of each week meets me as a class-leader on Sunday morning, to show me the way of life, and the path of salvation. He who sells my sister, for purposes of prostitution, stands forth as the pious advocate of purity. He who proclaims it a religious duty to read the Bible denies me the right of learning to read the name of the God who made me. He who is the religious advocate of marriage robs whole millions of its sacred influence, and leaves them to ravages of wholesale pollution. The warm defender of the sacredness of the family relation is the same that scatters whole families,—sundering husbands and wives, parents and children, sisters and brothers,—leaving the hut vacant, and the hearth desolate.[177]

The ideology of whiteness is idolatrous and anti-Christian. When whiteness is believed to be an absolute marker of superiority, and when, in the name of whiteness, nonwhite bodies are colonized, brutalized, murdered, raped, and, oppressed, then the ideology of whiteness is indeed anti-Christian.

After returning from Master Thomas, who threatened to beat Douglass if he did not return, Douglass faced his last flogging from Covey. Remember, at that time, Douglass had been under Covey's oppressive rule for six months and had six more to go. Douglass was questioning by then whether there was a God. He felt that he had indeed become transformed into a brute. He felt like taking his own life and Covey's. After Douglass returned home, Covey, because it was Sunday, pretended as if all was fine. Douglass: "His religion hindered him from breaking the Sabbath, but not from breaking my skin. He had more respect for the *day* than for the *man*, for whom the day was mercifully given; for while he would cut and slash my body during the week, he would not hesitate, on Sunday, to teach me the value of my soul, or the way of life and salvation by Jesus Christ."[178] On Monday morning, having ordered Douglass to go into the stable to feed and prepare the horses for the field, Covey attempted to subdue Douglass. In a pivotal passage, Douglass wrote: "The fighting madness had come upon me, and I found my strong fingers firmly attached to the throat of my cowardly tormentor; as heedless of consequences, at the moment, as though we stood as equals before the law. The very color of the man was forgotten."[179]

While fighting Covey, Douglass said he had forgotten "the very color of the man." Covey was, of course, white. However, for Douglass in that moment, whiteness had ceased to function as the transcendental norm; he rejected its superior status. In that moment of refusal, whiteness was placed under erasure.

Unlike in the situation involving Mr. Auld's refusal to allow Douglass to read, Douglass, in his own historical parlance, claimed his manhood / humanity; he did not just concede it. In his fight with Covey, Douglass not only resisted further potential physical brutality but he also resisted the entire ideological structure upon which whiteness was constructed. Not only did Douglass assert the materiality of his body but he also reclaimed his body in the name of freedom and self-definition, refusing to be fixed by a philosophical anthropology that profiled him within the framework of a set of intended meanings that collapsed his dark epidermis upon itself. He became *conscious of* his body as an active force, a moral site of resistance. In resisting Covey, in seeing through the sham of whiteness as sacrosanct, he saw whiteness as a cultural artifact, a power bloc held together through processes of collective and individual human choice and institutional social forces.

Although in the end Douglass won the fight, he realized that he was still institutionally enslaved. The Fugitive Slave Law of 1850 guaranteed this. Yet Douglass spoke of his freedom, saying: "however long I might remain a slave in form, the day had passed when I could be a slave in fact."[180] Through his act of challenging Covey's white authority, he was living the existential credo that one becomes a human being.[181]

Douglass had come to realize that the price of the social expression of his freedom was death; for he resisted being treated as a *thing*. He refused to wrap himself within the security of the serious world, but to risk. Beauvoir also realized the price of freedom, writing: "whatever the problems raised for him, the setbacks that he will have to assume, and the difficulties with which he will have to struggle, he must reject oppression at any cost."[182] He had resolved to embrace and affirm agency and came face-to-face with the anguish of his being-toward the future. He had become "a being of the distances, a movement toward the future, a project."[183] Douglass experienced the upsurge of the ontology of his freedom, though still a slave de jure. Had he not resisted Covey, Douglass would have reduced himself to a state where "living is only not dying."[184] He had succeeded in demystifying his situation; he realized it was a situation that white men/women and institutions imposed and sustained.[185] Indeed, fighting Covey was an act of Douglass surpassing himself, an act of war against the continuity of the normativity of whiteness.[186] As Beauvoir reminded us, "Revolt is not integrated into the harmonious development of the world; it does not wish to be integrated but rather to explode at the heart of the world and break its continuity."[187]

Douglass realized that he was not a thing fixed according to nature. He was metastable and transphenomenal. As the for-itself, he was always more than he appeared to be. Yet, as Sartre said, "the for-itself *is*. It *is*, we may say, even if it is a being which is not what it is and which is what it is not."[188] Moreover, Douglass was a significant and undeniable point of moral worth. "The freedom of a single man must count more than a cotton or rubber harvest."[189] Capturing his own sense of self-possession, Douglass said, "I am myself."[190] This did not mean Douglass now saw himself as an enclosed "monadic" consciousness. The point here is that he knew the truth of his existence; he knew he was not the "brute" seen through the aperture of the white gaze. He knew that his "freedom," in Beauvoir's words, "in order to fulfill itself, requires that it emerge into an open future," a future that he must claim.[191] Douglass said, "I was now my own master."[192] And while he realized that his body could be chained, he knew that did not mean he was ontologically a slave. He realized that being a "slave" was not a natural category, but one predicated upon the existence of "masters," just as the superiority of whiteness was inextricably linked to the inferiorization of Blackness. Having rejected the natural right of whites to enslave those deemed as dark others, Douglass had rejected the mythopoetic views of North American slavery.[193] Through his *lived* epistemic standpoint, and because of his iconoclasm against the images portrayed of "happy" and "cheerful" darkies living on plantations, Douglass made known to the world the atrocities of slavery and rendered visible the ideology of whiteness. As such, Douglass, along with others, created a significant epistemological rupture in the narrative lies deployed by whites to paint a history of white innocence in relationship to the actual brutalized Black body at the hands of white people.

NOTES

1. Jean-Paul Sartre was also influenced by the work of Richard Wright. As Robert Bernasconi notes, "Wright, as read by Sartre, not only gave Whites a glimpse of certain select aspects of Black life: he showed the oppressors how the oppressed regarded them. What Wright could do, over and beyond anything Sartre could accomplish, was not just write about the experience of being subject to racism, but also complete Sartre's project of showing the oppressor to himself." See Robert Bernasconi, "Sartre's Gaze Returned: The Transformation of the Phenomenology of

Racism," *Journal of the British Society for Phenomenology*, 18(2), 1995, 201–21, quotation on 207.

2. Margaret A. Simons, *Beauvoir and* The Second Sex: *Feminism, Race, and the Origins of Existentialism* (Lanham, MD: Rowman & Littlefield, 1999), 168.

3. . Simone de Beauvoir, *America Day by Day*, trans. Carol Cosman (1948; reprint, Berkeley and Los Angeles: University of California Press, 1999).

4. Simons, *Beauvoir and* The Second Sex, 181–2.

5. Simons, *Beauvoir and* The Second Sex, 176.

6. Simone de Beauvoir, *The Second Sex* (1949; reprint, New York: Vintage Books, 1989), 297–8.

7. Beauvoir, *Second Sex*, 297.

8. Some African chiefs participated in selling other African bodies to white enslavers. They did this for various trinkets of "value." Although the few African chiefs who participated in this ought to be held accountable, whether they fully knew the fate of those sold is unclear. During tribal warfare between Africans, there were those who were taken as "slaves." But this was not the same as the selling of Black bodies for capitalist/industrial profits. Indeed, "enslaved" in Africa had the opportunity to ascend within the new tribe. Moreover, a captured African could even eventually marry into the chief's family. In the case of white enslavers, Black bodies were reduced to chattel, discursively and nondiscursively constructed as intrinsically inferior according to their dark and physiologically perverse bodies. African chiefs' "gaze" was not structured according to a racialist/racist framework predicated upon the superiority of skin color. The "enslaved" African body by other African bodies was not believed, according to manifest destiny, to be fit for a lifetime of degradation. These bodies were not aimlessly murdered, lynched, or ritualistically castrated for viewing pleasure.

9. The ships left European ports, made violent incursions into Africa, captured and enslaved Africans, traveled to the so-called New World to deliver their goods, their "objects" of great financial value, and then sailed back to Europe.

10. Michel Foucault, *Discipline and Punish*, trans. Alan Sheridan (New York: Pantheon, 1995), 141.

11. Michel Foucault, *The Foucault Reader: An Introduction to Foucault's Thought*, ed. Paul Rabinow (London: Penguin, 1991), 173.

12. Bibi Bakare-Yusuf, "The Economy of Violence: Black Bodies and the Unspeakable Terror," in *Feminist Theory and the Body: A Reader*, ed. Janet Price and Margrit Shildrick (New York: Routledge, 1999), 313.

13. Bakare-Yusuf, "Economy of Violence," 314.

14. Emmanuel Chukwudi Eze, *Race and the Enlightenment: A Reader* (Malden, MA: Blackwell, 1997), 110.

15. Eze, *Race and the Enlightenment*, 124.

16. Simons, *Beauvoir and* The Second Sex, 217.

17. Frantz Fanon, *Black Skin, White Masks*, trans. Charles Lam Markmann (New York: Grove Press, Inc., 1967), 138.

18. Charles Johnson, "A Phenomenology of the Black Body," *Michigan Quarterly Review*, 32(4), 1993, 598–614, quotation on 605.

19. Bakare-Yusuf, "Economy of Violence," 318.

20. Hortense J. Spillers, "Mama's Baby, Papa's Maybe: An American Grammar Book," *Diacritics*, 17 (Summer 1987), 65–81, quotation on 72.

21. Bakare-Yusuf, "Economy of Violence," 317.

22. The act of choosing death over enslavement is a profound instance of self-consciousness and human agency. After all, animals do not kill themselves. As Lewis Gordon notes, "Blacks, it was believed, were incapable of committing suicide because, supposedly like the 'rest' of the animal kingdom, they lacked enough apperception or intelligence to understand the ramifications of their situation. This reasoning was based on the supposition of what a 'true' human being *would do* if treated as blacks are treated." See Lewis Gordon, "Introduction: Black Existential Philosophy," in his edited book *Existence in Black: An Anthology of Black Existential Philosophy* (New York: Routledge, 1997).

23. Some Africans actually feared they would be eaten, for they had not seen people with such ghost-like skin before. Enslaved Africans did attempt to resist their captors in the form of physically fighting for their freedom. Think here of those Africans who took control of the *Amistad* in July 1839. Sengbe Pieh or Joseph Cinqué led the resistance. And although he ordered Spaniards to return him and the other Africans back to Africa, they deceived him. Eventually, he and the other Africans were recaptured, stood trial, and were freed in 1841.

24. Bakare-Yusuf, "Economy of Violence," 318.

25. Spillers, "Mama's Baby, Papa's Maybe," 72.

26. Fred D'Aguiar, *Feeding the Ghosts* (Hopewell, NJ: The Ecco Press, 1997), 11.

27. D'Aguiar, *Feeding the Ghosts*, 38–9.

28. D'Aguiar, *Feeding the Ghosts*, 39–40.

29. bell hooks, *Ain't I a Woman: Black Women and Feminism* (Boston, MA: South End Press, 1981), 18–19.

30. Molefi K. Asante, *African American History: A Journey of Liberation* (Maywood, NJ: Peoples Publishing Group, Inc., 1995), 61.

31. Asante, *African American History*, 59.

32. Foucault, *Discipline and Punish*, 194.

33. Mary Prince's narrative is important in that it represents the voice and epistemic standpoint of the first Black British woman to have her experiences under slavery actually published. For Prince, like other Africans, the African diaspora, that space of rupture, dispersion, and displacement, forms the crucible in terms of which the experiential specificity of Black men's/women's lives took shape.

34. Mary Prince, *The History of Mary Prince: A West Indian Slave Related by Herself*, ed. Moira Ferguson (Ann Arbor: University of Michigan Press, 1997), 62.

35. Crispin Sartwell, *Act Like You Know: African-American Autobiography and White Identity* (Chicago: University of Chicago Press, 1998), 97.

36. Sartwell, *Act Like You Know*, 11.

37. Sartwell, *Act Like You Know*, 99.

38. Sartwell, *Act Like You Know*, 98.

39. Lillian Smith, *Killers of the Dream* (New York: W.W. Norton & Company, 1949/1961), 121. Of course, this does not deny how white women became prisoners

of the matrixes of forbidden desire, guilt, and profound repression when it came to the Black male body.

40. Smith, *Killers of the Dream*, 122–3.

41. George M. Fredrickson, *The Black Image in the White Mind: The Debate on Afro-America Character and Destiny, 1817–1914* (Hanover, NH: Wesleyan University Press, 1971), 279.

42. Fredrickson, *Black Image in the White Mind*, 279.

43. Fredrickson, *Black Image in the White Mind*, 277.

44. Stuart Hall, "Cultural Identity and Diaspora" in *Colonial Discourse and Post-Colonial Theory: A Reader*, ed. Patrick Williams and Laura Chrisman (New York: Columbia University Press, 1994), 394.

45. Graham Richards, *"Race," Racism and Psychology: Towards a Reflexive History* (New York: Routledge, 1997), 16.

46. Fredrickson, *Black Image in the White Mind*, 268.

47. Fredrickson, *Black Image in the White Mind*, 253.

48. Stephen Jay Gould, *The Mismeasure of Man* (New York: W.W. Norton & Company), 69.

49. Fredrickson, *Black Image in the White Mind*, 253.

50. Robyn Wiegman, *American Anatomies: Theorizing Race and Gender* (Durham, NC: Duke University Press, 1995), 53. According to European racist mythology, masculine domination was a clear marker of advanced civilization. Wiegman insightfully notes, "In this way, the binary structure of race—that rigorously defended emphasis on the incommensurabilities between black and white—took on, through anatomic analysis, a double ideological function: the European male's brain evinced not simply a racial superiority, but a quintessentially masculine one as well. Blackness, in short, was here feminized and the African (-American) male was disaffiliated from the masculine itself," 54.

51. Fredrickson, *Black Image in the White Mind*, 281.

52. Emmanuel Lévinas, "The Trace of the Other," in *Deconstruction in Context*, ed. Mark C. Taylor (Chicago: Chicago University Press, 1986), 346–7.

53. Quoted in Eze, *Race and the Enlightenment*, 33. Note that according to Gould, Hume held various political posts, "including the stewardship of the English colonial office in 1766," *Mismeasure of Man*, 72.

54. Eze, *Race and the Enlightenment*, 33.

55. In personal correspondence, Clarence Johnson argues that if this is correct, then Hume has no basis, inductively or otherwise, to suggest the contrary.

56. Clarence Sholé Johnson, *Cornel West and Philosophy: The Quest for Social Justice* (New York: Routledge, 2003), 156.

57. Johnson, *Cornel West and Philosophy*, 159.

58. Immanuel Kant, *Observations on the Feeling of the Beautiful and Sublime*, trans. John T. Goldthwait (1764; Berkeley: University of California Press, 1960), 110–11.

59. Kant, *Observations*, 113.

60. Johnson, although critical of Kant's position, insightfully formulates Kant's view regarding a Black person and the quality of being stupid in the form of a syllogism, *Cornel West and Philosophy*, 157.

61. Tsenay Serequeberhan, "The Critique of Eurocentrism and the Practice of African Philosophy," in *Postcolonial African Philosophy: A Critical Reader*, ed. Emmanuel Chukwudi Eze (Cambridge, MA: Blackwell Publishers, 1997), 153.

62. Immanuel Kant, "Review of Herder's Ideas for a Philosophy of the History of Mankind," in *Kant: On History*, ed. Lewis White Beck (Englewood Cliffs, NJ: Prentice Hall, 1963), 47.

63. Kant, "Review of Herder's Ideas," 47.

64. Serequeberhan, "Critique of Eurocentrism," 154.

65. Eze, *Race and the Enlightenment*, 48.

66. Eze, *Race and the Enlightenment*, 48.

67. I thank Jerry Miller for his insights here.

68. Charles W. Mills, *Blackness Visible: Essays on Philosophy and Race* (Ithaca, NY: Cornell University Press, 1998), 199.

69. Earl Conrad, *The Invention of the Negro* (New York: Paul S. Eriksson, Inc., 1966), 73–4.

70. Conrad, *Invention of the Negro*, 74. In their significant book *White Racism: The Basics* (New York: Routledge, 1995), Joe R. Feagin and Hernan Vera note: "Negative images of African Americans were accepted by the framers of the Declaration of Independence and the U.S. Constitution. Prominent European Americans in the early history of this nation were slaveholders, including the southerners George Washington, James Madison, and Thomas Jefferson. In an early draft of the Declaration of Independence, Jefferson attacked slavery but was careful to blame it on England's King George. However, because of slaveowners' opposition, Jefferson's anti-slavery language was omitted from the final version of that founding document. Despite his indictment of slavery, Jefferson himself was a slaveowner with racist ideas. Writing in *Notes on Virginia*, Jefferson argued that what he saw as the ugly color, offensive odor, and ugly hair of African American slaves indicated their physical inferiority and that their alleged inability to create was a sign of mental inferiority" (68–9). Given Jefferson's alleged relationship with Sally Hemings, one of his enslaved Black females, who is said to have given birth to seven of his children, the hypocrisy cries out.

71. *Macmillan Information Now Encyclopedia: The African-American Experience*, ed. Jack Salzman (New York: Macmillan Publishing, 1998), 56.

72. Conrad, *Invention of The Negro*, 75. Negroes were held to be inferior regardless of evidence to the contrary.

73. Georg Wilhelm Friedrich Hegel, "Anthropology," *Encyclopaedia of the Philosophical Sciences*, in *The Idea of Race*, ed. Robert Bernasconi and Tommy L. Lott (Indianapolis: Hackett, 2000), 40–1.

74. Emmanuel Chukwudi Eze, "Introduction," in *Postcolonial African Philosophy: A Critical Reader*, ed. Emmanuel Chukwudi Eze (Cambridge, MA: Blackwell Publishers, 1997), 9–10.

75. George Fredrickson, *Racism: A Short History* (Princeton, NJ: Princeton University Press, 2002), 59.

76. Fredrickson, *Racism*, 59.

77. Fredrickson, *Racism*, 59.

78. Fredrickson, *Racism*, 57.

79. Linda Martín Alcoff, "Merleau-Ponty and Feminist Theory on Experience," in *Chiasms: Merleau-Ponty's Notion of Flesh*, ed. Fred Evans and Leonard Lawlor (Albany: SUNY Press, 2000), 266.

80. Alcoff, "Merleau-Ponty and Feminist Theory on Experience," 266.

81. Frederick Douglass, *My Bondage and My Freedom*, with a new introduction by Philip S. Foner (New York: Dover Publications, 1969), vii.

82. Simone de Beauvoir, *The Ethics of Ambiguity* (New York: Citadel Press, 1976), 46.

83. Russell Ferguson, "Introduction: Invisible Center," in *Marginalization and Contemporary Cultures*, ed. Russell Ferguson, Martha Gever, Trinh T. Minh-ha, and Cornel West (New York: New Museum of Contemporary Art, 1990), 11.

84. Lewis R. Gordon. *Existentia Africana: Understanding Africana Existential Thought* (New York: Routledge, 2000).

85. Beauvoir, *Ethics of Ambiguity*, 83.

86. Beauvoir, *Second Sex*, 43.

87. Frederick Douglass, *Narrative of the Life of Frederick Douglass, an American Slave, Written by Himself*, ed. David W. Blight (New York: Bedford/St. Martin's Press, 1993), 39.

88. Douglass, *My Bondage and My Freedom*, 35.

89. Douglass, *My Bondage and My Freedom*, 34.

90. Douglass, *My Bondage and My Freedom*, 37–8.

91. Douglass, *My Bondage and My Freedom*, 48.

92. Douglass, *My Bondage and My Freedom*, 51.

93. Douglass, *My Bondage and My Freedom*, 53.

94. Bakare-Yusuf, "Economy of Violence," 320.

95. Justus Streller, *To Freedom Condemned: A Guide to the Philosophy of Jean-Paul Sartre*, trans. Wade Baskin (New York: Citadel Press, 1960), 126.

96. Beauvoir, *Second Sex*, 3.

97. Douglass, *Narrative of the Life of Frederick Douglass*, 64.

98. Beauvoir, *Ethics of Ambiguity*, 83.

99. Douglass, *My Bondage and My Freedom*, 60.

100. Beauvoir, *Second Sex*, xxix.

101. My point is not to deny the history of oppression shown toward white women within the context of white male hegemony. Black women were not shown the kind of respect shown toward white women. However, the "respect" shown toward white women was not a result of being valued equally with white men. As Marilyn Frye notes, "a woman who is chaste and obedient is called . . . 'respectable.'" Black women were deemed unchaste by nature. Frye is critical of the view that being white automatically grants raced white women political leverage over white men. She is also aware of how white women who have not critiqued the ways in which their "whiteliness" functions fail to form political alliances with nonwhite women, and how white women become partners in the oppression of nonwhites, and define themselves as possessions of white men. Nevertheless, she is cognizant of the benefits of being a raced white woman over being a raced Black woman in a context where white men occupy positions of power within a larger context of white racism: "Racism translates

into an aspiration to whiteliness. The white girl learns that whiteliness is dignity and respectability; she learns that whiteliness is her aptitude for partnership with white men; she learns that partnership with white men is her salvation from the original position of Woman in patriarchy. Adopting and cultivating whiteliness as an individual character seems to put it in the woman's own power to lever herself up out of a kind of nonbeing (the status of woman in a male-supremacist social order) over into a kind of Being (the status of white in white-supremacist social order). See "White Woman Feminist," in *Overcoming Racism and Sexism*, ed. Linda A. Bell and David Blumenfield (Lanham, MD: Rowman & Littlefield, 1995), 116.

102. Douglass, *My Bondage and My Freedom*, 52.

103. Smith, *Killers of the Dream*, 120.

104. Saidiya V. Hartman, *Scenes of Subjection: Terror, Slavery, and Self-Making in Nineteenth-Century America* (New York: Oxford University Press, 1997), 81.

105. Gayl Jones, *Corregidora* (Boston: Beacon Press, 1997), 54.

106. Douglass, *My Bondage and My Freedom*, 59.

107. Smith, *Killers of the Dream*, 121.

108. Joane Nagel, *Race, Ethnicity, and Sexuality: Intimate Intersections, Forbidden Frontiers* (New York: Oxford University Press, 2003), 106.

109. Douglass, *My Bondage and My Freedom*, 85.

110. Douglass, *My Bondage and My Freedom*, 87, emphasis added.

111. This in no way is designed to marginalize the many Black women who were policed, terrorized, and brutalized through acts of white sadistic lynching.

112. Beauvoir, *Ethics of Ambiguity*, 44.

113. See Grace Elizabeth Hale, *Making Whiteness: The Culture of Segregation in the South, 1890–1940* (New York: Vintage Books, 1999), 203–39.

114. Douglass, *My Bondage and My Freedom*, 233.

115. See *The Birth of Whiteness: Race and the Emergence of U.S. Cinema*, ed. Daniel Bernardi (New Brunswick, NJ: Rutgers University Press, 1996), 28.

116. Wiegman, *American Anatomies*, 99.

117. Sartwell, *Act Like You Know*, 110.

118. Sartwell, *Act Like You Know*, 36.

119. Sartwell, *Act Like You Know*, 89.

120. Douglass, *My Bondage and My Freedom*, 62.

121. Beauvoir, *Ethics of Ambiguity*, 49–50.

122. Beauvoir, *Ethics of Ambiguity*, 83.

123. Douglass, *My Bondage and My Freedom*, 56.

124. Simons, *Beauvoir and* The Second Sex, 218.

125. Beauvoir, *Second Sex*, 35.

126. Smith, *Killers of the Dream*, 130.

127. Beauvoir, *Ethics of Ambiguity*, 83.

128. Douglass, *My Bondage and My Freedom*, 57.

129. Beauvoir, *Ethics of Ambiguity*, 112.

130. Douglass, *My Bondage and My Freedom*, 132.

131. Douglass, *My Bondage and My Freedom*, 212.

132. Douglass, *My Bondage and My Freedom*, 75.

133. Beauvoir, *Second Sex*, xxxv.

134. Streller, *To Freedom Condemned*, 17.

135. William Barrett, *Irrational Man: A Study in Existential Philosophy* (Garden City, NY: Anchor Books, 1962), 245.

136. Sartwell, *Act Like You Know*, 34.

137. Streller, *To Freedom Condemned*, 127.

138. Beauvoir, *Second Sex*, xxvii.

139. Beauvoir, *Ethics of Ambiguity*, 13.

140. Jean-Paul Sartre, *Being and Nothingness*, trans. Hazel E. Barnes (New York: Pocket Books, 1956), 804.

141. Jean-Paul Sartre, *Existentialism and Human Emotions* (New York: Philosophical Library, Inc., 1957), 15.

142. Beauvoir, *Ethics of Ambiguity*, 31.

143. Douglass, *Narrative of the Life of Frederick Douglass*, 41.

144. Douglass, *Narrative of the Life of Frederick Douglass*, 49.

145. Douglass, *Narrative of the Life of Frederick Douglass*, 52.

146. Beauvoir, *Ethics of Ambiguity*, 100.

147. Douglass, *Narrative of the Life of Frederick Douglass*, 41.

148. Douglass, *Narrative of the Life of Frederick Douglass*, 53.

149. Douglass, *Narrative of the Life of Frederick Douglass*, 144.

150. Douglass, *My Bondage and My Freedom*, 178.

151. Susan J. Brison, *Aftermath: Violence and the Remaking of a Self* (Princeton, NJ: Princeton University Press, 2002), 39.

152. Prince, *History of Mary Prince*, 66.

153. Prince, *History of Mary Prince*, 74.

154. Bakare-Yusuf, "Economy of Violence," 317.

155. Beauvoir, *Ethics of Ambiguity*, 45.

156. Beauvoir, *Ethics of Ambiguity*, 47.

157. Douglass, *My Bondage and My Freedom*, 152.

158. Sartre, *Being and Nothingness*, 800.

159. Douglass, *Narrative of the Life of Frederick Douglass*, 57.

160. Douglass, *Narrative of the Life of Frederick Douglass*, 143.

161. Douglass had to develop sophisticated ways of *resisting* early on. In order to learn how to read, he had to deploy strategies that escaped the radar of the white gaze of Mr. and Mrs. Auld. "Seized with a determination to learn to read, at any cost," Douglass explained, "I hit upon many expedients to learn to accomplish the desired end. The plea which I mainly adopted, and the one by which I was most successful, was that of using my young white playmates, with whom I met in the street, as teachers. I used to carry, almost constantly, a copy of Webster's spelling book in my pocket; and, when sent on errands, or when play time was allowed me, I would step, with my young friends, aside, and take a lesson in spelling. I generally paid my tuition fee to the boys, with bread, which I also carried in my pocket," *My Bondage and My Freedom*, 155.

162. Beauvoir, *Ethics of Ambiguity*, 26.

163. Douglass, *Narrative of the Life of Frederick Douglass*, 75.

164. Foucault, *Discipline and Punish*, 214.

165. Gordon, *Existentia Africana*, 55.

166. Sartwell, *Act Like You Know*, 46.

167. Douglass, *My Bondage and My Freedom*, 216.

168. Douglass, *My Bondage and My Freedom*, 221.

169. Douglass, *My Bondage and My Freedom*, 225.

170. Douglass, *My Bondage and My Freedom*, 233.

171. Douglass, *My Bondage and My Freedom*, 230.

172. Douglass, *My Bondage and My Freedom*, 231.

173. Douglass, *My Bondage and My Freedom*, 229.

174. Some Black thinkers (e.g., Bishop McNeal Turner, and Reverend Alexander Crummell) endorsed the view that it was a form of providential inevitability that "benighted" Black people were to be "civilized" by those Europeans who had achieved "greatness." The argument, or so it would seem, was never that Africans should continue to suffer under slavery, but that the slave trade was providential as a means toward extricating Africans from their lived barbarity in Africa. This view, however, conceded the intellectual, religious, and moral superiority of Europeans over Africans, as well as upholding the idea that Africans ought to imitate Europe's understanding of what constituted "humanity" and "civilization." The view also implicated "divine intention" in the historical brutality of African people. Even assuming that the religious exegete maintains that it was never God's intention to prolong the suffering of Africans, but only to raise them up to the level of civilized humanity, it is reasonable to ask, "Why any suffering at all?" While this is not the place to explore the complexity of this issue, this raises the philosophical and theological issues that revolve around the problem of theodicy.

175. Sartwell, *Act Like You Know*, 38.

176. Douglass, *My Bondage and My Freedom*, 235.

177. Douglass, *Narrative of the Life of Frederick Douglass*, 105.

178. Douglass, *My Bondage and My Freedom*, 240.

179. Douglass, *My Bondage and My Freedom*, 242.

180. Douglass, *Narrative of the Life of Frederick Douglass*, 79.

181. Gordon, *Existentia Africana*, 46.

182. Beauvoir, *Ethics of Ambiguity*, 96.

183. Beauvoir, *Ethics of Ambiguity*, 102.

184. Beauvoir, *Ethics of Ambiguity*, 83.

185. Beauvoir, *Ethics of Ambiguity*, 85.

186. Bernard R. Boxill has written insightfully about Douglass's fight with Covey, and the larger issues around Douglass's transition from being a pacifist to believing in violent resistance. Boxill notes, "One explanation of his change from pacifist to advocate of violent slave resistance is that while he was always clear that the slaves had a right to resist their masters violently, before 1849 he warned against violent slave resistance because he believed it would delay the abolition of slavery and have bad consequences overall: after 1849 he changed his mind and began urging violent slave resistance because he believed it would hasten the end of slavery." See "The Fight with Covey," in Gordon, *Existence in Black*, 274.

187. Beauvoir, *Ethics of Ambiguity*, 84.

188. Sartre, *Being and Nothingness*, 127.

189. Beauvoir, *Ethics of Ambiguity*, 113.

190. Douglass, *Narrative of the Life of Frederick Douglass*, 137.

191. Beauvoir, *Ethics of Ambiguity*, 82.

192. Douglass, *Narrative of the Life of Frederick Douglass*, 103.

193. Within the institutional practices of American slavery, a few Black families also financially benefited from owning enslaved Black bodies. Thus when it came to making profits, class position and bourgeois values became the central organizing principles. In short, those few Blacks who financially benefited from slavery shared class values similar to elite whites who benefited from slavery. Such bourgeois Blacks were invested both in the accumulation of wealth and protecting their material interests, even if this meant upholding the continued enslavement of "fellow" Blacks. However, it is my sense that these bourgeois Blacks would have rejected the myths regarding the natural inferiority of African bodies as based upon the latter's dark epidermal constitution. Were this not the case, this would have placed such elite Blacks, despite their wealth, within the same negative ontological frame of reference as those Blacks who were caricatured as dumb animals fit for the field. Of course, light skin also functioned as a marker of the Black aristocracy. Indeed, Black abolitionists who were light in complexion and against the continued enslavement of Black bodies still looked down upon those masses of (dark complexioned) Blacks who were uneducated. The reader should also keep in mind that some Blacks were even disappointed by efforts to dismantle Jim Crow laws. The existence of such laws provided some Blacks, those who owned small stores and businesses, with the opportunity to exploit fellow Blacks who were legally prevented from shopping at "white only" stores.

Chapter 6

Desiring *Bluest Eyes,* Desiring Whiteness

The Black Body as Torn Asunder

It is the dominant race that can make it seem their experience is representative.

—bell hooks

Historically relegated to the auction block instead of the pedestal, the black female body has been constructed as the ugly end of a wearisome Western dialectic: not sacred but profane, not angelic but demonic, not fair lady but ugly darky.

—Vanessa D. Dickerson

When I teach Toni Morrison's *The Bluest Eye,* I find it necessary to provide students with a critical framework for understanding the ways in which whiteness as the transcendental norm is a contemporary global phenomenon, especially within the context of Africa. In many places in Africa, whiteness is valorized as a site of absolute beauty and with it the internalization of self-hatred. Skin-lightening products have sold well in many African countries. According to one study provided by the World Health Organization, "Nigerians are the highest users of such products: 77% of Nigerian women use the products on a regular basis. They are followed by Togo with 59%; South Africa with 35%; and Mali at 25%."[1] One Congolese man, who received injections to make his skin lighter, is reported to have said: "I pray every day and I ask God, 'God why did you make me black?' I don't like being black. I don't like black skin."[2] To invoke the theological here implies a kind of cosmic punishment; that Blackness is a stain of sin, that which is to be mourned. Indeed, the problem of theodicy is also invoked here. After all, why would an omnibenevolent God inflict upon someone a dark epidermis, that which is symbolic of "evil," "inferiority," "ugliness"? The reality is that whiteness is marketed. Consumers are created. A racialized economy of desire is produced and perpetuated as *normative*. It is that which is to be had, possessed. So, what Morrison writes about so brilliantly through the fictional character of Pecola Breedlove has larger nonfictional implications regarding the pain and suffering of real Black bodies that measure themselves according to the idol of whiteness, an idol that is worshipped. The result is physically devastating, often leaving Black bodies scarred from the toxicity of such skin bleaches. Of course, what happens to the souls of Black folk is also toxic, poisoning any sense of a healthy Black identity, leaving the Black body torn asunder, split, broken, doubled.

In this chapter, then, I expose a paradigm case of Du Boisian double-consciousness generated through the power of whiteness. As a manifestation of pathology, I theorize double-consciousness within the context of Toni Morrison's fictional text, *The Bluest Eye*. As did W. E. B. Du Bois, Morrison also engages in the process of exposing whiteness and its impact upon Black embodiment. Hence, this chapter functions as a form of "double exposure." Pecola Breedlove, the young and innocent protagonist of Morrison's text, does not manage psychologically to survive having her Black body "confiscated" and returned back to her as that which is problematic, ugly, wretched, and worthless.[3] Indeed, she comes to internalize the "thrown-back image"; she only "sees" her Black self as "seen" by the (white) one. Consequently, she comes to desire the attributes of the one. For want of the bluest eyes, she undergoes a psychological split so massive that she comes to imagine that she in fact *has* the bluest eyes.

As I have shown, whiteness is to goodness as Blackness is to evilness. Through the white imaginary, Blackness is ugly, dirty, uncivilized. Within the episteme of whiteness, "darker peoples," as W. E. B. Du Bois argued, "are dark in mind as well as in body; of dark, uncertain, and imperfect descent; of frailer, cheaper stuff."[4] Pecola Breedlove has fully internalized the myths of whiteness, particularly the myth of white beauty. She has come to see her dark skin, her non-blue eyes, as composed of "cheaper stuff." In Morrison's text, within the semiotic space of whiteness, blue eyes signify universal beauty. To possess blue eyes is to possess whiteness. Pecola sees herself "through the revelation of the other [white] world."[5] She has learned to measure herself by the bright eyes and white pure innocence of Shirley Temple. Within the process of becoming double, her fragile psyche could not sustain the constant warring. Her little dark body was torn asunder.

Pecola is a tragic figure who has *bleached* her identity "in a flood of white Americanism."[6] Unlike Emma Lou Brown, the Black female protagonist in Wallace Thurman's *The Blacker the Berry*, Pecola never gains a sense of "mental independence."[7] Initially, Emma thought of her skin as a curse.[8] "Not that she minded being black," Thurman wrote, "being a Negro necessitated having a colored skin, but she did mind being too black."[9] As mentioned before, from the perspective of whiteness, even if someone only has one drop of "Black blood" one is still *too* Black. And although Emma insisted upon using "an excess of rouge and powder" to whiten her too Black face, at the end of the text, she comes to accept her Black skin and learns how to fight "not so much for acceptance by other people, but for acceptance of herself by herself."[10] Pecola, however, never comes to accept herself. She finds salvation in blue eyes. The "salvation" of having blue eyes, however, means the psychological death of Pecola. In possessing the bluest eyes, she becomes the "bluest I," which indicates Morrison's powerful pun on the title of the book.[11]

Even before publication of Toni Morrison's seminal text *Playing in the Dark: Whiteness and the Literary Imagination*, from which critical whiteness theorists frequently quote and in which Morrison explores how the literary white imagination is parasitic upon various literary configurations of Blackness, there was *The Bluest Eye*. Although written over thirty years ago, the text is powerful in terms of its location, exposure, and interrogation of the semiotic spaces of whiteness. It is a crucial text that clearly demonstrates the psychological price paid for bleaching the Negro soul in a flood of whiteness.

Like *The Bluest Eye*, Morrison's *Playing in the Dark* critically exposes the white imaginary. As the title suggests, Morrison refuses to "play in the dark" but is interested in exposing "the serviceability of the Africanist presence" in white literary works.[12] Highlighting the significance of *Playing in the Dark*, Robert Gooding-Williams has noted that Africanist racial representations "were constituted through the ascription of multiple purposes and functions to individuals racially classified as black."[13] One such ascription is that of an enabler. Morrison notes that "Africanism is the vehicle by which the American [white] self knows itself as not enslaved, but free; not repulsive, but desirable; . . . not history-less, but historical; . . . not a blind accident of evolution, but a progressive fulfillment of destiny."[14]

Morrison uses the term *American Africanism* to describe "denotative and connotative blackness that African peoples have come to signify, as well as the entire range of views, assumptions, readings, and misreadings that accompany Eurocentric learning about these [Black] people."[15] In the white literary imagination, Black people have been treated as "standing-reserve," raw material just waiting to be used, exploited, spoken for, and validated by and through whiteness.[16] Morrison asks, "What does positing one's writerly self, in the wholly racialized society that is the United States, as unraced and all others as raced entail?"[17] The positing of oneself as unraced entails the presumption of a form of universality. It presumes that whiteness does not mediate one's vision or imagination. Indeed, such a white (read: unraced) writerly self is deemed normal, typical, superior, the standard, and the measure. Morrison notes that it was "Africanism, deployed as rawness and savagery, that provided the staging ground and area for the elaboration of the quintessential American identity."[18]

For example, in Willa Cather's *Sapphira and the Slave Girl*, Morrison shows how that text carries the weight of America's economy of racist discourse concerning Black women. The character Sapphira's very existential liveliness depends upon her need to denigrate the Black enslaved Nancy (imaginatively and possibly physically, using her nephew, Martin). According to a typical racist motif in North American history, one discussed throughout this text, not only were Black men thought to be bestial but Black women were also thought to be oversexed and always sexually available. The trope of the oversexed Black woman allows Sapphira to endow herself with value, virtue, and self-worth. Regarding Mark Twain's *Huckleberry Finn* along the same lines, Morrison wants to move beyond the interpretative framework that has stabilized the text within a sentimental nostrum about the innocence of Americanness. The text "becomes a more beautifully complicated work that sheds much light on some of the problems it has accumulated through traditional readings too shy to linger over the implications of the Africanist presence at its center."[19] For example, Morrison argues that the construction of the character Huck's identity is intertextually linked to the status of Jim as a "nigger." She exposes that "the agency, however, for Huck's struggle is the nigger Jim, and it is absolutely necessary . . . that the term nigger be inextricable from Huck's deliberations about who and what he himself is—or, more precisely, is not."[20]

Morrison brings a critical subjectivity (a kind of returned "gaze") to bear upon those white literary figures who have for so long constructed Blacks as incapable of critical thought and subjectivity. Although the textual foreground of *The Bluest Eye* explicitly portrays the deformation of the Black body/self of Pecola, the text "pecks away," according to Morrison, "at the [white] gaze that condemned her."[21] Hence, prior to *Playing in the Dark*, Morrison demands (in this case, by uncovering the secret of Pecola's "ugliness," psychopathology) that we turn our critical gaze toward the constituting activities, discursive field, and racist imaginary of whiteness. The metaphor of pecking away at whiteness suggests that it is concealed and *concealing*. Morrison's objective is to peck away at the powerful normative structure of whiteness.

Through *The Bluest Eye*, Morrison engages in a form of textual exposure of whiteness as a historically contingent set of practices. In this way, Pecola's so-called wretchedness is an effect of white racist power. Whiteness occupies a particular social, historical, material, and cultural position within a larger set of relationships. What is often masked, however, is the extent to which whiteness creates and sustains various social inequalities that are inextricably linked to the suffering of nonwhite people and the privileging of white people.

Whiteness is performed through what Du Bois referred to as "darker deeds."[22] Pecola did not ask to be born within a society that held up a mirror to her that exclaimed, "You are ugly and of 'lower grade.'" Rather, Pecola's *returned* (negatively epidermalized) Black body, objectified and negatively reconfigured by the normalizing white gaze, becomes the source of her existential and ontological contemptibility. I am reminded of African American artist and photographer Carrie Mae Weems's photographic work entitled "Mirror, Mirror," where a dark-skinned woman looks into a mirror only to be faced by what looks like a pale, older white woman. Beneath the photograph, the caption reads:

> Mirror, Mirror on the Wall
> Who's the Finest of them All?
> Snow White, you black bitch,
> And Don't You Forget it.[23]

Morrison characterizes the structure of the white gaze during a moment in *The Bluest Eye* where Pecola visits Yacobowski's store to buy some candy. Yacobowski is one of those whites, as Du Bois noted, who was taught "to believe that white people were so inherently and eternally superior to blacks, that to eat, sit, live or learn beside them [or even to sell them candy] was absolute degradation."[24] As an immigrant in America, Yacobowski had "paid the price of the ticket." The price of the ticket, according to James Baldwin, "was to become 'white.'"[25] Yacobowski's surveillance of Pecola is linked to the power to define. Dialectically, his immigrant status is diminished and the investment in his whiteness as a form of property is increased to the extent that he defines in negative terms this "poor Black thing" that stands before him. Operating from this site of white identity construction, Yacobowski has learned how to deny the active part he plays in constructing Pecola. His distorted construction of her body at the level of the imaginary only reinforces the illusion that he lives his own white identity/his body as real and stable. Intrapsychologically, his interaction with Pecola, which is really a relationship that he has with a fantasized object that he has projected outwardly from himself, is predicated upon the introjection of a false self that attempts to conceal its own instability, fears, and anxieties. As a performance, his gaze possesses the power to call forth, as it were, that which it sees.

Within this encounter, Yacobowski's *blue* eyes are devoid of curiosity. This lack of curiosity suggests that the little Black girl who stands before him is always already *known*. Her presence does not elicit interest, surprise, or inquisitiveness. His gaze passes over Pecola's uniqueness, her individuality. In his gaze, there is a vacuum that renders her of no particular interest. She might be said to be nondescript. To be nondescript, however, implies belonging to no particular class or kind. The reality is that Yacobowski does in fact recognize Pecola as belonging to a particular racial classification or kind. She is *Black*. Indeed, he sees her as a *racial* natural kind. She is recognized and yet unrecognized, visible in her invisibility. As Black, she constitutes the anonymous *they* of Blackness. The details of Pecola's life are irrelevant. It is enough that she is Black, typified, pure and simple. As Morrison writes: "Somewhere between retina and object, between vision and view, his eyes draw back, hesitate, and hover. At some fixed point in time and space he senses that he need not waste the effort of a glance. He does not see her, because for him there is nothing to see."[26]

Pecola, within the anonymous space of typification, does not even receive the respect that might be shown to a stranger. At least the stranger might loosen the cement of social typification in virtue of his/her not being from the same neighborhood. His/her strangeness has the potential of triggering at least a dialogue or curiosity. Pecola, however, is the ersatz human being. The structure of the social encounter has very little if anything to do with the fact that he is a grown man and she is a little girl. The encounter appears primarily shaped and mediated by Yacobowski's whiteness. Morrison locates part of the problem at the eyelid. Distaste is said to reside there. In fact, Pecola is said to be aware of this scopic distaste in all white people. She concludes that the distaste must be for her Blackness. Her Blackness is a signifier of distaste, dirtiness, aversion, and discontent.

Within the context of an existentialist frame of reference, Pecola is "flux and anticipation." She is transphenomenal and metastable. She possesses a sense of her being-toward-the-future. She is always already more than she is at any particular moment. As flux and anticipation, she exists as a *possibility*. Her Blackness is said to be "static and dread." Hence her Blackness is facticity, a thing to be feared, that which is the negation of values. Her Blackness is the embodiment of nihilism. Like Ralph Ellison's invisible man, Pecola no doubt aches with the need to convince herself that she does in fact exist in the real world, but she does not strike out with her fists, curse, or swear to force the likes of Yacobowski to recognize her. After leaving the store, she does feel angry. Indeed, the surge of anger that she feels has a humanizing dimension. After all, the white gaze has rendered her ontologically worthless. Her feeling of anger confirms that she experiences the world from an existential *here*. Her anger functions as a kind of a posteriori proof that *she is*. *I'm angry, ergo I am*. Like Ellison's invisible man, who often feels the need to bump people back, or Bigger Thomas, the protagonist in Richard Wright's *Native Son*, who actually and symbolically "slays whiteness," anger functions as a conduit through which some level of recognition is gained. As Morrison notes, "Anger is better. There is a sense of being in anger. A reality and presence. An awareness of worth."[27] Yacobowski's gaze is part of a larger accretion of white social forces that come to bear upon the denigration of her Black body/self, thus eradicating the space for a dialectics of recognition.

Pecola's Blackness as such does not cause the problem. "Blackness," after all, from the perspective of the white gaze, is a myth of whiteness. As she eagerly waits to purchase some candy, Pecola is not "seen" at all. However, she is visible just enough that "he hesitates, not wanting to touch her hand" as she holds out her hand containing three pennies to buy some candy.[28] Within this highly white-mediated semiotic space, his hesitation to touch her hand reduces her to an epidermal Blackness, something to be avoided. Also fascinating here is how the power of whiteness is performed through something as apparently benign as a hesitant reach for money from the hands of a little Black girl. This hesitant reach, however, embodies the larger white world that is even hesitant to "grant" the humanity of Blacks. In her careful narrative detail of Pecola's identity, Morrison is operating within a genealogical space of critique that "painstakingly exposes the tiny influences on a body that, over time, not only produce a subject of a certain sort [self-hating], [but] a subject defined by what it takes to be knowledge about itself and its world [that Black people were born inferior and ugly]."[29]

The problem is located in Yacobowski's white gaze, which has been shaped by the everyday, quotidian practices of whiteness and which thus generates and produces Pecola's Blackness as static and dread. And Pecola is learning to "see only what there was to see: the eyes of other people."[30] As Frantz Fanon would have said, the glance of others fixed her, sealing her "into that crushing object-hood."[31] Even after Pecola leaves Yacobowski's store, she feels a dart of affection that leaps out for some dandelions that she notices. Morrison is quick to note that the dandelions (like Yacobowski's white narcissism) "do not look at her and do not send love back."[32] Hence, the initial dart of affection is squandered and Pecola is unable to see the beauty in the dandelions; she is filled with Yacobowski's negative reactive value-creating force, his hatred of her. Thus, she begins to feel shame and self-loathing.

Carrying the weight of internalized white racism and the white gaze, Pecola has come to know all too well the "deficits" of her Black embodiment. As will be shown, moving in and out of white racist semiotic spaces, Pecola learns to relate to herself as inferior, dirty, limited, and somatically uglified. Unlike the idyllic (read: white) Dick-and-Jane reading primer that the reader encounters at the very beginning of the text—a narrative that Morrison brilliantly collapses into a maddening stream of sentences without punctuation—the reader becomes immediately aware of familial and ontological fractures in Pecola Breedlove's life when he/she encounters Pecola for the first time within *The Bluest Eye* (narrated by Claudia, one of the central characters in the text, and an omniscient voice[33]):

> Cholly Breedlove [Pecola's father], then, a renting black, having put his family outdoors, had catapulted himself beyond the reaches of human consideration. He had joined the animals; was, indeed, an old dog, a snake, a ratty nigger. Mrs. Breedlove was staying with the woman she worked for; the boy, Sammy [Pecola's brother], was with some other family; and Pecola was to stay with us. Cholly was in jail.[34]

The Dick-and-Jane reading primer tells the story of a house that is green and white. Mother, Father, Dick, and Jane reside therein with a dog and a cat and much happiness and laughter. Father is strong and Mother loves to play with her children. Jane is said to have friends who love to play with her. Opening the text with this Dick-and-Jane reading primer creates an artificial narrative text against which Morrison contrasts Pecola and her family. The words in the primer, as Theresa M. Towner writes, "scream their [white] simplistic morality, and their normalcy."[35] The primer creates the familiar Manichean divide that has been encountered throughout this project. Elliott Butler-Evans argues, "Contrasts between the Dick-and-Jane world and the 'real' world of the Breedloves are structured around several sets of binary oppositions: White/Black, affluence/ poverty, desirability/undesirability, order/chaos, valued/devalued."[36] In short, whiteness, as the transcendental norm, insidiously operates at the level of stories. These narratives fix Black bodies as "inadequate," yet as desirous of whiteness. Referring to Antillean children, Fanon notes that they wrote stories like real little (white) Parisians, "I like vacation because then I can run through the fields, breathe fresh air, and come home with *rosy* cheeks."[37]

Adding to an already dismal set of circumstances, Claudia adds, "She came with nothing."[38] In the Dick-and-Jane primer, the entire family appears to want for nothing. The familial space is replete with beauty, stability, cleanliness, safety, and wholesomeness. For Pecola, existentially speaking, she is just *there*, solitary and destitute. And like the flowers that Claudia later describes as having failed to grow, Pecola is also unyielding and barren. But what is also significant is the reality that Pecola had been put "outdoors." Within the text, being put outdoors signals a profound sense of having been ostracized. Indeed, it constitutes "the real terror of life."[39]

Capturing the finality of being outdoors, Claudia says, "But the concreteness of being outdoors was another matter—like the difference between the concept of death and being, in fact, dead. Dead doesn't change, and outdoors is here to stay."[40] So, the sense of being outdoors is not just a spatial relationship; it also connotes an ontological stasis, a sense of nothingness. Claudia goes on to say, "Knowing that there was such a thing as outdoors bred in us a hunger for property, for ownership."[41] In other words, in her state of "nothingness," which acts as a trope signifying both race and class, Pecola is desperate for something of value. She hungers for something that will provide her with a sense of being, belonging, and self-value. However, as Pecola fully comes to accept, being Black does not confer value; indeed, Blackness is tantamount to being property-less.

Du Bois understood whiteness as a wage that paid handsomely in terms of public deference, psychological uplift, protection from harm, access to public parks, and better schools.[42] "For the first two hundred years of the country's existence, the system of racialized privilege in both the public and private spheres," as Cheryl Harris argues, "carried through this linkage of rights and inequality, and rights and property. Whiteness as property was the critical core of a system that affirmed the hierarchical relations between white and Black."[43] Within the context of white greed, Du Bois asked himself why whiteness is so incredibly desirable and answers: "Then always, somehow, some way, silently but clearly I am given to understand that whiteness is the ownership of the earth forever and ever, Amen!"[44] For Black people, white ownership and greed implies making do within socioeconomic, ghettoized spaces of mere survival.

The Bluest Eye is set in 1941 Lorain, Ohio, the same place Toni Morrison actually grew up. Being Black, the Breedlove family, like Morrison's family, would have been hit hardest by the Great Depression. With descriptive clarity, indicating the degree to which Blacks were subjected to the greedy ways of white landlords, Morrison provides the reader with a view of the depressive physical environment within which Pecola lived. She describes the Breedlove family as "nestled together in the storefront. Festering together in the debris of a Realtor's whim."[45] The furniture and the spatial dimensions of their living space invoke a sense of aesthetic disgust: "In the center of the bedroom, for the even distribution of heat, stood a coal stove. Trunks, chairs, a small end table, and a cardboard 'wardrobe' closet were placed around the walls. The kitchen was in the back of this apartment, a separate room. There were no bath facilities. Only a toilet bowl, inaccessible to the eye, if not the ear, of the tenants."[46] Concerning the furnishings, there is really no more to be said. The furnishings "were anything but describable, having been conceived, manufactured, shipped, and sold in various states of thoughtlessness, greed, and indifference."[47] Having received a damaged sofa, which occurred during delivery, one of the white movers argue with Cholly, Pecola's father:

"Looka here, buddy. It was O.K. when I put it on the truck. The store can't do anything about it once it's on the truck . . . ." Listerine and Lucky Strike breath.

"But I don't want no tore couch if 'n it's bought new." Pleading eyes and tightened testicles.
"Tough shit, buddy. *Your* tough shit."[48]

Note the implied reference to Blackness as something dirty, as feces. But this is how whiteness fortifies its purity. Whiteness involves "the all-pervading desire to inculcate," as Du Bois said, "disdain for everything black, from Toussaint to the devil."[49]

Combining elements of class and race, and theorizing the fundamental dimensions of internalized (white) selfsurveillance, Morrison writes:

> The Breedloves did not live in a storefront because they were having temporary difficulty adjusting to the cutbacks at the plant. *They lived there because they were poor and black, and they stayed there because they believed they were ugly.* . . . Mrs. Breedlove, Sammy Breedlove, and Pecola Breedlove—wore their ugliness, put it on, so to speak, although it did not belong to them.[50]

What created in them the belief that they were ugly? What is it about their Black bodies that gets them returned to themselves in distorted form? If the ugliness does not belong to them, then to whom does it belong? In a passage rich with figurative language, Morrison provides a glimpse into the origins of this conviction. Relevant here is the argument that the self is *not* prior to the effects of a discursive field:

> You looked at them and wondered why they were so ugly; you looked closely and could not find the source. Then you realized that it came from conviction, their conviction. It was as though some mysterious allknowing master had given each one a cloak of ugliness to wear, and they had each accepted it without question. The master had said, "You are ugly people." They had looked about themselves and saw nothing to contradict the statement; saw, in fact, support for it leaning at them from every billboard, every movie, every glance. "Yes," they had said. "You are right." And they took the ugliness in their hands, threw it as a mantle over them, and went about the world with it.[51]

In short, the Breedloves' bodies were disciplined through the regime of whiteness, its values and dictates, which passes itself off, as Morrison says of political ideology, "as immutable, natural, and innocent."[52]

The point here is that within the context of white racist America, the Black self is always already formed through discourse, through various practices that "confirm" the Black self as ugly, bestial, dirty, and worthless. Commenting upon the ugliness of the Breedloves, Keith E. Byerman notes that the burden of this "'ugliness' is accepted without direct coercion. There are few white characters in the novel to impose the view. The ideological hegemony of whiteness is simply too overwhelming to be successfully resisted."[53] The reality of whiteness, however, expresses itself in the form of a conglomerate set of interlocking forces. These forces inhabit every nook and cranny of American life, possessing the power to make themselves representative. As Morrison implies, no matter how much one looks at the Breedloves, the ugliness cannot be located on the surface of their skin, as it were. Hence, it is their conviction that is the problem, which, of course, only begs the question of which Morrison is fully aware: what is the source of this conviction? The conviction did not emerge through a process of autogenesis. It is not as if the self comes into the world readymade, autonomous, and the absolute ground of its own meaning. By the time the self becomes critically self-reflexive, it has already become the effect of power such that "certain bodies, certain gestures, certain discourses, certain desires, come to be identified and constituted as individuals."[54] Power, then, need not function in ways that are noticeably "externally coercive." By the time Pecola works through the sociopsychological dynamics of the individual she has become (although within the text she never reaches this level of critical self-interrogation), the structure of her identity has already been constituted as an individual of a certain type—what she values, how she thinks about her eyes, her dark skin, the value of whiteness, and so on. In delineating such details, power has already been discerned. However, there is still a need to address the issue concerning the origin of the conviction that the Breedloves possess.

The (racist) force relations that constitute who the Breedloves are, although enduringly systemic and pervasive, have a sociohistorical genesis. This raises the issue of Fanon's conceptualization of the process of sociogenesis. Through various white practices, certain values and representations (like "Blackness is ugly") have come to appear as though they exist independently of human action and intersubjectivity. Hence, this sense of conviction is created within the context of white evasion, the serious attitude that reconfigures values as objects in the natural world. This is the *social context* within which Black people struggle with white identity orders, orders that sociohistorically speak to efforts on the part of whites to make sense of themselves through the denigration of Black people. As a master signifier, whiteness deems itself uncaused and unconditioned, that mysterious reality that has the absolute power to define difference.[55] Morrison's reference to "some mysterious all-knowing master" resonates with my earlier characterization of whiteness in chapter 5 as all seeing and all knowing.

The historical specificity and particularity of whiteness's knowledge of itself and "others" is presumed universal and ahistorical. On this score, the Breedloves are trapped within a semiotic space of white ("universal") aesthetical ideals, ideals according to which they are deemed different qua nonwhite and thereby indelibly stained by the disfiguring mark of Blackness.

Instead of values that owe their existence to various cultural practices, the Breedloves have come to accept certain values—through everyday forms of anti-Black racist practices—as material facts of the physical world. The Breedloves appear unable to cast off the white imposed cloak or veil. They have been split, doubled, through the measurement of their souls by the tape of a world (or by an outside gaze[56]) that says whiteness is ontologically and aesthetically supreme. Invoking the image of a master, Morrison is aware of the crippling impact of the institution of American slavery. She is cognizant of how deep white colonialism impacts the (dark) colonized, creating a double-consciousness in their very souls through the construction of a semiotic space designed to "confirm" their colonized status. Morrison is clearly aware of the circular logic and self-reinforcing structure of whiteness. "You are ugly people," when applied to Black people, carries an epistemic truth-value within a white discursive field that already comes replete with its own stipulated criteria for what constitutes beauty.

The mesmerizing power of whiteness, the sheer weight of its normativity and symbolic power, is clear in the novel when Frieda, Claudia's older sister, brings Pecola four graham crackers and some milk in a Shirley Temple cup. "She was a long time with the milk, and gazed fondly at the silhouette of Shirley Temple's dimpled face. Frieda and she had a loving conversation about how cuute Shirley Temple was."[57] Why is Pecola so obsessed with Shirley Temple? What does she see in her? What does Pecola *not* see in herself? Indeed, why does Pecola feel a deep sense of internal vacuity when looking at Shirley Temple? On the view developed thus far, Shirley Temple represents what Pecola is not. Indeed, Pecola's difference is defined relative to Shirley Temple's *whiteness* (as transcendental norm/master signifier). Pecola's Black body/self is returned to her phenomenologically, reconfigured as ugly in comparison with the ways in which Shirley Temple's body has been constructed as intrinsically beautiful. It is not just the image of Shirley Temple that holds Pecola's attention; it is also the white substance inside the cup. Only later in the narrative do we learn that Pecola drinks three quarts of milk. Milk symbolizes whiteness. Pecola does not consume so much milk out of greediness, however, as Claudia's mother, Mrs. MacTeer, believes; rather, it is out of her need to "become" white through the very act of consuming the milk. Perhaps the milk's whiteness will create a metamorphosis, changing her from Black to white, from absent to present, from nothing to something, from ugly to beautiful, from dirty to pure.

This theme involving the ingestion of whiteness is also clear in Pecola's selection of candy from Yacobowski's store. She buys Mary Janes. Even the innocent act of buying candy becomes an opportunity for racial self-resentment and selfdenigration. Something as presumably benign as a candy wrapper functions as a site of white cultural semiosis. Morrison writes:

Each pale yellow wrapper has a picture on it. A picture of little Mary Jane, for whom the candy is named. Smiling white face. Blond hair in gentle disarray, *blue eyes* looking at her out of a world of *clean comfort*. The eyes are petulant, mischievous. To Pecola they are simply *pretty*. To eat the candy is somehow *to eat the eyes, eat Mary Jane. Love Mary Jane. Be Mary Jane.*[58]

Even as Pecola is rejected and denigrated by the power embedded within Yacobowski's gaze, whose eyes, as I have noted, are blue, she seeks the power of Mary Jane's blue eyes through a process of "symbolic cannibalism."[59] Blue eyes are threatening and yet they also signify safety and solace.[60] Blue eyes constitute a metonymy for white hegemony as this is expressed through white cultural aesthetic ideals. Gunilla Theander Kester argues that "blue eyes stand as a *pars pro toto*, a synecdoche for a white little girl whom a racist culture would consider beautiful."[61] Like the whiteness of the milk, the piece of candy is believed to have the power to produce a genuine state of ontological change in Pecola, a change from Black to white, from a state of "racialized somatophobia,"[62] to a state of *clean somatic* comfort and "normalcy."

Through a process where reality and fiction are blurred, Pecola's mother, Pauline, is caught within a world of white filmic hyperreality, which further nurtures Pecola's inability to see through the farce of whiteness. Pauline:

The onliest time I be happy seem like was when I was in the picture show. Every time I got, I went. I'd go early, before the show started. They'd cut off the lights, and everything be black. Then the screen would light up, and I'd move right on in them pictures . . . . Them pictures gave me a lot of pleasure, but it made coming home hard, and looking at Cholly hard. I don't know. I 'member one time I went to see Clark Gable and Jean Harlow. I fixed my hair up like I'd seen hers on a magazine. A part on the side, with one little curl on my forehead. It looked just like her. Well, almost just like.[63]

Like Pecola, Pauline has internalized the fiction that whiteness is supremely beautiful. For Pecola and Pauline, whiteness, in psychoanalytic terms, has become an "object-cathexis," that in terms of which they have come to invest all of their mental and emotional energy. While at the picture show, Pauline is able to inhabit the filmic space of whiteness imaginatively. She is able to be the luminescent Jean Harlow.

Richard Dyer's work on the cultural uses of light, through lighting technology, argues that light in film is used to construct white people as individuals. He notes:

It is at least arguable that white society has found it hard to see non-white people as individuals; the very notion of the individual, of the freely developing, autonomous human person, is only applicable to those who are seen to be free and autonomous, who are not slaves or subject peoples. Movie lighting discriminates against non-white people because it is used in a cinema and a culture that finds it hard to recognize them as appropriate subjects for such lighting, that is, as individuals.[64]

Dyer's point is that even the technological uses of light can involve the exercise of power. The process of lighting becomes a medium of racial structuration, a technology of discipline that privileges white bodies/selves. Pauline is elevated by the medium of light used to enhance the whiteness of the characters on the screen; she partakes in the humanizing (read: white) and privileging powers of white light.

Elaborating on the powerful visual dimensions of Pauline's cinematic absorption of the value code of white aesthetics, Morrison is aware of the plenitudinous character of white light when she says that "there the black-and-white images came together, making a magnificent whole—all projected through the ray of light from above and behind."[65] Within a Platonic world, Pauline is like an artist's representation of a sensible object, a mere copy of a copy. Gary Schwartz has suggested this interpretation, arguing that "Pauline, as the viewer and learner, has absorbed the visions of light and darkness and becomes the engine of their reproduction. . . . Wittingly or otherwise, Pauline not only becomes the Imitation but, in turn, imitates it. She is an imitation of an imitation."[66] Living her life through cinematic white images, it is no wonder that Pauline, when Pecola was born, describes Pecola as "a black ball of hair."[67] Pauline adds, "But I knowed she was ugly. Head full of pretty hair, but Lord she was ugly."[68] Even that pretty hair will eventually give way to "tangled black puffs of rough wool to comb."[69] Even at birth, Pauline has already rendered Pecola's body problematic. Thus, "Pauline begins to distance herself from her child's body, identifying it as another strike against her own self, since the issue of her body cannot approximate the likes of Shirley Temple."[70]

As an ideal servant of whiteness, Pauline plays the part impeccably, super-imposing upon Pecola her own self-hatred. Although she neglects her own home, Pauline is obsessed with cleaning the Fisher house where she is a housemaid. There, she feels in control, happy, responsible, and *clean*. While working in the Fisher home, as when she sits mesmerized in the cinema, she feels a momentary reprieve from her Blackness (read: ugliness and dirtiness). After all, the Fisher home has "white porcelain, white woodwork, polished cabinets, and brilliant copperware."[71] Whiteness also provides Pauline with a false sense of existential meaning and emotional stability:

> Pauline kept this order, this beauty, for herself, a private world, and never introduced it into her storefront, or to her children. Them she bent toward respectability, and in so doing taught them fear: fear of being clumsy, fear of being like their father, fear of not being loved by God, fear of madness like Cholly's

mother's. Into her son she beat a loud desire to run away, and into her daughter she beat a fear of growing up, fear of other people, fear of life.[72]

In a scene where Frieda and Claudia go to visit Pecola at the Fisher home, where Pauline is on duty working, Pecola is exposed to her mother's vigilant obsession with and protection of the "purity" of whiteness. While waiting for Pauline to retrieve the wash, a young white girl—the little Fisher girl—came into the kitchen where Pecola, Frieda, and Claudia had been waiting. Anxious, she called for Pauline. Instead of calling her "Mrs. Breedlove," the formal address that her own children are required to use, the little white girl calls for "Polly." As she called for Polly, Pecola, Frieda, and Claudia noticed a deep-dish blueberry cobbler near the stove. Pecola decided to touch it to see if it was hot. As she did so, the blueberry pie fell by accident. The hot blueberries went everywhere, with most of the juice splattering on Pecola's legs. Claudia narrates how "in one gallop she was on Pecola, and with the back of her hand knocked her to the floor. Pecola slid in the pie juice, one leg folding under her. Mrs. Breedlove yanked her up by the arm, slapped her again, and in a voice thin with anger, abused Pecola directly and Freida and me by implication."[73]

Pauline calls Pecola a "crazy fool," as she worries about the dirtiness of the floor. In the meantime, the little white girl begins to cry. Immediately turning her loving attention to the white girl's pink sunback dress that the *blackish* blueberries had gotten dirty, Pauline repeats, "Hush. Don't worry none." She sooths the tears of the "little pink-and-yellow girl," reassuring her that all will be just fine, as "she spit out words to us like rotten pieces of apple."[74] In this context, the white body is a site of concern, love, and attention. The Black body, however, is vulnerable to insult, blame, and attack. Vanessa D. Dickerson notes:

> Pecola is one instance of the black child robbed of the affirmation of the caretakers of her body. She is one example of the black child whose need for his or her mother is sacrificed to the white child's pleasure or comfort in a mammy. . . . The little white girls (and boys) take to themselves relations, reflections, experiences, and feelings that ought rightfully belong to the Claudias and Pecolas of the world.[75]

Capturing the larger mutual exclusivity between Black bodies and white bodies, an exclusiveness based upon an essentialist, racial binary logic that valorizes the latter and devalorizes the former, Dickerson also notes:

> Unlike the body of the Fisher girl, which receives no concrete physical description, Pecola's is given a solidity and reality that brings it more sympathetically

near. Nevertheless, while the narrative represents Pecola's body as the real, embraceable body and the Fisher girl's as the specterized and distant body, Pecola's is socially assaulted, the Fisher's girl's held dear. To put it another way, the white child's body is what Mary Douglas in *Purity and Danger* would identify as the tidy body, the one associated with culture and civilization; Pecola's is the unruly body, the polluted or polluting body associated with nature.[76]

As the three girls leave, they can hear Pauline promise to make another pie for the little white girl. The white girl twice asks Polly who they were. Consistent with her own self-negation, Pauline refuses to answer. Symbolically, Pauline erases Pecola through the act of not identifying her. The white girl is left to internalize the image of Pecola, Frieda, and Claudia as unnamed and unnamable *problems*, Black phantoms whose existence is best left unknown and unknowable. Pecola is left to make sense of a mother who cherishes little white girls over little Black girls. She is left to conclude that whiteness guarantees love and affection, which explains why Pecola sits for hours "looking in the mirror, trying to discover the secret of the ugliness, the ugliness that made her ignored or despised at school, by teachers and classmates alike."[77] Of course, there is no ugliness intrinsic to Pecola to be discovered. Her "ugliness" is what emerges dialectically vis-à-vis whiteness. Whiteness is that silent norm, which manifests itself through her mother, through film, through small gestures and gazes.

Even when it appears that Pecola is "recognized," this recognition only further reinforces her status as denigrated other. For example, a young Black character named Junior, who is the son of Geraldine, recognizes Pecola only to traumatize her physically and emotionally. Like Pauline, Geraldine is obsessed with cleanliness. Unlike Pauline, however, she is a middle-class Black woman married to a predictable middle-class Black man, Louis. Geraldine's family reflects the "clean" and "pure" life depicted in the primer, cat and all. Geraldine is the embodiment of the "cult of true womanhood," ensuring that her son, husband, and cat are given the best comfort that she could provide. She practices "thrift, patience, high morals, and good manners." Seduced by a value-code shaped along an axis of both class and race, she is always trying to get rid of the "funkiness" of life. Morrison writes:

> Wherever it erupts, this Funk, they wipe it away; where it crusts, they dissolve it; wherever it drips, flowers, or clings, they find it and fight it until it dies. They fight this battle all the way to the grave. The laugh that is a little too loud; the enunciation a little too round; the gesture a little too generous. They hold their behind in for fear of a sway too free; when they wear lipstick, they never cover the entire mouth for fear of lips too thick, and they worry, worry, worry about the edges of their hair.[78]

From the above quote, what comes across clearly is a form of loathing toward the *Black* body, in particular, and embodiedness, more generally. Also clear is that Geraldine takes her cue from the model of dutiful and well-respected middle-class white women. Geraldine makes a concerted effort at deracinating any trace of funkiness. Funkiness is too "gaudy," aesthetically or otherwise. Gaudiness might be characterized as a "nigger" attribute. Geraldine takes the time to explain to her son the difference between colored people and niggers. For her, "colored people were neat and quiet; niggers were dirty and loud." Apparently, niggers did not concern themselves with cutting their hair as short as possible so as to get rid of any sign of wool. And despite the fact that Junior was light-skinned, she makes sure he received plenty of Jergens lotion "on his face to keep the skin from becoming ashen."[79] Clearly, Morrison is complicating received notions of what it means to be Black. She also explores how Black self-perception differs along an axis of class. Thus, in the mouth of Geraldine, there is an anti-Black racist discourse creating its own binary.

To the extent that Blacks imitate and valorize the behavior, thought, and feeling patterns of whites is the extent to which Blacks qua coloreds are able to reap the benefits of whiteness: order, cleanliness, respectability, income, stability, and so on. These are the code words, however, that inevitably return with an exclusionary sting. If one does not fit within the confines of these behavior, thought, and feeling patterns, one is then ridiculed for being a nigger, a result of having been characterized and fixed by a (white projected) negative image of what it means to be Black in the first place. Hence, "colored people" like Geraldine end up hating other Blacks who have been stereotyped and marked as disorderly, gaudy, destitute, savage, embodied, and emotional. One might say that just as the fabricated Black presence is important to the identity of whiteness, the fabricated presence of the "nigger type" is important to the "colored type."[80] Whiteness creates a fabricated nigger type, to which the colored type gives credence and from which it differentiates itself, and thereby creates a false and unachievable set of aspirations/goals for the colored type, getting them to behave as if they are substantially different, perhaps closer to being white. The irony here, though, is that the colored type never achieves the status of whiteness.

Hence, Pecola becomes the quintessence of all that is negative in the purview of whiteness, a perspective that Geraldine has internalized. Junior tricks Pecola to come to his house. He recognizes her to the extent that she is not like him. She is a nigger and is ugly.[81] He displaces his anger onto her, because of the lack of genuine affection he receives from his mother. After inviting Pecola into his house under the pretext of seeing some kittens, he throws his big Black cat in her face. The cat scratches her face and chest. After attempting to make Pecola his prisoner, and seeing that she has stopped crying and has taken an interest in the Black cat's blue eyes, he snatches the cat and begins to swing it around. When Pecola tries to stop him, he and Pecola fall, the cat lands on the radiator and then falls behind the sofa. At this moment, Geraldine comes through the door. Junior lies, saying, "She killed our cat."[82]

What happens to the cat might be said to foreshadow the devastating consequences that await Pecola as a result of being Black and desiring blue eyes. Although the black cat with blue eyes is not physically dead, *psychic* death awaits Pecola. After Junior targets Pecola as the source of the problem, a designation that Pecola has internalized as a result of having her very existence positioned as a problem by her family, the community, and other social forces, Geraldine's gaze fixes on Pecola, taking care to note her matted hair, her Black stained skin, dirty socks, old muddy shoes, her ugliness, her disorderliness, and her lack of postural refinement. Again, however, Pecola is not seen. She is assessed in terms of the ideals of white culture and found wanting. Geraldine's gaze has the capacity to "niggerize" Pecola. Geraldine's own self-hatred generates her hate for Pecola. Geraldine then speaks Pecola into existence; she further performs Pecola's sense of self-hatred using the power of words: "Get out," she says, her voice quiet. "You nasty little black bitch. Get out of my house."[83] Again, Pecola's Black body is returned to her. Only this time she does not return simply as the opposite of pretty Shirley Temple or as the object of distaste in the eyes of an older white man, she returns as a *nasty little black bitch*—the very negation of Shirley Temple and all that is white and pure.

Pecola is a site of disgust. She is a joke. Even her teachers try not to glance at her.[84] She is an object to be lampooned, a nasty little Black bitch used to solicit anger from young boys. Morrison explains: "She also knew that when one of the girls at school wanted to be particularly insulting to a boy, or wanted to get an immediate response from him, she could say, "Bobby loves Pecola Breedlove! Bobby Loves Pecola Breedlove!" and never fail to get peals of laughter from those in earshot, and mock anger from the accused."[85] She is the object of constant derision. For example, Claudia relates a story in which she and Frieda find Pecola surrounded by a group of boys hurling racial epithets her way: "Black e mo. Yadaddsleepsnekked. Black e mo black e mo ya dadd sleeps nekked. Black emo."[86] Whiteness is dutifully served. The boys, through their ritual performance of self-hatred, demonstrate their effective capacity of negative self-surveillance. Although Claudia and Frieda help break the circle of this ritual of self-denial, the theme of self-hatred is subtly and symbolically reintroduced through a mulatto character named Maureen Peal. Maureen, who only passively watches the events unfold, suddenly puts her arm through Pecola's and walks away as if they had been the best of friends:

"I just moved here. My name's Maureen Peal. What's yours?"

"Pecola."

"Pecola? Wasn't that the name of the girl in *Imitation of Life* ?"

"I don't know. What is that?"

"The picture show, you know. Where this mulatto girl hates her mother 'cause she is black and ugly but then cries at the funeral. It was real sad. Everybody cries in it.

Claudette Colbert too."

"Oh." Pecola's voice was no more than a sigh.

"Anyway, her name was Pecola too. She was so pretty. When it comes back, I'm going to see it again. My mother has seen it four times."[87]

The similarity between the name "Pecola" and "Peola," who played the self-hating mulatta in the 1934 film *Imitation of Life* is striking. Significant here is that the girl in *Imitation of Life* is called Peola, absent the "c." Schwartz suggests an interesting line of reasoning: "Pauline puts her own creative imprimatur on this child with a predestined name. The name with the 'c' has some suggestion of Latin *peccatum* (mistake, fault, error) while Peola sounds floral."[88] Having a name that phonetically sounds similar to "Peola," Pecola is nominally overdetermined. As it turns out, Pecola and Peola share the reality of internalized self-hatred. So, although Maureen is mistaken in terms of the correct pronunciation of the name, she is correct that Pecola is trapped by whiteness and would rather settle for being an imitation of whiteness than being Black. Misnaming Pecola also functions as a form of rejection. As John Bishop notes, "Maureen Peal's mistake has a larger relevance as well, for in Morrison's novels the act of (mis)naming signifies the community's power to deny individual autonomy." Bishop goes on to note that "they cannot see Pecola because only the pretty, pale Peola is deemed worthy of notice—they do not *c* the real girl."[89]

Pauline's obsession with whiteness functions as a problematic force that enables Pecola's self-hatred; she reinforces and cements the belief that whiteness is a mysterious *thing* of desirability. But it is Claudia's interrogation of this thing of desirability that provides glimpses of the possible source of Black self-hatred and perhaps, through Foucauldian problematization, provides a glimpse into possible ways of freeing thought in order to think differently.[90] During a heated exchange with Maureen, in which she also reveals her own self-hatred, calling both Claudia and Frieda "ugly black emos," Claudia reflects: "And all the time we knew that Maureen Peal was not the Enemy and not worthy of such intense hatred. The *Thing* to fear was the *Thing* that made *her* beautiful, and not us."[91] Here, Claudia demonstrates an awareness of the particularity (nonuniversality) of white beauty. This *thing*, this signifier of purity, cleanliness, and goodness, is the product of a generative context of white hegemony. This *thing* is not an unconditioned reality, but a socio-ontological reality. This *thing* is whiteness.

The power of whiteness (this *thing*) can be called upon in hours of need. Whiteness, on this score, is talismanic and soteriological. The theological implications are obvious. When we think of that which is unblemished, sinless, and pure, most of us unconsciously think of that which is white, resembling light, possessing luminosity. In popular movies, for example, we have automatically come to associate things dark with things evil. For example, the core narrative of the movie *Star Wars* is framed within a Manichean divide between the Dark Side of the Force and the Light Side. The Light Side defeats the Dark Side. And isn't it Luke ("bringer of the light") who defeats Darth (phonetically suggestive of dark)? My point here is that the construction of whiteness functions problematically in popular culture's imaginary in its relationship to Blackness (and, by association, Black people). Blackness signifies hopelessness, dread, and that which should be avoided. Whiteness, however, signifies hope, possibility, goodness, and has the power to solicit support and empathy.

Also, consider the movie version of John Grisham's *A Time to Kill*. After his young Black daughter Tonya Hailey, played by actress Rae'Ven Larrymore Kelly, is horribly raped and left infertile by two white men, Carl Lee Hailey, played by Samuel L. Jackson, takes the law into his own hands and shoots them as they are escorted through the courthouse. Because of his justified lack of trust in the justice system in the South, Hailey knew that he had to make the white male rapists pay. So he kills them. A white lawyer, Jake Brigance, played by Matthew McConaughey, takes on his case. Before Brigance delivers his closing statement to an all-white jury, he comes to Hailey expressing doubt about the possibility of getting Hailey off. At this point, Hailey tells Brigance he picked him because he thinks like all other white people and that this could prove to be an effective strategy. Tapping into the unseen and insidious dimensions of Brigance's whiteness, Hailey asks, "If you was on that jury, what would it take to convince you to set me free?" This forces Brigance to unearth levels of racism that he has left unexplored. This fuels Brigance's summation. He asks the jurors to close their eyes. He then proceeds to describe the horrible details of the rape of a young girl, detailing how her body was soaked in the rapists' urine, their semen, how they threw full beer cans at her body, tearing her flesh all the way to the bone, how she was hanged by the neck with a rope and the branch broke, and how she was left to die.[92] Brigance asks the jurors, "Can you see her?" At the very end of his powerfully moving description, one that is designed to put a human face on the victim, he says, "Now, imagine she's white." Hailey is found not guilty, and the movie ends with the Brigance family, his wife and young daughter, making an effort to cross the racial socioeconomic divide by going to an all-Black side of town to visit the Hailey family and their friends.

The tragedy here is that it is only through the process of imagining Hailey's young Black daughter as white that the jurors are apparently able to muster empathy for the young Black girl. The young girl's Black body alone, however, would not have justified Hailey's vigilante acts. The imagined young white girl's body was needed to elicit the necessary emotional and moral response to empathize with Hailey's actions. If "empathetic understanding *begins* with an appreciation of that person's situation," then the white jurors never really came to appreciate Hailey's situation, namely his love for his *Black* young daughter.[93] It would appear that the all-white jurors could only truly infer the other person's emotions (Hailey's emotions) if the young girl was white. Hence, since the young girl was Black, they could not have predicted he would have been so angry as to shoot and kill the white perpetrators. As Black, he had no right to kill white men, even if they brutally raped his daughter. After all, or so the white myth goes, as a Black girl, "she is always already ripe for the taking, [and] can-not be raped by white men."[94] Indeed, the young girl was Black, the "murderer" was Black, and those killed were white Southern boys out having a little fun. Instead of finding correspondences with Hailey's situation, the jurors had to *negate* an essential feature of his situation: that he was a Black man whose Black daughter was raped. The jurors never really give their verdict of not guilty based upon a Black father's "justified" course of action given the rape of his young Black daughter. They gave the verdict of not guilty based on an *imaginary* rape of a white girl. Through the power of the imagined raped white girl, and the moral despicableness, pain, and horror this image induced in the white jurors, the Black girl's actual rape was erased. Her humanity and inviolability were not conceded, but negated. Hence, in letting Hailey walk free, they really let their own white selves walk free. At the end of the movie, it is not justice that prevails; instead, whiteness saves the day. The movie only gives the pretense that there has been a victory over racism. The reality is that the hegemony of whiteness has been reinscribed.[95]

In *The Bluest Eye*, Pecola firmly believes in the saving powers of whiteness. During a scene where Cholly and Pauline are having one of their horrendous physical fights, fed by long-standing feelings of failure engineered by a society that systematically chisels away at their humanity, Pecola calls upon the "omnipotence" of whiteness. Claudia narrates, "If she looked different, beautiful, maybe Cholly would be different, and Mrs. Breedlove too. Maybe they'd say, 'Why, look at prettyeyed Pecola. We mustn't do bad things in front of those pretty eyes.'"[96] Pecola firmly believes that she, that is, her *Blackness*, is responsible for the irascible and violent behavior of her parents. However, it is the internalization of epistemic violence that leads her to believe this.

Susan Bordo's contention that anorexia nervosa is linked to androcentric disciplinary technologies of the body is key here. For like many who suffer from this condition, Pecola is also subject to her own "ghosts," who speak and confirm her wretchedness and ugliness.[97] She *knows* herself as the degraded other, she *knows* herself as a problem, and this knowledge causes her to wish for her own disappearance: "Please, God," she whispered into the palm of her hand, "please let me disappear."[98] Indeed, "each night, without fail, she prayed for blue eyes."[99] Praying for blue eyes is Pecola's way of attempting to deproblematize her identity. Her wish is not to be seen as ugly, as Black, but as beautiful and desirable. In short, her desire is to be seen as white.

The wish to disappear might also be interpreted as a trope of whiteness. As I have argued, whiteness, as normative, deems itself unmarked, invisible, and transparent. Pecola's rejection of her body functions on at least three different levels. First, she wishes she could disappear as the Black cause of her parent's turmoil. Second, there is a sense in which she wishes for some form of corporeal death. She at least desires to be unburdened of her epidermal racial schema, a form of embodiment she sees as synonymous with being cursed. Third, her wish to disappear suggests the desire to be unrecognized in her normalcy, to disappear within a flood of whiteness and thereby lose the stain of Blackness, that which makes her hypervisible.

Pauline, by example, teaches Pecola to deny herself and to deny life. Denying her own Blackness, unconsciously wishing for the love and protection of a man like Clark Gable, trying her best to look like Jean Harlow, and finally learning to be content with the mantle of ugliness that the power of whiteness imposed upon her, Pauline learns to settle. She becomes a "Black hole," as it were, the penetration of which comes to mark her worth and her closeness with Cholly. In fact, the only time Pauline seems close to him is when her "flesh is all that be on his mind." In these moments of bodily objectification, Pauline believes she is beautiful: "Not until he has let go of all he has, and give it to me. To me. To me. When he does, I feel a power. I be strong, I be pretty, I be young."[100] Mixed with overtones of masochism, has Pauline come to accept her self-value through being sexually objectified? Pauline is most happy when she is either under the control of filmic white images, dutifully fulfilling the needs of white folk, or being sexually objectified by Cholly. In all three situations, Pauline undergoes a form of erasure.[101]

Cholly Breedlove's affections are also hermetically sealed from his children: "Having no idea of how to raise children, and having never watched any parent raise himself, he could not even comprehend what a relationship should be."[102] Cholly spends most of his time in a drunken stupor, reflecting the pangs of racism and feelings of rejection that he had experienced in his own life. Unlike the father in the Dick-and-Jane primer, Cholly is thrown within a world of rejection, existential malaise, and anti-Black racism. He is the Black father who does not measure up to the Dick-and-Jane primer. Like Pauline, he too undergoes very powerful experiences of erasure. Like Pecola and Pauline, Cholly's identity is situated within a racial and racist context of unequal power relations. Cholly's identity is given birth to, as it were, within various contexts that never really generate a positive sense of self-definition.

Cholly's life begins with rejection. When he was only four days old, "his mother wrapped him in two blankets and one newspaper and placed him on a junk heap by the railroad."[103] His Great Aunt Jimmy saved and raised him. Indeed, his mother never even gave him a name at birth. As Aunt Jimmy says, "Your mama didn't name you nothing."[104] Thrown out like trash by his mother and left unnamed, Cholly is born into a society within which the power structure is "controlled by traditional white patriarchs."[105] One can imagine the degree of repression required to fight back memories of being thrown away like junk and being unloved by his mother. Within a society where Blackness is already devalued and rejected a priori, Cholly already has a tremendous burden to carry.

We learn that years later, as told by the omniscient narrator, Cholly undergoes a devastating encounter with whiteness as he experiences his first sexual act. Instead of directing his anger toward the larger white social structure partly responsible for what he has become, Cholly's anger becomes implosive, impacting all those closest to him. While attending a gathering in honor of his recently deceased Great Aunt Jimmy, Cholly and a girl named Darlene clandestinely go off to copulate. As they begin, they are startled by an "invasive presence":

> There stood two white men. One with a spirit lamp, the other with a flashlight. There was no mistake about their being white; he could smell it. Cholly jumped, trying to kneel, stand, and get his pants up all in one motion. The men had long guns. "Hee hee hee heeeee." The snicker was a long asthmatic cough. The other raced the flashlight all over Cholly and Darlene. "Get on wid it, nigger," said the flashlight one. "Sir?" said Cholly, trying to find a buttonhole. "I said, get on wid it. An' make it good, nigger, make it good."[106]

In the above passage, Morrison's reference to the effusion of light is reminiscent of Pauline's experience at the movie house. Schwartz, directing attention to the pornographic overtones of this scene, writes, "Flashlight and Spiritlamp, two sources of white light, looking at what looks most fascinating to them: what is not white. What is not white is obscene."[107] As stated in chapter 3, this "attraction-repulsion" dynamic was played out by French men as they gazed upon the "nonwhite obscenity" of Sarah Ba(a)rtman(n)'s Black body. Like Ba(a)rtman(n), Cholly has his behind literally exposed, with the flashlight making a moon on it.[108] Again, within this context, Morrison captures the significance of the relationship between the performance of the white gaze, power, and context. With his behind exposed, Cholly feels vulnerable to white penetration, symbolically and literally. By shining the *light* on his buttocks, a light that does not provide greater clarity, but greater distortion, his masculine somatic schema and body integrity are challenged.

Through the structure of white male spectatorship, Cholly is reduced to fragments of flesh. After all, he is on top of Darlene, and the white onlookers never demand to see her. Hence, it is Cholly who is reduced to, "feminized" as, a gyrating "piece of ass." The implications of mixed race homoerotic desire are prevalent in this scene. One might also argue that the intrusiveness of the white men disrupts Cholly's sense of generative, sexual agency just as enslaved Blacks were forced to copulate at the behest of whites ("Get on wid it, niggers") in order to replenish more pieces of property, that is, Black bodies. Cholly becomes just another indistinguishable Black animal in estrous, performing before the white gaze.

The white gaze, as a ritual performance, as I have argued, is inextricably bound up with objectifying, exoticizing, and sexualizing the Black body, inscribing it with myths and codes that function to ontologize it, thus returning it as that which it is not. Cholly experiences "the degradation of having this very private act of affirming his manhood turned into a sideshow, into a spectacle of two animals rutting in the woods."[109] He and Darlene are symbolically returned to themselves as libidinous animals on display in a public zoo. This is indicative, as I have argued throughout this text, of the white gaze's power of socio-ontological constitutionality. The white gaze reconstitutes the innocence of the sexual act into something dirty through a mode of representation (partly created through verbal and nonverbal white male actions) that renders the sexual performance of the two Black bodies pornographic. Forced by the voyeuristic white onlookers to continue, Cholly can only pretend: "Cholly, moving faster, looked at Darlene. He hated her. He almost wished he could do it—hard, long, and painfully, he hated her so much."[110] Symbolically, the white gaze has disrupted Cholly's show of his "manhood." The white gaze not only sees, but generates Cholly's impotence. The white male gaze has symbolically emasculated Cholly.

It is also important to keep in mind the very real historical association of Black male sexuality as a threat to white female "purity." The ritual of castrating Black men can be interpreted as the manifestation of the need for white men to prove their masculine prowess, to protect their women from contamination resulting from the so-called unnatural practices of miscegenation, and to possess the large and threatening object—the Black male penis—that they themselves had created through myth. In Cholly's situation, the two white males have successfully challenged his "masculine" identity where this identity is linked to his inability to protect Darlene and his inability to maintain an erection.

This process of Black male emasculation is not an uncommon experience that Black males have had to deal with within contexts where white male authority could prove deadly. In a scene in the movie *Crash*, two Los Angeles police officers stop a Black married couple on their way home. Cameron (Terence Howard), who is a Black male television director, and his wife Christine (Thandie Newton), who comes across as a Black woman who possesses a sense of social superiority, are told by one of the police officers (Matt Dillon) to get out of their vehicle. There is no other explanation for them to get out of their vehicle other than to be harassed. Dillon's character is the quintessential white racist cop. Despite their cooperation, the fact that they are married, and various markers of social achievement, he instructs both of them, although they clearly pose no threat, to put their hands on the vehicle. He then proceeds to check them for weapons. This plays itself out against the racist presupposition that all Blacks are armed and dangerous. His partner, the "good white cop," clearly does not completely approve of what is taking place. As Christine is being "frisked," Dillon's character puts his hands up her dress. We are led to believe that he forces his finger(s) into her vagina. Cameron, aware of this, does absolutely nothing. Begging Cameron to do something, Christine can only cry in complete humiliation. As with Cholly, Cameron's masculinity, defined as a man's ability to protect his woman, is completely erased. Like an enslaved Black male who knows his wife has just been raped by a white man, Cameron remains passive, facing his helplessness. After the event, the blame falls on Cameron's head as not being "man enough." So not only is he emasculated by the white cop but he is further emasculated by his wife. He could have physically tried to defend her, but this, in all reality, particularly given the history of racism in the LAPD, easily could have led to his death. This phenomenon justifiably pushes Cameron eventually to take a counterviolent approach toward those who hold the power. Given the reality of the power structure up against which he is determined to fight, he must be prepared to die.

Like Cameron, Cholly does not direct his anger toward the white gazers. "They were big white, armed men. He was small, black, helpless."[111] As a result of feeling helpless yet again, Cholly instead turns his hatred toward Darlene, a hatred he also feels toward himself. Dickerson observes:

> Unable to protect, to fight, to hide, Cholly cannot manifest the patriarchal prowess, benevolence, or obscurity (after all, his backside is literally exposed) that is traditionally associated with maleness and manhood. Like Darlene he

is accessible, weak, and naked. And to be thus naked is to share not only the tenderness and the plight of the female, but also to share a role traditionally assigned to her. The naked male is feminized, if not humanized.[112]

At one level of analysis, the threat to Cholly's masculinity and manhood is real, particularly in a culture so incredibly ideologically phallocentric in its values and practices.[113] The concept of masculinity, though, is by no means historically stable.[114] Given the past and present historical context in which men prove themselves through dominating women, Cholly has become the vehicle through which the power of this ideology is performed. Within the framework of the masculine ideology, the symbol of the erect penis means masculine power. What is significant to note is that once Cholly's masculinity is challenged and he feels threatened, he reinscribes phallocentric power through his desire to fuck Darlene "hard, long, and painfully." Because the white men have exposed his weakness, an attribute that male culture has stipulated as feminine, which is another unstable concept, Cholly feels the need to regain a sense of male power, a form of power he thinks is retrievable through further humiliation and sexual domination of Darlene.

Feeling exposed, weak, and emasculated, Cholly goes in search of his father, Samson Fuller, in Macon. Only 14, Cholly finds his father playing a game of craps. When Cholly sees a man whose name is Samson Fuller, he feels a certain level of affection. As Cholly attempts to identify himself, he cannot recall the name of his mother, a name he wonders if he had ever known. His father is more interested in the game. Almost as if his father had been confronted with this scenario before, he responds to Cholly with indifference. In an unforgettable and powerful act of rejection, Morrison writes: "But Fuller had turned back to the game that was about to begin anew. He bent down to toss a bill on the ground, and waited for a throw. When it was gone, he stood up and in a vexed and whiny voice shouted at Cholly, 'Tell that bitch she get her money. Now, get the fuck outta my face!'"[115] Initially feeling utterly paralyzed, Cholly finds the strength to run away. Mastering all of his strength not to cry, "his bowels suddenly opened up, and before he could realize what he knew, liquid stools were running down his legs."[116] Having "soiled himself like a baby," Cholly assumes the role of an infant, unprotected and unable to control basic bodily functions. The theme of infantilism is significant here. Not only has he been thrown away on a junk heap by his mother when he was an infant and had his bare behind exposed to white male onlookers, but now, neglected by his father, he soils his pants and runs away only to physically assume a fetal position under a pier. Morrison notes, "He remained there in fetal position, paralyzed, his fists covering his eyes, for a long time. No sound, no sight, only darkness and heat and the press of his knuckles on his eyelids. He even forgot his messed-up trousers."[117]

As a Black man in America, Cholly is "stripped by his past of the possibilities of material accumulation and of social standing."[118] Destitute and Black, living in poverty and squalor that was typical and socioeconomically and existentially overbearing for Black folk, being sold inferior furniture and then being identified as "shit" for not wanting it, having lost his self-esteem, rejected by his biological parents, violated by the white male gaze, having no sense of positive self-empowerment, and being an alcoholic to boot, which no doubt functions as a crutch to deal with so much pain and suffering in a white man's world that constantly holds up to him an image that he is not, Cholly is the epitome of the white man's burden. Perhaps "there was nothing more to lose." He is described as being "truly free" and without bounds, "alone with his own perceptions and appetites, and they alone interested him."[119] This "freedom," however, is only symbolic; it is born of powerlessness. Feeling god-like and omnipotent, which is the inverse reality of his once real and remembered sexual impotence, which also functions as a trope for economic, affective, and parental impotence and his powerlessness as a Black man in white America, he attempts to control everything within his immediate grasp, although with reckless irresponsibility and devastating consequences.

"So it was on a Saturday afternoon, in the thin light of spring [*a time of new and joyous beginnings*], he staggered home reeling drunk and saw his daughter [Pecola] in the kitchen."[120] Reeking with self-doubt, self-hatred, feeling like a failure in the white man's world, Cholly undergoes a process of implosion, a process that expresses itself inward as well as outward: He rapes Pecola. "No longer merely a site of ugliness," as Dickerson says, "Pecola's body has become a vessel of sin."[121] Pregnant with her father's child, having *dark* skin, which symbolically represents evil, having the habit of drinking three quarts of milk, which Mrs. MacTeer says is "downright *sin*ful,"[122] Pecola's sinfulness is multiplied. Part of the Dick-and-Jane primer opens up the chapter within which Pecola's rape is described. The words run together in unpunctuated sentential madness:

"SEEFATHERHEISBIGANDSTRONGFATH
ERWILLYOUPLAYWITHJANEFATHER
ISSMILINGSMILEFATHERSMILESMILE."[123]

Again, the powerful irony is that the primer reads like a fairy tale/fake narrative in comparison with the life of the Breedlove family.[124] The sentential structure of the primer also clearly lacks boundaries, a reality reflected in Cholly's relationship with Pecola. Unlike the father in the primer, Cholly does not smile, and his act of "playing" with his daughter becomes a site of unspeakable violence, physical and psychological trauma. Pecola needed to be loved, to feel it, to know its gentleness, to know its unconditionality and warmth, to reciprocate it. "Your brown eyes are beautiful, Pecola." "Now, what kind of candy can I get the beautiful little girl in the pretty dress?" "Pecola, you're special and your father and I love you so much." Unfortunately, from the narrative, these words were never spoken. Then again, Pecola did wonder what love felt like. Overhearing her mother and father copulating in bed, she came to think of love as "choking sounds and silence."[125]

Describing the horrible experience of Pecola's rape, the reader is told, "the gigantic thrust he [Cholly] made into her then provoked the only sound she made—a hollow suck of air in the back of her throat."[126] Perhaps Pecola was correct all along. Love *was* silence (words of parental affection lacking) and choking sounds (having your body invaded, and forced to emit sounds of profound distress). Pecola needed eyes that refused to see her as ugly, that could not possibly see her as ugly. She needed genuine familial affection and affirmation, but Cholly could only manage to push her legs apart violently and drop "his seeds in his own plot of black dirt."[127]

Doubly stained (being Black and physically sullied by her father), Pecola's Black body returns to her as *fucked*, both literally and figuratively. She has come to learn multiple messages about being embodied. As a young Black female, she learns the pain and terror of not only what it means to live-her-body-as-Black within a culture where the standard of beauty is indelibly marked by whiteness but she also lives her body in a world where the female body always already "makes one prey" within the context of male dominance.[128] Susan J. Brison notes, "Those who endure long periods of repeated torture often find ways of dissociating themselves from their bodies, that part of themselves which undergoes the torture."[129] Pecola's body is tortured through the process of abusive words, denigrating performative gazes, and redirected self-hatred. Pecola does not appear to resist the inscriptions of white racist discourse, inscriptions with which she has thoroughly identified. Wherever she goes, she encounters projective fantasies that construct her dark body as destiny, fixed and timeless.

Pecola's rejection of her body has absolutely nothing to do with Platonic metaphysics. It is not pure *disembodiment* that she desires. Rather, she seeks *white embodiment*, and, of course, by extension, *dis*embodiment from her Black body. Cholly only quickens her desire to cast off the dark nuisance she calls her body. Linda Alcoff provides a phenomenological description of sexual abuse as traumatically experienced by a young child, insightfully referencing feelings of corporeal dislocation:

> The child . . . feels shame marked on the body itself, as a thing to be used, a kind of living spittoon. The flesh of one's own body envelops and incorporates

the dreaded other, with its disregard for oneself and its capacity for psychic or physical violence. No wonder these events often produce a psychic dislocation from one's own corporeal present and one's ability to accept inhabiting this body, which is the continued site of the other. One's body now will forever retain a layer of remembered experience as the colonized space for a monstrous subjectivity.[130]

Cholly only adds to the profound loathing Pecola feels for her dark embodied *immanence* (etymologically, the sense of "remaining in place," stasis).

On the symbolic order, to be embodied-in-white is to transcend the autochthonous "black static dirt" she has become. Symbolically, white embodiment is paradoxically a form of *dis*embodiment. Whiteness is beauty transcendent, pure, clean, untainted, brilliance, genius, above and beyond the dirt and filth of the earth. Whiteness is associated with forms of angelic embodiment typically represented in iconographic depictions as luminescent "bodies" descending from the heavens. For Pecola, to be white, to have blue eyes that are the color of the sky is to escape the world of choking sounds and silence. It is to escape Yacobowski's dehumanizing gaze and to be loved like the young Fisher girl. It is to live a life that actually breeds love. Cholly Breedlove, contrary to his name, does not *breed love*, but hate, fear, trauma, and incest. Similar to the white gaze, he is a body snatcher. Reminiscent of the 1956 science fiction film *Invasion of the Body Snatchers*, both the white gaze and Cholly are invaders of bodies. They confiscate bodies. After taking possession of them, the bodies are then returned, although reconfigured, alien, and often monstrous.

Given the tenor of *The Bluest Eye*, the reader feels sympathy for Cholly over and above the inexcusable and unconscionable act of raping his daughter. After all, Cholly has been the object of systemic forces of white racism and profound levels of parental neglect. However, immediately leading up to the rape, the actual rape itself, and immediately thereafter, the reader is aware of the stark irony displayed. The entire scene is filled with contradictions and oppositions such that the reader's attention and empathy are shifted toward Pecola. Elliott Butler-Evans captures the significance of such irony in his analysis of the juxtaposition of contradictory terms used during this tragic moment within the text:

> Central . . . is the recurrent use of tender and tenderness in a context that is clearly intended to be ironic. Cholly envisions "tenderly" breaking his daughter's neck, fantasizes about violating her body with "tenderness," and wants to "fuck" her "tenderly." The oxymoronic construction itself undermines whatever sympathies one has for Cholly. The fusion of tenderness with acts of fantasized and real violence is experienced by the reader as a contradiction. Consequently, Cholly's antiheroic stature is significantly diminished in the text.

This is reinforced at the end of the description, when the narrative focus shifts to Pecola: "So when the child regained consciousness, she was lying on the kitchen floor under a heavy quilt, trying to connect the pain between her legs with the face of her mother looming over her."[131]

It would appear that for all of his life Cholly had been "fucked." What else, then, does he have to offer? White racist society placed him and many other Black males in the position of "fuckees." Being so placed, perhaps the only logical response is to "fuck" the world out of which they were spawned. Raping his daughter, Cholly has become the very quintessence of the how the white imaginary envisioned the Black body. Cholly is weak, wild, and irresponsible, and he beats his wife and neglects his children. He is economically destitute. He is sexually rapacious and bestial. As noted earlier, Cholly is described as being beyond the reaches of human consideration. He is said to have joined the animals, described as an old dog and a snake. Indeed, before he rapes Pecola, the reader is told that he crawls toward her on all fours.[132]

Although other Black males within *The Bluest Eye* are poor and struggle to create lives for themselves and their families (e.g., Claudia and Frieda's father, Mr. MacTeer), Cholly's life stands out as the tragic outcome of living in a society where Blacks have been systemically bombarded with (physical, psychological, and semiotic) racial violence. It is not the "successful" Black males within the text against which we should measure Cholly. This can lead to the simplistic conclusion that Cholly could have done otherwise, that he could have risen above his circumstances. While true in theory, and while one should continue to think Cholly's rape of Pecola morally abhorrent and unacceptable, there is more to be critiqued than Cholly. The process of critiquing the power of whiteness and phallocentric conceptions of masculinity (two central antagonists within the text) is far more significant than leaving the system intact and continuing to expect that someone like Cholly will succeed *in spite of* the larger systemically anti-Black racist context into which he was thrown, a context where options are seriously truncated.

Having been racially othered, rejected, uglified, put outdoors and taught to hate herself, and humiliated by people within the community (e.g., Yacobowski, Maureen Peal, Junior, Geraldine, teachers, and students), Pecola's rape and subsequent impregnation by Cholly decisively breaks her fragile spirit, forcing her to seek refuge in bluest eyes, the obtaining of which leads to a complete split in the fabric of her psyche. One way of understanding the Black community in Lorain, Ohio, is that they could not prevent this devastating psychological split. The community also suffered from measuring its soul by the tape of a world that measured whiteness as supreme. "The novel's central paucity," as Cat Moses argues, "is the community's lack of self-love, a lack precipitated by the imposition of a master aesthetic that privileges the light skin and blue eyes inherent in the community's internalization of this master aesthetic."[133] Perhaps this internalization explains why it is so easy for Pecola to seek out and find a light-skinned character named Soaphead Church, who is said to be capable of helping the unfortunate to "overcome Spells, Bad Luck, and Evil Influences [read: Blackness]."[134]

Church, like Pecola, hates his Blackness. In fact, he comes from an English lineage of "mixed blood" and is a strong Anglophile. Morrison says that the entire family "married 'up', lightening the family complexion and thinning out the family features." The family is described as "hoping to prove beyond a doubt De Gobineau's hypothesis that 'all civilizations derive from the white race [and], that none can exist without its help.'"[135] Church feels he has to do something for this "little black girl who wanted to rise up out of the pit of her blackness and see the world with blue eyes."[136] Ironically, he is also a pedophile, although he never makes a sexual advance toward Pecola. Hence, Pecola moves cyclically within a social space of pathology, a space of actual and potential trauma. What is it about a community, indeed an entire society, such that a young Black girl who had been recently molested by her biological father can only receive help to overcome her corporeal malediction through the care and understanding of another pedophile?

At a deeper level, Morrison is raising the issue of theodicy, the problem of how to account for profound suffering and injustice within a universe where God is said to exist. In fact, once Pecola successfully performs the necessary task that will grant her blue eyes (killing a dog that Church despises), Church writes a letter to God, exclaiming: "I did what You did not, could not, would not do: I looked at that ugly little black girl, and I loved her. I played You. And it was a very good show."[137] When the reader encounters Pecola again she has become *double*. Her "body, which has been the vortex of a hateful social prejudice and a devastating paternal love, is reinscribed in a self-reflexive dialogue of italicized and roman print that constitutes a fleshing out of double consciousness."[138] We find Pecola happily engaged in a lively conversation with herself about her new "blue eyes":

Sure it is. Can you imagine? Something like that happening to a person, and nobody but nobody saying anything about it? They all try to pretend they don't see them. Isn't that funny? . . . I said, isn't that funny? *Yes.* You are the only one who tells me how pretty they are. *Yes.* You are a real friend. I'm sorry about picking on you before. I mean, saying you are jealous and all. *That's all right.* No. Really. You are my very best friend. Why didn't I know you before. *You didn't need me before.* Didn't need you? *I mean . . . you were so unhappy before. I guess you didn't notice me before.* I guess you're right. And I was so lonely for friends. And you were right here. Right before my eyes. *No, honey. Right after your eyes.*[139]

Finally, Pecola has undergone a process of complete psychological trans-mogrification. She has entered "a twilight zone of being."[140] Like a bird long-ing to fly high and envelope itself within the blueness of the sky, Pecola can be observed "beating the air, a winged but grounded bird, intent on the blue void it could not reach—could not even see—but which filled the valleys of the mind."[141]

After Du Bois's encounter with the tall white newcomer, he also found himself living within a region of blue sky, but it was not "the blueness of the sky" that metaphorically spoke to the fanciful flight of insanity. Rather, after having his Black body/self negatively returned by the white gaze, Du Bois said, "I had thereafter no desire to tear down that veil, to creep through; I held all beyond it in common contempt, and lived above it in a region of blue sky, and great wandering shadows."[142] Pecola does not hold what is beyond the veil in contempt. To do so would imply a certain level of indigna-tion, a certain level of resistance to white power. In her soul, Pecola becomes white. But in Pecola's agony and sorrow, where are the sorrow songs, as Du Bois said, that breathe hope? Where are those comforting cadences that should have emboldened and enabled her to see that there is an ultimate justice? There was no release from existential angst and despair that resulted in victory, triumph, or confidence marked by inner peace. Du Bois asked, "Do the Sorrow Songs sing true?"[143] Answer: For Pecola, not in this world. *Not in this world!*

It is important to note that of all of the characters in *The Bluest Eye*, Claudia is most resistant to the epistemic regime of whiteness. Although Pecola is the "Bluest I" in the novel, it is Claudia who enacts a *blues* ontology, who bears witness in the African American tradition of testifying to the horrors that have befallen Pecola.[144] Unlike Pecola's family, Claudia's family has greater cohe-sion and order, although there is a paucity of material wealth. And although there were days, like Sundays, that were "full of 'don'ts' and 'set'cha self downs,'" there were also days of singing and delight.[145] Claudia says:

> If my mother was in a singing mood, it wasn't so bad. She would sing about hard times, bad times, and somebody-done-gone-and-left-me times. But her voice was so sweet and her singing-eyes so melty I found myself longing for those hard times, yearning to be grown without "a thin di-i-ime to my name." I looked forward to the delicious time when "my man" would leave me, when I would "hate to see that evening sun go down . . . 'cause then I would know "my man has left this town." Misery colored by the greens and blues in my mother's voice took all of the grief out of the words and left me with a conviction that pain was not only endurable, it was sweet.[146]

Here, Morrison brilliantly and insightfully has Claudia reference her mother, Mrs. MacTeer, singing lyrics from W. C. Handy's "St. Louis

Blues."[147] Although there is specific reference made to "St. Louis Blues," Mrs. MacTeer's blues repertoire could have included songs by Gertrude "Ma" Rainey, Bessie Smith, and others. Songs by these Black women would have provided Claudia with examples of strong Black women who were capable of directly confronting emotional pain—articulating the edges and curves of such pain through song—and mustering the courage to transcend it, if not simply to live with it in all of its complexity, but never to become a prisoner of it. Handy's piece is filled with pain, but also *movement*. "St. Louis Blues" opens with:

> I hate to see de evenin' sun go down
> I hate to see de evenin' sun go down
> Cause mah baby, he done lef' dis town
> Feelin' tomorrow lak I feel today
> Feelin' tomorrow lak I feel today
> I'll pack mah trunk, an' make mah getaway[148]

Hating to see "de evenin' sun go down" is just one movement on the rung of existential angst, and *intra*personal sorrow. Being linked to a larger process of resistance and movement, the depression experienced by the "evenin' sun going down" does not constitute stasis. It is only momentary. Anticipating tomorrow the same feelings of angst that she feels today, she knows what she must do: "I'll pack mah trunk, an' make mah getaway." She knows that she must move on and resist the angst. Making her getaway is emblematic of her metastability, and her capacity to take charge, make a radical change, and redirect her life. In other words, the meaning of angst is not fixed, but can be renarrated over and over again in song "like a certain Derridean notion of ceaseless movement and play."[149] The message Claudia receives is that Black women need not accept their lives as a given but can resist the conditions that attempt to deplete their longing for a better life and for something different. Through her mother's musicking, Claudia feels empowered with a sense of infinite possibility.

Theorizing this leitmotif of movement in the blues songs of Gertrude Rainey, Angela Davis notes that "A good number of Rainey's songs that evoke mobility and travel encourage black women to look toward 'home' for consolation and inspiration. In these songs the activity of travel has a clear and precise goal. Travel is not synonymous with uncertainty and the unknown but rather is undertaken with the aim of bringing certainty and stability into the women's life."[150] Consider Rainey's "Lost Wandering Blues." Davis points out that the first stanza, "leavin' this mornin' with my clothes in my hand," is indicative of "an absolute rupture with the old conditions the protagonist is rejecting." Davis argues that the theme of getting away and

rupturing old conditions is even stronger where Rainey "transforms a recur-
ring male blues image into one with a specifically female content."[151] Unlike
where the matchbox is used as a metaphor to indicate both baggage and being
poor, Rainey reconfigures the meaning of the matchbox to fit her precise
determination to leave a troubled situation. Davis cites the lyrics of Blind
Lemon Jefferson's "Matchbox Blues" to make the point of contrast. A verse
from "Matchbox Blues" reads:

> I'm setting here wondering will a matchbox hold my clothes
> I'm setting here wondering will a matchbox hold my clothes
> I ain't got so many matches but I got so far to go.[152]

Davis insightfully notes that "when Ma Rainey sings, 'I got a trunk too big
to be bothering with on the road,' the matchbox emerges as a metaphor for the
protagonist's conscious decision to strip herself down to the bare essentials,
leaving behind everything that may have defined her place under former conditions. What once served as a sign of impoverishment and want becomes for
Rainey an emancipatory vehicle."[153]

Thinking about the blues as part of the same African American musical
tradition as sorrow songs, which functioned as sites through which the Black
embodied spirit could both sing of its pain and yet move beyond it, listening to her mother sing the blues instilled in Claudia a profound sense of
existential hope and indefatigability. This hope is characteristic of enacting a
blues ontology. What is important to this way of *being blue* is the ability to
improvise during moments of pain and sorrow. Singing the blues is a way of
making a way out of no way.

Even if Pecola had been within earshot of Mrs. MacTeer's musicking
of the blues, she may not have been receptive to the influences of how the
blues carried and communicated motifs of resistance and didacticism and
how they could be heard in terms of their functionality to disclose a field of
possibility and resoluteness. After all, Pecola was already showing profound
signs of self-hatred when she arrived at the MacTeer home. Moreover, unlike
Claudia, Pecola may have received subtle messages from Mrs. MacTeer
that her presence was an intrusion, which would have functioned as just
one more instance of feeling unwanted, one more experience of having her
bodily presence rejected.[154] "Although Mrs. MacTeer does what Geraldine
would never do—take Pecola into her home—she clearly experiences
Pecola's body as economically and morally intrusive," as Dickerson notes.[155]
Recalling the magnitude of her mother's complaints, articulated in dramatic
monologues, Claudia says: "My mother's fussing soliloquies always irritated
and depressed us. They were interminable, insulting, and although indirect
(Mama never named anybody—just talked about folks and *some* people),

extremely painful in their thrust. She would go on like that for hours, connecting one offense to another until all of the things that chagrined her were spewed out."[156]

The complexity of Black musicking should be understood as signifying a "nexus of musical pleasure, religious zeal, sensual stimulation, and counterhegemonic resistance."[157] In short, African American musical forms are multifaceted. Of interest here is the counterhegemonic aspect of the blues. One might say that blues musicking was a form of resilience and identity formation for Black people. The image of railway junctions signifies impermanence, agency; "they symbolize sharecroppers, in the late 19th and early 20th centuries, migrating by trains to the North in search of jobs, safety, and a less racist environment."[158] As Houston A. Baker, Jr., notes, "The railway juncture is marked by transience," a form of transience that is physical, emotional, and existential.[159] Enacting a blues ontology speaks to the subjunctive mode of being, it speaks to human reality as *Seinkonnen* (an ability to be). The blues, then, as a site of *becoming*, de-paralyzes the spirit. Baker writes that "even as they speak of paralyzing absence and ineradicable desire, their instrumental rhythms suggest change, movement, action, continuance, unlimited and unending possibility. Like signification itself, blues are always nomadically wandering. Like the freight-hopping hobo, they are ever on the move, ceaselessly summing novel experience."[160]

Africans were enslaved and forced to come to the so-called New World, only to recreate themselves through processes of improvisation, movement (physical and psychological), syncretism, and bricolage, processes that possess family resemblances. Through a process of bricolage, Claudia appropriates the blues lyrics her mother sang, which are immediately available to her; she is able to feel the tragic sense of which they speak and yet is also attentive to their alternative possibility to transcend. Unlike Pecola who was not exposed to blues music, the blues frees Claudia from the stultifying impact of internalized whiteness.

Claudia's resistance to the epistemic regime of whiteness, and its seductive powers, is demonstrated in terms of a white doll given to her one Christmas. She relates:

> When I took it to bed, its hard unyielding limbs resisted my flesh—the tapered fingertips on those dimpled hands scratched. If, in sleep, I turned, the bone-cold head collided with my own. It was a most uncomfortable, patently aggressive sleeping companion. To hold it was no more rewarding. The starched gauze or lace on the cotton dress irritated any embrace. I had only one desire: to dismember it. To see of what it was made, to discover the dearness, to find the beauty, the desirability that had escaped me, but apparently only me. Adults, older girls, shops, magazines, newspapers, window signs—all the world had

agreed that a blue-eyed, yellow-haired, pink-skinned doll was what every girl child treasured.[161]

Unlike so many of the Black children in Kenneth and Mamie Clark's famous experiments who showed a distinct preference for white dolls over Black/brown ones, Claudia rejects the white doll, preferring to dismember it, to ascertain what makes it so special by virtue of being white.[162] Claudia literally destroys the white doll by breaking off parts. Of course, adults do not understand why she does this. After all, how could a young Black girl not want to possess a beautiful white doll? "Grown people frowned and fussed," Claudia reports: "You-don't-know-how-to-take-care-of-nothing. I-never-had-a-baby-doll-in-my-whole-life-and-used-to-cry-my-eyes-out-for-them. Now-you-got-one-a-beautiful-one-and-you-tear-it-up-what's-the-matter-with-you?"[163] Referring to the doll as "a beautiful one," the adults reveal the core of their longing. As they would cry out their eyes over not having *something beautiful* (read: white), one gets the impression that they are really crying out their eyes over being Black, the negation of beauty. They long for beauty qua whiteness. To embrace the beautiful white doll is an important way of vicariously possessing an aspect of whiteness. "How strong was their outrage. Tears threatened to erase the aloofness of their authority. The emotion of years of unfulfilled longing preened in their voices," notes Claudia.[164]

Claudia longs for familiar experiences, quotidian joys and pleasures that are achievable within the confines of her own Black family culture. Had they asked her what she desired, she would have been forthright. According to Claudia, she just wants "to sit on the low stool in Big Mama's kitchen with my lap full of lilacs and listen to Big Papa play his violin for me alone. The lowness of the stool made for my body, the security and warmth of Big Mama's kitchen, the smell of the lilacs, the sound of the music, and, since it would be good to have all of my senses engaged, the taste of a peach, perhaps, afterward."[165] Claudia's body screams out against the Dick-and-Jane reading primer. She hates milk and moves against the desired "cleanliness" (i.e., desired whiteness) of Pauline and Geraldine.[166] Claudia "looked with loathing on new dresses that required a hateful bath in a galvanized zinc tub before wearing."[167] She finds herself "slipping around on the zinc, no time to play or soak, for the water chilled too fast, no time to enjoy one's nakedness, only time to make curtains of soapy water careen down between the legs. Then the scratchy towels and the dreadful and humiliating absence of dirt. The irritable, unimaginative cleanliness. Gone the ink marks from legs and face, all my creations and accumulations of the day gone, and replaced by goose pimples."[168] The cleanliness is not just a passing moment of dislike. It is irritable and unimaginative. Bathing feels more like a ritual of bleaching, leaving one as white as snow, simple, clean, cold, chilly, perhaps even scary, leaving her with goose pimples. There is something about "dirt" that suggests the opposite of being sullen, which gives character to Claudia's body. She sees something humiliating in being so clean, perhaps so "white." She would rather the dark ink creations and accumulations to remain, marking her body's identity with countersigns that militate against cleanliness (whiteness). To forge an interpretive leap, perhaps this was Morrison's way of having Claudia engage in her own self-scripting, putting up a fight against the "washed cleanliness" of the Black body as symbolic of whiteness.

Although acknowledging Claudia's resistance to whiteness, Keith E. Byerman argues that within *The Bluest Eye*, "the ideological hegemony of whiteness is simply too overwhelming to be successfully resisted."[169] Byerman thinks that, "Claudia, the strongest character in the book, cannot defy the myth and is even made to feel guilty for her childhood doubts. Knowing full well that the myth is a lie, she must nonetheless bow before its idol."[170] Byerman points to a passage in which Claudia is critical of her own ruminations about causing whites pain by literally pinching their eyes. She says:

> When I learned how repulsive this disinterested violence was, that it was repulsive because it was disinterested, my shame floundered about for refuge. The best hiding place was love. Thus the conversion from pristine sadism to fabricated hatred, to fraudulent love. It was a small step to Shirley Temple. I learned much later to worship her, just as I learned to delight in cleanliness, knowing, even as I learned, that the change was adjustment without improvement.[171]

I am not convinced, however, that Claudia has given into the myth/idol of whiteness. She realizes that rituals such as worshipping Shirley Temple and delighting in cleanliness do not lead to any improvement—only an adjustment. Perhaps there is something of greater value that Claudia is after, something according to which a small adjustment might secure. Perhaps by worshipping Shirley Temple and delighting in cleanliness Claudia feels she might be even more desirable to her mother/other Black women. Recall that Claudia witnessed Pauline turn her loving attention to the little white girl, not to Pecola, during the blueberry pie incident. Indeed, perhaps there is also a peculiar form of Black mother-daughter identification formation at play. Concerning this point, Anne Anlin Cheng argues: "Claudia thus eventually learns to love Shirley Temple, I would argue, not merely or even primarily as a gesture of social compliance, but rather as a response to the call of the mother, as a perverse form of maternal connection. Only by learning to love little white girls can little black girls be like their mothers."[172]

Claudia's treatment of white dolls resonates symbolically with one of the significant objectives of this text, that is, to see how whiteness is constituted, to see its entrails, so as to discover what makes it so special. Pecola's tragedy suggests that at the very core of the alleged universal status of whiteness—and the negative reactive value-creating power linked to whiteness's assimilative capacity to reduce the otherness of the other to its own sameness—resides the reality of madness. Whiteness is a form of madness predicated upon the construction of differences against the metanarrative voice of its self-appointed status as the one. However, as I have argued, the socially constructed allure, power, and hegemony of whiteness are passed off as the "natural" order of things. This so-called natural order is maintained through various practices that attempt to conceal whiteness's historically contingent status and cultural particularity. For Pecola, even blue eyes were not enough. She was after the *bluest* eyes. However, this aesthetic and ontological feat is achievable, as Morrison makes clear, at the very expense of sanity itself.

As stated, Pecola is a tragic figure. She at once reflects the many existential realities of everyday Black life and functions as a powerful fictional character through whom we are able to gain imaginative access to a life of trauma.[173] Morrison does not describe an abstract conception of the self, delineating the ideal epistemic circumstances under which all cognitive agents (regardless of race, gender, class, or global geography) come to know x in some objective fashion. Rather, she provides the narrative of an embodied, young, raced, gendered, and sexed self; a self that is indexed to a particular historical, social, and cultural space. Morrison is not depicting abstract and universal truths, but "accidents of private [and public] history" that philosophically shed light on what it means to be a self (in this case, a Black female child) that cuts against the grain of metaphysical speculation regarding the nature of the self as "whatever it is whose persistence accounts for personal identity over time."[174]

As has been shown, Pecola's identity is severely ruptured. Even Pecola's memory, another usual philosophical candidate for maintaining personal identity, has been partly destroyed and reconstructed through her experience of trauma, racial degradation, and sexual molestation. Indeed, even her body, at the phenomenological level, is *not* the same body. Hence, because of the massive rift in her consciousness, that is, through the emergence of her double-consciousness, she is no longer that ugly Black body. For Pecola, there is a lived or phenomenological severance of bodily continuity; she has *become* someone else. Male gendered language aside, Fanon placed his finger on Pecola's "hallucinatory whitening" when he wrote: "If he is overwhelmed to such a degree by the wish to be white, it is because he lives in a society that makes his inferiority possible, in a society that derives its stability from the perpetuation of this complex, in a society that proclaims the superiority of one race; to the identical degree to which that society creates difficulties for him, he will find himself thrust into a neurotic situation."[175]

In an interview describing how she understands her own literary efforts, Morrison says that her "books are about very specific circumstances, and in them are people who do very specific things." She continues that "the plot, characters are part of my effort to create a language in which I can posit philosophical questions. I want the reader to ponder those questions not because I put them in an essay, but because they are part of a narrative."[176] Within the context of a narrative, as opposed to a philosophical architectonic system, Morrison is able to place the reader into an imaginative *lived* space, a powerful narrative space that is able to articulate modalities of lived existence where bodies are raped, racially brutalized, dehumanized, marginalized, and traumatized. In short, through narrative, Morrison moves the reader through the messiness of the impact of contingent history upon the body. Hence, one might say that Morrison posits philosophical questions that are linked inextricably to narrative. After all, our lives are lived narratives, journeys of pain, endurance, contradiction, death, intersubjectivity, suffering, racism, sexism, terror, trauma, joy, and transcendence. Avoiding abstract and non-indexical discourse, Morrison reveals the power of literature to embody the flesh and blood reality of what it means to-be-in-the-world.[177]

Morrison is also writing out of her own unique lived context. Her narrative embarkation toward exposing what it means for a young Black girl to experience profound levels of self-loathing (in this case, desiring blue eyes) is linked to an actual experience. Morrison reflects:

> We had just started elementary school. She said she wanted blue eyes. I looked around to picture her with them and was violently repelled by what I imagined she would look like if she had her wish. The sorrow in her voice seemed to call for sympathy, and I faked it for her, but, astonished by the desecration she proposed, I "got mad" at her instead.[178]

It would appear that it was during this early stage in Morrison's life that she began to feel the weight, at least emotionally, of what it would mean for a young Black girl to wish for blue eyes. One might say that *The Bluest Eye* was the narrative site through which she came to terms with the deeper philosophical implications of such a wish.

There is a fundamental link between Morrison's own lived embodied experiences and how she eventually renders such experiences intelligible through her narrative constructions. For example, she talks about cleaning the homes of white people when she was thirteen, homes that had very nice things that her family did not have. "Years later," she notes:

I used some of what I observed in my fiction. In "The Bluest Eye," Pauline lived in this dump and hated everything in it. And then she worked for the Fishers, who had this beautiful house, and she loved it. She got a lot of respect as their maid that she didn't get anywhere else. If she went to the grocery store as a black woman from that little house and said, "I don't want this meat," she would not be heard. But if she went in as a representative of these white people and said, "This is not good enough," they'd pay attention.[179]

Hence, it is not only the context of her lived experiences that enables Morrison to expose significant features of whiteness but her lived context also forms the backdrop against which she creates various plots and characters that function as part of her effort to forge a language in which certain philosophical questions might be posited. *The Bluest Eye* is ripe with an abundance of philosophical questions regarding the semiotics of whiteness and Blackness, the self in relation to the community and its responsibility for those who are vulnerable in an anti-Black world, issues of male hegemony and the reality of sexual trauma experienced by females of all ages, and questions of agency and the various ways in which the subject is shaped vis-à-vis various sites of interpellation.

Of course, it is one thing to pose these questions in the abstract or to respond to them in the abstract. Morrison's narrative depictions have a way of taking the reader beyond the abstract, enveloping her imaginative characters in flesh and blood, pain and sorrow, and thereby creating an emotional vortex through which readers are forced "to pose living metaphysical questions to themselves."[180]

NOTES

1. Pumza Fihlani, "Africa: Where Black Is Not Really Beautiful." See: http://www.bbc.com/news/world-africa-20444798 (accessed on June 3, 2016)
2. Fihlani, "Africa: Where Black Is Not Really Beautiful."
3. Perhaps Sara(h) Ba(a)rtman(n) comes close to the fictional character Pecola Breedlove in terms of having her psyche torn asunder through the regulatory power of the white gaze.
4. W. E. B. Du Bois, "The Souls of White Folk," in *W. E. B. Du Bois: A Reader*, ed. David Levering Lewis (New York: Henry Holt and Company, 1995), 460.
5. W. E. B. Du Bois, *The Souls of Black Folk* (1903; reprint, New York: New American Library, Inc., 1982), 45.
6. Du Bois, *Souls of Black Folk*, 45.
7. Wallace Thurman, *The Blacker the Berry* (1929; reprint, New York: Simon & Schuster, 1996), 217.
8. With regard to the association of Blackness with being cursed, note the narratives of the curse of Ham or the curse of Canaan.
9. Thurman, *Blacker the Berry*, 21.

10. Thurman, *Blacker the Berry*, 210, 217.

11. John Bishop, "Morrison's *The Bluest Eye*," *Explicator*, 51(4) (Summer 1993), 252–5, quotation on 254.

12. Toni Morrison, *Playing in the Dark: Whiteness and the Literary Imagination* (New York: Vintage Books, 1993), 76.

13. Robert Gooding-Williams, "Look, A Negro!" in *Reading Rodney King, Reading Urban Uprising*, ed. Robert Gooding-Williams (New York: Routledge, 1993), 160–1.

14. Morrison, *Playing in the Dark*, 52.

15. Morrison, *Playing in the Dark*, 6–7.

16. "Standing-reserve" is an expression Martin Heidegger used to understand/critique technology. The point here is that Blacks within the context of the white imaginary are not conceptualized as instantiations of *Dasein*, but as things merely present-to-hand, things available for exploitation. The white imaginary functions as a kind of framework, a world-picture, in terms of which the Black body shows itself, as it were, as that which is usable and can be manipulated. The implication is that whites can become so entrapped within white norms that the Black body is not capable of being seen, as showing up, as anything other than standing-reserve. See Martin Heidegger, *Basic Writings*, 2nd ed., ed. David Farrell Krell (San Francisco: H arperSanFrancisco, 1993).

17. Morrison, *Playing in the Dark*, xii.

18. Morrison, *Playing in the Dark*, 44.

19. Morrison, *Playing in the Dark*, 54.

20. Morrison, *Playing in the Dark*, 55.

21. Toni Morrison, *The Bluest Eye* (1970; reprint, New York: Alfred A. Knopf, 1998), 210.

22. Du Bois, "Souls of White Folk," 454.

23. See Carrie Mae Weems, "Mirror, Mirror," from the *Ain't Jokin'* Series, 1987–1988, http://www-personal.umich.edu/~tirtzae/weems.html (accessed, April 5, 2008)

24. W. E. B. Du Bois, "Sex and Racism," in Levering, *W. E. B. Du Bois: A Reader*, 313–14.

25. James Baldwin, "On Being 'White' . . . and Other Lies," in *Black on White: Black Writers on What It Means to Be White*, ed. David R. Roediger (New York: Schocken Books, 1998), 178.

26. Morrison, *Bluest Eye*, 48.

27. Morrison, *Bluest Eye*, 50.

28. Morrison, *Bluest Eye*, 49.

29. C. G. Prado, *Starting with Foucault: An Introduction to Genealogy* (Boulder, CO: Westview Press, 1995), 36.

30. Morrison, *Bluest Eye*, 47.

31. Frantz Fanon, *Black Skin, White Masks*, trans. Charles Lam Markmann (New York: Grove Press, Inc., 1967), 109.

32. Morrison, *Bluest Eye*, 50.

33. The omniscient voice is more knowledgeable than Claudia. After all, she is only nine years old. The omniscient voice provides information about life and the Breedloves to which Claudia would not have had access.

34. Morrison, *Bluest Eye*, 18.

35. Theresa M. Towner, "Black Matters on the Dixie Limited: *As I Lay Dying* and *The Bluest Eye*," in *Unflinching Gaze: Morrison and Faulkner Re-Envisioned*, ed. Carol A. Kolmerten, Stephen M. Ross, and Judith Bryant Wittenberg (Jackson: University Press of Mississippi, 1997), 124.

36. Elliott Butler-Evans, *Race, Gender, and Desire: Narrative Strategies in the Fiction of Toni Cade Bambara, Toni Morrison, and Alice Walker* (Philadelphia: Temple University Press, 1989), 68.

37. Frantz Fanon, *Black Skin, White Masks*, 162, n25.

38. Morrison, *Bluest Eye*, 18.

39. Morrison, *Bluest Eye*, 17.

40. Morrison, *Bluest Eye*, 17–18.

41. Morrison, *Bluest Eye*, 17.

42. Cheryl Harris, "Whiteness as Property," in Roediger, *Black on White*, 116.

43. Harris, "Whiteness as Property," 118.

44. Du Bois, "Souls of White Folk," 454.

45. Morrison, *Bluest Eye*, 34.

46. Morrison, *Bluest Eye*, 35.

47. Morrison, *Bluest Eye*, 35.

48. Morrison, *Bluest Eye*, 36.

49. Du Bois, *Souls of Black Folk*, 50.

50. Morrison, *Bluest Eye*, 38, emphasis added.

51. Morrison, *Bluest Eye*, 39.

52. Toni Morrison, "Unspeakable Things Unspoken: The Afro-American Presence in American Literature," *Michigan Quarterly Review*, 28, 1989, 1–34, quotation on 8.

53. Keith E. Byerman, "Intense Behaviors: The Use of the Grotesque in *The Bluest Eye* and *Eva's Man*," *CLA Journal*, 25(4) (June 1982), 447–57, quotation on 449.

54. C. G. Prado, *Descartes and Foucault: A Contrastive Introduction to Philosophy* (Ottawa: University of Ottawa Press, 1992), 159.

55. Concerning the sui generis and causi sui status of the settler, Fanon noted, "The settler makes history; his life is an epoch, an Odyssey. He is the absolute beginning." See Frantz Fanon, *The Wretched of the Earth* (New York: Grove Press, 1963), 51.

56. Morrison, *Bluest Eye*, 210.

57. Morrison, *Bluest Eye*, 19.

58. Morrison, *Bluest Eye*, 50, emphasis added.

59. Jacqueline de Weever, "The Inverted World of Toni Morrison's *The Bluest Eye* and *Sula*," *CLA Journal*, 22(4) (June 1979), 402–14, quotation on 406.

60. The use of the term *threatening* is to suggest that blue eyes not only constitute beauty and safety for Pecola, but they also carry overtones of negativity, harsh criticism, and degradation. After all, it is not abstract, detached blue eyes that Pecola ever sees. She sees blue eyes within the context of a disapproving face, a demeaning look. In this way, for Pecola, blues eyes carry traces of association with feelings of being threatened.

61. Gunilla Theander Kester, *Writing the Subject:* Bildung *and the African American Text* (New York: Peter Lang, 1995), 77.

62. Vanessa D. Dickerson, "Summoning SomeBody: The Flesh Made Word in Toni Morrison's Fiction," in *Recovering the Black Female Body: Self-Representation*

by African American Women, ed. Michael Bennett and Vanessa D. Dickerson (New Brunswick, NJ: Rutgers University Press, 2001), 196.

63. Morrison, *Bluest Eye*, 123.

64. Richard Dyer, *White* (New York: Routledge, 1997), 102.

65. Morrison, *Bluest Eye*, 122.

66. Gary Schwartz, "Toni Morrison at the Movies: Theorizing Race through Imitation of Life," in *Existence in Black: An Anthology of Existential Philosophy*, ed. Lewis R. Gordon (New York: Routledge, 1997), 123.

67. Morrison, *Bluest Eye*, 124.

68. Morrison, *Bluest Eye*, 126.

69. Morrison, *Bluest Eye*, 127.

70. Dickerson, "Summoning SomeBody," 199–200.

71. Morrison, *Bluest Eye*, 107–8.

72. Morrison, *Bluest Eye*, 128.

73. Morrison, *Bluest Eye*, 108–9.

74. Morrison, *Bluest Eye*, 109.

75. Dickerson, "Summoning SomeBody," 214, n5.

76. Dickerson, "Summoning SomeBody," 199.

77. Morrison, *Bluest Eye*, 45.

78. Morrison, *Bluest Eye*, 83.

79. Morrison, *Bluest Eye*, 87.

80. Morrison, *Playing in the Dark*, 6.

81. Morrison, *Bluest Eye*, 88.

82. Morrison, *Bluest Eye*, 91.

83. Morrison, *Bluest Eye*, 92.

84. Morrison, *Bluest Eye*, 45.

85. Morrison, *Bluest Eye*, 46.

86. Morrison, *Bluest Eye*, 65.

87. Morrison, *Bluest Eye*, 67–8.

88. Schwartz, "Toni Morrison at the Movies," 123.

89. Bishop, "Morrison's *The Bluest Eye*," 253–4.

90. For Foucault, the concept of problematization involves encouraging new forms of subjectivity through the process of interrogating and changing the truths, knowledges, and discourses within which we currently define ourselves. See Prado, *Starting with Foucault*, 112–15, 162–4.

91. Morrison, *Bluest Eye*, 74.

92. See Ann duCille's very insightful analysis of this movie within the larger context of her interpretation of whiteness in relation to Shirley Temple in "The Shirley Temple of My Familiar," *Transition* (The White Issue) Issue 73, 7(1), 1998, 10–32, esp. 31–2.

93. See Janine Jones, "The Impairment of Empathy in Goodwill Whites for African Americans," in *What White Looks Like: African-American Philosophers on the Whiteness Question* (New York: Routledge, 2004), 71.

94. duCille, "The Shirley Temple of My Familiar," 32.

95. For a lengthier engagement of this movie, see George Yancy's " 'Now, Imagine She's White,' The Gift of the Black Gaze and the Re-inscription of Whiteness as Normative in *A Time to Kill*" in *Race, Philosophy, and Film*, ed. by Dan Flory and Mary Bloodsworth-Lugo (London and New York: Routledge, 2013), 134–148.

96. Morrison, *Bluest Eye*, 46.

97. Jana Sawicki, "Foucault, Feminism, and Questions of Identity," in *The Cambridge Companion to Foucault*, ed. Gary Gutting (Cambridge, UK: Cambridge University Press, 1999), 292.

98. Morrison, *Bluest Eye*, 45.

99. Morrison, *Bluest Eye*, 46.

100. Morrison, *Bluest Eye*, 130.

101. I thank Linda Alcoff for a counter reading of Pauline's relationship with Cholly. In personal communication, she wrote, "In the description of Pauline's sex with Cholly, I wonder if you read this too negatively. She is getting attention, after all, and a kind of positive valuation in his desire for her. Being sexually objectified is not equivalent to rape. Here is where Sartre's characterization of sexual activity lacks complexity."

102. Morrison, *Bluest Eye*, 160.

103. Morrison, *Bluest Eye*, 132.

104. Morrison, *Bluest Eye*, 133.

105. Vanessa D. Dickerson, "The Naked Father in Toni Morrison's *The Bluest Eye*," in *Refiguring the Father: New Feminist Readings of Patriarchy*, ed. Patricia Yaeger and Beth Kowaleski-Wallace (Carbondale: Southern Illinois University Press, 1989), 110.

106. Morrison, *Bluest Eye*, 147–8.

107. Schwartz, "Toni Morrison at the Movies," 124–5.

108. Morrison, *Bluest Eye*, 148.

109. Dickerson, "The Naked Father," 111.

110. Morrison, *Bluest Eye*, 148.

111. Morrison, *Bluest Eye*, 150.

112. Dickerson, "The Naked Father," 112.

113. Even in discourse communities where Black men come to terms with their own understanding of what it means to be a "Black man," according their own normative criteria, there is the understanding among Black men that white men fear this sense of identity and deploy strategies for rendering them powerless.

114. See Gail Bederman, *Manliness and Civilization: A Cultural History of Gender and Race in the United States, 1880–1917* (Chicago: University of Chicago Press, 1995), esp. chapter 1.

115. Morrison, *Bluest Eye*, 156.

116. Morrison, *Bluest Eye*, 156–7.

117. Morrison, *Bluest Eye*, 157.

118. Dickerson, "The Naked Father," 117.

119. Morrison, *Bluest Eye*, 160.

120. Morrison, *Bluest Eye*, 161.

121. Dickerson, "Summoning SomeBody," 202.

122. Morrison, *Bluest Eye*, 25.

123. Morrison, *Bluest Eye*, 132.

124. Another way of theorizing the "fakeness" of the Dick-and-Jane primer is in terms of whiteness. In other words, just as the primer moves from a level of sentential coherence and then transforms into something incoherent, whiteness, at its heart, is unstable, incoherent, a sham. As such, whiteness breaks apart, it falters, and fails to support its façade of universality and impregnability. I would like to thank Gloria Jirsaraie for this insight.

125. Morrison, *Bluest Eye*, 57.

126. Morrison, *Bluest Eye*, 163.

127. Morrison, *Bluest Eye*, 5.

128. Susan J. Brison, *Aftermath: Violence and the Remaking of a Self* (Princeton, NJ: Princeton University Press, 2002), 44.

129. Brison, *Aftermath*, 47.

130. Linda Martin Alcoff, "Merleau-Ponty and Feminist Theory on Experience," in *Chiasms: Merleau-Ponty's Notion of Flesh,* ed. Fred Evans and Leonard Lawlor (Albany: State University of New York Press, 2000), 268. This quotation is taken from a larger context within which Alcoff critiques Michel Foucault, calling into question his "claim that discourses can alter the experience of events like sexual relations between adults and children to such a degree that they can become 'inconsequential pleasures'" (see esp. 266–9).

131. Butler-Evans, *Race, Gender, and Desire*, 79.

132. Morrison, *Bluest Eye*, 162.

133. Cat Moses, "The Blues Aesthetic in Toni Morrison's *The Bluest Eye*," *African American Review*, 33(4) (Winter 1999), 623–36, quotation on 634.

134. Morrison, *Bluest Eye*, 173.

135. Morrison, *Bluest Eye*, 168.

136. Morrison, *Bluest Eye*, 174.

137. Morrison, *Bluest Eye*, 182.

138. Dickerson, "Summoning SomeBody," 202.

139. Morrison, *Bluest Eye*, 196. During the conversation with herself, Pecola implies that her father either attempted or actually raped her at least one other time (199–200).

140. Dickerson, "Summoning SomeBody," 202.

141. Morrison, *Bluest Eye*, 204.

142. Du Bois, *Souls of Black Folk*, 44.

143. Du Bois, *Souls of Black Folk*, 274.

144. Moses, "The Blues Aesthetic in Toni Morrison's *The Bluest Eye*," 624.

145. Morrison, *Bluest Eye*, 25.

146. Morrison, *Bluest Eye*, 25–6.

147. Angela Davis is critical of the 1929 motion picture *St. Louis Blues*. Davis argues that the film "deserves criticism not only for its exploitation of racist stereotypes but for its violation of the spirit of the blues. Its direct translation of blues images into a visual and linear narrative violates blues discourse, which is always complicated, contextualized, and informed by that which is unbroken as well as

by that which is named. St. Louis Blues, the film, flagrantly disregards the spirit of women's blues by leaving the victimized woman with no recourse." See Angela Davis, *Blues Legacies and Black Feminism: Gertrude "Ma" Rainey, Bessie Smith, and Billie Holiday* (New York: Pantheon Books, 1998), 61. African American literary critic Houston A. Baker, Jr., also is critical of W. C. Handy's rendering of the blues. Baker writes, "But the autobiographical account of the man who has been called the 'Father of the Blues' offers only a simplistic detailing of a progress, describing, as it were, the elevation of a 'primitive' folk ditty to the status of 'art' in America. Handy's rendering leaves unexamined, therefore, myriad corridors, mainroads, and way-stations of an extraordinary and elusive Afro-American cultural phenomenon." See Houston A. Baker, Jr., *Blues, Ideology, and Afro-American Literature: A Vernacular Theory* (Chicago: University of Chicago Press, 1984), 8.

148. Moses, "The Blues Aesthetic in Toni Morrison's *The Bluest Eye*," 635.

149. Diana Fuss, *Essentially Speaking: Feminism, Nature, and Difference* (New York: Routledge, 1989), 88.

150. Davis, *Blues Legacies*, 80.

151. Davis, *Blues Legacies*, 78.

152. Davis, *Blues Legacies*, 78.

153. Davis, *Blues Legacies*, 78–9.

154. It is interesting to note that Pecola does not feel rejected by the three black whores who resided in an apartment above the storefront where the Breedloves lived. Although China, Poland, and Miss Marie did not play any special role in liberating Pecola from her psychological death, they did offer a sense of temporary reprieve. One might ask: what has happened to the nurturing functions of a larger community when a young Black girl finds delight in the fact that she gains some form of recognition in the eyes of prostitutes?

155. Dickerson, "Summoning SomeBody," 200.

156. Morrison, *Bluest Eye*, 24.

157. Guthrie P. Ramsey, Jr., *Race Music: Black Cultures from Bebop to Hip Hop* (Berkeley: University of California Press, 2003), 41.

158. Fuss, *Essentially Speaking: Feminism, Nature, and Difference*, 88.

159. Baker, *Blues, Ideology, and Afro-American Literature*, 7.

160. Baker, *Blues, Ideology, and Afro-American Literature*, 8.

161. Morrison, *Bluest Eye*, 20.

162. These experiments were used as evidence to demonstrate that segregation was deleterious to Black children's self-images. The evidence was cited in *Brown v. Board of Education* that proved segregation was unequal and thereby unconstitutional. See Adelbert H. Jenkins, *Turning Corners: The Psychology of African Americans* (Needham Heights, MA: Allyn and Bacon, 1995), 27.

163. Morrison, *Bluest Eye*, 21.

164. Morrison, *Bluest Eye*, 21.

165. Morrison, *Bluest Eye*, 22.

166. Morrison, *Bluest Eye*, 23.

167. Morrison, *Bluest Eye*, 22.

168. Morrison, *Bluest Eye*, 22.

169. Byerman, "Intense Behaviors," 449.

170. Byerman, "Intense Behaviors," 449–50.

171. Morrison, *Bluest Eye*, 23.

172. Ann Anlin Cheng, "Wounded Beauty: An Exploratory Essay on Race, Feminism, and the Aesthetic Question," *Tulsa Studies in Women's Literature*, 19(2), 2000, 191–217, quotation on 200. On the same page, Cheng also provides an insightful spin on Claudia's claim that this movement toward cleanliness and Shirley Temple was "adjustment without improvement." She notes: "Beauty for Claudia is a convoluted lesson in desire that, even as it reaches a goal (the new object of desire, Shirley Temple), nonetheless never quite achieves stable meaning. This last claim—'it was adjustment without improvement'—is also slightly puzzling. Is it a statement mourning the self's continued inability to assume fully that white ideal; an acknowledgment of the emptiness of such compliance; or even a larger allusion to the nature of social 'improvement' in African-American communities? The answer can in fact be all of the above, or, at least, the statement's ambiguity informs us that, for the object of discrimination, it is impossible to disentangle these meanings. Claudia's relationships to ideal white beauty, to her own self-perception, to other black women, and to the larger African American community bespeaks desire and critique—or desire in spite of critique."

173. Brison, *Aftermath*, 25.

174. Brison, *Aftermath*, 24, 40.

175. Fanon, *Black Skin, White Masks*, 100.

176. Claudia Dreifus, "Chloe Wofford Talks about Toni Morrison," http://www. en.utexas.edu/amlit/amlitprivate/texts/morrison1.html (accessed, April 5, 2008)

177. See Eleanore Holveck, *Simone de Beauvoir's Philosophy of Lived Experience: Literature and Metaphysics* (Lanham, MD: Rowman & Littlefield, 2002), 7–8, 151, 161–2.

178. Morrison, *Bluest Eye*, 209.

179. Dreifus, "Chloe Wofford Talks about Toni Morrison."

180. Holveck, *Simone de Beauvoir's Philosophy of Lived Experience*, 8.

Chapter 7

Whiteness as Ambush and the Transformative Power of Vigilance

As an antiracist racist I believe that I should always feel conflicted, full of contradictions, never as though I have "arrived."

—Christine Clark

Whites are, after all, still accorded the privileges of being White even as they ideologically renounce their whiteness, often with the best intentions.

—Peter McLaren

Some readers may be shocked to see a white person contritely acknowledge that she is a racist. I do not say this with pride. I simply believe that no matter how hard I work at not being racist, I still am. Because part of racism is systemic, I benefit from the privilege that I am struggling to see.... All whites are racist in this use of the term, because we benefit from systemic white privilege.

—Stephanie M. Wildman

"Bullshit!" That was the immediate response of a white student after I gave a lecture exploring the complex "race" dynamics theorized in the elevator example, explored in chapter 2, where my body is confiscated and marked as dangerous. I was invited to a class on multiculturalism to talk about whiteness and the Black body. The majority of the class was white. Having given a variation of this lecture before, I had become used to hands being raised in eagerness, if only then to have my interlocutor launch into a diatribe aimed at finding holes in my presentation, but never a definitive "Bullshit!" I was particularly struck by the harsh tone of her response and the look of self-certainty that appeared on her face. Much needs to be explored in terms of the communicational dynamics that arise within contexts where Black bodies (in this case, a Black male body) speak openly and honestly about issues of whiteness to a mostly white audience. On the one hand, because I am Black, I am already the racially marked body that is expected to be able to say something knowledgeable, meaningful, and important about race. On the other hand, when that knowledge exposes the racist operations of white bodies, marks them as raced and racist, I am deemed either overly sensitive or too quick to generalize to all whites what I have experienced on the basis of a "few unfortunate events" or "exceptional cases."

The female student did not accuse me of having committed a non sequitur or having failed to define my terms adequately. She effectively created a dialogical space within which I became the "bullshitter," one who has absolutely no interest in the truth. She, of course, positioned herself as the discerner of bullshit and so as one who ought to be believed. She did go on to explain how my example did not describe her as *she* would not have responded to the presence of a Black male body on an elevator with such fear, stiff bodily comportment, and suspicion. While addressing her objection, I continued to think about the vitriolic nature of her initial response. After all, the elevator example is not intended to indict white women as such but to theorize and make sense of the phenomenon of being alone on elevators with white women as experienced by Black men, many of whom have shared how they have had white women respond to them in precisely the way that I describe. A Black university president once disclosed to me that he too has experienced what he aptly referred to as the "elevator effect."

"Bullshit!" functioned as a form of erasure of the experiences of Black men who have indeed encountered the white gaze within the contexts of elevators and other social spaces. She assumed no "responsibility to marginalized people and to the understanding developed from their lives."[1] There was no suspension of her sense of self-certainty regarding the dynamics of race and racism and how Black men struggle daily to deal with issues of racism in their lives. She did not *listen* to me and did not take any steps toward conceding my understanding of the social world as legitimate. As Joe Feagin and Hernan Vera state, "White racism involves a massive breakdown of empathy, the human capacity to experience the feelings of members of an out-group viewed as different."[2] In addition to the fact that "bullshit" functioned as a form of erasure, not unlike the humiliating experiences that I have had in the presence of certain white bodies, it also pointed to various ways in which the manifest function of certain objections may very well operate to obfuscate profound modes of living in bad faith. In other words, she was lying to herself, concealing from view the reality of her own racism in relationship to those moments on elevators or in other social spaces where she engaged in perceptual practices that criminalized or demonized the Black body.

However, I am careful here to note that the epistemic validity of an objection must not be reduced to its emotional delivery or aim to insult.

In fact, one philosopher pointed out to me that if he and I held very different views regarding the ontology of numbers that an objection from him ought to be judged on the basis of its validity and nothing more. In the case of the white student, however, the context of the lecture was not about the ontology of numbers, it was about race and racism. Discussions involving the ontology of numbers, while I imagine can get very passionate, do not implicate the self in the same way discussions around race and racism do. The self is not similarly exposed, made potentially vulnerable. The white female student was not passionately invested in defending an ontological theory regarding numbers, but conceivably invested in protecting hidden and threatening aspects of her white self that she would rather avoid. She was far more interested in protecting her sense of "goodness," which functioned to mask how she is implicated in the subtle workings of white racism.

The white student's objection raised the issue of how white interlocutors, when in discussions involving race and racism, may (more than they realize) deploy theory as a way of not being forced to examine aspects of their own white subject position. Indeed, the deployment of theory can function as a form of bad faith. Whiteness, after all, is a master of concealment; it is insidiously embedded within response s, reactions, good intentions, postural gestures, denials, and structural and material orders. Etymologically, the word "insidious" (*insidiae*) means to ambush—a powerful metaphor, as it brings to mind images and scenarios of being snared and trapped unexpectedly. Whiteness as a form of ambushing is not an anomaly.[3] The operations of whiteness are by no means completely transparent. This is partly what it means to say that whiteness is insidious. The moment a white person claims to have arrived, he/she often undergoes a surprise attack, a form of attack that points to how whiteness ensnares even as one strives to fight against racism. Shannon Sullivan states, "Rather than rest assured that she is effectively fighting white privilege, when engaging in resistance a person needs to continually be questioning the effects of her activism on both self and world."[4]

Although there are many white antiracists who do fight and will continue to fight against the operations of white power, and it is true that the regulatory power of whiteness will invariably attempt to undermine such efforts, it is important that white antiracists realize how much is at stake. While antiracist whites take time to get their shit together, a luxury that is a species of privilege, Black bodies and bodies of color continue to suffer, their bodies cry out for the political and existential urgency for the *immediate* undoing of the oppressive operations of whiteness. Here, the very notion of the temporal gets racialized. My point here is that even as whites take the time to theorize the complexity of whiteness, revealing its various modes of resistance to radical transformation, Black bodies continue to endure tremendous pain and suffering. Doing theory in the service of undoing whiteness comes with its own snares and seductions, its own comfort zones, and reinscription of distances. Whites who deploy theory in the service of fighting against white racism must caution against the seduction of white narcissism, the recentering of whiteness, even if it is the object of critical reflection, and, hence, the process of sequestration from the real world of weeping, suffering, and traumatized Black bodies impacted by the operations of white power. As antiracist whites continue to make mistakes and continue to falter in the face of institutional interpellation and habituated racist reflexes, tomorrow, a Black body will be murdered as it innocently reaches for its wallet. The sheer weight of this reality mocks the patience of theory.

Jane Lazarre, a white Jewish mother of interracial sons, relates the story of how one of her son's Black friends was harassed right outside her home by police who thought the car he was driving was stolen. Lazarre shouted, "But this is unbelievable!"[5] Her son responded angrily, reminding her that being stopped by police and questioned because he is driving a nice-looking car is something that happens to him all the time. After all, he is a Black man and as such suspect a priori. Lazarre, while certainly committed to fighting against an anti-Black racist world, was ambushed. As white, as privileged, she can remain innocent of such travesties. Her state of disbelief as she later realizes, "signifies the vast space of white blindness to the dailiness of racism."[6] Lazarre became aware that she was ambushed by her whiteness, as she realized that her subject position is productive of a form of ignorance.

While antiracist activist Tim Wise continues to make a conscious effort at eradicating racism, he realizes how trapped he is within the vortex of white power and how whiteness waylays the white self even as one fights against racism with all good intentions. He relates a story that gets at the core of how racism operates in very insidious ways. In 2003, he boarded a 737 headed to St. Louis. He notes, "I glanced into the cockpit . . . and there I saw something I had never seen before in all the years I had been flying: not one but two black pilots at the controls of the plane."[7]

Despite all the antiracist work that he had done, Wise admits that he thought: "Oh my God, can these guys fly this plane?"[8] Wise points out that what he knew to be true was of little help. In short, Wise was ambushed by whiteness. This example points to how racism is embedded within one's embodied habitual engagement with the social world and how it is weaved within the unconscious, impacting everyday mundane transactions. This raises the issue of the sheer magnitude of the work that is necessary to challenge the insidious nature of racism. It points to how racism eats away, as W. E. B. Du Bois might say, at the souls of white folk.

Wise tells another story, of his grandmother, Maw, who had been diagnosed with Alzheimer's. He shares the horrible narrative of the last stages of her life, how Maw began "to forget who people were, confusing me with my father on a pretty much permanent basis." Wise poses this important question: "What does a little old lady with Alzheimer's tell us about whiteness in America?"[9] He makes a point of sharing with his readers that she was antiracist and tried to teach this to his parents and by extension to him. What makes the story even more tragic is that her father was a member of the Ku Klux Klan. He eventually quit the Klan because of her antiracist fortitude. After all, at age fifteen, she had fallen in love with Leo Wise, who was Jewish. Wise provides these details in order to give readers an example of the degrading magnitude involved in the insidious nature of racism and how it wounds the soul. As her condition worsened, she forgot her former self, which is one of the powerful tragedies of Alzheimer's. She began to call her nurses "niggers." Wise explains: "She could not go to the bathroom by herself. She could not recognize a glass of water for what it was. But she could recognize a *nigger*. America had seen to that, and no disease would strip her of that memory. Indeed, it would be one of the last words I would hear her say, before finally she stopped talking at all."[10]

As has been argued throughout this book, whiteness is a powerful *embodied* form of being-in-the-world, where "ignorance of white domination is not just an empty gap in knowledge nor the product of a mere epistemological oversight."[11] One might say that being a white antiracist is never completely in one's control because such an identity is deferred by the sheer complexity of the fact that one is never self-transparent, that one is ensconced within structural and material power racial hierarchies, that the white body is constituted by racist habits that create a form of racist inertia even as the white body attempts to undermine its somatic normativity, and that the white self undergoes processes of interpellation even as the white self engages in agential acts of racist disruption. This does not mean, though, that all is hopeless or, as one white student commented, that "since racism is so powerful that we [whites] just might as well be racists." One ought to exercise vigilance and DuBoisian "long siege" even while complicity with whiteness is still possible or precisely because one is always already complicit with whiteness.

Comedian Michael Richards (known as the character "Cosmo Kramer" on the sitcom *Seinfeld*) may not have realized the significance of his insight when he attempted a televised apology for his explosive racist tirade at the Laugh Factory in 2006. Pointing to a group of Blacks in the audience who allegedly had been talking during his performance, with a great deal of anger and vitriol he shouted: "Shut up. Fifty years ago, we'd have you upside down with a fucking fork up your ass. You can talk, you can talk, you can talk.

You brave now motherfucka. Throw his ass out, he's a nigger! He's a nigger! He's a nigger! A nigger, look it's a nigger!" After this tirade, people actually began to leave the show. On his way out, one of the Black men shouted back at Richards, saying how unfair it was that he used such language. Richards responded, "That's what happens when you interrupt a white man, don't you know?"[12] Particularly revealing about Richards's language is his reference to the spectacle of lynching Black male bodies with themes of unashamed sodomy, in this case with a fork. Moreover, as a *white man*, he marked his identity as a site of threatening power over and against the inferior, uncultured, and disruptive identity of the "nigger." In short, to interrupt a white man, to look a white man in the eyes, to disagree with a white man, is to forget one's place in the natural scheme of things. To think that you are more than a "nigger" requires some reminding. Richards asked, "Don't you know?" His question reminded the "niggers" in the audience that they should have known better than to interfere with a white man, whose voice and presence are sacrosanct and hegemonic. Richards used the "n-word" six times, seven if you include where he pronounced it "nigga." Later, he appeared via satellite on the *Dave Letterman Show* (with Jerry Seinfeld on the show) and offered an apology, saying "I'm not a racist. That's what's so insane about this." How does one reconcile his understanding of himself as not a racist in the light of his blatant racism? Insightfully, he adds, "And yet, it's said. It comes through. It fires out of me."[13]

Richards could be lying about not being a racist in order to redeem his image. In short, he simply got caught. My sense though is that he was *ambushed*. Even as he thinks he is not a racist—perhaps because he has Black friends and other "friends of color" and does not use the notorious "n-word" on a daily basis, and because he does not identify as a skinhead or associate with Klan groups—his remarks belied his self-understanding. In fact, he may see himself as a "good white." Being a good white, however, does not mean that one has *arrived*. In fact, being antiracist does not mean that the white self has arrived. There are many good whites who continue to participate in structures of racial power from which they benefit, who fear for their lives while walking down the street with Black young men walking in their direction, and who have conniptions when their young daughters (and sons) bring home "persons of color" as potential dates. For many, embedded within the construction of the notion of the "good white" and the antiracist white is the sense of stasis and self-glorification. This form of self-understanding actually obstructs the necessary deeper critical work required to unearth the various ways in which one is actually complicit in terms of racist behavior. Monique Roelofs echoes this point when she is suspicious of "a supposedly achieved 'insightful', 'sophisticated', 'cool', 'courageous', 'humorous', 'morally remediable', 'humane' whiteness." She worries "about the capacities of self-aestheticization to pass off my whiteness as more critical than it can be."[14]

Dismantling whiteness is a *continuous* project. As Clevis Headley writes, the suspension of whiteness "must come in the form of a continuously affirmed refusal to prolong the ontological and existential project of whiteness."[15] John Warren notes that even as he attempts to perform whiteness differently, he "cannot rest under the banner of the transformed."[16] He realizes he cannot escape whiteness, nor can he discount the various ways in which he actually reproduces and reinscribes whiteness. Similarly, Lisa Heldke notes, "Expanding responsibility involves recognizing that over-privilege takes everlastingly new forms, requiring traitors [to whiteness] constantly to reinvent themselves."[17] And as Alison Bailey writes, "It is a mistake to think that becoming traitorous is tantamount to completely overcoming racism."[18] This, however, is the *ambiguous* reality of white racism. Antiracist whites must not flee this ambiguity, but continue to undo white racism even as it repositions them as privileged. The discourse of "undoing" whiteness, as used here, does not mean that one is capable of undoing whiteness as one might remove one's shirt. Whiteness is not a flimsy category such that one can simply decide to cast it aside. In other words, while "undoing" whiteness is clearly a performative metaphor, it does not presuppose an ontology of the self that is capable, through a single act of will and intention, of rising above the white discursive streams within which that self is embedded. Even in the movie version of *To Kill a Mockingbird*, Atticus Finch (played by Gregory Peck) has a Black maid, a Black mammy figure whose sole purpose appears to be to serve whiteness. As a "good white," he still reaps the ontological surplus of a larger white system that segregates and denigrates Black people. After all, one's whiteness involves a "reproducing of a historical situation."[19] This speaks to the multifaceted social reality of racism and to how the white self is implicated in complex social matrices that involve the self in preexisting racial power relations. Because white racism is so incredibly rooted in the fabric of white America, there is no place called "innocence." As whites become conscious of the pervasive and systemic operations of whiteness, they are already within the fray of it all, entangled in webs of meaning and forms of white racial and racist hailing to which they have already implicitly been produced as an effect, though there is always space for renegotiating, renarrating, and destabilizing their white identity.[20] This partly speaks to the notion that the self is always already historically ensconced in frames of reference that render the social world intelligible and meaningful. As this white self is prereflectively constituted through various racial and racist discursive regimes, the sedimentation of experience shapes perceptions of, and mediates embodied transactions with, the social world in ways that reinforce the social order of things as normative and stable. Hence, the white racial and racist self emerges within a context where the racial and racist actions and discourse of others are anterior to it. In this sense, then, it is more accurate to talk about the white self as always already given as whitely, for it has already "gotten done," as it were, by whiteness.

Disrupting whiteness is not confined to a set of antiracist beliefs. The commitment to being an antiracist involves a continual choice, though one often filled with tensions, contradictions, and ambushes. As Richards admits: "And yet, it's said. It comes through. It fires out of me." Richards, despite his claim that he is not a racist, is effectively hailed and produced by racist habits and practices that are long-standing and constitute historical racist sedimentation. Warren writes, "If I am a product of history, a genera-tion after generation construction, then the notion of undoing that performa-tive work in my lifetime totally simplifies the complexity that is race."[21] Even as one attempts to shift the white gaze, as if it were solely a question of removing tinted glasses, one continues to "see" the "violent" Black body (i.e., "nigger") as it approaches, the "thug" Black body, the "armed" Black body, though it is unarmed, the "Black rapist" as he crosses the street at night in one's direction, the Black "welfare queen" as she walks with her children, and "lazy" Black bodies as they commune on street corners. Within this context, "seeing" is not merely a private and isolated performance but the repetition of a collective performative gazing, the reproduction of the weight of a racist oracular epistemic order sustained by "a culturally and structurally racist society."[22] The reality of racism is that it is, as Richards says, insane. It is insane because it is so incredibly insidious. Richards fails to compre-hend how his own self-understanding is incongruent with the subtlety of his racist performance. This, again, speaks to the false notion that the self is completely in control of its own meanings and the contexts within which it is located. My guess is that Richards would not have gone into a long and vicious tirade had the persons talking in the audience been white women/ men. And if he had, his racism would have gone undetected. Examples such as the Richards case ought to force antiracist whites who fight for social justice to interrogate the sedimentation of their own racism. Furthermore, the Richards example should force antiracist whites to admit that their efforts are always incomplete, particularly as the dynamics of self-in-context are not transparent and/or simply a case of willful management. It is one thing to remain in the company of whites and proclaim oneself an antiracist. It is another to throw oneself in the social fray where people of color move and have their being. It is within such *lived* social spaces of transacting with Black bodies, for example, that one's commitment to antiracist praxis is tested. It is so easy to hide behind antiracist rhetoric when one limits oneself to predictable social encounters that are already predicated upon social trans-actions that do not challenge or complicate the white self. However, in social transactions that do challenge the white self, conditions obtain that are ripe for ambush. As Richards warns, "That's what happens when you interrupt a white man, don't you know?" While being ambushed by one's whiteness can occur in the absence of people of color, as when one deems oneself an antiracist white and yet laughs hysterically at a racist joke while bonding with one's white friends, actually transacting with flesh and blood bodies of color can function as a powerful catalyst that can trigger an ambush. "You're a prolific *Black* philosopher." And yet, there is the mantra: "I'm not a racist. That's what's so insane about this."

My students are often taken aback when I ask them to raise their hands if they think that they are racist. The question itself is perceived as a threat, as it implies that one of them could actually be a racist. At this point, I ask them to close their eyes and imagine their wedding day. I encourage them to imagine the smell of the flowers, the colors of their matching wedding attire, all of the friends and family members who have been invited, and so on. Before they say, "I do," I ask them to open their eyes and disclose the "race" of their bride/groom. The response is always, with perhaps one exception, a resounding, "white!" Because I teach in a majority white university, my objective is to get the students to see just how insane it is that whiteness is being reproduced by them even though each failed to raise his/her hand when asked if anyone in the class is a racist. My example shows that whiteness even shapes the object of love and desire. One female student got particularly upset by this suggestion. "I just don't desire Black men. This doesn't mean that I don't like them or that I'm a racist." When asked to elaborate, she reiterated that it was simply about desire, not race. I tried to get her to see that desire was not the explanatory end point, but the explanandum, that which is to be explained. On further exploration, many of my students began to talk about how there was only one Black student in their classes and how there were only other whites to date in their neighborhoods. At first, none of my students finds this strange. After further critical discussion, a few of my students do begin to make broad connections between racial segregation, the reproduction of whiteness, white bonding, the perpetuation of "normalcy," the repetition of white sensibilities and values, the encouragement of white solipsism, and the phenomenon of desire.

To encourage whites to avoid idealizations of themselves as antiracists and therefore in some sense see their subject positions as marginal in relationship to the larger structure of white power, it is important to remind them that in racist white America there is simply no place where they can remain *permanently* marginal. This social realist position militates against any unproblematic notions of having achieved a so-called color-blind perspective, which can function as another way of avoiding challenging white structural power. While antiracist whites may anger other whites, the former still "Bear a socially privileged racial identity."[23] Even so-called poor white trash identities are *white*. As Bryant Keith Alexander notes, "Disregarding issues of class and location, they [white trash identities] engage a performance of 'better than thou' in the presence of non-Whites; a performance of privilege that they assume to be either a birthright or a historically perceived sanction."[24] I would argue that "Black trash" might be said to be a tautology. Dispose, as it were, of the trash in "white trash" and one has whiteness. Dispose of the trash in "Black trash" and one is left with Blackness, which is more of the same, the disposable, the wretched, the socially unpalatable refuse. White trash might be marked by class, and inflected by class, but whiteness still allows entrance into The Gap without being followed. In other words, whiteness is interpellated as innocence as it enters into those larger social and semiotic spaces where it is constituted as "one of us." Addressing the issue of poor whites who embrace their whiteness as an ontological stamp of superiority, Marilyn Frye notes: "Many poor and working-class white people are perfectly confident that they are more intelligent, know more, have better judgment, and are more moral than black people or Chicanos or Puerto Ricans or Indians or anyone else they view as not white, and believe that they would be perfectly competent to run the country and to rule others justly and righteously if given the opportunity."[25] And while it is true that the white bourgeoisie deployed divide-and-conquer tactics to sustain divisions and tensions between poor Blacks and poor whites and that this prohibited/prohibits the recognition of shared interests, "we must tell the full story of white racism in all of its complexity, and this complexity cannot be fully resolved through a class analysis that sequesters the guilty as only among the rich."[26]

To be white in America is to be always already implicated in structures of power, which complicates what it means to be a white ally (or *alligare*, "to bind to"). For even as whites fight on behalf of people of color, that is, engage in acts that bind them to people of color, there is also a sense in which whites simultaneously "bind to" structures of power. Some whites argue that white supremacy is something that existed in the past and that, therefore, while there are still white people who are certainly prejudicial, the oppression of Black bodies no longer exists. My white students often argue this way, assuring me that they therefore must be on the side of racial justice. According to Aimee Carrillo Rowe, " 'History', as it is written through the assumption that 'oppression' could only have occurred within the rubric of overt white supremacy, becomes the narrative mechanism through which contemporary whiteness can be severed from its own genealogy. That is, white supremacy is displaced from the present and reassigned to the past through a temporal logic of white dislocation."[27] This temporal displacement, as Rowe notes, involves the investment in a narrative of white innocence. This functions to shift the emphasis away from many of my students' whiteness and how it implicates them in *present* structures of white power. However, rather than discussing issues of deep structural racism, I have had white students complain that if only Blacks and whites could stop all of the insults and stereotyping then all would be fine.

Weeks after a guest lecture I gave, one white male student provided me with a copy of the paper he had written for the course. The paper was very articulate and poignant, showing a great deal of insight into issues of white privilege. Parts of the paper explicitly described levels of frustration that he felt as I lectured. He wrote, "I felt a growing sense of uneasiness rising inside of me. It grew to a point where my stomach began to ache and my hands began to quiver." He describes going for a run after the lecture to let out some energy. He wrote that he "felt the inchoate brew of uneasiness intensify and then take the form of anger." He imagined himself back in the classroom with me and imagined himself throwing his notebook against the wall, flipping the desk in front of him and having it whirl in the air before it hit the ground. It is my sense that this heightened emotional reaction indicated a form of bad faith. While he is certainly someone who takes pride in developing an antiracist mode of being-in-the-world, he fails to accept the complex ways in which, despite this, his whiteness undergoes a process of interpellation whereby he is implicated in complex social processes that privilege his whiteness beyond his intention to the contrary. In other words, there is a sense in which he is lying to himself, masking the extent to which he is implicated in whiteness by taking a moral high ground and placing too much emphasis on his genuine antiracist efforts.

In order to work through some of his feelings, he then wrote a large portion of his paper as an imaginary conversation with me. He wrote, "Don't write me off as just a white male. If you do that, I will be more poised to write you off as just an Other. I do not want this, but it's something I've felt in me recently." Earlier in the paper, he wrote, "You don't know *me*!! Don't freaking tell *me* who I am!!" The student clearly conflates our histories. Given the history of white racism in America, it is not unreasonable that Blacks have come to find wanting white antiracists who are willing to fight against racism and who claim to have "lost" some level of power in the process. The student flattens out our differential histories. In fact, he asserts his power to write me off as an Other, performing a threat that has literally taken the form of the killing of Black bodies. The fact of the matter is that white America has already written me off as an Other. He simply reiterates the history of white power and arrogance. In short, if I desist from pointing out to him how he is implicated in structures of white power and how his whiteness can function as a significant site of blindness, he will accept me, bestow upon me the wonderful status of non-other. He also falsely assumes an equality of power whereby Blacks really have the same form of power to write *him* off as an Other. He felt labeled "the white male," that new group that attempts to shift victimization away from people of color. He added, "But I'm telling you, staying on the level of labels and stereotypes without getting to know me—calling me out as just a white male—will keep me on the level of labels as well." The problem is that Black denigration has never purely functioned at the level of labels and mythos. Labeling is part and parcel of a history of castration, rape, lynch mobs, being beaten beyond recognition, sold from auction blocks, and so on. His willingness to be an ally was predicated upon a conditional, that was based upon a false equivalence of historical power. This move is indicative of what Charles Mills calls "a mystificatory obfuscation of the clearly *a*symmetrical and enduring system of white power."[28] And "You don't know *me*!!" functioned to erase my own insights, my subjectivity and epistemic grounding regarding the ways of whiteness. It also communicated that he (as an atomistic consciousness) knows and controls the meaning of *his* identity. This effectively conveys who has the real power. It is important though that this student's positive efforts to identify and work through his blinkers are *not* crushed, but nurtured and critically engaged. I would agree with Gloria Yamato, when she says, "Do not blame people of color for your frustration about racism, but do appreciate the fact that people of color will often help you get in touch with that frustration," especially when that frustration takes the form of humility.[29]

To be white in America and to be an ally must involve a self-reflexive moment of realization that people of color don't owe white people anything. As Wise notes, "And if all they [Blacks] do is respond to our efforts with a terse 'about time', then that's too bad. Get over it."[30] To be a white ally is a problematic identity when motivated by paternalism or moral narcissism. Confessions of giving generously to the United Negro College Fund or that one has never used the "n" word or that one is currently dating someone Black or Latino(a) or that one just hired a person of color in one's philosophy department[31] are perfectly consistent with a failure to explore deeper layers of what it means to be a white antiracist ally. In fact, such confessions often function to ease the conscience of whites.

Being an ally does not mean slumming around people of color, eager to eat their food, dance to their music, rub against their "exotic" bodies. The racial politics of gentrification can achieve this end, while simultaneously keeping the "darkies" within a circumscribed space. Being a white antiracist ally is not simply a commitment to helping Black people and other people of color. As Gloria Yamato says, "Work on racism for your sake, not 'their' sake."[32] It involves an active commitment to relinquishing white power. It entails accountability, where this "involves taking responsibility *for* one's social location, and for the way that understanding flows from that location."[33] A white ally is one who fights injustice even as "it costs them something personally."[34] This fight must be done precisely through the recognition that one *is* a white person, "rather than attempting to step outside that identity, in order to rebuild it from without, as it were."[35]

White people who are sincere about antiracism need to pay critical attention to the ways in which they can relinquish white power. Merely rearticulating whiteness beyond white guilt and deep feelings of angst is not sufficient. There must be the call, the continuous effort, to *disarticulate* whiteness from those juridico-political, economic, institutional, aesthetic, and other locations that will resist disarticulation to ensure the maintenance of white power. The point here is that the white body is not simply implicated in and productive of racialized spaces that have profoundly destructive psychological implications for Black bodies. Rather, the white body is tied to the operations of the state as a powerful site of white hegemony. White people and critical whiteness studies theorists must remain cognizant of the fact that Black people critiqued whiteness and struggled against whiteness (and continue to do so) because whiteness is oppressive; it systemically excludes, derails, polices, segregates, and murders. Deploying critical pedagogies in the name of valorizing cultural heterogeneity in schools as a strategy for disrupting whiteness as normative is one thing. Fighting the police, the prison system—the repressive apparatus of the state—de facto residential segregation, bank lending practices, and racialized global capitalism, where the white imperial subject continues to expand its reach and control over nonwhite others according to its mythos of manifest destiny, is another. Hence, "to bind to" Black people and other people of color involves fighting to undo the racialized material structures, discursive orders, and semiotic fields according to which the power of one's whiteness is purchased.

As whites attempt to undo power and privilege, they find themselves confronting a world in which whiteness is not only around them but also working through them.[36] Given this, disrupting sites of whiteness will require that white allies cultivate identities "rooted in understandings of themselves and their relations to others."[37] And given the pervasive and structural complexity of whiteness to reposition one's identity as center, and, hence, over and against those of people of color, undoing whiteness "is a project in process, always becoming, always in need of another step."[38] Even as one tries, one's efforts will be thwarted by unconscious habits of white privilege, forming roadblocks as one attempts to expose whiteness.[39] What this means is that one cannot, through a sheer act of will, cast off one's whiteness, particularly as whiteness qua "race" is not a thin covering laid over a fundamentally non-raced identity.[40] To combat whiteness effectively requires an understanding of social ontological constitutive spaces wherein others can cite you "as white and thus contribute to the performative reiteration of racial difference."[41]

This raises the issue of the role of historical agency on the part of phenotypic whites to transgress habituated modes of being-in-the-world, while remaining cognizant of the multiple ways in which whiteness is invested in its own self-concealment. Indeed, I would argue that whites *ought* to transgress their investments in whiteness. If whiteness was a fixed essence, the discourse of ought would be meaningless. The discourse of ought, however, speaks to the condition of *lack*. This not only raises the issue of whiteness to that of the ethical level but also raises the issue of whiteness to the existential ontological level. To invoke the ethical and the existential ontological within this context raises the motifs of anguish and anxiety. If whiteness is not an essence, then the reality of choice, the cultivation of "a certain kind of identity,"[42] and the nurturing of new habits, dispositions, and responsiveness[43] become *the* pressing issues. Frye also calls for new ways of whitely-being-in-the-world, particularly in those social spaces where whiteliness is required or rewarded. She argues that antiracist whites know they must "practice new ways of being in environments that nurture different habits of feeling, perception, and thought, and that we will have to make these environments for ourselves since the world will not offer them to us."[44]

While I use the term *identity* within the context of antiracist white identity, there is no attempt to specify that which is fixed; rather, an antiracist white identity is what is reclaimed and constantly refashioned. But even here, the notion of cultivating a certain kind of identity must not be reduced to a form of *apolitical* aesthetic *s*elf-fashioning. There is the reality of the larger racist social processes to which one is inextricably tied; hence, the importance of sociogeny, where one does not lose sight of the social in its constitutive role in the formation of the individual.[45] I would also argue that the cultivation of new habits and dispositions—while never losing sight of the socio-structured and structuring world—which presuppose the notion of an ontological *lack*, speaks to the dynamics of existential conversion in relation to whiteness. For Simone de Beauvoir, as argued in chapter 5, existential conversion involved the rejection of grounding values in any putative absolutes. Existential conversion in relation to whiteness is indispensable in terms of militating against whiteness as it takes itself to be unconditioned and as a site of universal value. "Like the mytho-maniac who while reading a love-letter pretends to forget that she has sent it to herself," whiteness is a form of bad faith.[46]

The point here is that "learning how to stop regarding one's overprivilege as natural and inevitable" or as an absolute value is an important propaedeutic to undertake as one attempts to "undo" whiteness.[47] It is also important to note that whiteness as a repetition of acts takes on the appearance of something permanent, when in fact such repetition can be fissured and cracked. It is difficult to nurture these fissures in whiteness as long as one remains safe in one's white comfort zone. You "must actively place yourself in situations that challenge your biases and preconceived notions," travel to those lived spaces where whiteness is understood very differently.[48] As a border crosser, one does not travel to these spaces as colonizers, paternalists, and do-gooders. Rather, as María Lugones notes, "by traveling to their 'world' we can understand *what it is to be them and what it is to be ourselves in their eyes.*"[49] Fissuring whiteness involves a form of white double-consciousness, though maintaining a self-reflexive posture to guard against a sense of white "ontological expansionism." *What it means to be them* can easily slip into a form of romanticizing through white subject positions. In this way, Blacks become only stereotyped "by the [white] arrogant perceiver and are pliable, foldable, file-awayable, classifiable."[50] And *what it is to be ourselves in their eyes* always borders on distortion, defensiveness, and self-protective arrogance. The possibility of being *ambushed* by unexplored layers of one's whiteness is always there. But this is how power works; it shifts even as one attempts honest efforts to resist it. This is the way those whites who struggle to undo whiteness as a multiple complex structure must "expand responsibility as they flush out new 'pockets of incompleteness', and discard strategies and understandings that have lost their effectiveness."[51]

This is why it is important that the dynamics of white racism not solely be left in hands of whites to theorize. Whites' insights must be challenged and corrected by those bodies of color that stand to suffer from the subtle blinkers that inhibit the efforts of antiracist whites. People of color must keep whites cognizant of the limits of their visions, their "certainty" regarding how to tackle whiteness. The assumption is that one is capable of learning from the so-called other "who can open up a world aspired to by the self. The Other also provides us with objectivity, not in a hostile sense, but in the sense of correcting the limitations of our own perspective."[52]

Learning from people of color, opening oneself to them, also places one in relationship to the possibility of being ambushed in new and radical ways.[53] Whites must respectfully position themselves in relation to people of color such that whites will learn to expect to be ambushed, to be open to it. Whites who are open to life-affirming and transformative transactions with people of color are not simply waiting defensively in fear of new information that may threaten to destabilize their sense of self. Rather, there is an openness to having one's world transformed and cracked. Being ambushed within such transactional contexts can lead to profound experiences of liminality, throwing the white self into spaces of rich uncertainty and the actual phenomenological experience of the white self as permeable. Hence, the reality of being ambushed should be regarded as valuable to growth, not a sign of defeat. Indeed, there are transformative possibilities in the valorization of an ambush experience as a mode of surprise, as an experiential opening from which one learns and teaches about the insidious nature of whiteness. Hence, *thankfulness* ought to be the attendant attitude as one is ambushed. For in that moment, whites come to learn more about themselves, expanding knowledge of the self, revealing how the white self is other to itself. In this way, not only does the humility of thankfulness on the part of whites function as a bridge to others, but it also functions as a bridge to the white self. This type of trans-formative possibility was clearly exemplified in the above examples of Wise and Lazarre. Wise was able to utilize the ambush experience, embracing it as a surprise, as a challenge to his own antiracist practices. Lazarre also was able to turn her ambush experience into something positive, realizing that her construction of the police harassment of the innocent Black male as unbeliev-able was a function of her being blinded by her own white "innocence" and privilege.

Theorizing ambush as a form of surprise in the case of Michael Richards' tirade helps to demonstrate the transformative possibilities inherent in this idea. While Richards noted that his racism came through and fired out of him, even though he said he believes he is not a racist, he did *not* use that moment of ambush as a moment of productive disclosure. He could have used that moment to focus on how whiteness snares good-intentioned white people. Self-reflexively, he could have stopped himself and redirected his anger toward the shock of his own racism, creating a disruptive space of com-municative power that addressed both the unconscious operations of racism and how the operations of racism can be temporarily fissured and silenced. At the moment of realizing he had been ambushed, there would have been an interval of space in which the repetition of whiteness could have been proven unreliable. Even as he shouted "nigger" six times, there was still space for that moment of realization that he was being ambushed, and, hence, a moment of redemptive possibility. Such a moment of recognition would require the thematization of just how incredibly frustrated and outraged he felt as he had spoken those words and had dehumanized those Blacks in attendance while also positioning those whites in attendance as racists as well. After all, to shout, "A nigger, look it's a nigger!" presupposed a com-municative act addressed to those who would readily recognize the presence of a "nigger." Moreover, he does say "we'd" have you upside down. This is an implied reference to whites in the audience and a form of historical refer-ence to the reality of the spectacle of *collective* white gazers vis-à-vis lynched Black bodies. Nevertheless, the ambush would have provided the opportunity for creative intervention, for assuming the subject position of an ally.

The white ally engages in a form of relationality that requires a suspension of self-certainty, arrogance, fear, and other-blaming. Inherent in the ambush experience is the possibility of fissure and suspension, a counter-hailing for antiracist action. This suspension can simultaneously involve new imagin-ings, daring spontaneity, and a form of world-traveling that does not seek to assimilate or to intrude.[54] Indeed, the incipiency and development of alliances require "leaping" forward beyond various agonistic, supercilious, and procrustean presuppositions. And as long as the white self qua "superior" is defined dialectically in relation to the Black self qua "inferior," the possibility of a genuine alliance is precluded. White parasitism must be revealed, *shaken* and *cracked* at its core. When the fractures and fissures begin to show themselves, "it's best to avoid denial . . . wait for new possibilities to emerge. Isn't that what white folks need to allow? Must [white folk] not crack up in order to be something new?"[55] Indeed, "as long as whites are in bad faith and phobogenic constructions of blacks provide needed reinforcements of ego determinations," according to Paget Henry, "antiblack racism will be with us."[56] It is important to note, though, that while the above conceptualization and requirement of a form of suspension is necessary to transformative praxis on the part of whites, suspension does not wipe away, as if by magic, the force of white racist effective history and the ingrained and habituated practices of white people or the racist institutional structures that privilege them. In this case, suspension is both tactical and ethical, but it does not obviate all of the messy work ahead.

There is also the issue of the meaning of alliances that—while grounded in mutual respect and the deployment of suspension—are still shaped by radically differential social power positions that are buttressed by material distribution along racial lines. That is, even as one demonstrates disaffiliative efforts in relation to whiteness, one's whiteness is recuperative through mobility back to the vanilla suburbs. The larger issue, one I do not address here, is whether the ultimate aims of undoing whiteness involve making sure that people of color have greater opportunities to get a piece of the American pie (in short, having liberal democracy work for them in more effective ways) or whether undoing whiteness requires redistributing wealth and power. The point is that many whites may be willing to do the necessary work to engage in new and transformative ways of undoing whiteness without any concern for tackling issues around disparity of wealth along racial lines. However, undoing whiteness is inextricably linked to undoing those structural power relationships that continue to privilege whites, even as they strive to perform whiteness differently within the context of transacting with people of color on a daily basis. While undoing whiteness in elevator encounters is one thing or deploying critical pedagogies that challenge white teachers to trouble their whiteness in the classroom is another, doing these things does not necessarily lead to strong advocacy on the part of whites for broader systemic structural change. Undoing whiteness must also involve undoing structural power as defined along racial lines.

While existential conversion is *not* sufficient for undoing the various ways in which whiteness reasserts power and privilege, it functions as a necessary

critical process in terms of exposing the contingency and historicity of whiteness and challenging and troubling its ideological constitution as absolute
and permanent. This raises the issue of the serious man/world of whiteness
as developed in chapter 5. Consider the traumatic experience Du Bois had
with the tall white newcomer who refused to exchange visiting cards with
him at school. She refused it peremptorily, as Du Bois says, with a glance. As
a basis upon which to give critical attention to ways of disrupting whiteness
as absolute consider the tall newcomer's phenomenological or lived mode of
relationality to her own sense of identity. While many scholars have critically
explored how significant this experience was for Du Bois, the white tall newcomer's mode of being is often left undertheorized.

When the white girl refused to exchange cards with Du Bois, she performed her identity through negation, establishing her space both physically and psychologically. She lived her body in an expansive modality. Her
identity is lived with epistemic certainty. She lived her body as a readymade
sacrosanct site that defined and excluded differences. Her embodiment was
itself a site of white racist dramaturgy, an enactment of a role, which actually differentially *valued* and exaggerated differences. For the newcomer,
she simply *acted* with an always already sense of entitlement. She lived her
body "as a corporeal entitlement to spatiality."[57] As she moved through space,
she racially carved it up, as it were, distorting it, marking it with her white
presence. Embodying space in this raced way, she demarcated her immediate
lived space as clean, untouchable, privileged. Her *refusal*, although clearly
disclosed, simultaneously involved a process of concealment. In other words,
there is a white racist dominant history of knowledge production that established her white identity as secure.

Having unconsciously internalized what it means to be "normal" (i.e.,
white), her identity was sealed, "leak-proof"; she had become a site of a
monadic structure who came to believe that her identity and her whiteness
were *nonrelational*. Of course, to remain ignorant of the dynamic relational
basis upon which her white identity was actually predicated functions as the
desideratum of whiteness. Indeed, she has come to live her whiteness, her
identity, as an unconditioned state of being. But her identity was already connected to those nonwhite identities that she judged abhorrent. On my view, as
I have argued previously, existential conversion addresses the unconditioned
presumption of white identity. White identity, in other words, constitutes a
site of value-creating force that elides the historical contingency of such values. Through existential conversion, whites are encouraged to come to terms
with the reality that white identity is created within a socially situated context
and not grounded in some transcendental source.

The tall newcomer has become *absorbed* in the world of whiteness. Within
the process of "being-in" the world of whiteness, she *lives* its fantasies,

psychologically projecting them outwardly and inwardly, all the while unaware of how she is both duped by whiteness and has become a vehicle through which whiteness is performed. She animates white racist scripts on cue, because they have become habituated modes of bodily enactment.

She has learned to enact particular somatic responses characteristic of white bodies that transact with nonwhite bodies within normative spaces that are designed to demarcate and create a wedge between normative white bodies and "anomalous" nonwhite bodies. Like the white woman in the elevator, she lives her body through inherited legitimation narratives and unconscious habits.[58] She lives her body within the framework of a narrative that projects her forward, placing her ahead of herself, forming calcified readymade responses to those nonwhite others.[59] Her narrative is structured by an overarching myth that provides the necessary axiological and epistemological frame of reference to make sense of her identity. In short, the tall newcomer has come to inhabit the serious world of whiteness. The serious world of whiteness functions as a pre-established axiological and ontological cartography that imposes fixed coordinates that both reward and punish whites. The white order of things appears to place categorical demands on human reality.[60]

On the other side of whiteness as a serious mode of engaging and transacting with the world is the existentially converted white who recognizes the ideological grounds upon which whiteness is a farce and that whiteness is a site of values that are existentially founded. "Existentialist conversion," as Eleanore Holveck notes, "cancels the grounding of values in any absolute, whether that absolute be a god, a church, a state, etc. By existentialist conversion, one sees that all values refer to choices made by someone who is finite and limited."[61] Deemed an absolute, whiteness is a perfectly seductive trap for the (white) serious man/woman to take flight in the face of his/her freedom. Of course, other forms of white flight (the privilege of mobility) literally provide whites with safe spaces in terms of which white bonding and white fear are reproduced. In the case of the tall newcomer, she has come to embody her whiteness as it "permanently confers value upon [her]."[62] What is required is "an affectivity which would throw [her] dangerously beyond [her whitely self]."[63]

The process of existential conversion has implications for profoundly new forms of relationality. Not only are phenotypic whites faced with the anxiety of relating to nonwhites in terms that render problematic their previous racialized epistemic certainty regarding the nonwhite other, but existential conversion calls into question, indeed disrupts, their previous certainty regarding how they understand and value themselves. The fundamental premise of existential conversion is that one is not condemned to whiteness, but that there are always other ways of grounding one's identity, performing one's whiteness, even as one's whiteness is interpellated within the larger social world of white power. Existential conversion holds out the possibility that the tall newcomer may come to terms with the reality that whiteness is not an absolute value.[64]

Whiteness, in this context, does not refer to that which functions as a phenotypic marker. In choosing freedom, the newcomer chooses against acting in the world whitely. While I have heard whites express the desire to tear off their white skin, choosing freedom does not mean that one chooses against one's phenotypic white body *as such*. To deny one's white body is to fall into bad faith. Hence, the newcomer should not reject her body. In choosing freedom, she embraces her facticity and also rejects the privilege of *exclusive transcendence*, a privilege that whites have claimed for themselves. In rejecting her whiteness as exclusive transcendence, since this is dialectically linked to the reduction of Blacks to mere facticity and immanence, she affirms not only the facticity of Blacks but their transcendence as well. She comes to realize that the *serious* world of whiteness can be opposed and that what she previously took to be inevitable—the supremacy and superiority of whiteness—has turned out to be a *particular historically* contingent formation predicated upon a lie that passed itself off as the truth through white performative repetition. Through this repetition, white orders of power appear "natural." In other words, white forms of life constitute a framework of intelligibility "that helps whites interpret their experience and that influences behavior, alters emotions, and shapes what whites see and do not see."[65] Through existential conversion in relation to whiteness, the newcomer is able to live her body as a "calling out to the other" in his/her otherness as opposed to forms of communicative practices that occlude, seal off, and stereotype. She creates cracks within the prison house of whiteness's *sameness*, rejecting the ideological structuring of her identity as fixed and superior, thus unsettling and troubling habituated perceptual practices and fixed (racialized) spatial modes of bodily comportment in relation to nonwhite bodies. Disrupting various racialized spatial modes of bodily comportment further troubles and challenges the ways in which she/whites live her/their spatiality, productively contributing to the undoing of "the racial and racist civilized 'we' from the wild 'them.'"[66]

Hence, to live her phenotypic white body in freedom, which is a continuous act of reclamation, is to live her body in ways that facilitate the freedom of nonwhite bodies; whereas, living one's whiteness in the mode of the serious attempts to occlude the nonwhite from speaking, from exercising greater spatial mobility, and, in many cases, from being. To challenge the serious world of whiteness is to question, to counter what one sees, even as the field of one's white gaze continues to construct the social world falsely. It is to welcome a form of "distortion" that sees through what has been constituted via white racist orders as "clarity." Hence, as the body of color enters various racialized spaces, indeed, elevator spaces, one must valorize the cracks, one must valorize the experience of ambush. "Don't repair them. Instead, welcome the crumble of white supremacist lies."[67] In other words, one strives to disrupt the hail of whiteness. This raises the issue of ambiguity that I raised earlier. One is at once an expression of whiteness, but its possibility for cracking, disrupting, and resignification renders problematic such an expression. As Alecia Y. Jackson notes, "I am produced through certain power relations, but I am also a site for reworking those power relations so that something different and less constraining can be produced."[68]

I conceptualize existential conversion in relation to whiteness as a constant affirmation of new forms of responsiveness, new forms of challenging unearned privileges, and assiduous attempts at founding anti-whiteness values. After all, one has to live in the everyday world in which whiteness—despite one's commitment to live one's body in freedom, that is, contrary to the expectations and readymade meanings that always already exist in the serious world of whiteness—continues to be seductive. To "live one's body in freedom" therefore does not mean that one lives one's body outside various situational constraints and historical forces but that one continues to achieve those self-reflexive moments that attempt to destabilize various habituated white normative practices. Hence, existential conversion, at least with respect to whiteness, must involve a self-reflexive way of being-in-the-world where the tall newcomer continually takes up the project of disaffiliation from whitely ways of being, even as she undergoes processes of interpellation. My point here is that as she lives her body in freedom, as she challenges the white racialized and racist world, its discourses and power relations, as she attempts to forge new habits and new forms of self-knowledge, she does not live her body outside of history. There is no nonracial Archimedean point from which she can unsettle racism. Hence, while a process of constant destabilization that cracks away at whiteness is indispensable as a value and a form of praxis, there is the realization that "a cartography of race would better describe a white race traitor as 'off center', that is, as destabilizing the center while still remaining in it."[69] So, even as the newcomer conceivably extends her hand across the color line, reaching out to the young W. E. B. Du Bois, thus throwing her whiteness off center and situates herself in that space of liminality, she will, at some point, leave the classroom and be thrown back into the serious world of whiteness where the rich possibilities of ambush are covered over.

Concerning the insidious forms of whitely modes of being, Bailey's distinction between privilege-cognizant and privilege-evasive white scripts proves helpful. Within the framework of this discourse, the newcomer must constantly reaffirm her commitment to enacting a privilege-cognizant white script; that is, she must remain cognizant of the ways in which she is privileged (or privileges herself) because of her phenotypic whiteness. According to Bailey, privilege-cognizant whites are race traitors "who refuse to animate the scripts whites are expected to perform, and who are unfaithful to worldviews whites are expected to hold."[70] In this way, privilege-cognizant whites are committed to "doing whiteness differently."[71] If "race is constituted through the repetition of acts, verbal and nonverbal, that continue to communicate difference," then whites must engage in counter-stylized iterative anti-whitely acts.[72]

It is not easy to discern the subtle and yet pervasive ways in which the ideology of whiteness profoundly distorts mutually flourishing forms of human relationality. Contesting the normative status of whiteness "means living in constant struggle, always working with self and those around you. . . . It is a process that . . . [builds on] the notion that all benefit when whiteness inflicts less violence [on] others in the world."[73] But it is important to note, in Beauvoirian terms, that whiteness is like an "inhuman [idol] to which one will not hesitate to sacrifice" all that is of value, even the white body itself. Therefore, the serious world of whiteness is a very dangerous world. Whiteness makes tyrants out of human beings. The white elides "the subjectivity of his [her] choice" through the constitution of whiteness as an absolute value that "is being asserted through him [her]." This is done at the expense of white accountability. In this way, one is able to deny "the subjectivity and the freedom of others, to such an extent that, sacrificing them to the [idol of whiteness]" means absolutely nothing. On this score, it is accurate to describe whiteness as a form of fanaticism that is "as formidable as the fanaticism of passion."[74] Whiteness as fanaticism occludes other voices from speaking, and other bodies from being, and other ways of revealing and performing the depths of, and the promises inherent in, human reality as *homo possibilitas*. So, don't be fooled. Whiteness is *not* the best that history has to offer. This conclusion signals the historical bankruptcy of whiteness as an ethical exemplar, the problematic self-certainty and narcissism of whiteness, the profound historical contingency of whiteness, and the possibility for rethinking new and nonhegemonic hermeneutic horizons of whiteness.

NOTES

1. Lisa Heldke, "On Being a Responsible Traitor," in *Daring to Be Good: Essays in Feminist Ethico-Politics*, ed. Bat-Ami Bar On and Ann Ferguson (New York: Routledge, 1998), 96.

2. Joe R. Feagin and Hernan Vera, *White Racism: The Basics* (New York: Routledge, 1995), 16.

3. I now theorize the ambush experience within the conceptual framework of what I call the opaque white racist self and the embedded white racist self. See: George Yancy, *Look, a White! Philosophical Essays on Whiteness* (Philadelphia, PA: Temple University Press, 2012), especially chapter 6.

4. Shannon Sullivan, *Revealing Whiteness: The Unconscious Habits of Racial Privilege* (Bloomington: Indiana University Press, 2006), 197.

5. Jane Lazarre, *Beyond the Whiteness of Whiteness: Memoir of a White Mother of Black Sons* (Durham, NC: Duke University Press, 1999), 33. The reader should note that since the publication of the first edition of this book, Jane has become a wonderful friend. Her work is incredibly important and I think should be read by all of us.

6. Lazarre, *Beyond the Whiteness of Whiteness*, 33.

7. Tim Wise, *White Like Me: Reflections on Race from a Privileged Son* (New York: Soft Skull Press, 2005), 133.

8. Wise, *White Like Me*, 133.

9. Wise, *White Like Me*, 128.

10. Wise, *White Like Me*, 131.

11. Sullivan, *Revealing Whiteness*, 189.

12. "Kramer's Racist Tirade Caught on Tape"; www.tmz.com/2006/11/20/kramers-racist-tirade-caught-on-tape (accessed, April 5, 2008)

13. "Mean Michael Richards"; http://www.youtube.com/watch?v=k2gzv-fy7ro

14. Monique Roelofs, "Racialization as an Aesthetic Production: What Does the Aesthetic Do for Whiteness and Blackness and Vice Versa?" in *White on White/Black on Black*, ed. George Yancy (Lanham, MD: Rowman & Littlefield, 2005), 112.

15. Clevis Headley, "Delegitimizing the Normativity of 'Whiteness': A Critical Africana Philosophical Study of the Metaphoricity of 'Whiteness,'" in Yancy, *What White Looks Like*, 103.

16. John T. Warren, "Performing Whiteness Differently: Rethinking the Abolitionist Project," *Educational Theory*, 51(4), 2001, 451–66, quotation on 465.

17. Heldke, "On Being a Responsible Traitor," 97–8.

18. Alison Bailey, "Locating Traitorous Identities: Toward a View of Privilege-Cognizant White Character," *Hypatia*, 13(3), 1998, 27–42, quotation on 39.

19. Warren, "Performing Whiteness Differently," 454.

20. Being produced as an effect does not mean that one is nomologically determined.

21. Warren, "Performing Whiteness Differently," 454.

22. Feagin and Vera, *White Racism*, 13.

23. Bailey, "Locating Traitorous Identities," 31.

24. Bryant Keith Alexander, "Black Skin/White Masks: The Performative Sustainability of Whiteness (With Apologies to Frantz Fanon)," *Qualitative Inquiry*, 10(5), 647–72, quotation on 657.

25. Marilyn Frye, "White Woman Feminist," in *Overcoming Racism and Sexism*, ed. Linda A. Bell and David Blumenfield (Lanham, MD: Rowman & Littlefield, 1995), 123–4.

26. Linda Martín Alcoff, "What Should White People Do?" *Hypatia*, 13(3), 1998, 6–25, quotation on 19.

27. Aimee Carrillo Rowe, "Feeling in the Dark: Empathy, Whiteness, and Miscegenation in *Monster's Ball,*" *Hypatia*, 22(2), 2007, 122–42, quotation on 129.

28. Charles W. Mills, "White Supremacy as Sociopolitical System: A Philosophical Perspective," in *White Out: The Continuing Significance of Racism*, ed. Ashley W. Doane and Eduardo Bonilla-Silva (New York: Routledge, 2003), 40–1.

29. Gloria Yamato, "Something about the Subject Makes It Hard to Name," in *Making Face, Making Soul Haciendo Caras: Creative and Critical Perspectives by Feminists of Color*, ed. Gloria Anzaldua (San Francisco: Aunt Lute Books, 1990), 23.

30. Wise, *White Like Me*, 98.

31. In fact, I have suspected some philosophy departments hire Blacks that will play the white party line or whose philosophical views will make other whites in the department feel more comfortable with themselves.

32. Yamato, "Something about the Subject Makes It Hard to Name," 23–4.

33. Heldke, "On Being a Responsible Traitor," 98.

34. Christine Clark, "The Secret: White Lies Are Never Little," in *Becoming and Unbecoming White: Owning and Disowning a Racial Identity*, ed. Christine Clark and James O'Donnell (Westport, CT: Bergin & Garvey, 1999), 93.

35. Heldke, "On Being a Responsible Traitor," 93.

36. Warren, "Performing Whiteness Differently," 465.

37. Heldke, "On Being a Responsible Traitor," 90.

38. Warren, "Performing Whiteness Differently," 466.

39. Sullivan, *Revealing Whiteness*, 197.

40. Sullivan, *Revealing Whiteness*, 32.

41. Warren, "Performing Whiteness Differently," 459.

42. Heldke, "On Being a Responsible Traitor," 90.

43. Drawing from the work of Minnie Bruce Pratt and Marilyn Frye, Audrey Thompson theorizes the importance of antiracist whites developing new modes of responsiveness. See her article "Tiffany, Friend of People of Color: White Investments in Antiracism," in *Qualitative Studies in Education*, 16(1), 2003, 7–29.

44. Frye, "White Woman Feminist," 131.

45. Sullivan, *Revealing Whiteness*, 108.

46. Simone de Beauvoir, *The Ethics of Ambiguity* (1948; reprint, New York: Citadel Press, 1976), 47.

47. Heldke, "On Being a Responsible Traitor," 93

48. Derald Wing Sue, *Overcoming Our Racism: The Journal to Liberation* (San Francisco: Jossey-Bass, 2003), 192.

49. María Lugones, "Playfulness, 'World'-Travelling, and Loving Perception," in Anzaldua, *Making Face, Making Soul*, 401.

50. Lugones, "Playfulness, 'World'-Travelling, and Loving Perception," 402.

51. Heldke, "On Being a Responsible Traitor," 98.

52. Margaret A. Simons, *Beauvoir and* The Second Sex*: Feminism, Race, and the Origins of Existentialism* (Lanham, MD: Rowman & Littlefield, 1999), 224.

53. I now refer to this opening as a form of un-suturing. See George Yancy's "Introduction: Un-Sutured," in *White Self-Criticality beyond Anti-Racism: How Does It Feel to Be a White Problem?* ed. George Yancy (Lanham, MD: Lexington Books, 2015), xi–xxvii.

54. I thank Christina Rawls for her emphasis upon spontaneity as a way of developing new forms of relating in a racially divisive world.

55. Chris Cuomo, "White and Cracking Up," in Yancy, *White on White*, 30.

56. Paget Henry, "African and Afro-Caribbean Existential Philosophies," in *Existence in Black: An Anthology of Black Existential Philosophy*, ed. Lewis Gordon (New York: Routledge, 1997), 33.

57. Shannon Sullivan, "The Racialization of Space: Toward a Phenomenological Account of Raced and Antiracist Spatiality," in *The Problems of Resistance: Studies in Alternate Political Cultures*, ed. Steve Martinot and Joy James (New York: Humanity Books, 2001), 94.

58. Alcoff, "What Should White People Do?" 7.

59. Linda Alcoff notes that "racism, as Eduardo Mendiata has put it, feels as if one finds oneself in the world ahead of oneself, the space one occupies as already occupied." See Alcoff, "Who's Afraid of Identity Politics," in *Reclaiming Identity: Realist Theory and the Predicament of Postmodernism*, ed. Paula M. L. Moya and Michael R. Hames-García (Berkeley: University of California Press, 2000), 338.

60. Lewis Gordon, *Bad Faith and Antiblack Racism* (New York: Humanity Books, 1999), 61.

61. Eleanor Holveck, *Simone de Beauvoir's Philosophy of Lived Experience: Literature and Metaphysics* (Lanham, MD: Rowman & Littlefield, 2002), 94.

62. Beauvoir, *Ethics of Ambiguity*, 46.

63. Beauvoir, *Ethics of Ambiguity*, 47.

64. The *critical* dimension of existential conversion presupposes that through the process of historicizing whiteness, exposing the non-transcendental basis upon which it is grounded, revealing its pernicious historical practices, and destroying its idols and illusions, whites will deploy strategies to disrupt the various ways in which whiteness continues to reassert itself. In revealing the pernicious historical practices of whiteness, I am presupposing as an aftermath the nurturing and development of the sort of person committed to new forms of ethical relationality, one engaged in the nurturing of new habits and dispositions. This speaks to the *affirmative* dimension of existential conversion whereby the tall newcomer disrupts whiteness not only because of its oppressive effects upon people of color, but because of its deep and problematic ethical implications for a parasitic identity and a form of social existence that leads to the atrophy of forms of sociality that encourage modes of engagement that mutually reinforce existential forms of upsurge that are freeing and not oppressive. There is still the messiness of transaction, confrontation, negotiation, dialogue, mistakes, interpellation, reinscription, and ambush. Also, there is no guarantee that the majority of whites—and history is our guide here—will be prepared to engage transformative modes of relationality that seek to eliminate various complex ways in which the privilege and power of their whiteness is secured at the expense of people of color, even as they expose the value-laden historical and social construction of the category of whiteness.

65. Feagin and Vera, *White Racism*, 12.

66. Sullivan, *Revealing Whiteness*, 143.

67. Chris Cuomo, "White and Cracking Up," in *White on White/ Black on Black*, ed. George Yancy (Lanham, MD: Rowman & Littlefield, 2005), 32.

68. Alecia Youngblood Jackson, "Performativity Identified," *Qualitative Inquiry*, 10(5), 2004, 673–90, quotation on 685.

69. Sullivan, *Revealing Whiteness*, 162.

70. Bailey, "Locating Traitorous Identities," 28.

71. Warren, "Performing Whiteness Differently," 453.

72. Warren, "Performing Whiteness Differently," 460–1.

73. Warren, "Performing Whiteness Differently," 466.

74. Beauvoir, *Ethics of Ambiguity*, 49.

Chapter 8

White Embodied Gazing, the Black Body as Disgust, and the Aesthetics of Un-Suturing

Body aesthetics, when theorized through the racist historical sedimentation of the white gaze, can yield insights into processes of racialized valence that have deep social ontological and existential implications. To come to terms with this claim, I begin with the white gaze in its active form, implicative of a site of white power, hegemony, and privilege, one that comes replete with an assemblage of "knowledge" or a racist episteme regarding the Black body.[1] White *gazing* is a violent process. It is not an atomic act or an inaugural event that captures, in an unmediated fashion, the bareness, as it were, of "objects." Indeed, white gazing is an historical achievement. In other words, white gazing is a specific historical practice, socially collective and intersubjective, a process that is dutifully maintained. Whether consciously or unconsciously enacted, white gazing is an achievement that is synonymous with an accomplishment, that which is the result of actions, deeds (*pragma*), practices.

By emphasizing the concept of achievement, the aim is also to belie the implication that white gazing is somehow an ahistorical phenomenon. Rather, white gazing is a deeply historical accretion, the result of white historical forces, values, assumptions, circuits of desire, institutional structures, irrational fears, paranoia, and an assemblage of "knowledge" that fundamentally configures what appears and the how of that which appears. On this score, the white gaze involves the correlative constitution of a racialized field[2] that normalizes the marking of Black bodies through a relationship of white power. Hence, the discourse of achievement or accomplishment vis-à-vis the white gaze or white gazing thematizes and thereby undercuts the obfuscatory structure of whiteness, a structure that normalizes its practices. Theorizing his racialized "white" skin tone, John Warren argues, "The fact of my whiteness is not accidental. Rather, my whiteness is an accomplishment of a history of discursive, normalized moments that worked together to make me appear this skin tone."[3] In stream with Warren's argument regarding whiteness as a history of discursive moments, while lecturing at conferences and teaching in classrooms I have often asked white people to examine their racially white bodies in mirrors and to think beyond the frame of that single visual moment, to read that visual moment through the reality of a specifically configured sociohistorical temporality, one that is inextricably expressive of white supremacy, purity, privilege, and power. The objective is to get them to enlarge their frame of reference, come to terms with the ways in which their bodies are marked by a history that they did not create, but will perpetuate in often banal ways. More important, sociohistorical temporality enlarges the meaning of that visual moment, revealing the fact that their white bodies have racial meanings that they could not have were they to bracket out historical temporality through a fictive and imaginary self that is an absolute law unto itself. In this way, the past lives in their present bodies "just as in melody the first notes are transformed by those which follow and are given a value they could not have had by themselves."[4]

In terms of a relevant Foucauldian conceptual register, the discourse of *achievement or accomplishment* is consistent with *genealogical* inquiry, which attempts to uncover that which obscures its origins. In short, a genealogical inquiry critiques hegemonic orders that mask themselves as "natural processes," thus demonstrating their contingency and thereby their openness to transformation. Indeed, by emphasizing the historical achievement of the white gaze, the notion of agency is preserved as the white gaze is sociohistorically constituted, that is, contingent, not ontologically fixed. In terms of white gazing, when white bodies look out upon the world, they not only see what has been put there for them to see, and see it in a specific way, but they cooperate, consciously or unconsciously, with broader processes of normative and epistemic accretion, in assisting to bring certain objects into view in particular configured ways. My point here is that the white gaze is an embodied phenomenon, a mode of social engagement, a form of practice that presupposes a thick, historical sedimentation or encrustation of white supremacy. Again, however, as a site of historical practice, an historical accomplishment, the white gaze is contingent and thereby open to be disrupted, undone.

The process of white gazing might be said to be a species of attunement (*stimmung*) that discloses as well as cancels. This process of gazing is not simply limited to the ocular sphere but functions as a synecdoche that implicates white embodiment, more generally. In this case, white embodiment, its expansions and contractions through space vis-à-vis Black bodies or bodies of color, signals the white body's complex repertoire of racial responsiveness. As Jean-Paul Sartre notes, "the whiteness of his skin was another look, condensed light. The white man—white because he was man, white like daylight, white like truth, white like virtue."[5]

White embodiment is the site of whiteness as the transcendental norm: a norm that takes itself to be fungible with "daylight," "truth," and "virtue." Whiteness deems itself un-raced and universal. Yet, these features of whiteness, along with their tropes, constitute a lie; that lie is part of its structure. There is contained within whiteness another lie, one that is dialectically linked to the brutalization, dehumanization, and violence imposed upon Black bodies and bodies of color. That lie is that the Black body *is* night, doom, darkness, and danger; it *is* deceptive and devious; it *is* a site of vice and moral depravity. Hence, the meaning of whiteness, as universal, contains within itself an obfuscated parasitism that reduces the Black body to a wretched particularity. It is this sense of damned particularity that implies hierarchical *difference*, a form of difference that is defined through the normative structure of whiteness that defines itself as ontologically self-sufficient. It is precisely this sense of ontological self-sufficiency and axiological universality that installs the Black body as ersatz, aesthetically deformed, morally disabled (think here of the curse of Ham or Canaan), excessive, monstrous, disgusting, that is, *distasteful*.

Lillian Smith, who wrote with courage and deep insight regarding the racist vitriol within the Southern United States, especially within the context of the pre–Civil Rights Movement, provides an insightful example of just how white embodiment has inherited a history that resides *in* and *through* the white body, a white racist history that saturates white modes of being. More accurately, whiteness as the transcendental norm is the very expression of white embodied existence; orientation; modes of comportment, style, emotion, aesthetic responses; feelings of threat, neuronal activity; the activation of sweat glands, breathing patterns, heart rate, auditory and olfactory responses. In short, *whiteness is all the way down.* Smith tells the story of a white church woman who desired to break the racist segregationist taboo of eating with Black people. Smith writes, "Though her conscience was serene, and her enjoyment of this association was real, yet she was seized by an acute nausea which disappeared only when the meal was finished. She was too honest to attribute it to anything other than anxiety welling up from the 'bottom of her personality', as she expressed it, creeping back from her childhood training."[6]

Kristina DuRocher also provides an example where this sort of white embodied revulsive response was activated vis-à-vis Black bodies. DuRocher notes that Alice Harris Kester, the wife of Howard Kester, a prominent white preacher who was influenced by the Social Gospel movement, "confronted one of the southern 'sins', at a Negro Baptist Publishing House lunch. She tried to eat at the same table as African Americans, but could not keep her

food down, running home in tears."[7] Both white women appear to be sincere
in their efforts at political activism. Yet, their bodies responded in ways
contrary to their intentions. The former was hit with severe stomach distress
that dissipated only after she left the presence of those Black bodies. The
latter, literally, could not keep her food down. Given the white distorted
imaginary vis-à-vis the Black body, it is my sense that she perceived the
Black bodies present as "disgusting Black beasts," "hyper-sexual animals,"
sites of "uncleanliness," "filth," "feces," which are the antitheses of white
normativity qua purity. In the language of Frantz Fanon, it is as if both white
women had already "sketched a historico-racial schema"[8] below their corporeal schemas. In the case of Alice, she gags, retches, vomits up what the
logics of her white embodiment refuse to endure through what she sees and
perhaps smells and hears. Indeed, perhaps her entire bodily sensorium reacts
negatively to the "disgusting" and "revolting" Black body, eliciting a visceral
white embodied response that is grounded within the historical sedimentation of racist myths and representations. Yet, to puke because of the presence
of the Black body reveals a greater truth: it is evidence of a white corporeal
contract, as it were, that agrees not to concede that white racist mythopoetic
constructions are products of white fabulous (as in fable) embodied self-
aggrandizement: smelly Negroes, hypersexed Blacks, ugly baboons, coons,
Black savages, and dirty niggers.

Dan Flory notes that "famous nineteenth-century naturalist Louis Agassiz
had a 'pronounced visceral revulsion' to being in close proximity with
blacks, in spite of being opposed to slavery."[9] It was, after all, Immanuel
Kant, the *critical* philosopher par excellence, who said that "Negroes
stink"[10] and that they have "no feeling beyond the trifling."[11] In the former
case, the Black body is philosophically authorized by Kant as a site of putre-
faction. In the latter case, the Black body is philosophically authorized by
him as devoid of the "feeling of the beautiful and the sublime."[12] Such white
aesthetic sensibilities, fueled by the distorted racist imago of the Black body
in the white imaginary, are sites of violence. Cornel West writes, "The myths
offer distorted, dehumanized creatures whose bodies—color of skin, shape
of nose and lips, type of hair, size of hips—are already distinguished from
the white norm of beauty and whose feared sexual activities are deemed
disgusting, dirty or funky and considered less acceptable."[13] Think here
of the tragic reality of the fictional protagonist Pecola Breedlove, in Toni
Morrison's *The Bluest Eye*,[14] who, through a kind of racialized dysmorphia,
came to hate her Black body, wanting to be white at the expense of her own
sanity. As Emmanuel Levinas writes, "But violence does not consist so much
in injuring and annihilating persons as in interrupting their continuity, making them play roles in which they no longer recognize themselves, making
them betray not only commitments but their own substance, making them

carry out actions that will destroy every possibility for action."[15] James Baldwin speaks directly to the problem of white racist historical sedimentation, and a certain fabricated sense of white self-mastery, and white atomic neoliberalism.

> White man, hear me! History, as nearly no one seems to know, is not merely something to be read. And it does not refer merely, or even principally, to the past. On the contrary, the great force of history comes from the fact that we carry it within us, are unconsciously controlled by it in many ways, and history is literally *present* in all that we do. It could scarcely be otherwise, since it is to history that we owe our frames of reference, our identities, and our aspirations.[16]

In the case of the two white women (or Louis Agassiz), it is not the case that they failed to bracket epistemologically false beliefs. It was not as if either one was morally torn regarding the ethics of racial oppression. In both cases, intentionality and ethical fortitude were of little help in terms of staving off the disruptions of the habituated white body, a white body that is constituted within a white supremacist historical matrix that is present in the white body's modes of engagement. In other words, simply having a serene conscience or having epistemologically correct beliefs made little or no difference in terms of the white body's iterative "sociomoral disgust reactions."[17] Flory notes:

> In general, individuals who react thusly do not even know on a conscious level the character of or reasons for their responses. Such reactions are primarily what we used to call 'non-cognitive'; that is, not an aware, rational choice, but rather a cognitively opaque response. Thus in the vast majority of cases they are phenomenologically experienced as 'automatic' rather than thoughtful or reflective. Disgust, as a direct affect, is generally unmediated by ratiocinative thought processes or explicit propositional content.[18]

It is precisely the white body as racially habituated vis-à-vis the Black body that occludes the crucial instigation necessary for rupturing "racialized disgust."[19] Yet, it is this racial and racist habituation that renders the feeling of disgust " 'natural', which would serve to reinforce the presumed appropriateness of this kind of [disgust] response."[20]

The Black body vis-à-vis the process of white gazing can assume all sorts of transmogrified dimensions. As theorized in chapter 1, think here again of the eleven cries from the forty-three-year-old Black male, Eric Garner. What *did* the white police officers hear as Garner called out for help? What *didn't* they hear? What *couldn't* they hear? Perhaps they heard nothing at all, perhaps unintelligible groans, perhaps gobbledygook. After all, he was allegedly engaged in criminal activity; he was perceived as the ethically derelict, the big Black smelly beast in need of taming; a walking, talking King Kong in New York

City threatening the nation-building efforts of white police officers. And like King Kong, he met his dreadful fate at the hands of white bodies. From the perspective that I'm theorizing, Eric Garner was a site of disgust like a piece of meat wedged prominently between one's front teeth, hard on the eyes. We don't want to look, but we somehow must.

Garner, with his "I can't breathe" cry of help, can be compared to nineteen-year-old Black female Renisha McBride, who was shot in the face and killed by fifty-five-year-old white male Theodore Wafer on November 2, 2013, in Dearborn Heights, Michigan, as she banged on his front door for help after being in a car accident. Innocent and unarmed, McBride sought safety, a place of protection within what is demographically a predominantly white suburban space. And while it is unclear whether or not Wafer knew that McBride was Black or female, we do know that his defense said that he saw a "shadowy figure."[21] We also know that Wafer complained of "crime" and how his neighborhood had become increasingly "dangerous" and how he had discovered "drug" paraphernalia there.[22] We also know that Wafer initially said that his shotgun had gone off by accident, but later said that he defended himself because of the pounding at his door. While he may not have seen that McBride was Black, the suggestive power of racist and racial signifiers is present. "Crime, "drugs," and "danger" are racially coded terms; their racial operational intelligibility is linked to a racial Manichean divide where "shadowy figures," "death," "doom," and "danger" reside, where Black bodies are racially overdetermined. Joe Feagin notes, "In the English language of the colonists, prior to the development of African American enslavement, the word 'white' had uses that were mostly positive, such as 'gleaming brightly', as for a candle, while the word 'black' had mostly negative meanings like 'sooted'. The word 'black' had long been used by the residents of England metaphorically, to describe evil and the devil. It was soon adopted by the early English colonists for the purpose of naming dark-skinned Africans."[23] Examining the toxicity of deep cultural, racial semiotics, Frantz Fanon notes that "Satan is black, one talks of shadows, when one is dirty one is black—whether one is thinking of physical dirtiness or of moral dirtiness."[24] So, what did Wafer "hear" as he was awakened from his sleep? It is important to note that Wafer's response—the feeling of threat, the eagerness to stand his ground, his white space, moving to retrieve his shotgun, the urgency to eliminate the outside threat, perhaps "contaminant," opening the front door, and shooting through the actual closed and locked screen door at the "shadowy figure"—is a deeply corporeal response, one that white bodies enact through habituation, because of media saturation of Black stereotypes. In other words, Wafer performs and perpetuates racial spatial logics, racial affective logics, and racial judgmental logics; these logics constitute white modes of being-in-the-world that reflect what Fanon calls "the unreflected imposition of a culture."[25] Hortense

Spillers reminds us that as a Black woman she is a "marked woman."[26] As McBride sought help, perhaps disorientated because of the car crash, she was always already marked: a Black female body in the wrong place. Spillers further notes, "I describe a locus of confounded identities, a meeting ground of investments and privations in the national treasury of rhetorical wealth. My country needs me, and if I were not here, I would have to be invented."[27] On another day and time, McBride might have been needed to be a "prostitute," a "Welfare queen," or a "nappy-headed ho,"[28] but on November 2, 2013, she was a "shadowy figure," a "spectral sight", "a phantasmatic production."[29] She was shot and killed not because she posed a real threat; she was shot in exchange for the robbery she never committed, the physical violence she never caused, but which she is, by virtue of her Blackness, always already about to commit or cause.[30] What is important to note is that were it up to Cheryl Carpenter, a defense attorney for Wafer, a postmortem racist narrative would have been invented to "prove" that McBride "was aggressive. She was violent. She broke part of Mr. Wafer's house."[31] Carpenter also wanted to create a narrative based upon McBride's text messages that would help to "demonstrate" that her character was morally questionable by revealing her possession of provocative photos and her use of apparent "slang" references to marijuana.[32] Like Eric Garner, McBride, through the white imaginary, was guilty and had to be taken down. Both were part of a white America, a sham democracy, "whose state apparatus, including judges, attorneys, 'owners', 'soul drivers', 'overseers', and 'men of God', apparently colludes with a protocol of 'search and destroy.'"[33]

Or think here again of seventeen-year-old Black male Trayvon Martin who was profiled, and epistemologically totalized, by George Zimmerman, who decided to get out of his car and track down Martin. Doing discursive violence to Martin's body before the actual confrontation with Martin, Zimmerman said that he looked "suspicious," was "up to no good" and looked like he was "on drugs." Notice how it is Zimmerman's description (or, more accurately, *ascription*) of Martin's body that eats away at its somatic integrity and also supplants Martin's first-person understanding of himself. Zimmerman's words, then, not only violated Martin's embodied-being-in-that-space of Sanford, Florida, but violated Martin's epistemic integrity. As we know, Martin's young Black body, because it was "up to no good," had to be controlled. As he innocently traversed the streets back to be with his younger brother, with his juice and candy, he was not met by *Thanatos*, whose touch of death is gentle. Rather, as by the *Keres*, who imposed violent and cruel death on their victims, Martin's young life was *brutally* taken; he was shot in the chest by George Zimmerman whose touch was deadly and violent. When asked if he regretted that he got out of his car to follow Martin, or regretted that he had a gun that night or if there is anything that he would do

differently retrospectively, Zimmerman's response was a resounding, "No."
In fact, like the "divine" teleological assumptions undergirding the doctrine
of manifest destiny, Zimmerman declared, "I feel that it was all God's plan."[34]
In this case, Martin's Black body was destined to be killed; he had it coming.
Like white colonizers, Zimmerman had a "divine" mission to fulfill—his job
was to exterminate, to unburden white America of one more problem, one
more misfortune, and one more "nigger."

Garner, Martin, and McBride were sites of imminent disaster, calamitous,
threatening like an astrological omen.[35] After all, Garner was big and he was
Black, an object that offended the "civilizational" sensibilities/tastes of the
white police officers. Like Martin vis-à-vis Zimmerman,[36] Garner was always
already suspicious. Both Martin and Garner were "out of place," a blight that
needed to be profiled and removed from sight. Their bodies disrupted the harmony and symmetry of white space, functioning as a *shocking* presence that
had to be stopped; indeed, stopped dead. Think here also of Jordan Davis who
was killed by white male Michael David Dunn, who exercised his whiteness
within a public space to control and police what he called "thug music" or
"rap crap." The Black young male bodies playing the aesthetically "cacopho-
nous music" did not have a right, from Dunn's perspective, to express sonic
freedom, *taste*, and their own *aesthetic agency*. Then again, I guess that those
Black young male bodies had "no feeling beyond the trifling." For Dunn, or
so I would argue, rap music and those young Black male bodies were inter-
changeable: both excessive, a needless surplus of sorts, and, thereby, disposable. Once they are removed, symmetry returns, things are back as they ought
to be; one now *feels* good, corporeally unstressed, at ease.

When one thinks about the history of the Black body within white America,
the theme of racialized immobility is a salient one; it is a form of violence
exercised through the corporeal and spatial policing of the Black body. The
history of slavery, Black codes, Jim Crow, white neighborhood covenants,
lynching, and stop-and-frisk are some of the ways in which the Black body's
agency has been militated against. Davis and his friends exercised embodied
agency when they refused to turn down their music. Garner exercised his
embodied agency when he told police officers, who accused him of selling loose
cigarettes, "I'm tired of this. This stops today!"[37] However, given white fear of
Black embodied mobility, agency, and self-definition, which constitutes a threat
to white power, such agency undergoes a process of "transposition and fabrication of dangerous intention."[38] This reversal of who constitutes the perpetrator
of danger is clear in the tragic case of Sandra Bland, a twenty-eight-year-old
Black woman who was stopped by white male trooper Brian Encinia in Prairie
View, Texas, on July 10, 2015. Bland, after being arrested, was mysteriously
found dead in her jail cell from an apparent suicide. While the investigation of
the "suicide" is at the time of this writing ongoing, what is clear to me is that

Encinia exercised white panoptic surveillance and state power/violence.[39] As in the cases of Garner and Davis, Bland was punished (and eventually died) for exercising her agential voice, for taking a stand against white power and presumed white impunity when it comes to the brutalization of Black bodies. What is clear from the dashcam video[40] is that Bland knew that she was being followed. Knowing this, she pulled over, apparently failing to signal. Counterfactually, one is led to believe that Bland would have been alive today had Encinia not pursued her *while driving Black*. Once stopped, she says, "You were speeding up, tailing me."[41] When framed through the recent deaths of unarmed Black men, women, and children by white police officers and their white proxies, one can understand that Bland might change lanes. She no doubt felt intimidated and angry, knowing that she was being followed though she had not done anything wrong. So, she exercised agency by pulling over. Perhaps Encinia, through a racist episteme, *already knew* that Bland was about to do something wrong. Given Encinia's white epistemic authority, he could "see" this. Butler notes, "The visual field is not neutral to the question of race; it is itself a racial formation, an episteme, hegemonic and forceful."[42] Encinia's asking Bland "What's wrong?" and "You okay?" sounds more like an imputation of guilt than concern. Those questions seem to function as part of an eventual discovery of what he already knows. Understandably, Bland is upset because she feels as if she was put into a situation for which she did not ask, even if it is true that she failed to signal. Bland tells Encinia as much after he says that she seems really irritated. She says, "I am. I really am. I feel like it's crap what I'm getting a ticket for. I was getting out of your way. You were speeding up, tailing me, so I move over and you stop me. So yeah, I am a little irritated, but that doesn't stop you from giving me a ticket." If it is true that white people have created a world in which their understanding is expressly thwarted, then Encinia is living in a state of profound white bad faith. Yet, this is how white power functions; it lies to itself. Encinia was following closely a Black woman who was minding her own business, and excited, we are told, about a new job. Encinia appears to live in a world in which the brutal history of white male treatment of Black women was nonexistent. Yet, the history of whiteness, its sedimentation, created the conditions for what would ensue. After checking her driver's license, Encinia returns to Bland's car and says, "Okay, ma'am." From what we discover later, Encinia was going to give Bland a warning. So, why didn't he give the warning and let her go? My contention is that he was already angered by her agency, her freedom to express how she felt angered by *his actions*. She was not the problem; he was. It was her lack of silence that insulted his white male and white state authority. After all, the history of white supremacy is a history of silencing Black voices—some having their tongues cut from their mouths. Thus, the silencing is not only hegemonic, but perverse and sadistic. Framing this silence vis-à-vis anger, Audre Lorde writes, "Women of color in America [sic] have grown up within a symphony of anger, at being silenced, at being unchosen, at knowing that when we survive, it is in spite of a world that takes for granted our lack of humanness, and which hates our very existence outside of its service."[43] With white state authority and arrogance spilling from his lips, Encinia asks, "You mind putting out your cigarette, please? If you don't mind?" Bland, laying claim to her spatiality and embodied freedom within her own car, says, "I'm in my car, why do I have to put out my cigarette?" Encinia then gives a "lawful order," "Well, you can step on out now," one that is inextricably linked to Bland's direct exercise of agency. In short, Encinia, angered by this Black women's agency and defiance of white male power and, by extension, the hegemony of white state power, is able to express and simultaneously obfuscate his frustrated white male megalomania through the declaration of a lawful order. This provides the grounds for lawful arrest, but reframes and distorts the narrative sequence that led to the lawful order. Any resistance on the part of Bland, who is painfully aware of how the events actually unfolded and who is grounded by her own epistemic authority, will now constitute "aggression" and "violence" against Encinia and the state, which helps to construct the racist assumption that the Black female body needs to be placed under control, in need of white discipline because of its *natural* proclivity toward ire. Refusing to follow orders that are really the result of Encinia's white male authority being challenged, he threatens to *light her up* with a stun gun, and *drag* her from her car. After getting out of the car, Bland accuses him of *slamming her head* to the ground, something that is outside the purview of the dashcam. When Bland complains of having epilepsy, Encinia says, "Good. Good," implying that he would not give a damn if Bland had an epileptic seizure as a result of her head being slammed to the ground. This insensitivity is reminiscent of the shooting death of Eric Harris. As shown in chapter 1, as he cried out, "Oh my God. I'm losing my breath," one of the white male police officers shouts, "Fuck your breath!"[44] Butler notes, "Certain lives will be highly protected, and the abrogation of their claims to sanctity will be sufficient to mobilize the forces of war. Other lives will not find such fast and furious support and will not even qualify as 'grievable.'"[45] To grieve suggests the sense of gravitas, to weigh heavy, as laying heavy upon one's heart. In short, Harris's claim to the inviolability of his life was rendered of no consequence.

Bland had a right to be where she was; she had a right to speak her frustration into existence; she had a right to be angry; she had a right to continue smoking her cigarette. She had a right to and an obligation to pull from the history of Black women who have refused and continue to refuse silence and injustice. Bland's voice and her demand for respect were denied. Encinia failed or refused to understand how white supremacist history, power, and privilege structured his encounter with Bland; he failed to understand how his white body was the site of a particular legacy, a site of specific white regulatory values and perceptual habits. He did not "see" or "hear" Bland on her terms, thus placing her epistemic authority under erasure. Bland's *life did not matter*. There was no recognition of Bland's alterity as the site of an opportunity for Encinia to engage his whiteness differently, to recognize the promise of the beauty obtainable by relating to a fellow human being with respect.

Returning to the tragic moments of Eric Garner's socio-existential plight, his cry, his call, is intelligible within the framework of a relational ontology. "I can't breathe" is a call for help, a crying out to others, a call that says, "Please *hear* me." It implicates the white other. "I can't breathe" challenges white perceptual practices, ones that have become *sutured*, held intact, seemingly impregnable. Like Encinia, the white police officers at the scene have seemingly closed off the possibility of self-interrogation. Garner's cries for help were absorbed into an "established [white] ontology."[46] To have heard his cries should have solicited (etymologically, to disturb) an urgent response from the police. To hear pounding on one's door at three in the morning does not ipso facto signify danger. The meaning of the pounding isn't predetermined, but open for interpretation, deferred through the workings of a different moral imagination. The pounding can also function as an invitation, a call to respond to a desperate Black teenager, a stranger in the early morning, a fragile soul in search of help. Hers was a frantic plea for help. Exposed to the will of another, she sought out a "neighbor," someone who might have the will to *dwell near* her; someone who might respect her alterity; someone who might courageously ask, "Are you in danger?" But Wafer had nothing more than death for McBride—the silencing of another Black life. Similarly, to see Trayvon Martin as a young Black boy traversing with effort through the street, after realizing that he was being watched, profiled, and surveilled, would require something more from Zimmerman. But Zimmerman had nothing more than death for Martin—the silencing of another Black life. To hear the so-called rap crap differently, and to see those young Black males as exercising their aesthetic sensibilities, and not as "thugs" with crude musical tastes, would require more from Dunn. But Dunn had nothing more than death for Davis—the silencing of another Black life. Bearing upon their white bodies is effective white history, white systemic interpellative forces, white implicit alliances, white discursive regimes, white iterative processes of habituation, and white power and privilege. Baldwin argues that "it is with great pain and terror"[47] that one begins to realize that history has shaped, in this case, those white police officers, and those white self-appointed protectors of all things white and pure. It is with great pain and terror that they will come to understand that they have inherited and continue to perpetuate their *white* frames of reference. Yet, those white bodies (Daniel Pantaleo, George Zimmerman, Michael David Dunn, Theodore Wafer, and Brian Encinia) avoided that great pain and terror.[48] I would argue that they remained sutured; sewn up and sealed, unable or unwilling to understand their relationship to white effective history; to understand the ways in which they have already been dispossessed by history, which already presupposes sociality and therefore vulnerability. More accurately, they fled from (covered over) their vulnerability; they refused to come to terms with the un-sutured selves that they are: corporeal selves that are always already exposed and beyond mastery. If only trooper Encinia had entered into battle against his historically created white self and challenged the racist epistemic and axiological frames of reference through which he encountered Bland, he would have possibly been hailed from a different place, "undone" by having truly heard Bland's anger, a form of justified anger rooted in a white racist system that he helps to perpetuate. The violence done to Bland should not be restricted to what happened *after* she exited her car, since it originates from the moment when Encinia initially follows her. It is the violence toward and violation of her integrity that is also at issue here; she was made to suffer the consequences of a racist imago of the Black body ingrained in four centuries of this country's existence. "What's wrong?" and "You okay?" did not bespeak concern, did not communicate an un-suturing. Encinia was not prepared to be moved by the epistemic testimony of a Black woman being pursued within a country that legally sanctions the thesis that Black lives don't matter—unless, of course, they serve the interests and desires of white power.

The terms "sutured" and "un-sutured," as I deploy them here, are not only *practices* that respectively occlude change and engender change, but they are also indicative of what it means to be a human subject at all, that is, indicative of what it means to be *homo possibilitas* (un-sutured) and to be thrown within the context of historical facticity (sutured). In other words, to be a subject is indicative of what it means to be "subjected to" or "constituted by," and indicative of what it means to resist certain forms of being "subjected to," "constituted by" or interpellated. I would argue that this is precisely *our* ontology, one that speaks to who and what we are as human beings—we are both constituted (sutured) and un-constituted (un-sutured) realities. Yet, historically, there will be ways in which we are specifically constituted (sutured), and there will be specific ways in which we might find it necessary to challenge (un-suture with respect to) that form of specific constitution—none of which is determined a priori. As Judith Butler argues, "From the outset, what relation the self will take to itself, how it will craft itself in response to an injunction [a mode of interpellation, historical structuring], how it will form itself, and what labor it will perform upon itself is a challenge, if not an open question."[49] As noted earlier, Baldwin argues that history is literally present in all that we do. He is specifically addressing white people within the context of white supremacist history. Given this history, what white people will do is indeed an open question. Also, what labor the white self will perform upon itself is a challenge. Baldwin points in the direction of a process of laboring that attempts to disrupt or "undo" white supremacist history. White modes of being-in-the-world, white bodily forms of comportment, whites ways of occupying space, and white gazes, are precisely the ways in which white supremacist and hegemonic power is literally present in all that white people do. Baldwin theorizes a space for white people to battle with their historically contingent, created white selves. He provides us with a specific framework that will shape the relation that the white self will take to itself. The discourse of battle presupposes processes of rupture, agency, and the capacity to resist (etymologically, to take a stand against) certain processes of white racist interpellation.

In short, while it is true that whiteness is a site of power, an assemblage of "knowledge," and an effective history, it does not follow that white people are *determined* or devoid of agency qua white, that there is no space for counter-iterative, white antiracist practices. In other words, there is a space for the practice of un-suturing, where this is both a site of a specific form of antiracist practice and a way of being all too human, always already a site of the given (facticity) and the taken (possibility)—a self that is not created ex nihilo, but a self that both understands its historical facticity and can "engage in an aesthetics of the self that maintains a critical relation to existing [problematic and heteronomous] norms."[50] On this score, then, when it comes to Daniel Pantaleo, George Zimmerman, Michael David Dunn, Theodore Wafer, and Brian Encinia, there was no effort on their part to embody (or recognize) a radically different aesthetics of dwelling, of being-in-the-world, of being near, a different way or style of somatic comportment, sensing, feeling, emoting, perceiving—an aesthetics that realizes the futility of *total closure*, where the body, in this case, the white body, is already exposed to the touch of the Black body; indeed, where they are already *touching* across a racialized social integument/skin.

While the *aesthetics* of un-suturing, which here refers to a form of practice, sounds counterintuitive, especially as aesthetics has come to denote and connote that which is beautiful, I argue that it is precisely in being un-sutured, exposed, vulnerable, open to be wounded that there is a profound element of the beautiful, the ecstatic, to be experienced and engaged—where the body trembles in its contingency, responsibility, and restlessness; where it stands in awe, which is an instantiation of an aesthetic response, where the perceptual and sensorial are shaken, unhinged.[51] White bodies need to undergo processes of undoing, processes of disorientation; whites must come to relate to their own bodies/embodiment in ways that will install experiences of the uncanny, the strange. They must come to terms with the fact that, at a fundamental ontological level, their embodiment is already un-sutured, which points to the reality that as human subjects we are always already beyond ourselves, dispossessed by forces of interpellation, where the idea of the atomic self and *absolute* self-mastery is deeply problematic. Moreover, within this context, the concept of un-suturing points to the importance of being undone through the cultivation of practices that disrupt our relationship to various problematic forces and existing norms, practices that cultivate different ways of being-in-the-world, different ways of understanding embodiment as extended through a shared social integument as opposed to a form of rigid spatial enclosure. So, it is important that white people, within the context of a white suprema-cist, neoliberal social and political context, which is indicative of our current historical moment in the United States, come to realize that they were never the site of *mastery* in the first place. To use Judith Butler's discourse, which points to what I theorized earlier in terms of what it means to be human per-sons, the reality is that all of us are in the precarious situation of *"having been given over from the start."*[52] So, whites must begin to recognize that they are un-sutured and that being un-sutured points to a reality fundamental to who and what we are as human beings. As Butler notes, "One seeks to preserve oneself against the injuriousness of the other, but if one were successful at walling oneself off from injury, one would become inhuman. In this sense, we make a mistake when we take 'self-preservation' to be the essence of the human, unless we accordingly claim that the 'inhuman' is constitutive of the human."[53] Butler's use of 'inhuman' is pertinent here, especially given the inhuman ways in which white people have learned to suture themselves vis-à-vis Black bodies (Jim Crow, redlining, anti-miscegenation laws, gated communities). Within this context, whiteness is historically installed as the site of "racial purity" and as the human qua human. Given this problematic, racialized understanding of the human, we are left with the category of the human as morally bankrupt, especially as whiteness is a site of racial self-preservation which is, in this case, a species of the inhuman.

As white people nurture practices of un-suturing vis-à-vis Black bod-ies, they dwell within the space of the human. "White man, hear me!" is Baldwin's plea to redirect the attention of white people toward understand-ing that they have failed to understand themselves within a history of their own making and failed to understand how this history installs sites of flee-ing, of seeking shelter, of self-preserving, of suturing. In failing or refusing to understand the vicious history of anti-Blackness of which whites are the principal architects, the Black body has, by extension, become a site of tera-tology which white people deny any responsibility for creating. As a result, white bodies approach Black bodies with a form of suturing (somatic and psychic closure) that they both inherit and perpetuate. Coming to terms with the vicious history of white supremacy requires a practice of un-suturing, a critical distancing from (or disruption of) various hegemonic norms, that enables an anti-hegemonic way of crafting a different (white) self and thereby recrafting/de-problematizing Black embodiment.

Because white people collectively engage in habituated embodied white racist practices that are mutually reinforcing within the context of socially quotidian spaces and that are further supported by deeply ingrained and sedimented historical, institutional structures, the assumption that white people can engage in practices of un-suturing solely through a single act of intention, as one might change his/her clothes at will, is misleading. The ingrained history of white supremacy, its habits and its insidious nature, will require constant *striving*; it will require practice, a reiterative opening and wounding, habits of uncovering the stench of white mendacity. Yet, it will be a form of practice accompanied by an awareness of the ways in which white identity formation is still connected to and complicit with white supremacist structures. In this regard, "the mechanisms of [white] social systems are much more insidious, fluid, and difficult to pinpoint"[54] even as white people engage in acts of un-suturing qua resistance. The system of anti-Blackness is a pervasive systemic structure and is etched into the embodied lives of white people. Un-suturing is not an act of magic but requires "the active repetition of acts, verbal and nonverbal, that continue to communicate"[55] the responsibility to engage opportunities for creating fissures in the system, disruptions in one's mode of being white. The white self that engages responsibly within this practice is not an atomic self but a deeply historically embedded self. As such, then, un-suturing will involve a form of white antiracist *Bildung* that takes seriously the gravitas of collective white history and white collective practices that sustain white collective suturing. This process of *Bildung* will involve the indispensability of installing *antiracist* forms of configured subjectivation, discursive practices, and regimes of antiracist intelligibility that call/hail an un-sutured self or a white self that critically engages in unmasking and fissuring white historical sedimentation.

The process of un-suturing ultimately means, as John Warren states, "listening to others and trying to find ways of hearing how I [as a white person] help to constitute whiteness in ways that build from and reinstitute my own privilege."[56] Being sutured, then, Zimmerman failed/refused to be undone by Martin's presence. He did not hear Martin; he did not see Martin. In the presence of Martin, Zimmerman became the "master" of the meaning of his corporality; indeed, he also became the master of the meaning of Martin's embodiment. Martin was, for Zimmerman, up to no good, suspicious. Martin wore the mark, the stain. Martin was the site of "terror" through Zimmerman's gaze. Yet, there is a different experience of terror, one that expresses a form of exuberance, one that promises more than that projected upon Martin's Black body; it is the terror or the sublime to be recognized in Martin's *precarious* existence and in Zimmerman's own existence or in one's own existence. Etymologically, the word "precarious" denotes *dependency*. Therefore, to say that Martin's existence is precarious is to say that his embodiment expresses a form of dependency, a form of *asking*, an *entreaty*; a form of *prayer*, of *supplication*. So, if what we are is ontologically a site of *asking*, then what is required is a response. Think of the unfolding of the potential of something profoundly beautiful and yet "terrifying," had Zimmerman become un-sutured vis-à-vis Martin's body, a body that is an *asking*: "Will you help me?" "Will you take care of me as I walk in this unfamiliar space?" "Will you support me as I walk here with effortless grace?" "Can you see my Black body as one that matters?" Given the racial asymmetrical power relations between Black bodies and white bodies, Martin's body all the more stands out as a site of *enfleshment* in the mode of beseeching. And the terror is the realization on the part of Zimmerman that *he alone* is being asked to respond, and to respond in such a way that he becomes vulnerable; to recognize his mutually precarious (and therefore dependent) existence in relationship to Martin's. In that moment of un-suturing, Zimmerman would come to understand the meaning of his own being in the mode of deferral: he is not a monad, but is already out there, as it were, entangled in the life of Martin.

In this un-suturing, this wounding, I want Zimmerman to understand that he is always already an "answer" to Martin's presence qua an asking. The point here is that, given the ontology that I'm suggesting of embodiment as a mode of asking, Zimmerman is already an answer to Martin's presence within that mutually shared space. And while the answer was initially in the mode of epistemic violence (and later actual physical violence), there is, or so I'm arguing, something deeper ontologically that Zimmerman misses. The dyadic relationship called for a kind of "unobtrusive vigilance,"[57] where Zimmerman is on the lookout for Martin's safety, but it called for even more than that. I theorize and envision a dyadic relationship both where Zimmerman is on the lookout for Martin's safety and where Zimmerman, the site of an always already un-sutured corporeal interconnectedness, is ontologically compelled to respond in a mode of care expressed as a presumption of entreaty on the part of Martin.

There are some forms of terror, as I'm theorizing the concept here, that point to a kind of awe, where one stands in the presence of an embodied other qua *entreaty* that demands a freely given response, one that is thereby anxiety-ridden, filled with risk, uncertainty, a sense of corporeal unsettling, and deep ontological and existential gravitas. It is *not* the kind of terror waiting to be unleashed, as in a lynch mob; rather, it is a form of terror that is experienced in the form of being unhinged vis-à-vis the other. It is not the intentional mobilization of expressible/ expressed terror to do harm, but the demobilization of expressible/expressed uncertainty and joy. Neither

Renisha McBride's nor Sandra Bland's existence unhinged the suturing practices of Theodore Wafer or Brian Encinia. McBride's *entreaty* was met with swift and horrific deadly violence. And Sandra Bland's effort to assert her integrity and to articulate her *lived* experience of frustration and anger at being stopped while driving while Black was met by white male police arrogance in the name of white state power, control, and brutality. Both Wafer and Encinia missed the profundity of having their whiteness challenged vis-à-vis encounters with Black bodies that could have prompted a new way of seeing, a new way of knowing, a new way of being. Similarly, in the case of George Zimmerman, he turned inward, sutured himself, became centripetal and all the more self-certain, failed or refused to understand his relationship to a white metanarrative history, to grasp the ways in which he was always already linked to the social and ontological integument that subtends (literally, to stretch beneath) his relationship to Martin. Gearing up, preparing for a battle, not an embodied entreaty, Zimmerman, as we know, *pursued* Martin.[58] Zimmerman was on the prowl, his physical gait uninviting; a body in the mode of taking a stand, upright, with no intention of genuflection (etymologically, to bend the knee). As such, Martin *became* the enemy, monster; the stranger and infestation unworthy of life itself, an infinitely disposable life. After all, Martin was supposedly there to take, to pillage. In other words, Zimmerman chased Martin, *pursued* him, which is etymologically linked to the term "prosecute," to hold a trial. It was Zimmerman's bodily style and comportment, being on the hunt, as it were, that positions Martin as the one who is about to commit a crime, who is to be feared, and who is to be tried. As such, Martin's being, in the form of an *asking*, was met with a bullet, fired from a gun by a sutured self that failed to lose itself in that moment or to come to terms with its being as always already dispossessed. As Butler writes, "I think I have lost 'you' only to discover that 'I' have gone missing as well."[59] Yet, it is within the framework of whiteness as the transcendental norm that Zimmerman will be enabled to "find" himself, to reclaim himself, that is, to live the illusion of a form of mastery and ontological independence that was never his to claim. Un-suturing disrupts; it troubles and unsettles; it is not afraid of forms of genuflection and humility that get expressed through a panoply of *open* or centrifugal embodied gestures; un-sutured gestures that are linked to the ways in which the world reveals itself differently. As an aesthetic gesture/site, un-suturing is a form of exposure, an opening, a corporeal style, and a dispositional sensibility that troubles the insularity of whiteness; that troubles and overwhelms the senses, revealing our somatic porosity and instigating instability; that sense of being thrown off balance, off center, and exposing different (and counterhegemonic) ways of being attuned to our inter-corporeal existence, our mutual touching.

NOTES

1. The reader should note that when I refer to the "Black body," I am privileging those Black bodies that in some sense became "black" qua problematic as they moved across the Middle Passage. I am, however, aware of the "terrain of Blackness" in terms of the changing landscape of Blackness, for example, Black African immigrants and their children. However, I point to the Middle Passage as the crucible in terms of which Black identity is marked. It functions as that space of death, docility, amalgamation, and resistance that is important to understanding Black people in North America. So, it becomes a central existential and ontological motif through which I theorize what it means to be Black. Yet, it is important to note that those bodies were scattered and not confined to North America. So, I think that it is important to theorize the ways in which that oceanic experience shaped other Black bodies that were dispersed throughout the world. As such, then, one must examine the different genealogies and phenomenological configurations that speak not only to those bodies that were not enslaved in North America, though came through the Middle Passage, but also speak to those Black bodies that did not arrive at their "destinies" through the transatlantic slave trade at all. This raises important questions regarding the lived meaning of "Blackness" and how Blackness is differentially defined diachronically and in terms of points of geographical origin. Furthermore, this raises questions about how Blackness is permeable and protean. This also raises the issue of the meaning of 1619 and how Black identity and Black subjectivity can be erroneously tied to that moment in time, which then raises the issue of how a specific Black historical narrative can function monolithically and thus exclude those Black bodies that don't narrativize 1619 in the same way or even at all.

2. Todd May, *Between Genealogy and Epistemology: Psychology, Politics, and Knowledge in the Thought of Michel Foucault* (University Park: The Pennsylvania State University Press, 1993), 69.

3. John T. Warren, "Performing Whiteness Differently: Rethinking the Abolitionist Project," *Educational Theory*, 51(4), 2001, 451–66, quotation on 462.

4. Gabriel Marcel, *Metaphysical Journal*, trans. Bernard Wall (Chicago: Henry Regnery, 1952), 150.

5. Jean-Paul Sartre, "Black Orpheus," in *Race*, ed. Robert Bernasconi (Malden, MA: Blackwell Publishers, 2001), 115.

6. Lillian Smith, *Killers of the Dream* (New York: W.W. Norton, 1949), 148.

7. Kristina DuRocher, *Raising Racists: The Socialization of White Children in the Jim Crow South* (Lexington: The University Press of Kentucky, 2011), 169.

8. Frantz Fanon, *Black Skin, White Masks*, trans. Charles Lam Markmann (New York: Grove Press, Inc., 1967), 111.

9. Dan Flory, "Imaginative Resistance, Racialized Disgust, and *12 Years A Slave*," *Film and Philosophy*, 19, 2015, 75–95, quotation on 80.

10. Immanuel Kant, "On the Different Races of Man," in *Race and the Enlightenment: A Reader*, ed. Emmanuel Chukwudi Eze (Malden, MA: Blackwell Publishers, 1997/1775), 46.

11. Immanuel Kant, "Observations on the Feeling of the Beautiful and Sublime," in *Race and the Enlightenment: A Reader*, ed. Emmanuel Chukwudi Eze (Malden, MA: Blackwell Publishers, 1997/1764), 49.

12. Kant, "Observations on the Feeling of the Beautiful and Sublime," 49.

13. Cornel West, *Race Matters* (Boston: Beacon Press, 1993), 83. Of course, the reality here is that the same "disgusting" Black body also implicates a white libidinal economy of desire.

14. Toni Morrison, *The Bluest Eye* (New York: A Plume Book, 1970). I philosophically engage Morrison's text earlier in this book in chapter 6.

15. Emmanuel Levinas, Preface to *Totality and Infinity*, trans. Alfonso Lingis (Pittsburgh, PA: Duquesne University Press, 1969), 21.

16. James Baldwin, *The Price of the Ticket: Collected Nonfiction, 1948-1985* (New York: St. Martin's Press, 1985), 410.

17. Flory, "Imaginative Resistance, Racialized Disgust, and *12 Years A Slave*," 85.

18. Flory, "Imaginative Resistance, Racialized Disgust, and *12 Years A Slave*," 80–1. For an extended philosophical commentary on whiteness as a site of psychic opacity, see George Yancy, *Look, a White! Philosophical Essays on Whiteness* (Philadelphia, PA: Temple University Press, 2012), especially chapter 6.

19. Flory, "Imaginative Resistance, Racialized Disgust, and *12 Years A Slave*," 80.

20. Flory, "Imaginative Resistance, Racialized Disgust, and *12 Years A Slave*," 80.

21. http://www.nbcnews.com/news/us-news/unjustified-opening-arguments-heard-porch-shooting-death-n162851 (accessed on July 31, 2015)

22. http://legalinsurrection.com/2014/08/homeowner-takes-the-stand-in-detroit-front-porch-murder-trial/ (accessed July 28, 2015)

23. Joe R. Feagin, *The White Racial Frame: Centuries of Racial Framing and Counter-Framing* (New York: Routledge, 2010), 49.

24. Fanon, *Black Skin, White Masks*, 189.

25. Fanon, *Black Skin, White Masks*, 191.

26. Hortense Spillers, "Mama's Baby, Papa's Maybe: An American Grammar Book," in *Feminisms: An Anthology of Literary Theory and Criticism*, ed. Robyn R. Warhol and Diane Price Herndl (New Brunswick, NJ: Rutgers University Press, 1997), 384.

27. Spillers, "Mama's Baby, Papa's Maybe," 384.

28. http://mediamatters.org/research/2007/04/04/imus-called-womens-basketball-team-nappy-headed/138497 (accessed July 28, 2015)

29. Judith Butler, "Endangered/Endangering: Schematic Racism and White Paranoia," in *Reading Rodney King: Reading Urban Uprising*, ed. Robert Gooding-Williams (New York: Routledge, 1993), 18.

30. Butler, "Endangered/Endangering," 19.

31. http://www.theguardian.com/world/2014/jul/21/renisha-mcbride-shooting-trial-detroit (accessed July 28, 2015)

32. http://www.hngn.com/articles/34967/20140630/judge-blocks-renisha-mcbride-cellphone-pictures-in-trial.htm (accessed July 28, 2015)

33. Spillers, "Mama's Baby, Papa's Maybe," 387.

34. See https://www.youtube.com/watch?v=eZxpwb0UYuk (accessed on April 3, 2015)

35. Thanks to Jane A. Gordon for helping me to think about the concept of disaster in this way.

36. And while it is true that Zimmerman is mixed-race, I would argue that he internalized the logic of the white gaze. The point here is that the white gaze is mobile.

37. http://www.theguardian.com/us-news/video/2014/dec/04/i-cant-breathe-eric-garner-chokehold-death-video (accessed July 29, 2015)

38. Butler, "Endangered/Endangering," 21.

39. See Joy James, *Resisting State Violence: Radicalism, Gender, & Race in U.S. Culture* (Minneapolis: University of Minnesota Press, 1996).

40. http://www.washingtonpost.com/lifestyle/style/the-deeper-meaning-in-the-sandra-bland-video-that-has-so-many-deflated/2015/07/25/5fb47db8-30e4-11e5-8353-1215475949f4_story.html (accessed July 29, 2015)

41. http://www.huffingtonpost.com/entry/sandra-bland-arrest-transcript_55b03a88e4b0a9b94853b1f1 (assessed July 29, 2015)

42. Butler, "Endangered/Endangering," 17.

43. Audre Lorde, *Sister Outsider: Essays & Speeches* (New York: The Crossing Press, 2007), 129.

44. http://www.theguardian.com/us-news/2015/apr/12/video-shows-tulsa-police-pursuing-and-shooting-man-killed-in-alleged-mistake (accessed July 29, 2015)

45. Judith Butler, *Precarious Life: The Powers of Mourning and Violence* (New York: Verso, 2006), 33.

46. Butler, *Precarious Life*, 33.

47. Baldwin, *Price of the Ticket*, 410.

48. Judith Butler, *Giving an Account of Oneself* (New York: Fordham University Press, 2005), 18.

49. Butler, *Giving an Account of Oneself*, 17.

50. I would like to thank Deepika Bahri for the discourse of the sensorial within this context.

51. Butler, *Giving an Account of Oneself*, 77.

52. Butler, *Giving an Account of Oneself*, 103.

53. Warren, "Performing Whiteness Differently," 458.

54. Warren, "Performing Whiteness Differently," 460.

55. Warren, "Performing Whiteness Differently," 464.

56. I would like to thank Sherri Irvin for this term and for creatively talking through this section of the chapter with me. Susan Hadley is also to be thanked for her assistance as I struggled to express what felt inexpressible.

57. For a critical analysis of the racialized policing of Trayvon Martin and the implications for Black bodies, more generally, see George Yancy and Janine Jones (eds.) *Pursuing Trayvon Martin: Historical Contexts and Contemporary Manifestations of Racial Dynamics* (Lanham, MD: Lexington Books, 2014).

58. Butler, *Precarious Life*, 22.

Index

About the Author

George Yancy is professor of philosophy at Emory University. He received his PhD (with distinction) in philosophy from Duquesne University where he was the first McAnulty Fellow. He received his first MA in philosophy from Yale University and his second MA in Africana Studies from NYU, where he received the prestigious McCracken Fellowship. He received his BA (*cum laude*) in philosophy from the University of Pittsburgh. His work focuses primarily in the areas of critical philosophy of race, critical whiteness studies, and philosophy of the black experience. He has authored many academic articles and book chapters. He has authored, edited, or coedited numerous books, including *Our Black Sons Matter: Mothers Talk about Fears, Sorrows, and Hopes* (coedited with Maria De Guadalupe Davidson and Susan Hadley, 2016); *White Self-Criticality beyond Anti-Racism: How Does It Feel to Be a White Problem?* (2015); *Exploring Race in Predominantly White Classrooms: Scholars of Color Reflect* (coedited with Maria Del Guadalupe Davidson, 2014); *Pursuing Trayvon Martin: Historical Contexts and Contemporary Manifestations of Racial Dynamics* (coedited with Janine Jones, 2013); *Look, A White! Philosophical Essays on Whiteness* (2012); *Christology and Whiteness: What Would Jesus Do?* (2012); *Reframing the Practice of Philosophy: Bodies of Color, Bodies of Knowledge* (2012); *Therapeutic Uses of Rap and Hip-Hop* (coedited with Susan Hadley, 2011); *The Center Must Not Hold: White Women Philosophers on the Whiteness of Philosophy* (2010); *Critical Perspectives on bell hooks* (coedited with Maria Del Guadalupe Davidson, 2009); *Philosophy in Multiple Voices* (2007); *Narrative Identities: Psychologists Engaged in Self-Construction* (coedited with Susan Hadley, 2005); *White on White/Black on Black* (2005); *What White Looks Like: African American Philosophers on the Whiteness Question*

(2004); *The Philosophical I: Personal Reflections on Life in Philosophy* (2002); *Cornel West: A Critical Reader* (2001) and *African-American Philosophers: 17 Conversations* (1998). Yancy's work has been cited nationally and internationally. The first edition of *Black Bodies, White Gazes* received an honorable mention from the Gustavus Myers Center for the Study of Bigotry and Human Rights and three of his edited books have received *CHOICE* outstanding academic book awards. He is editor of the *Philosophy of Race Book Series* at Lexington Books and is known for his influential interviews on the subject of race at *The Stone, New York Times*. In 2014 and 2016, Yancy won the American Philosophical Association Committee on Public Philosophy's Op-Ed Contest.